THE SITCOM READER

Second Edition

THE
SITCOM
READER

America Re-viewed, Still Skewed

Edited by

Mary M. Dalton and Laura R. Linder

Published by State University of New York Press, Albany

For information, contact State University of New York Press, Albany, NY
www.sunypress.edu

Production, Eileen Nizer
Marketing, Anne M. Valentine

Library of Congress Cataloging-in-Publication Data

The sitcom reader : America re-viewed, still skewed / edited by Mary M. Dalton and Laura R. Linder. — Second edition.
    pages cm
Includes bibliographical references and index.
ISBN 978-1-4384-6131-1 (hardcover : alk. paper)
ISBN 978-1-4384-6130-4 (pbk. : alk. paper)
ISBN 978-1-4384-6132-8 (e-book)
    1. Radio comedies—United States—History and criticism.   I. Dalton, Mary M., 1962– editor.   II. Linder, Laura R., editor.

PN1991.8.C65S57 2016
791.45'617—dc23   2015030787

10 9 8 7 6 5 4 3 2 1

For everyone who makes me think and laugh at the same time.

—MMD

For my super-smart granddaughters, Taylor and Kate.

—LRL

Contents

Illustrations

Introduction

Long gone are the days when scholars had to justify writing about television. The pervasiveness and persuasiveness of television programming has continued to evolve and now may be accessed on a variety of media in almost any imaginable locale. The continued relevance of the form makes critical and historical analyses of series, meanings audiences may find there, and the industry that produces these cultural artifacts an enterprise of continuing significance. This volume features twenty-one chapters—some included in the first edition of this anthology, some significantly revised, and eight new essays—on American situation comedies, one of the oldest and most ubiquitous forms of television programming.

The chapters are arranged into six chronological sections by decade from the 1950s to the 2010s, essays that have been carefully considered as the anthology was conceptualized to address landmark series as well as the following topics: origins and conventions of the genre; the family; gender; sexuality; race and ethnicity; work and social class; production practices; cultural resonances; and ideology. Perspectives represented here include critical media studies, cultural studies, historic surveys, feminist theory, queer theory, and a number of interdisciplinary approaches. The range of theoretical and critical tools employed by the authors of chapters is an intentional choice on the part of the editors to parallel the richness and range of the programming itself.

This project originated as a way to help fill a void in the television literature, and more than ten years after the publication of the first edition, it is time for a revised look at sitcoms, which continue to thrive as a genre. From our examination of the scholarship of sitcoms and broader topics related to television, we found these proposed areas of inquiry have been well established and represented in media studies. What has been missing, however, is a single updated volume that comprehensively and chronologically examines the genre of situation comedy and applies sets of critical lenses to contextualize the programs and help readers think about the shows and, perhaps, even about themselves in new contexts.

Origins of the Genre

In Search of the Radio Sitcom

DAVID MARC

The introduction of a mass communication medium normally occurs when an economically viable commercial application is found for a new technology. A third element necessary to the launch, content (i.e., something to communicate), is often treated as something of an afterthought in this process. As a result, adaptations of popular works and of entire genres from previous media tend to dominate the introductory period, even as they mutate under the developing conditions of the new medium. Such was the case in the rise of the television sitcom from the ashes of network radio.

While a dozen or more long-running network radio series served as sources for early television situation comedies, it is in some ways misleading to describe these radio programs (e.g., *Father Knows Best, Amos 'n' Andy*, or *The Life of Riley*) as "radio sitcoms." According to the *Oxford English Dictionary*, neither the term "situation comedy" nor "sitcom" achieved common usage until the 1950s, the point at which this type of entertainment had become completely absent from American radio.

TV Guide appears to be among the first general circulation publications to use the term "situation comedy" in print with the following passage cited by the *Oxford English Dictionary* from a 1953 article: "Ever since *I Love Lucy* zoomed to the top rung on the rating ladder, it seems the networks have been filling every available half-hour with another situation comedy" (*TV Guide*). The abbreviated form, "sitcom," which probably enjoys greater usage today, has an even shorter history. It is dated in print by the *OED* only as far back as a 1964 *Life* magazine article announcing Bing Crosby's upcoming (and ill-fated) attempt to work in the genre: "Even Bing has succumbed . . . and will appear in a sitcom as an electrical engineer who happens to break into song once a week" (*Life* magazine).

The integration of the term "sitcom" into the American language, like much of popular culture, was driven by the promotional needs of the entertainment industry. The *Life* article cited above provides a case in point. One of the most popular singers in early twentieth-century American show business, Crosby was well known to the public, first through his records and then as a radio personality and movie star. As the star of a radio variety show in the 1930s and 1940s, he demonstrated abilities to deliver gag lines, play the straight man, and trade snappy banter with guests that led to his pairing with Bob Hope in the Paramount "road" pictures.[1] While variety programming was as popular on early television as it had been on radio, the genre went into a gradual decline in the 1960s, which eventually led to its virtual absence from prime time.[2]

With feature film production also in decline during the 1960s, many aging, studio-era movie stars—including Crosby, Donna Reed, Robert Young, Ida Lupino, Fred MacMurray, and Jimmy Stewart—attempted to reinvest their celebrity in situation comedy, a genre that had been experiencing a continuous surge of growth since 1951, when *I Love Lucy* sprinted past Milton Berle's *Texaco Star Theatre* and half a dozen other comedy-variety shows to the top of the prime-time ratings. Furthermore, residual fees from reruns of sitcoms were proving to be an extraordinary cash cow (Schatz).

Though a situation comedy may be accurately described as a "comic drama" or a "narrative comedy" to distinguish it from variety (or comedy-variety) programming, such terms were no doubt considered too eggheaded for promoting the product. Thus, "situation comedy" emerged from its origins in back-office show-biz lingo to become part of popular discourse.[3] Its abbreviation to "sitcom" was perhaps all but inevitable in accordance with the grammar of public relations.

DIALECT COMEDIES

Two of the longest-running and most popular "radio sitcoms" to be adapted for television were *The Goldbergs* (premiering on the NBC radio network in 1929 as *The Rise of the Goldbergs*) and *Amos 'n' Andy* (premiering locally in Chicago in 1928 and going national on NBC the following year). Both series began as live 15-minute programs that aired Monday through Friday, a broadcast format more akin to radio soap opera than television sitcom, and both were restructured into weekly half-hour series during the early 1940s. Both were adapted for television early in the life of the medium (*The Goldbergs* in 1949; *Amos 'n' Andy* in 1951) as weekly, half-hour, filmed series with audience response tracks, all characteristics that became basic to the genre. The two programs shared significant content attributes as well. Both made primary use of ethnic dialect comedy, a source of popular humor traceable in American culture to the nineteenth-century minstrel and vaudeville stages.[4]

The Goldbergs was written and produced on both radio and television by its star, Gertrude Berg, one of only a very few women who produced their own network programs.[5] The thick Ashkenazic (i.e., eastern European) Jewish accents of the program's immigrant generation characters provided much of the show's humor while the younger, born-in-America characters spoke something more akin to standard radio English, sporadically adding inflections to acknowledge the series' Bronx location. Plotting was generally based on the exploitation of character stereotypes, especially live-in Uncle David's failure to catch the gist of things American (in one episode we learn that he has named his goldfish "Karl Marx" because of his respect for philosophers). But, despite its reliance on stereotyping, *The Goldbergs* could rarely be accused of anything more noxious than a kind of chicken-soup sentimentality in its content.

Amos 'n' Andy, centered on African American characters living in Harlem, was written, produced, and performed on radio by Freeman Gosden and Charles Correll, Whites who had grown up in the Jim Crow South. The pair had performed blackface "race humor" onstage in vaudeville and had done stints with several of the surviving minstrel shows of the early twentieth century. Their *Amos 'n' Andy* radio series—loosely based on "Sam and Henry," two earlier characters they had created—grew from a local program on WMAQ-Chicago to what was arguably the most listened to prime-time entertainment series in the history of radio.[6]

When the television adaptation of *Amos 'n' Andy* came under attack by the NAACP and other civic organizations following its 1951 premiere, Gosden and Correll claimed to be nonplussed, even hurt, by claims made about the show's perpetuation of negative stereotypes. They argued that they were performing the same type of dialect humor in their depiction of "Negroes" as other sitcoms used in their comic depictions of any number of ethnic groups (*The Goldbergs*' Jewish characters being a prime example; *I Love Lucy*'s Hispanic character, Ricky Ricardo, being another). In viewing *Amos 'n' Andy* today, it is difficult to ignore the series' unrelenting focus on negative stereotypes derived from the slavery era. The level of stupidity that emerges from the relentless use of farfetched malapropisms makes it

Figure 1.1. Spencer Williams, Jr. as Andy Brown, Tim Moore as George "The Kingfish" Stevens, and Alvin Childress as Amos Jones in *Amos 'n' Andy*. 1951–1953. Photo courtesy of Movie Star NewsFair.

difficult to characterize the effect of the sitcom as anything but racist at its core (Cripps 33–54).

The efforts of civil rights organizations to pressure CBS into canceling *Amos 'n' Andy* in 1953, despite the program's bankable Nielsen ratings, is counted by some as among the first battles won in the post-World War II Civil Rights Movement. If there is tragedy in the incident, it fell upon the African American performers. Gosden and Correll, who had performed as the title characters in three feature films for MGM, were dissuaded from taking on the roles in the television series and had replaced themselves and others in the cast with African American actors.[7] As these performers had predicted in arguing for the continuation of the show, the cancellation left them without any role to play in "all-White" television.[8] An ensemble of masterful African American comedians, including Tim Moore (as The King-fish), Ernestine Wade (as Sapphire), and Johnny Lee (as Algonquin J. Cal-houn), simply disappeared from public view. Amanda Randolph (Mama), Kingfish's hilarious "battle ax" mother-in-law, was the sole exception. She took the part of the family maid on *The Danny Thomas Show*.[9]

Sitting atop the radio ratings with audiences numbering in the tens of millions, comedies such as *The Goldbergs* and *Amos 'n' Andy* seemed obvi-ous choices for television, as were other radio hits that depended heavily on dialect humor. These included *Life with Luigi* (Italians in Chicago); *I Remember Mama* (Norwegians in San Francisco); and *Beulah* (African American servants in Middle American suburbia).[10] While dialect humor was a natural for an aural medium, what had had been a staple on radio proved to be a short-lived phenomenon on television and a poor fit for the emerging culture of postwar America.

The ethnic sitcoms suffered from the popular promotion of assimi-lationism that accompanied the mass migration of immigrant and second-generation White families from inner-city neighborhoods to suburban tracts. The exaggerated accents and malapropisms of radio comedy might have become more embarrassing than funny to a significant segment of the early television-viewing audience, which was located almost exclusively in large metropolitan areas.[11] Thomas Cripps has suggested that African American war veterans played a significant role in opposing the television adaptation of *Amos 'n' Andy*, which they saw as an instrument for perpetuation of the longstanding stereotypes that stood behind Jim Crow laws.

Though it had run for two decades on radio, *Amos 'n' Andy* was gone from television in two seasons. *The Goldbergs* managed to remain on the air for six seasons, but this was largely due to Gertrude Berg's savvy as a pro-ducer. She repeatedly made new deals to save the show, switching television networks three times and even agreeing to change the 25-year-old format by moving the family from the Bronx to the suburbs and renaming the sitcom *Molly*. In the end, ridding the show of what was now seen as its Depression-era, immigrant baggage left it a limp imitation of itself. Following *Molly*'s

Figure 1.2 Gertrude Berg as Molly Goldberg in *The Goldbergs*. 1929–1954 (radio 1929–1948 & television 1949–1954). Photo courtesy of Photofest.

cancellation in 1955, not a single radio dialect comedy was left on the air. Suburban families with names such as Stone (*The Donna Reed Show*) and Anderson (*Father Knows Best*) moved in to dominate the genre.

THE SITCOM-VARIETY SHOW HYBRIDS

Like *The Goldbergs* and *Amos 'n' Andy*, *The Jack Benny Program* and *The George Burns and Gracie Allen Show* were among radio's most popular hits.

These shows present complex genre problems when considered as sources for the television programs of the same name. On radio, *Benny* and *Burns and Allen* made frequent use of seamless aural segués to shift rhetorical modes between direct-address presentation (i.e., the vaudeville-derived variety format) and representational narratives of domestic life that seem very much like radio prototypes of contemporary television sitcoms.[12] Genre theory has thus far been unable to account for these shows in any satisfying way, and so they are treated as "radio sitcoms" by a kind of critical default.[13]

The purposeful confusion of the two principal genres of broadcast comedy (sitcom and variety), which radio accomplished by a mere shift of language, required much more work for presentation on television. *I Love Lucy* and *The Adventures of Ozzie and Harriet*, two sitcoms featuring bandleaders as husband-fathers, made use of "backstage" narrative in order to work variety elements, such as music, song, and dance, into the dramatic framework.

In *I Love Lucy*, Lucy's husband Ricky is a nightclub performer, and she is a hopeless showbiz wannabe. A plurality of episodes concerns her efforts to sneak into shows at the Tropicana. The nightclub stage functions to allow variety segués. In *Ozzie and Harriet*, Ozzie's son, Ricky Nelson, has a garage band and performs at parties or practice sessions. *Ozzie and Harriet* was a pioneer in cross-media promotion with Ricky Nelson launching a string of Billboard Top Ten hits on the show.

It is worth noting that *The Bing Crosby Show* (1964–65), which inspired *Life* magazine to use the word "sitcom" in print, incorporated a backstage device as well. A closer look at the failed effort reveals an evocatively frenzied attempt at generic, masscult cookie-cutting with subgeneric elements borrowed from a half-dozen sitcom hits of the period. Like Danny Thomas (Danny Williams in *The Danny Thomas Show*) and Andy Griffith (Andy Taylor in *The Andy Griffith Show*), Crosby invokes persona in the sitcom narrative as "Bing Collins." His character is a suburban suit-and-tie professional, married with children (á la Robert Young in *Father Knows Best* and other archetypal sitcom dads). His daughters are a study in contrast between boy-crazy, bobby-soxer Janice and child prodigy Joyce in what seems to be a nod to the contrast between Patty and Cathy Lane of *The Patty Duke Show*.

The narrative thrust of the series has Bing eschewing stardom for the higher calling of being a "normal" family man, a familiar and popular theme in American mythology that perhaps reached its film apogee in Frank Capra's *It's a Wonderful Life* (1942). Using Bing Collins's aversion to fame and fortune as a diversion, the storyline incorporates Bing Crosby through the backstage door. Bing's wife (Beverly Garland) is, like Lucy, an incorrigible show business wannabe. She attempts to drag Bing back onstage as a way of realizing her suppressed ambitions. Borrowing another tactic from *The Danny Thomas Show* for the episode finish, Bing breaks into song as he delivers dad's weekly words of wisdom, with appropriate musical accompaniment rising from behind kitchen appliances, living room furniture, or garden tools.

IMPROVING THE HORSE AND CARRIAGE

When searching for the roots of situation comedy and other television genres in radio, it is worth remembering that radio enjoyed an extremely short moment as a primary (or *the* primary) medium for commercial American entertainment, perhaps too short to fully realize any genres of its own. Invented just before the turn of the twentieth century as a "wireless tele-graph" whose purpose was to provide two-way communication systems for ships at sea and for places not reachable by telegraph cable, it was improved to carry analog sound in the 1910s. This led to a wave of hobbyists (known as "hams," another word for "showoffs") who began performing for each other with the new desktop communication system: telling jokes, reading poems, creating false identities, and otherwise prefiguring Internet chatting by the better part of a century.

It was not until after World War I that the mass production of cheap, downstream receivers for the consuming public was attempted. The first commercially owned local radio stations were put on the air in the 1920s by electronics manufacturers to stimulate sales of these models. In 1927, the Radio Corporation of America, the country's biggest maker of sets, launched its subsidiary, the National Broadcasting Company, thus imposing centralized quality control on broadcasting entertainment products by feed-ing content to a network of cross-country stations from its corporate studios.

Radio achieved a position at center stage of American culture during the national traumas of the Great Depression and the Second World War but went into decline after 1948, as the three major network broadcast-ing companies (NBC, CBS, and ABC) accelerated their commitment of the medium's profits to the development of another medium—television. Radio's "golden age" ends with a whimper in 1953 when its last great star, Jack Benny, gets the word from CBS that his radio show must go. Dying in its twenties and dead at around thirty, prime-time entertainment radio was only beginning to define its generic texts when they were either killed, kidnapped, or subjected to forced mutation in the service of the needs of visual representation on television.[14]

The case can be made that the artistic life of radio was hampered throughout most of its existence by the anticipation of television, which was patented in 1927, the very same year that network radio went on the air.[15] As early as 1929, David Sarnoff, the RCA executive who founded NBC, gave an address at the Harvard Business School in which he announced the existence of television, expressing a belief that it would "replace" radio (Morgenthau). By 1939, television broadcasting was within the capabilities of RCA, which publicly demonstrated it through daily telecasts from the New York World's Fair. There were more than a thousand set owners in the New York metropolitan area at the time, though most were employees of either RCA and/or several other companies at work on the technology.

World War II delayed television's implementation as a mass medium until after 1945, but the handwriting was already on the cue cards for radio. At the very height of its popularity, with daily audiences for specific programs numbering in the tens of millions, radio was functioning as little more than a stepping stone to television for the people who controlled the money that might have been used to develop radio art.

Henry Morgenthau, III, a pioneer maker of documentary films for television and the producer of Eleanor Roosevelt's syndicated television talk show during the 1950s, heard Sarnoff express his views on the future of radio in person in 1947. Morgenthau had just read Charles A. Siepmann's *Radio's Second Chance*, in which the author argued that radio was only beginning to suggest its artistic and educational potentials. Inspired to want to work in radio by Siepmann, Morgenthau had his father, then Secretary of the U.S. Treasury, arrange a meeting for him with Sarnoff, who was now chairman of the board at RCA. Morgenthau described it this way:

> I have a memory of walking down endless corridors, sort of like approaching the Sun King at Versailles, and meeting Sarnoff and talking to him briefly about my ambition to go into FM radio, which was new. I talked about the static-free sound and the opening of new channels and how exciting this all seemed to me. He stopped me and said that he thought going into radio was the worst possible thing to do. He said FM radio was like inventing an improved horse carriage just at the time that automobiles were coming in. "Forget radio and get into television!" he said and walked away, as if I were the mad man.

Though radio was already being dismissed as an obsolete technology in the late 1940s, the phenomenon it had done so much to create—mass audiences—had grown more valuable than ever to those who had the future of radio in their hands. Accordingly, they cannibalized the medium for its content. It is remarkable, however, to see how little attention was paid to the intricacies of adaptation, even for hit shows.

According to Paul Henning, who began writing radio scripts for *The George Burns and Gracie Allen Show* in 1942, the show's staff was sent a memo in April of 1950 informing them that they would be doing "the show" on television beginning in October. "I remember George saying, 'Let's all go down to Palm Springs and we'll sit around the pool and talk about what we're going to do for television,'" Henning said. "Ralph Levy, the producer, evolved the idea for the show: a simple situation comedy with the cut-out set of the Burns's house, and another one for their neighbors, and, downstage, an area where George could stand and talk directly to the audience, to explain about his wife, Gracie, and predict what was going to happen [in the plot], and comment on his daily life in and around their neighborhood" (Wilk 176–77).

When Henning's wife, Ruth, suggested to Levy and Burns that they might need something more "visual" to interest audiences that were *seeing* the action, Burns came up with the idea of placing a television in the "den" of George and Gracie's television house. When the plot of the sitcom got too convoluted, the writers had the option of sending George up to the den to watch an action picture on television, usually a Western, which played on the screen during broadcasts for as long as ten seconds. "You could do that kind of stuff back then, because nobody knew what a sitcom was," Paul Henning said. "We just did comedy."

NOTES

1. The *American Heritage Dictionary* lists "variety show" but does not list "comedy-variety" or "comedy-variety show." The *Oxford English Dictionary* lists neither. What we would today call a "comedy-variety show" was, during the radio era, usually called either a "comedy show" (if hosted by a comedian) or a "variety show." The term "comedy-variety" became useful or perhaps necessary during the television era to distinguish this type of programming from two proliferating forms: the situation comedy (e.g., *I Love Lucy*) and the variety show (i.e., "vaudeo" shows hosted by noncomedians, such as *The Ed Sullivan Show*, also known as *Toast of the Town*).

2. While dormant in English-language American television, the comedy-variety and variety genres remain vital in Spanish-language programming in the United States and elsewhere.

3. Several radio comedy writers, including Everett Greenbaum and Paul Henning, recall the use of terms such as "situational comedy" and "situation com-

edy" in shop talk as early as the 1930s as a way of distinguishing comic drama from the more popular vaudeville style of that era, which today is remembered as comedy-variety. See the oral history collections of the Center for the Study of Popular Television, Syracuse University.

4. See Robert Toll, *Blacking Up: The Minstrel Show in 19th Century America* (NY: Oxford University Press, 1974) for a detailed discussion of the minstrel show and its extraordinary role in American culture.

5. Irna Philips (1901–1973), who virtually invented the daytime soap opera for radio and single-handedly adapted it for television, was the most prolific and influential of the handful of women producers in broadcasting. For a useful concise biography of Philips, see the entry concerning her in Oxford University Press's *American National Biography Online*.

6. For more detail on *Amos 'n' Andy*, see Melvin Patrick Ely, *The Adventures of Amos 'n' Andy: A Social History of an American Phenomenon* (NY: Free Press, 1991).

7. There were three "Amos 'n' Andy" movies, with the title roles performed by Gosden and Correll in blackface: *Check and Double Check* (1930), *The Rasslin' Match* (1934), and *The Lion Tamer* (1934).

8. See J. Fred Macdonald, *Blacks and White Television* (Chicago: Nelson Hall, 1983) for the most comprehensive history of African Americans on early American television.

9. No criticism of *The Danny Thomas Show* is meant here. The show's producers, Danny Thomas and Sheldon Leonard, insisted on employing African American performers at a time when almost none were on television. Leonard and Thomas made another political statement by knowingly employing writers who had been blacklisted for their political beliefs. For example, Frank Tarloff (credited with the pseudonym "David Adler") wrote for at least three of their sitcoms, *The Danny Thomas Show*, *The Andy Griffith Show*, and *The Dick Van Dyke Show*. Tarloff recounts this in an interview in the oral history collections of the Center for the Study of Popular Television at the Syracuse University Library.

10. *Beulah* (ABC, 1951–53), whose title female character had been played by a White man on radio, was less popular than *Amos 'n' Andy* and was therefore less of a *cause celebre*. It was also cancelled in 1953, however, under similar circumstance. After its first season on television, the program's star, Ethel Waters, had quit because of the negative stereotypes she felt were perpetuated in her character.

11. The FCC issued 108 television station licenses before 1948, almost all of which were allocated to cities in three megalopolitan regions: the northeast coastal corridor stretching from Boston to Washington, D.C.; the Great Lakes rim, from Cleveland to Milwaukee via Chicago; and urban California, including Los Angeles and San Francisco. In 1948, the FCC put a freeze on new licensing that lasted until 1952.

12. For a detailed discussion of modes of television narrative, see the author's *Demographic Vistas* (Philadelphia: University of Pennsylvania Press, 1996), pp. 11–33.

13. In the 1990s, *Seinfeld* attempted to reintroduce the technique of creating genre tension between situation comedy and comedy-variety by opening and sometimes closing the show with stand-up clips.

14. For a rare account of the process of imagining content for television, see Gilbert Seldes, "The Errors of Television," *The Atlantic Monthly* (May 1937), pp. 531–41. Seldes, a Harvard-educated popular culture and radio critic, was hired by CBS in 1935 as a consultant to its television development program.

15. In 1927 Philo T. Farnsworth patented his image dissector, which included key elements of the cathode ray tube. That same year, the Radio Corporation of America, whose company research and development team was led by Russian emigré Vladimir Zworykin, patented its *eikonoscope*.

The 1950s

In the early years of television, broadcasters were preoccupied with technological development and jockeying over patent claims. Entertainment programming was a secondary consideration, with most content being imported from radio. This is true in the entrepreneurial stage of almost every new medium, but the overwhelming popularity of television put a lot of pressure on broadcasters to improve the quality of the product being delivered to people's homes. NBC had become the first network to launch a commercially sponsored broadcast in 1941, with CBS and others following, but the onset of World War II led the Federal Communication Commission (FCC) to ban the commercial production of television equipment for the duration of the war. Once the fighting ended, the American middle class entered into a period of unprecedented expansion, including greater reliance on the automobile, rapid suburbanization, and a love affair with time-saving appliances. But, perhaps the most common ritual to take place in the domestic sphere, regardless of geography or class, was the replacement of the radio by the television as the centerpiece of the family living space. It is estimated that there were fewer than 10,000 television sets in 1945, about six million in 1950, and almost 60 million by the end of the decade.[1]

The 1950s saw steady improvement in the quality of transmission and an expansion in programming. The FCC lifted its four-year "freeze" on the licensing of new television stations in 1952, which allowed nearly thirteen hundred communities to enter the TV age. This coincided with the approval of transmission via UHF (ultra high frequency), which allowed TV sets to receive more channels. And, after an earlier system developed by CBS proved incompatible with most existing black-and-white sets, RCA introduced a system in 1954 that brought color to the small screen. Two other advances, one technological and the other methodological, are worth noting: in 1955, Robert Adler invented a remote control called the Zenith Space Commander, setting the stage for a new kind of viewer known as

the couch potato; and, in 1959, overnight local market ratings were introduced by Nielsen Media Research in New York, yielding reasonably accurate
measurements of audiences for particular programs and giving networks and
advertisers their most powerful tool for setting prices for commercial spots
and making programming decisions.

As David Marc argues in the Introduction to this volume, the early
days of television represented more of a shift of technology than content
as popular radio genres often made the transition to the new medium with
little to no change except for the addition of pictures. Sitcoms that made
the transition, such as *Our Miss Brooks*, sometimes recycled radio scripts
verbatim. The airwaves were filled with Westerns, variety shows, anthologies,
detective series, dramas, quiz shows (prescandal), and, of course, sitcoms. In
fact, a sitcom legend dominated the decade: *I Love Lucy* was the top-rated
series four seasons (1952–53, 1953–54, 1954–55, and 1956–57) and ranked
second and third two additional seasons. Only after the zany redhead left the
air (temporarily) did the Western gallop toward the height of its popularity,
with *Gunsmoke* taking the top slot for the last two seasons of the 1950s.
Other popular sitcoms that landed among the top thirty shows during the
decade are *The Aldrich Family*; *Amos 'n' Andy*; *The Ann Southern Show*; *The
Danny Thomas Show*; *December Bride*; *Dennis the Menace*; *Father Knows Best*;
The Gale Storm Show; *The George Burns and Gracie Allen Show*; *The Honeymooners*; *I Married Joan*; *Life with Luigi*; *The Life of Riley*; *Mama*; *My Little
Margie*; *Our Miss Brooks*; *Private Secretary*; *The Real McCoys*; and *Topper*.

Some tend to think of 1950s television programs as bland, even boring, because of their predictability. Some series undoubtedly fit that description, but it is an incomplete characterization on two levels: first, it does not
acknowledge the innovation within the genre, and, second, it fails to apply
critical readings to conventional series. While some series replicated what
was already an established form on radio, or copied television hits as new
conventions emerged and then became codified, others, such as *The George
Burns and Gracie Allen Show*, experimented boldly with the format and
juxtaposed sitcom scenes with cutaway scenes of George Burns breaking the
fourth wall (a technique employed again in later shows such as *The Bernie
Mac Show*, *The Office*, and *Modern Family*). Burns would speak directly to
the studio audience about the characters and situations unfolding in the
episode and would also frequently acknowledge the technical apparatus and
crew necessary for broadcasting the show. In some ways, the 1950s were
a time of experimentation and innovation because the rules had not been
firmly established. In this regard, there are similarities to the 2010s, a time
when technology was once again presenting opportunities for the sitcom

to continue with popular, tried and true patterns while also expanding the parameters of what constitutes the genre and occasionally reinventing itself.

Television, like culture overall, is more complex than we convey when we rely solely on broad strokes to paint an expansive landscape. We might think of the 1950s as a calm period of postwar prosperity, suburban growth, and innocent pastimes, a time when father really did know best and mother vacuumed the (already spotless) carpet while wearing heels and pearls, two of the familiar character types Judy Kutulas explores in her expansive chapter on the sitcom family. But, there are many other cultural narratives and competing readings of popular television shows. After all, postwar prosperity had the effect of pushing women out of the workplace to make room for returning GIs, sending them to the domestic sphere and relegating them to tasks that many found less fulfilling than the jobs they performed during the war. Gradually, these housewives' malaise, which Betty Friedan would later term "the problem that has no name" in *The Feminine Mystique*, would be recognized as a significant social issue, but connections among gender, race, sexuality, and class issues would not be widely acknowledged or discussed for another twenty-five to thirty years.

Many women of color always worked outside of the home, and often inside someone else's home, but they had to confront both economic realities that limited their employment options *and* social conditions that often stripped them of dignity. Television in the 1950s "dealt with" the tyranny of separate and unequal conditions, and the lack of opportunity for Blacks by not dealing with it at all, even though the Civil Rights Movement started to hit its stride by the middle of the decade. Some have argued that the exclusion of Blacks was more of an economic decision than the expression of bias. Although this is a rationalization for an inexcusable practice, considerable pressure was applied by advertisers to avoid subjects and characters that might alienate mainstream audiences. In order to keep sponsors on board, executives curtailed shows with immigrants and working-class characters in addition to those with Blacks.

Looking at these programs and policies through a contemporary lens allows us to take stock of historical progress, but it can forestall a full appreciation of the television texts. We return to the idea that the most constructive approach to television texts is holistic, recognizing that they are complex rather than monolithic. Accordingly, Lori Landay instructs us on contextual and subversive readings of *I Love Lucy*; Lucy might be confined to the domestic sphere, but she continues her madcap attempts at escape because she yearns for something more. The fact that uncomfortable truths, such as those Steven Sheehan writes about in his chapter on *The*

Honeymooners, are seldom foregrounded on television should not obscure the fact that they can be found there. Hidden truths, uncomfortable truths, reading against the grain, and challenging our tacit understandings of the sitcom are essential tools for explicating situation comedies, the most familiar and ubiquitous genre of television programming.

NOTES

1. Specific estimates vary by source, but a surge in television set sales throughout the 1950s is constant across sources. These figures are from "Television," *The World Book Encyclopedia.* Chicago: World Book, Inc. 2003:119.

2

Who Rules the Roost?

Sitcom Family Dynamics from the Cleavers to *Modern Family*

JUDY KUTULAS

At the heart of the American sitcom lies the family—nuclear, extended, blended, and created. We've seen it all, from families headed by automotive matriarchs to astronauts married to genies. Family is the one experience to which virtually all viewers can relate. It evokes symbols and images advertisers like. And, its plot possibilities are endless. According to Stephanie Coontz, "our most powerful visions of traditional families derive from images that are still delivered to our homes in countless reruns of television sit-coms" (23). Yet, the modern audience is conflicted about those images. We see in the Cleavers (*Leave It to Beaver*) and other TV families a vision of perfection, the embodiment of security, stability, and togetherness that haunts us as we grapple with our real, less-than-perfect families. At the heart of these TV families is the clear articulation of roles and responsibilities and the gentle lines of authority that flow from wise dad and understanding mom to obedient children (May 208). Objectively, we know that the Cleavers represent an ideal rather than a norm, and one that confines and constricts individuality. Emotionally, though, we cannot escape the sense that life would be so much better if our lives were just like the Cleavers' lives.

The 1950s sitcom family idealizes a "qualitatively new phenomenon" (Coontz 25). The Depression and World War II blurred American memories of "normal" family life even as these events induced intense longing for stability. The Cold War introduced a new set of social expectations; family was to be a secure, consumerist, conformist bulwark against communism (May 10–11). TV provided an intimate family prototype, beamed weekly into domestic space, natural, didactic, but still theatrical (Spigel *Make Room* 157), starring a white-collar father, a stay-at-home mother, and a flock of children all nestled in their safe, small-town cocoon. Material affluence contributes to the alluring image, but it is the TV family's dynamic that remains

Figure 2.1. Hugh Beaumont as Ward Cleaver, Barbara Billingsley as June Cleaver, Jerry Mathers as Theodore "Beaver" Cleaver, and Tony Dow as Wally Cleaver in *Leave It to Beaver*. 1957–1963. Photo courtesy of Photofest.

so seductive. In these series, everybody gets along, everybody is happy, and everyone wants to be together. There is just enough conflict to drive plots. By the time the half-hour is over, everybody is happy again. The Cleavers and other 1950s TV families are the wish fulfillment of several decades of social disruption, economic dislocation, and political fear.

The ethnic and racial sitcoms that made the transition from radio to television—*The Goldbergs, I Remember Mama* (called *Mama* on TV), and *Amos 'n' Andy*—could not compete with these new middle-class White family stories. Their focus on hardship, ethnic difference, or the conflicts that exist between husbands and wives or parents and children started to seem old-fashioned. *I Love Lucy* marked the transition. Originally a battle-of-the-sexes comedy set in a New York City apartment, the series adds a child to the mix, which softens the title character. Eventually, it is reset in suburban Connecticut (Gerard Jones 73). A new dynamic emerges post-*Lucy*, one in which TV families respect authority, model conformity, and follow social rules.

In the new TV families, dad is the leader but not the boss. Only ethnic hotheads like Ricky Ricardo (*I Love Lucy*) or Danny Williams (*Make Room for Daddy*) (who, TV name aside, was Lebanese) believe in the Old-World patriarch. Sociologists noted the transformation from the "positional" family to the "personal" one that is more democratic and less authoritarian (Skolnick 167–68). The new ideal, reinforced by several decades of social fears about too-powerful women, rested on complementary gender roles in marriage (Weiss 18–19). The modern husband was involved in family life, helping out by occasionally drying the dishes, playing with his children, and modeling appropriate gender roles for his sons (Spock 254–55). In real life, dad's centrality to the family was slipping away as the family became more of a consumer entity, mom's specialty, and as dad worked longer hours and learned to fit into a corporate culture (Kimmel 236–37). On TV, however, dad was always around, the impeccable reflection of the new ideal. Meanwhile, mom was supposed to be dad's complement, the "steady, loving person" who met children's day-to-day emotional needs and cooked their suppers (Spock 484). On TV, she was more invisible to help prop up dad's declining household status (Leibman 121–33). Stability was the result of carefully balanced roles: father knew best, mother nurtured, and children learned their place within the family. In TV households without such division of labor—the households of TV neighbors, sidekicks, and friends—chaos prevailed. The problem child on *Leave It to Beaver*, Eddie Haskell, lived in a dysfunctional family with a father who (depending on the episode) hit, yelled, criticized, or ignored his son. But, in successful

1950s TV families, members worked together, understood their individual roles, and did what was expected of them.

By the middle 1960s, networks became willing to disturb this domestic harmony for a particular segment of the audience. Advertisers instinctively recognized the potential of the baby boom, that vast postwar demographic bulge of Americans born between 1947 and 1960, and TV courted it with a host of kiddie shows, such as *The Mickey Mouse Club* and *The Flintstones*. The spending possibilities of boomers as they moved into adolescence did not escape the TV industry. Certainly, *The Adventures of Ozzie and Harriet* benefited from the simple expedient of tacking a song by son, and teen singing sensation, Ricky, at the end of episodes. The popularity of the Beatles, including records, movies, magazines, bubblegum cards, and a Saturday morning cartoon show, reminded network programmers that teens had money and, unlike other components of the audience, were eager to spend it. But, immersed in a postwar peer culture, teens did not always believe that father knew best, either on sitcoms or in real life (Gilbert *Cycle* 17).

The emerging generation gap was treated gently on two mid-1960s shows, *Gidget* and *The Patty Duke Show*. On *The Patty Duke Show*, Duke played, as the theme song explained, "identical cousins" who were "different as night and day," sedate, studious, English Cathy and all-American, boy-crazy, frug-dancing Patty. Cathy rarely found herself at odds with her uncle and aunt, but Patty lived in a world of peers and peer temptations. She fell in and out of love, tried on new roles, and often drove her parents crazy. She didn't, to the disproportionately teen and preteen audience's delight, always do what her parents wanted her to do. As the first boomers edged into adulthood, their conflicts with real-life parents were likewise refracted on late 1960s series, such as *The Mothers-in-Law* and *That Girl*. In both programs, the younger generation politely rejects their parents' lives. Ann Marie's (*That Girl*) decision to move to New York City and become an actress is about finding her own way in the world rather than meeting parental expectations or following social rules. By the late 1960s, a few sitcoms began to undermine TV parents' authority by privileging the independence of their adult or nearly adult children.

Within the next few years, the generation gap would split wide open, both in real life and on TV. College students rebelled against their parents' authority and materialism. The counterculture, the women's liberation movement, and the sexual revolution alienated youth from traditional institutions including the family. By 1970, one-third of America's college-aged population rejected marriage and having children (Schulman 16). TV stereotypes symbolized much of what they rebelled against. Young women feared becoming like *Leave It to Beaver* matriarch June Cleaver—sweet, servile, and invisible, vacuuming in her pearls and high heels. Young men were equally dubious of patriarch Ward Cleaver, particularly his relationship with his boss and the psychological costs of keeping the Cleaver family ensconced in white picket fences and new Fords. This generation defied the networks' previous assumptions about audience. They were, as a group, freer spending, certainly by comparison to their Depression-raised parents. They were single longer, so less of their income was given over to fixed expenses such as mortgages and car payments. They were, in short, a highly desirable audience for advertisers. But, they were also less likely to watch TV than their elders because their lives were more self-absorbed, their time less structured into TV-watching routines, and they saw little around the dial that resonated with their lives (Gerard Jones 187–88).

As in so many aspects of American society, the baby boomers had the numerical weight to force change. Networks began to privilege them as a desired audience, and advertisers pitched their ads at them. CBS dumped stories about well-meaning but eccentric rural families like *The Beverly Hillbillies* and *Green Acres*, replacing them with more sophisticated "relevance" fare geared toward a freer-spending younger audience (Gerard Jones 192). In January of 1971, *All in the Family* premiered, sending shock waves through the culture because of its rendering of a family decidedly unlike the Cleavers. Its main characters are Archie and Edith Bunker, their daughter Gloria, and Gloria's husband, Michael. Gloria and Michael are baby boomers, open to the new political, social, and cultural possibilities of the 1960s. Archie and Edith represent the older generation, raised on the deprivation and sacrifice of the Depression and the unabashed patriotism of World War II. These two generations fight all the time about the war in Vietnam, sexual attitudes, race, religion, and women's roles, but the subtext is nearly always the same. Archie expects to be the patriarch of his family with all the attendant status and power of that position. Gloria and Michael reject both his authority and his model of family, actions privileged by the show's presentation of Archie as ignorant and bigoted (Marc *Comic* 1989, 183). Even though his wife is subservient (offering the can of beer, saving his chair in front of the TV), Archie is clearly not the lord and master of his castle.

All in the Family legitimated youth's rebellion against its elders. Its implicit subject was boomers' critique of the 1950s family dynamic. Edith trots after Archie, smoothing over conflict, yet Archie treats her like a servant, not a partner or an equal. She tries to bolster his authority; he keeps telling her to "stifle." He uses similar tactics to keep his wayward daughter and son-in-law in line. The invisible, automatic hierarchy of the Cleaver household, however, is neither as normal nor as easy for the Bunkers. *All in the Family* replicates the real-world collapse of authority that followed the war in Vietnam and the counterculture. A generation of Americans became as sensitive to power and authority dynamics as are Gloria and Michael. Archie symbolizes the abuse of power and the unreasonable expectation of obedience that young people saw everywhere from the White House to their universities. *All in the Family* also reveals the seamy underside of the 1950s family, the hurt, disappointment, and denial that are sometimes all that hold the Bunkers together. The series serves a different function than do happy family sitcoms, mocking rather than modeling, offering up a deliberately imperfect vision of family life to replace the perfect Cleaver model.

The show spawned a host of so-called relevancy family comedies by creator Norman Lear: *Good Times, Maude, Sanford and Son, The Jeffersons,* and *One Day at a Time.* MTM Productions, founded by Mary Tyler Moore and her then-husband, Grant Tinker, followed suit with their own set of relevant domestic comedies, including *The Mary Tyler Moore Show, Rhoda, Phyllis,* and *The Bob Newhart Show.* None is as shocking as *All in the Family* had been, but none features families like the Cleavers, either. Reality intrudes—divorce, unemployment, crime—and plots aren't happily resolved in half an hour. Dad and mom don't have all the answers. Families don't live in harmony, or balance. Sometimes their economic or physical existence is in jeopardy. By the 1973–74 season, relevancy comedies occupied half of the top-ten Nielsen spots, and they were the only sitcoms to make that list. Their target demographic was "a young, liberal upscale audience making the transition from turbulent college campuses to the workplace" (Taylor 56)—in other words, baby boomers. While Saturday night, America's traditional date night, used to be a big family broadcast night that included such family-friendly shows as *My Three Sons, Green Acres,* and *Petticoat Junction,* CBS drew bigger ratings with a 1974 Saturday night lineup aimed at the baby boomers: *All in the Family, The Mary Tyler Moore Show,* and *M*A*S*H.* College students and young singles watched in dorms and apartments. Young women, particularly, became a desirable audience segment, not as wives and mothers, but as single women pursuing education, independence, and careers (Rabinovitz 145). This baby-boomer audience had the numerical and social weight to expect that their critical view of family life would prevail.

In 1970s relevancy family shows, fathers' authority disappears because, to baby boomers, fathers weren't central family members. The boomer audience might have grown up watching Ward Cleaver, but its lived experience and the counterculture's social critique suggested that real fathers were rarely as available or engaged as Ward Cleaver. They were too busy at the office to make time for family (Weiss 108). Relevancy sitcoms didn't so much question whether father knew best as whether he had any power in a domestic space ruled by mom. Unlike Archie, other 1970s TV fathers only rarely bother to claim authority, having long since learned that a kind of domestic ignorance is bliss. So superfluous were some of them that, like Phyllis' husband, Lars, on *The Mary Tyler Moore Show*, they aren't even shown or, if they are, they make occasional appearances in their children's lives, such as Julie and Barbara's divorced father on *One Day at a Time*. As boomer children aged, they came to suspect that Ward Cleaver's den was a retreat away from the actual domestic power figure: mom.

Since moms are presented as the true authority figures on 1970s relevancy sitcoms, they became prime targets for ridicule and attack. Females were disproportionate viewers of sitcoms, and the "single-female household" was a valuable 1970s demographic target (Marc, *Comic*, 1989, 169). Thanks to the Women's Movement, young women looked at their mothers and saw "models to avoid" (Breines 77), women who parlayed domesticity into power they extracted via guilt. If fathers disengage in 1970s sitcoms, then mothers wage constant passive-aggressive guerilla actions to legitimate the housewife's role, a role that, in 1970s currency, had been significantly devalued. TV housewives in series of the 1970s fervently believe in the value of what June Cleaver did all day, so fervently that they want their daughters to be like her (and them). There is a constant tug-of-war on shows like *Rhoda* between those mothers and their daughters, who are more attracted to liberation and the workplace than to marriage to a nice doctor and a house in the suburbs. Such struggles exaggerate the real-life generational break delineated by the Women's Movement while allowing the all-important young, female demographic the vicarious thrill of besting mom.

As parental authority declined on 1970s relevancy TV, family is redefined. There have always been truncated families on sitcoms—widows and widowers and bachelor uncles—but off-camera death forces those structures. On *Rhoda, One Day at a Time*, and *The Mary Tyler Moore Show*, family comes apart when family members opt out. Biological family no longer offered the security of 1950s sitcoms because, for many prized boomer viewers, family is not a stable institution. A lot of 1950s families stayed together out of necessity; by the 1970s, however, women had economic options other than marriage, and the singles lifestyle tempted both men and women. The divorce rate rose, the marriage rate dropped, and the baby boom gave way to the birth dearth (Frum 73–81). Lifestyle choices also alienated many boomers from their parents. Sitcoms in the 1970s culturally explore these facts of modern life. The more fragmented and unstable TV's biological families become, the more TV representatives of the target demographic seek out alternatives to biological family. Constructed family composed of peers, friends, or coworkers who function as "support group[s]" (Marc *Comic* 1989, 169) provide the kinds of affirmation biological families didn't always give. Originally a radical idea with roots in the counterculture (communal living), the sitcom's quick embrace of constructed family helps normalize it thanks to such hits as *WKRP in Cincinnati*, *M*A*S*H*, and *Three's Company*. Unlike biological family, constructed family is family by choice, family without the hang-up of family roles, family without hierarchy.

TV in the 1970s was antiauthoritarian in style as well as structure, reflecting the influx of boomers into the production process. The result was programming that embraced 1960s values and was irreverent, topical, and mocking of institutions and traditions. *Saturday Night Live*, itself a constructed family of boomer performer/writers, epitomizes the style of TV made by and aimed at people "who had grown up watching television" (Marc *Demographic* 151). Its most popular target is TV and, especially, 1950s family stereotypes, which appear in segments as diverse as a Hearst family Christmas and the Coneheads. In one classic sketch, guest host Rick Nelson (*The Adventures of Ozzie and Harriet*) finds himself trapped in a series of 1950s family sitcom homes, endlessly doomed to circulate from the set of *Leave It to Beaver* to *Father Knows Best* to *Make Room for Daddy*. Boomer TV uses the Cleaver metaphor as a generational touchstone, a nostalgic cultural reference point, and a sacred cow to be prodded and poked. No longer a model, the happy family ideal can be rendered sweetly in *Happy Days* or sarcastically in *Mary Hartman, Mary Hartman*, but always with a nudge and a wink toward the boomer audience.

By the end of the 1970s, the young, single TV market became less important, largely because "it was simply difficult to keep those affluent, educated young people at home in front of the set" (Gerard Jones 244). The demographic center of gravity shifted as more boomers began their own families and as "family values" became a 1980s political catchphrase. The family sitcom revived in the early 1980s with two enormous hits, *The Cosby Show* and *Family Ties* (Thompson 45). These shows feature neither the complementary parental roles of the 1950s nor the frustrated housewives and invisible dads of the 1970s. Their dynamic is modern. Clair Huxtable (*The Cosby Show*) and Alyse Keaton (*Family Ties*) work outside the home, their husbands cook and clean, and parenting is a shared enterprise. Both shows also play on boomers' generational identities. The Huxtables had marched on Washington in 1963, and the Keatons had been hippies. But, what most distinguishes these programs from 1970s family stories is that the boomers are now in charge, both behind the scenes and in front of the camera. Family sitcoms in the 1980s reveal how boomers intend to do family differently.

In the 1950s, parents raised their children to be crowd followers and people pleasers, conformist and obedient (Breines 68). In the 1980s, boomer parents cultivated independence in their children. TV parenting styles also changed. Ward and June Cleaver know what is right for their children; Cliff and Clair Huxtable want their children to learn it for themselves. Families are run democratically as parents help to educate and advise but rarely lay down the law. Most of all, parents practice tolerance, a value rebellious boomers wished their parents had shown them. The ideal in 1980s family sitcoms created by boomers is what sociologist Arlene Skolnick describes as a "personal, democratic style" of childrearing, in which "an emphasis on autonomy" replaces obedience as a parenting goal (Skolnick 170). Family comedies aspire to model a more flexible and autonomous family unit in the 1980s, even if, as Cliff Huxtable discovers frequently, children raised in such an environment aren't always respectful of parental authority.

While boomers often controlled the sitcom production process and, thereby, family representations on 1980s sitcoms, they had to take into account the broader audience for family stories. In addition to boomer parents, the primary audience for the new generation of family comedies was kids and young teens. Indeed, on *Family Ties* and another 1980s family comedy, *Growing Pains*, the teenage sons, played by Michael J. Fox and Kirk Cameron, respectively, became so popular with preteen girls that they gained more airplay and, at some point, more dominance in shows originally about their TV parents. The bifurcated audience meant that 1980s family sitcoms had an undercurrent of youthful subversion, even though the rebels Cameron and Fox played were of very different sorts: Cameron, the epitome of the underachieving male, and Fox, the yuppie Republican. Younger viewers, identified as Generation X (defined as those born between 1961 and 1981), were well acquainted with the happy family sitcom ideal, thanks to reruns of *Leave It To Beaver* and *My Three Sons* on Nickelodeon and late afternoon showings of *The Partridge Family* and *Happy Days*. Their interaction with family sitcoms was different, however.

If their boomer parents grew up in families influenced—for better or worse—by the Cleaver ideal, then Gen X's primary interaction with the Cleavers was through TV. As Gen Xers grew up, old reruns often served both a babysitting and escapist function. Watching TV, many longed for "a happier, more simple time when families weren't as dysfunctional" (Owen 18), even though, as an age cohort, they had assimilated their parents' anti-authoritarian values. In an episode from the second season of *Blossom*, the title character, whose mother is pursuing a singing career in France, dreams that her mother is Clair Huxtable, dressed in a frilly apron and standing in the kitchen prepared to explain menstruation by drawing in icing on a sheet cake, an interesting blending of 1950s ideals and a more modern sensibility. In the end, whether or not the Cleaver family model could possibly be realized, Gen Xers knew they would never themselves live it and for that their parents' generation was to blame. Like their parents before them, they blamed *their* parents for whatever deficiencies they found in their upbringings and represented the result in sitcoms they helped write and direct for their peers. The Gen X response to the happy family ideal first appeared on the margins of mainstream TV, partially fueled by producers' desire to attract and keep the youngest edge of the young, single demographic. *The Simpsons* and *Married With Children*, two Gen X visions of family, were crucial to the success of a new network, FOX, which targeted the "young-adult audience" (Jamie Kellner, president of FOX, cited in Owen 57). The adults in these shows were boomer parents, not as boomers might see them but as their children did.

The classic Gen X representation of a boomer parent is Homer Simpson. Homer's creator, Matt Groening, is a boomer, not a Gen Xer, but, like most members of both age groups, he "grew up completely overwhelmed by TV" (Doherty 36). Although Homer lives in Springfield, a name borrowed from *Father Knows Best*, he bears little resemblance to any 1950s father, a fact that tickles both boomer viewers and their children. But, members of the two generations enjoy Homer for slightly different reasons. For boomers, he's an example of bad parenting, of what would happen if fathers simply indulged themselves rather than being responsible for their children. For Gen Xers, Homer represents the illogical extension of the boomer pursuit of autonomy, what pollster Daniel Yankelovich describes as the "ethic of self-fulfillment (qtd. in Skolnick 167). Homer seeks immediate gratification and is completely governed by his id. Yet, viewers of both generations like watching the show because Homer is a bad role model. *The Simpsons* is naughty, rebellious fun, a breath of fresh air in a TV world where families richer and more perfect than our own predominate. Father, not mother, is the problematic character, although Marge Simpson's strength comes from her determination to reproduce the June Cleaver ideal in a far-from-perfect family. We can all feel superior to the Simpson family. Still, they survive, sometimes thrive, and certainly love each other, and that is reassuring to anyone whose family seems flawed.

In the 1990s, most sitcoms about families were pitched at older audiences, so a show like *Everybody Loves Raymond* isn't about the kids, as the voiceover under the opening credits declares during the first season. Instead, it is about grown-ups who continue to fight with their parents and each other, mainly over the lines of responsibility, both generational and gendered. In one episode, the adults turn on one another, each blaming the others when one of the kids-the-show-wasn't-about writes a story called "The Angry Family" for school. Teachers, counselors, and the local priest all meet with the family, clearly disapproving of their behavior and eager to set them straight. Yet, after much finger-pointing and soul-searching, the story ends with the discovery that the "Angry Family" is actually a TV program the child likes, not a commentary about his actual family. Like the Simpsons, the Barones of *Everybody Loves Raymond* are flawed, hurtful, and selfish, but they love each other, and that premise ensures that everything will work out in the end.

As a new generation of sitcom viewers, Millennials (those born after 1980), emerged and Gen Xers increasingly took control over the production process, boomers lost their power to dictate how family looked on TV. When they appear at all on programs like *Will & Grace* and *Friends*, sitcom boomers play the parents of main characters, inappropriately randy and prone to divorces that shock their adult children, who must rely on one another within their constructed families to get by. These TV boomer parents of young adults tell us how actual young people feel about their parents: that they have been either too involved or not involved enough in their lives. *Friends*, however, ended its 11-year run in 2004 with five of six characters in families of their own: Rachel and Ross together with baby Emma, Monica and Chandler married with a house in the suburbs and newborn twins, and Phoebe and Mike married and contemplating children. Happily-ever-after for these Gen Xers is some version of nuclear family even if, as Rachel observes in the series finale, we never get to see Monica and Chandler actually handle twins, two jobs, and a house in the 'burbs.

As more Gen Xers and Millennials began coupling up, a new form of sitcom structure, often called postmodern, suggests that, once again, the relationship between audience and program has changed, this time with the audience demanding more power to view and interpret TV independently of network schedules. On *Scrubs*, new interns mature over the nine seasons from goofy medical students to adults with real jobs and families—but never families that look like the Cleavers, or even the Huxtables. The families constructed on *Scrubs* are more temporary and regularly threatened by individuals' impulsive wants. The same is true on *How I Met Your Mother*, whose frame is a father telling the prolonged story of the couplings of himself and four of his friends as they move from college to old age, thanks to flash-forwards, sometimes offering alternative versions of the same reality, including inappropriate details. The series is the first deliberately structured for binge-watching, allowing for prolonged exploration of family themes like marriage, having children, and settling in the suburbs (Carter C1). Lily and Marshall marry, and with a child by 2012, struggle with issues Monica and Chandler might have had if *Friends* progressed, finding nannies, claiming couple time, and acquiring a house, all stories never covered by *Father Knows Best*. And, their occasionally featured, baby-boomer parents behave just like Chandler and Monica's, which is to say they often misbehave. Even the mother referred to in the series' title turns out to be a red herring, as in the last moments of the last episode we learn that the true object of the narrator's affections wasn't the mother at all, but Robin, an ongoing character whose wedding to someone else was the focus of the last season.

Another postmodern family sitcom, *Modern Family*, spans the generations, among both characters and viewers. Its cast is diverse and multigenerational, featuring a gay couple with an adopted daughter from Vietnam; a blended, multigenerational family with an older father, stereotypical hot Colombian trophy wife, and her fussy, young teen son; and, a more traditional nuclear family with a stay-at-home wife who begins to transition back into the workplace by taking a job with her father. Its pseudo-documentary style allows characters to comment on the actions of others as well as offer signs to the audience, such as rolling eyes, that express their points of view. Consequently, what makes *Modern Family* modern isn't just its diversity but also our responsibility as viewers to negotiate among competing perspectives and find our own "truth." The series blends the self-documentation and analysis of a Facebooking, Instagramming, tweeting society with the snarky tone that begins with shows like *All in the Family* and has never really left the sitcom since. *Modern Family's* invisible "normal," though, echoes decades of American sitcoms with its posh and well-appointed homes and its stereotypical assumptions about gender roles, sexuality, and ethnic identity. We don't feel superior to the Prichett-Dumphy clan so much as we understand them, largely because we recognize their foibles and their conceits in our loved ones and, perhaps, in ourselves. What distinguishes *Modern Family* from other contemporary family sitcoms is that everyone is wonderfully fallible, and someone always offers us a moral at the end of the half-hour.

Our families today look and function differently from the way they did when the family sitcom began, as does the relationship between series and audience. We are more diverse as a nation and able to control when and how we watch any show, which naturally influences the sitcom's presentation. Family sitcoms no longer really model or teach how to be good—

Figure 2.2. Ty Burrell as Phil Dunphy, Sofia Vergara as Gloria Delgado-Pritchett, Ed O'Neill as Jay Pritchett, Eric Stonestreet as Cameron Tucker, Aubrey Anderson-Emmons as Lily Tucker-Pritchett, (middle row) Sarah Hyland as Haley Dunphy, Julie Bowen as Claire Dunphy, Rico Rodriguez as Manny Delgado, Jesse Tyler Ferguson as Mitchell Pritchett, (bottom row) Nolan Gould as Luke Dunphy, and Ariel Winter as Alex Dunphy in *Modern Family*. 2009– . Photo courtesy of Photofest.

"normal"—American families. Instead, they confirm our flaws, reveal our differences, and yet still support the unconditional love at the heart of families, whether the families are biological, blended, or otherwise constructed. Although Netflix, specialized channels, and DVD sets allow anyone to watch virtually any show at any time, modern TV seems simultaneously less and more obsessed with the happy 1950s sitcom family ideal. Like the Prichett-Dunphys, we aspire to be the best that we can be as fathers, mothers, sons, and daughters, aspirations shaped in part by those hovering 1950s norms only the oldest audience members can actually remember.

The culture of the 1960s has triumphed in American society to the extent that we accept American families that are diverse and constructed. The 1970s and 1980s television series have debunked a lot of the myths and stereotypes about how mothers, fathers, and children ought to behave. But, the reference point of the Cleavers remains the cultural ideal in American society; whether accepted, rejected, or reconfigured, it does always seem to loom over TV's renderings of family. Like Rick Nelson, we as viewers seem forever trapped in a *Twilight Zone* of 1950s family sitcoms, never quite at home but always hopeful.

3

I Love Lucy

Television and Gender in Postwar Domestic Ideology

LORI LANDAY

"Lu--cy! You've got some 'splainin' to do!" Ricky Ricardo exclaims, demanding an explanation for yet another of Lucy's tricky schemes to get into the act, make money, outdo the "girls" in her women's club, or in some other way escape being just a housewife. *I Love Lucy* ran Monday nights on CBS as a half-hour situation comedy from October 1951 to May 1957 and as monthly, hour-long specials from November 1957 until April 1960. It is the show in which the conventions, structure, and style of the sitcom genre were codified, and it might well be the most popular situation comedy ever. Of course, the genre of the television sitcom has antecedents, and *I Love Lucy* was based not only on conventions of comedy established in romantic comedy, vaudeville, film, radio, and the earliest television shows in general but also reworked material from Ball's hit radio show, *My Favorite Husband. I Love Lucy* was innovative, however, in both its sense of the *situation* and the *comedy*; the situation was based in a comic tension between everyday life and comic exaggeration, and the comedy was based on the unrivaled comedic talents of Lucille Ball and the excellent supporting cast. At its height, *I Love Lucy* redefined what it meant for a television show to be popular, being the first television show to be seen in over ten million American homes and setting many new ratings records. Not only did the show help develop the situation comedy into a genre, it contributed to the construction of postwar domestic ideology.

I Love Lucy could be this influential because it was created when television was inventing itself and its place in American culture. Recorded on black-and-white 35mm film before a live studio audience, edited, and then broadcast, the show set the standard for television aesthetics; the flat lighting style invented by legendary cinematographer Karl Freund gave depth and realism to the studio sets. Stylistically, the show set a new standard for the broadcast audiovisual medium by incorporating key aspects of both radio and film—a live studio audience and continuity editing, respectively. The live studio audience enabled the actors to play off and to their audience and helped blur the boundaries between the worlds of the home and the television screen. Viewers at home laughed along with the unseen studio audience. The editing between shots captured with three cameras running simultaneously facilitated the style of classical Hollywood cinema, establishing intimacy and identification through use of the close-up.[1] Moreover, when these spectatorial practices of classical Hollywood cinema were combined with the domestic exhibition of television, the sense of intimacy and closeness was even more pronounced. The medium of television had an immediacy and sense of presence that far outstripped radio and film. Whether live or, like *I Love Lucy*, filmed "live," the discursive patterns of early television encouraged viewers to feel as if they were actually present at the event or performance. As the 1946 book *Here Is Television, Your Window on the World* suggests, founding discourses represented television as both transparent and magical in that it not only extended the home but brought the world into the family living room.

The genre of situation comedy was at a crucial stage in its development. *I Love Lucy* and *My Favorite Husband* producer and writer Jess Oppenheimer explained that he and writers Madelyn Pugh and Bob Carroll, Jr. had broken new ground with their radio sitcom: "We just weren't writing what was then considered the 'in' kind of radio comedy show, where you have a series of comedy characters, each of whom comes in, does his own shtick, and then exits. Instead, we did whole stories—*situation* comedy" (127–28). Indeed, each episode of *I Love Lucy* has a rational setup, and the emphasis on storytelling rather than shtick focused the show's content on cultural discourses of home and family life. The *situation* of *I Love Lucy* was the domestic life of Lucy and Ricky Ricardo, who were not stars but ordinary people (although in later seasons Ricky's career takes the gang to Hollywood and Europe). When the writers wrote the initial scripts for the series, they based the everyday details of the Ricardo marriage on the Arnaz's marriage, and many scenes set in the Ricardo bedroom as the characters wake up, get dressed, or get ready for bed have an intimacy that is grounded in the mundane details of everyday life and in the audience's knowledge that the actors were really married.

In portraying everyday domesticity grounded in realism, *I Love Lucy* brought a representation of home life into American homes at a time when many families were buying televisions and working out their own versions of domestic life. After World War II, Americans were, to use Elaine Tyler May's phrase, "homeward bound," both moving toward domesticity and also restrained by domesticity. The boundaries between home and the world, long a demarcater of gender, were in flux. The ideology of domesticity— an idealization of marriage, family, and the home prescribed, albeit differently, to both men and women—was an inherently unstable one (like the other postwar ideologies of containment) that tried to legitimate traditional

Figure 3.1. Lucille Ball as Lucy Ricardo and Desi Arnaz as Ricky Ricardo in *I Love Lucy*. 1951–1961. Photo courtesy of Movie Star NewsFair.

definitions of gender and the separation of spheres at a time when those divisions were breaking down. At the core of the ideological construct of femininity in the postwar era were women's roles as housewives. High marriage rates, the explosion of suburban housing, the baby boom, emphasis on traditional gender roles, and a renewed belief in the importance of the home all bolstered a domestic revival in the 1950s. This revival informed the cultural context in which *I Love Lucy* struck such a chord, though with a twist that evolved from the real lives of Ball and Arnaz.

The origin of the series would have been well known to most television watchers, because it was repeated relentlessly in the popular publications of the time—*Life, Newsweek, Time, Look*—women's magazines, and daily newspapers. The series originated in Ball and Arnaz's desire to work together so they could stop the work-caused separations that had characterized their marriage. CBS was interested in making a television version of Ball's radio show, *My Favorite Husband*, but balked at the idea of casting Arnaz as the husband because his Cuban ethnicity did not fit into the successful formula centered on the radio show's Midwestern family. Ball and Arnaz took matters into their own hands with a vaudeville tour intended to prove to CBS that they could find and please an audience.

The pilot and then the series kept the dizzy housewife character and the older couple foils relatively intact, but it changed the setting to New York and the husband's profession from banker to bandleader. In shifting the situation from middle-class domesticity to the world of show business, *I Love Lucy* tapped into the television trend of stars playing versions of themselves (George Burns and Gracie Allen; Ozzie and Harriett Nelson) and enabled musical numbers to be performed. The pilot centered on Larry Lopez, a bandleader who wanted as normal life as possible, and his wacky wife, Lucy, who wanted to get into show business. In the pilot, Larry laments, "I want a wife who's just a wife." And, so a major conflict of *I Love Lucy* was articulated: the dissatisfied housewife eager to escape the home versus the world-weary husband who wants his wife to provide him the comforts of home—characters clearly not based on Ball and Arnaz's real-life image or experience, although perhaps on some fantasy of the domestic bliss that postwar discourses promised would come from a conventional home life based on polarized gender roles.

How typical was the restlessness and frustration that Lucy embodied? According to Betty Friedan's *The Feminine Mystique*, "the problem that has no name" was unspoken yet widespread, and the comic treatment of women's desires for a life outside the home is more a precursor of 1960s–70s feminism than typical of the 1950s. It might be that Ball and Arnaz (and their writers) were continuing to perform the cultural work suggested by a 1938

Photoplay magazine poll of Hollywood stars, which found that 93 percent of female stars and 78 percent of male stars believed in women having careers after marriage in contrast to the general population that disapproved of wives having jobs (May 41). *I Love Lucy* gives us both the actors' vanguard perspective, which obviously Ball and Arnaz shared, *and* the more conventional perspective of the population at large, which the show mimicked. Ball and Arnaz and the writers, including Madelyn Pugh, one of very few women television writers, based their work on their experiences as gendered people in the postwar era; they were surrounded by the domestic revival sweeping America, yet separate from it as part of Hollywood's more egalitarian culture.

Seen in this light, *I Love Lucy* resonated so loudly in the early 1950s because the show suggested the failure of the domestic ideal—based on the rigid gender roles portrayed in popular culture to match up with people's real experiences of everyday life. The gap between domestic ideology and social experience was larger in the 1950s than in the earlier half of the twentieth century. Historian William Chafe summarizes some evidence to support this: "The poll data showed that most citizens preferred to retain traditional definitions of masculine and feminine spheres, even while modifying the content of those spheres in practice" (171). When Lucille Ball is quoted as saying, "I'm just a typical housewife at heart" in an article on "America's top saleswomen," she is indeed holding a traditional definition of femininity while in practice having an unconventional career by excelling in the physical comedy that had been the province of men.

Of course, *I Love Lucy* was not a social realist critique of gender roles—it was *comedy*. But, comedy in American culture in general, and in television sitcoms in particular, is a major forum for reflecting and shaping cultural ideals; it is a testing ground for social formations from the simplest performance of mannerisms to the *situation* that gives the comedy its premise. In order for a sitcom to be popular, it does not have to depict how life really is, but it does have to portray a life that the audience likes.

Audiences not only liked *I Love Lucy*, they *loved* it, and they embraced not only the series but a range of Lucy and Ricky commodities, including his and hers matching pajamas, jewelry, nursery sets, aprons, smoking jackets, dolls, diaper bags, and furniture for every room. As Ball explains in her autobiography, "It was possible to furnish a house and dress a whole family with items carrying our *I Love Lucy* label" (224). One ad proclaiming "Live Like Lucy!" indicates how television brought the world into the home and the home into the world with commodities. Clearly the vision of domesticity enacted in the Ricardo's apartment was, for Lucy, a commodified one with many episodes centering on the struggle to get the money to buy something for herself or the home, perhaps most hilariously exemplified in the episode "The Freezer." Although Ball and Arnaz were in a far-different financial situation from the Ricardos, or most of their middle-class viewers, the show's emphasis on love—on emotions, marriage, friendship, and the pleasures of domestic life—outweighed the dissonance between Ball-Arnaz and the Ricardos. At no point was this more apparent than when the off-screen and on-screen lives of Ball and Arnaz were at their closest—when the writers worked Ball's real-life pregnancy into the show by making Lucy Ricardo pregnant, too.

On January 19, 1953, two babies were born—in the morning, Ball and Arnaz had a son, and in the evening, Lucy and Ricky Ricardo also had a son. "Lucy Goes to the Hospital" hit an all-time high rating, with an estimate of more than 44 million viewers. In blurring the line between reality and artifice with the synchronic "real-life" and "fictional" births, *I Love Lucy* was a metaphor for what television as an institution and apparatus was doing anyway: making more permeable the traditional demarcations between public and private, truth and artifice, and representation and social experience.

The seven pregnancy shows, culminating in "Lucy Goes to the Hospital" (which barely had Lucy in it at all) built on the previous season and a half when *I Love Lucy* established itself as a phenomenon. Many of the most brilliant episodes are from this early period, including "Job Switching" with the hilarious candy factory conveyor belt scene and "Lucy Does a TV Commercial" with the Vitameatavegamin scene. These episodes and many more lesser-known ones followed the successful formula of building up to comic climaxes that showcased the comedic talents of Ball and her co-stars. *New York Times Magazine* writer Jack Gould explained the appeal in March 1953:

> "I Love Lucy" is as much a phenomenon as an attraction. Fundamentally, it is a piece of hilarious theatre put together with deceptively brilliant know-how, but it also is many other things. In part it is a fusion of the make-believe of the footlights and the real-life existence of a glamorous "name." In part it is the product of inspired press agentry which has made a national legend of a couple which two years ago was on the Hollywood side-lines. (16)

The "inspired" publicity machine to which Gould refers was indeed industrious and effective. By February 1952, just four months after *I Love Lucy* premiered, the show was not only number one but also hit all the major newspapers and magazines, making connections between the real-life actors and their on-screen characters and intertwining their personal and professional stories.

Of the hundreds of magazine and newspaper articles and features that I have researched, hardly any stray from the Desilu publicity machine's story of how television saved their marriage. The story goes like this: After their 1940 marriage, they were so busy with their careers that they barely saw each other, and they tried to find a vehicle in which they could work together. Even though producers would not develop projects for them because of Arnaz's Cuban ethnicity and strong accent, Ball and Arnaz were convinced they could be a success. The vaudeville act they took on the road was well received, but they canceled the second half because of 39-year-old Ball's pregnancy. That pregnancy ended in a miscarriage, but soon she was pregnant again, and they filmed the pilot episode when she was six months pregnant. CBS and sponsor cigarette company Philip Morris picked up the show, and they began production one month after their daughter Lucie was born. The innovations of the production context figure largely in the articles—that Ball and Arnaz owned the show through their company Desilu Productions and filmed it before a live audience in Hollywood—but the articles always stress the love story. As a March 1952 *Chicago Sunday Tribune* article put it, "Desi and Lucille are particularly grateful to TV because it has given them an opportunity to live a normal family life." An April 6, 1952, *L.A. Examiner* article ran a picture of the couple smooching in bed with the caption, "When Desi and Lucille do scenes like this in their TV show, they aren't just play-acting—they really mean it." Or as "a friend" of Ball's explained in a July 1952 *Look* article, "The trouble with Lucy is that her real life is so much like her reel life" (Silvian 7).

Of course, despite the PR copy that the show was based on the Ball and Arnaz marriage, clearly it was not. In particular, the divergence between talented, successful, and famous Lucille Ball and thwarted, unfulfilled, unknown Lucy Ricardo is huge, and although the actors had a daughter, the Ricardos were childless. But, it allowed Ball and Arnaz a bizarre public fantasy of a private life closer to traditional gender roles than their real-life partnership.

The situation of *I Love Lucy* articulated the contradictions of marriage, gender, the battle of the sexes, and middle-class life—concerns of the majority of television watchers and buyers. Ball attributed the series' success to identification:

> We had a great identification with millions of people. People identified with the Ricardos because we had the same problems they had. Desi and I weren't your ordinary Hollywood couple on

TV. We lived in a brownstone apartment somewhere in Manhattan, and paying the rent, getting a new dress, getting a stale fur collar on an old cloth coat, or buying a piece of furniture were all worth a story. (qtd. in Andrews 225–26)

Note that the things Ball lists as ordinary problems all deal with domestic, private life; the problem solving leads back to the core of the show, the "love" between the couple. The actors' collaborative marriage filters through the comic representation of the demands of the companionate marriage, the postwar ideal that imagined the husband and wife as a team supporting the husband's work in the public sphere with the wife stationed in the private sphere.

This aspect of the conflation of Ball-Arnaz and the Ricardos emerged even more when the show incorporated Lucille Ball's real-life pregnancy into the fictional world of the series. When Ball and Arnaz revealed her pregnancy to the show's producer, they transformed what could have been the end of the series into a new arena for comedy; not only had television "saved" their marriage, but it enabled Ball to maintain her career and have a family. Moreover, Ball performed the cultural work of a trickster in mainstream America by being the first openly pregnant woman to perform on television, which challenged accepted ideas about the impropriety of public representations of pregnancy. For example, even though the censors would not allow anyone to say the word "pregnant" on the show (the French "enceinte" was used instead), Arnaz refused when Philip Morris wanted Lucy's pregnant body hidden behind furniture. Instead of hiding Ball's pregnancy, they made comedy from Lucy's cravings and mood swings, aspirations for the baby's future, Ricky's sympathetic morning sickness and important role as father, and cute maternity clothes (available at a store near you).

The intertwining of fictionality and "reality" in the pregnancy episodes resulted in an emotional intensity that allowed the viewer to participate in a highly mediated but nevertheless moving enactment of expecting a baby. Throughout these reality-based episodes, the audience is privy to a re-enactment of personal events, or rather, Ball and Arnaz turned their private experience into a public representation that reflected and shaped the popular pursuit of marriage and family.

The episode in which Lucy tells Ricky she is expecting was foreshadowed by media coverage of Ball's pregnancy and reports that the baby would be incorporated into the show. In the episode, Lucy tries to tell Ricky the news, things interfere, and the dramatic irony builds because the viewer knows what Ricky does not. The climax of the show occurs in

Ricky's nightclub—and Ball and Arnaz were understandably emotional as they filmed the scene. Ricky gets an anonymous note that a woman wants to tell her husband they are expecting a "blessed event," and Ricky goes from table to table looking for the couple as he sings "Rockabye Baby." He finally comes to a table where Lucy is seated. After an emotional moment of realization, Ricky sings "We're Having a Baby" as he walks around the stage with a tearful Lucy, and he flubs the lyrics of the song. The episode ends with a close-up of the couple crying and laughing. Producer Oppenheimer recalls that they did another take, filming a more upbeat scene as had been originally scripted, but they decided to use the first one.

This moment is significant because it is Lucille Ball and Desi Arnaz we are watching, not the characters. The fiction of the television series becomes, for a moment, transparent. Most striking, however, is the intimacy of this scene, a familiarity felt by the audience for the people on the screen that had been forged in a television series that revolved around the intimate moments of marriage and everyday life. In order for the creative team to choose the take in which the actors are choked up and have it work, there had to have been a long setup to this moment paved with a hybrid of fictionality and reality that transcends both.

The scene itself plays with the line between reality and artifice and between public and private. As Ricky goes from table to table in search of the parents-to-be, the camera is positioned in the audience, encouraging our identification as a live audience member (reinforced by the laughter of the studio audience that blurs with the diegetic laughter of the club audience). The mise-en-scène of the nightclub stage and incorporation of musical performance into the plot is typical of how early television oscillated between domestic and theatrical space in shows such as *The George Burns and Gracie Allen Show*, *The Adventures of Ozzie and Harriet*, and *Make Room for Daddy*, as well as *I Love Lucy*. As Lynn Spigel explains, "By acknowledging its own artifice and theatricality, the family comedy encouraged viewers to feel as if they had been let in on a joke, while at the same time allowing them to take that joke seriously" (*Make Room* 165). The strategy of letting the audience in on both the joke and the seriousness runs through the pregnancy episodes and makes comedy out of reality—including Ball's pregnant body and what it could and could not do. Although there is not a great deal of Ball's trademark physical comedy in the episodes filmed while she was six and seven months pregnant, there are scattered moments. Not only is Ball a pregnant woman seen in public and continuing to work, but also in the scenes that showcase her pregnant body, Lucy is competent and resourceful in getting around its limitations.

The convergence of reality and fictionality suggested by Ball's physical comedy peaked on January 19, 1953, when the two babies were born. The *Newsweek* cover story of the same date, "Desilu Formula for Top TV: Brains, Beauty, Now a Baby," describes the schedule of the blessed events, "If all goes well, newspaper readers all over the country will be treated on Jan. 20 to the story of Mrs. Arnaz having a baby—the morning after they see Mrs. Ricardo go to the hospital on TV. All this may come under the heading of how duplicated in life and television *can* you get" (56). Because no one knew the sex of the Ball-Arnaz baby, they could not duplicate that piece of reality for the November filming of the episode "Lucy Goes to the Hospital," and it was kept secret that the Ricardo baby would be a boy. The pregnancy episodes play on this uncertainty, and the sex became a topic of popular speculation, culminating in the dual births. Examples of the headlines reporting the births foreground the collision of reality and fictionality—with fictionality winning out over reality: "Lucy Sticks to Script: A Boy It Is!" (*NY Daily Mirror,* 1/20/53); "TV Was Right: a Boy for Lucille" (*Daily News,* 1/20/53); "What the Script Ordered" (*Life,* 2/2/53).

Unlike the celebratory melding of real-life and fiction in the babies, other real-life events were kept carefully away from the television text. Although *I Love Lucy* was subversive about domestic containment, Ball, Arnaz, the producers, and CBS downplayed the Red Scare accusation that Lucille Ball was a Communist. A full discussion of the media representations of how Ball had, in fact, registered as a Communist in 1938 in order, she insisted, to please her grandfather, is beyond the scope of this chapter, but Ball's red hair almost had a very different—and career-ending—connotation. The news of Ball's 1953 hearings before the House Un-American Activities Committee leaked out, leading to a *Los Angeles-Herald Express* headline, in three-inch red letters: "LUCILLE BALL NAMED RED." That night, before the filming of the 1953–54 season premiere, Arnaz gave a serious speech denouncing communism and labeling the rumors lies. The crowd cheered. He ended as he always did, with, "And now, I want you to meet my favorite wife," but then he continued, "my favorite redhead—in fact, that's the only thing red about her, and even that's not legitimate—Lucille Ball!" (Sanders and Gilbert 81) Not surprisingly, the television series also eschewed the real-life unrest in the Ball-Arnaz marriage, which ended in divorce in 1960, about when the series ended. It seems that television could not really save their, or anyone's, marriage.

"There's no dream she wouldn't reach for, and no fall she wouldn't take." This is how Walter Matthau described the universal appeal and comedic genius of Lucille Ball, and indeed Lucille Ball's comic genius continues to entertain and amaze in its embrace of both hopeful aspiration and often subsequent plummet (Sanders and Gilbert 368). In the role of Lucy, Ball and her collaborators created one of the most beloved and central kinds of cultural figures: a trickster, a subversive, paradoxical fantasy figure who does what we cannot or dare not by moving between social spaces, roles, and categories that the culture has deemed oppositional (Landay *Trickster*). When faced with a situation that appears to have only two choices, the trickster is the kind of hero/ine who creates a third possibility. But, the trickster's schemes often backfire, and then the trickster becomes the dupe. Lucy is specifically a female trickster because her attempts to circumvent the limitations of postwar domesticity oscillate between "masculine" and "feminine" social roles, spaces, practices, and metaphors.

By calling attention to the power relations of the sexes in everyday domestic life, *I Love Lucy* participated in a proto-feminist current building in American culture. The continued appeal of *I Love Lucy* in reruns is due not only to comic brilliance but also to how it offers contemporary audiences a fitting precursor to the women's movement of the 1960s–70s. Scholar George Lipsitz's term "memory as misappropriation" suggests a show can be popular because it represents the past as people wish it had been. *I Love Lucy* recasts the domestic prison of the 1950s into the easily escapable terrain of the female trickster. Lucy's daring pursuit of her desires and her irrepressible insistence that Ricky—and everyone else—acknowledge her as a talented individual provide a model that may be radically different from our impressions of our mothers, grandmothers, and great-grandmothers. Moreover, by wiggling under, vaulting over, and sneaking past the boundary between reality and fictionality, by playing fast and loose with the various windows between the world and the home that television promised and failed to be, Lucy the trickster delighted postwar Americans, and *I Love Lucy* shaped situation comedy forever.

NOTES

Thanks to my husband, Richard Cownie, for editing help, as well as for seeing the humor in things.

1. Despite the myth it started, Desilu did not invent the three-camera system still used in television today. Arnaz and cinematographer Karl Freund (who shot the German expressionist *Metropolis* in 1926 and was Ball's cinematographer on the 1943 MGM musical *DuBarry Was a Lady*) adapted the system pioneered by Jerry Fairbanks but kept all three cameras rolling simultaneously. See Christopher Anderson, *Hollywood TV: The Studio System in the Fifties*, 53–56 and 65–68.

To the Moon!

Working-Class Masculinity in *The Honeymooners*

STEVEN T. SHEEHAN

Ralph Kramden and his wife Alice are troubled. Having just received a telegram, they stand in the main room of their Brooklyn apartment and worry because telegrams usually bring bad news. Finally, Ralph musters the courage to read it and discovers that Alice's mother plans to come for a visit. The two express relief, and Ralph leaves the room. A split-second later, Gleason barrels back. The gravity of the situation has dawned on Ralph, and he bellows, "Your mother?! Now listen. Your mother is not stepping one foot in this house!" The two descend into a familiar pattern of bickering. Ultimately, Alice states flatly that her mother will always be welcome to visit *her* house. At this assertion, Ralph reels back, half out of amazement and half out of amusement. His eyes bug, and the rotund comedian skips lightly around the stage softly lilting, "Your house? Your house?" Suddenly he plants his feet, drops his voice several octaves and affirms that the apartment is, in fact, *his* house. Therefore, he determines who can and who cannot visit.

In response, Alice launches into a facetious tribute to Ralph and the "lap of luxury" in which he keeps her. Ultimately, she settles on an extended metaphor that, by sarcastically paralleling their apartment to Disneyland, contrasts the couple's lack of consumer commodities and cramped unpleasantness with the amusement park that opened earlier that year and that the scholar Karal Ann Marling has argued serves as a symbol of the possibilities of limitless consumer pleasure and family togetherness. Alice glides to the apartment's kitchen window. Only a small opening is visible, densely packed with a backdrop of gray, Brooklyn, tenement buildings. While Alice claims to see slightly more than the scope available to the viewer, her description of that "view," which she calls her "Fantasyland," includes garbage cans, the rear of a nearby Chinese restaurant, and a neighbor's long underwear hanging out to dry. The tenement window and Alice's description of it underscore the Kramdens' life in a confined urban space in contrast to the expansive, picture window suburbs of postwar America. From the window, Alice sashays to the sink, where she turns the tap. As the faucet emits knocking sounds rather than water, she cries, "This! Now this is my Adventureland." Nodding her head to the other side of the kitchen, she draws attention to the aged stove and traditional icebox. Knowing that the kitchen appliances are always fodder for her most biting sarcasm, the audience snickers in anticipation of the punch line. When she delivers it, that the appliances are her "Frontierland," they let loose with laughter. As the laughter drops off, she notes that the apartment lacks only one of the four "lands" that make up the larger Disneyland complex. She has no "World of Tomorrow." Gleason, who has remained steadfast at the center of the living space through Alice's monologue, comes alive. He bugs his eyes, blows out his cheeks, and puffs his chest. "You want a world of tomorrow?!" he bellows. Again the audience laughs in anticipation of the familiar punch line. He brings a fist up to his wife's chin and shouts, "You're going to the moon!" The audience laughs uproariously.

The comedic treatment of material deprivation and domestic violence in this 1955 episode of *The Honeymooners* titled "Hello Mom" is typical of the show. The couple argues in nearly every episode. Alice often gains the upper hand by pointing to the material evidence scattered throughout the apartment of Ralph's failure to achieve the standard of living that had increasingly come to define success for the postwar American working class. Following a series of pointed barbs, Ralph often becomes enraged and threatens his wife. The sketch, and the Ralph character in particular, resonated with audiences because it foregrounded the frustrations many felt attempting to negotiate a postwar cultural landscape that celebrated domesticity and material abundance not only as sources of individual pleasure and fulfillment but as key aspects of citizenship and national identity. Sitcoms like *The Honeymooners*, which are based on the frustrations of working-class characters, have been wildly popular, but they are also relatively infrequent visitors to prime-time network television. The intrusion of material deprivation into the homes of working-class characters, and their resulting sense of anger and isolation, runs counter to the prosperity assumed in typical sitcoms. Angry, isolated characters like Ralph Kramden are found more frequently in the vigilante films of the 1960s and beyond than in domestic situation comedies.

The Honeymooners debuted in 1951 as a sketch on the Dumont television network's *Cavalcade of Stars* variety show hosted by Jackie Gleason. Gleason jumped to the Columbia Broadcasting System (CBS) for the 1952–53 season to host *The Jackie Gleason Show,* bringing the sketch with him. By the 1953–54 season, Gleason's show had become one of television's most broadly viewed programs, and *The Honeymooners* sketch its most popular segment. Indeed, the sketch became so popular that Gleason pushed to make it a half-hour episodic series independent of the variety show for the 1955–56 television season. The sketch returned to *The Jackie Gleason Show* for a final season in 1956–57 (Simon). Throughout its run, the sketch focused on the domestic dramas and squabbles of the working-class Kramden couple, a New York City bus driver and his stay-at-home wife, who live in a ramshackle Brooklyn tenement.

Figure 4.1. Jackie Gleason as Ralph Kramden, Art Carney as Ed Norton, and Audrey Meadows as Alice Kramden in *The Honeymooners*. 1955–1956. Photo courtesy of Wikipedia.

The show's popularity and its major themes were not merely coincidental. *The Honeymooners* resonated with postwar audiences because it addresses important concerns about working-class masculinity in what historian Lizabeth Cohen has termed "A Consumers' Republic"—a postwar America in which national and personal identities were increasingly defined by the ability to produce, purchase, and accumulate consumer pleasures. Pointedly, Cohen chooses the word "republic" rather than the simpler "nation" to describe postwar America. In doing so, she indicates that the postwar consumer society is built on the republican political and social traditions sewn into the fabric of American history. Stretching back to the Revolutionary era, the ideology of republicanism glorified the financially independent, politically virtuous head of the family. The original republican man was conceived as a farmer, whose land allowed him to produce what he would consume and to consume only what he could produce. Thus, he possessed *virtue*, an economic and social independence that servants, slaves, women, and children lacked. Given his financial and social independence, he could govern in the interest of the republic rather than in his own economic self-interest. He was at once individualistic, cultivating his own economic and social status, and self-sacrificing, serving the interests of the republic and his dependents. In the postwar era, the ability to wisely and generously provide consumer goods established men as family heads and productive members of the polity. To be a citizen of the consumers' republic, the individual man needed not only to maintain an income but to spend it wisely on big-ticket consumer items, thereby affirming his role as head of household and fueling the production-consumption cycle on which national well-being depended (Cohen).

In his analysis of real and fictional middle-class men in postwar America, the historian James Gilbert argues that, in contrast to the conventional belief that Americans simply reaffirmed a traditional, breadwinner masculinity in the postwar era, the period actually saw more fluid gender boundaries and the emergence of myriad masculinities. Both Cohen and Gilbert demonstrate that rather than simply bringing home the breadwinner's paycheck, postwar men were expected to take increasing responsibility for spending it, particularly in consuming household durables in order to care for dependent families in the postwar world (*Men*). This essay builds on Gilbert's notion of multiple masculinities and the demonstrated importance of consumption to postwar masculinity while expanding the framework to examine what happens to gender discourses when they focus on *working-class* masculinity. Unlike most middle-class television patriarchs, Ralph Kramden never embraces his role in the consumers' republic. *The Honeymooners* repeatedly stresses both the burdensome nature of the material obligations of family life and Ralph's inability to meet them. When Ralph does participate in consumer culture, he does so purposefully to distance himself from his wife and home, thereby creating more marital strife.

Like most situation comedies, storylines on *The Honeymooners* usually rotate around the domestic lives of its main characters. Yet, the show's dramatic tension is premised on the fact that the couple cannot enjoy the consumer pleasures of the contemporary middle class. As a result, the show often reminded its audience that Ralph's public failures make him an inadequate breadwinner and thus constitute the root causes of his domestic distress. Ralph often finds himself intimidated and overwhelmed by authority figures, particularly his boss, in public situations. For example, in a 1956 episode titled "Opportunity Knocks, but . . . ," Ralph stands outside the Gotham Bus Company, his employer, confidently jawing with a coworker. With his shoulders rolled back and chest jutted out proudly, he gestures firmly with his hands and brags that he always speaks his mind to the boss to whom he refers casually by his last name: Marshall. As the coworker leaves the scene, an older well-dressed man walks up to him. Kramden literally shrinks as his shoulders roll forward, his chest caves, and his mouth convulses in involuntary tremors before croaking out, "*Mister* Marshall." Throughout the ensuing sequence, Ralph, with hands folded respectfully over his lunchbox, makes a seemingly neutral statement with which the boss disagrees. In turn, Ralph immediately reverses his original statement. We see the social distance between the two men, and its clearly demoralizing effect on the previously boastful Kramden. In addition, the scene affords Mr. Marshall an unmistakable air of institutional authority as the sign for the Gotham Bus Company, which he commands and for which Ralph labors as a driver, looms over them and further intimidates Ralph.

Ralph's public failures and cowardice in the face of institutional power are not confined to his relationship with the Gotham Bus Company and do not stop at his apartment door. In another 1956 episode titled "The Worry Wort," Ralph receives a letter from the Internal Revenue Service requesting his presence at the local office. He spends the ensuing episode pacing about the apartment, poring over tax documents, fretting about what he has done wrong, and plotting an escape. Ultimately, after determining to throw himself on the mercy of the IRS, he discovers that he has merely forgotten to sign his otherwise legally completed tax return. Ralph's working-class status cuts him off from the center of public power in postwar America, and when he does encounter representatives of that power structure, he often literally collapses under what he perceives as their intimidation.

At first glance, *The Honeymooners* seems to demonstrate that a public failure like Ralph Kramden can maintain his self-esteem and manhood by serving as the final authority in his home and over his wife. Ralph's oft-repeated claim to be "king of the castle" is one of the show's comic mantras. Yet, as Cecilia Tichi has argued in her study of postwar television, the ability to possess, display, and gaze upon consumer goods played a fundamental role in establishing male authority within the postwar home as the representation of the "comfortable suburban interior [paid] tribute to the man as good provider and master of family and property" (17). Thus, Alice frequently undermines Ralph's claims to patriarchal authority by pointing to his inadequacies as a provider and consumer. For Ralph, the domestic setting is neither a haven from public failure nor the foundation for citizenship in a consumers' republic. Their barren kitchen/dining/living area constantly reminds Ralph, the show's other characters, and the viewer of Ralph's inadequacies as a provider and consumer.

Over and over, Alice points out Ralph's inability to provide and his outright refusal to purchase household commodities. Implicitly, and sometimes quite explicitly, she points out that their sparsely furnished apartment and her husband's inability or unwillingness to update it has locked the couple in prewar Brooklyn as the postwar world grows around them. Thus, in a 1955 episode titled "A Woman's Work Is Never Done," Alice brags sarcastically about her "atomic kitchen," referring to contemporary notions of postwar America as part of the atomic age. In its postwar context, the idea of the atomic age held forth that cutting-edge science and technology could be applied to everyday material life to foster comfort and efficiency. Alice labels her kitchen "atomic" not for its streamlined technological comfort but because it looks "like Yucca Flats," the bleak landscape that served as the site of numerous nuclear test explosions in the 1940s and 1950s. Indeed, rather than resembling the typical, celebrated, postwar living space, the décor could best be characterized as Alice sarcastically describes it, "early Depression."

In a rich, qualitative postwar study of the lives of working-class couples, the sociologist Mirra Komarovsky found similar tendencies among her subjects. "The poor providers," she reports, offer "their wives too obvious a weapon to be used in a fit of anger" (291). For example, one husband told of an occasion on which he supported his daughter's refusal to eat dinner because he agreed with her distaste for a particular dish. According to the man's recollection, his wife then "hollered at [him] at the table and said if [he'd] make enough money she could get the food they liked" (292). *The Honeymooners* offer a humorous fictionalization of the contradictions that gave rise to the poignant, real-life stories found in Komarovsky's work.

argues, "*The Honeymooners* would never be popular in France, Germany, Italy, Scandinavia, or the Baltic States, where the man already is undisputed boss of the home" (15). Komarovsky also found such violent frustration linked to domestic squabbles over family finances and men's ability to provide. She notes, "economic failure is likely to magnify shortcomings. The poor providers are themselves frustrated and anxious. Not many men can handle these destructive emotions without further consequences, such as drinking, violence, irritability, increased sensitivity to criticism, and withdrawal" (291). *The Honeymooners* confronts these areas of tension within the working-class home and provides an identifiable, humorous, and cathartic outlet in Ralph Kramden's anger.

The Honeymooners attempts to contain and resolve its depiction of domestic conflicts over the rights and resources of consumption with humor and pathos. Inevitably, the couple ends violent arguments by gradually sliding into fits of uncontrollable laughter and embracing one another. Ralph will look at Alice and utter one of the show's stock phrases, "Baby, you're the greatest," before the scene fades out. Yet, by making Ralph's desire to escape his tenement, and frequently his marriage, a central component of the show, *The Honeymooners* nudges at the lid of a Pandora's box of gendered conflict at the core of postwar consumer culture and domesticity.

There have been relatively few domestic situation comedies based on working-class characters like the Kramdens. In a series of quantitative studies, Richard Butsch finds that middle-class characters, particularly from such prestige professions as medicine and the arts, have been overrepresented in prime-time sitcoms. Working-class characters have been underrepresented, especially blue-collar workers. Butsch notes that only 11 percent of major characters from the dawn of television through 1990 could be characterized as working class. Other scholars have corroborated Butsch's findings and updated them to cover the 1990s (Butsch and Glennon 1983; Butsch 1992; Scharrer 2001). Moreover, periods with greater (but never proportional) working-class representation in network sitcoms occur only during eras of transition and crisis in network programming. Butsch finds three small peaks for working-class representation during these transitional periods: the middle of the 1950s, when networks were still making the shift from radio to television; the early 1970s, when networks sought to replace older rural audiences with younger, urban audiences more attractive to advertisers; and in the late 1980s and early 1990s, as the networks hemorrhaged audience shares to cable television. Thus, for network programmers, middle-class affluence is the norm, and working-class characters are experiments for abnormal times.

Risk aversion partially explains the relative lack of working-class characters. Network executives, producers, and writers seek to create and sell a product to one another and the public. That product, a domestic situation comedy, is both time-consuming and expensive to produce. Failure can cost months of time and millions of dollars, so networks produce a familiar product that has been a proven seller in the past. During periods of transition and upheaval in television viewing, because the proven formula no longer seems to work, networks have found room for more working-class characters. Of course, with the proliferation of nonbroadcast options available now, there is a greater range of sitcoms in style and content than at any previous time in the history of the form, though blue-collar workers still lag behind other types of representations.

The most important explanation for the dearth of working-class characters and settings in situation comedies is that they are not amenable to an advertiser-sponsored art form that highlights domesticity on a historically domestic medium. For most sitcom families, and for their program sponsors, middle-class affluence is an unspoken, all-pervasive assumption. Conflicts over children's behavior and personal relationships emerge and are resolved before the backdrop of well-appointed living areas, bedrooms, and kitchens that never figure into the plot narrative. Characters do not fret about unfulfilled material desires; they do not bicker over how to distribute limited financial resources. In working-class situation comedies, the harsh material reality of the outside world too often intrudes into the domestic sphere. Ralph and Alice fight over his inability to meet cultural expectations about commodity consumption. To demand a new refrigerator, as Alice does, and to become enraged at the thought of losing scarce income to household purchases, as Ralph does, is to question the very nature of the consumers' republic. The tensions in the Kramden's apartment, though they resemble the conflicts in middle-class sitcoms, stem from the overt, harsh reality of material scarcity. No amount of closing-scene hugs or utterings of "Baby, you're the greatest" can overcome the reality that the Kramdens are broke, live in a sparsely furnished tenement, and that Ralph has no realistic opportunity to lead them out.

The Honeymooners foreshadows the iconic frustrated, defeated working-class man of the late 1960s and beyond. As Mark Nicholls points out in his examination of masculinity in the films of Martin Scorsese, while we have traditionally focused on the rage and violent actions of "Scorsese's Men," their emotions and behaviors stem from a fundamental point of inadequacy and self-loathing that earlier appears in Gleason's performance of Ralph Kramden. In analyzing Travis Bickle's dialogue with his mirrored reflection in *Taxi Driver*, Nicholls argues:

For all the manic violence this celebrated scene may suggest, Travis's mirror rehearsal suggests not action but retreat . . . Placing himself as a morally superior "man apart" from the corruption and confusion of the urban mob, Travis is playing out his fantasy scenario of destroying evil, saving the virtuous, and redeeming the community. A bloody and violent self-sacrifice is central to his mission. Public validation of that mission is implicit. The mirror reminds us, however, that the fantasy scenario is a response to the inadequate self. Travis's routine thus looks less like a moment of empowering action than a melancholic marker of loss—of that gap which . . . sits at the center of our being. (1–2)

Travis Bickle's melancholia ultimately provides some justification for his murderous rampage at the end of the film, just as male melancholy often "is frequently used to validate and protect certain forms of male desire . . . particularly against claims of misogyny" (Nicholls xiv). Travis Bickle and his melancholic, angry brothers can be seen as Ralph Kramden's progeny. Just as *Taxi Driver* invites empathy for Travis Bickle, *The Honeymooners* invites empathy for Ralph, a man who fails to meet the demands of mid-century masculine consumer citizenship and who approaches the line separating melancholia and violence without crossing it.

Ultimately, Ralph Kramden and *The Honeymooners* are significant because they shed insight into a specifically working-class, mass-mediated masculinity that is angrier and more alienated than middle-class models of masculinity in the 1950s. In addition, like other gender discourses in the 1950s, this angry working-class masculinity marks the historical root of a gender ideology that becomes more apparent and more prominent by the late 1960s. While scholars have discovered the roots of the progressive and countercultural movements of the 1960s and 1970s in such 1950s popular cultural phenomena as the Beats, James Dean, and Elvis, Ralph Kramden points the way toward Travis Bickle and Archie Bunker. The character and the show demonstrate that rather than emerging simply in reaction to the upheaval of the late 1960s, the archetype of the lonely, frustrated working-class man also grows from the battles over gender, consumption, and authority in the living rooms and in the popular culture of the 1950s. While popular with audiences, that working-class character type has resided uneasily and only intermittently in the advertiser-sponsored consumer utopia of the domestic sitcom.

The 1960s

If the surface calm of the 1950s masked various underlying tensions, the 1960s—especially by the middle of the decade—put those conflicts out in the open where they became undeniable. Battle lines were drawn across political, military, social, and cultural terrain. Television tried to keep the peace by soothing the wounds and by bridging the generation gap by pretending serious differences did not exist. The decade started with the first televised presidential debate in 1960, and in hindsight, that event provided a clue about the huge cultural shift about to take place. A majority of people listening on the radio thought Richard Nixon won the debate, but those watching on television felt that John F. Kennedy had prevailed; clearly, TV viewers were influenced by John F. Kennedy's handsomeness and ease in front of the camera, which contrasted markedly with Nixon's sweaty pallor. As Daniel Boorstin noted, the imagery of media events was becoming more influential than the actual events. Television was ushering the nation into the Age of Celebrity.

Kennedy won the election and became the country's first Catholic president. The following year, he issued an executive order establishing the Peace Corps. But, not every problem could be solved by presidential charisma and clout. The Berlin Wall, the foremost symbol of the Cold War, was erected in 1961, and the Cuban Missile Crisis occurred the following year when President Kennedy demanded that the Soviet Union remove its missiles from Cuba. The country went into collective shock when President Kennedy was assassinated in November 1963, and people turned to their television sets for comfort. Kennedy's assassination and funeral were telecast nonstop for four days with producers and technicians overcoming technological constraints to create a type of immersive programming that had not been seen previously. The sense of national insecurity was only exacerbated by three subsequent assassinations: Malcolm X in 1965, and Martin Luther King, Jr. and Robert Kennedy in 1968.

During the 1960s, the Women's Movement gained strength, spurred by the publication of Betty Friedan's book *The Feminine Mystique* and the formation of the National Organization for Women. Traditional constructions of gender were beginning to collide with new ideas and opportunities for women, but this was not the only value framework that was undergoing challenges within the larger culture and on television. John O'Leary and Rick Worland explore ways rural sitcoms, especially the early seasons of *The Doris Day Show*, draw on the comfort some viewers took in the ways that traditional values of rural America were upheld while also making small acknowledgments of the arrival of modernity. As ineffectively as television may have addressed women's rights (prefiguring what Judy Kutulas discusses in the next section as a growing acceptance of women's liberation but not feminism), there was, at least, an acknowledgment of women's emerging power in the way that Doris Day reinvented her character (Doris Martin) to adapt to changes in the cultural landscape and better resonate with viewers. And, it is hard to deny that the most powerful women on television during the decade were Samantha (*Bewitched*) and Jeannie (*I Dream of Jeannie*), even if they did try to harness their powers (with limited success). The Stonewall Riots in New York City in 1969 marked the acknowledged inception of the Gay Rights Movement, but it would be decades before openly gay characters would assume starring roles on sitcoms. Television was not yet ready for serious discussions about race, class, gender, and sexuality.

As the Vietnam War escalated with huge troop buildups in the second half of the decade, antiwar demonstrations became increasingly fervent, and when the avuncular Walter Cronkite went on the *CBS Evening News* in February 1968 to declare the war unwinnable, it was clear that President Lyndon Johnson had lost the support of mainstream America. But, the real-world devastation of Vietnam was but a distant distraction in sitcom-land; the majority of 1960s sitcoms remained locked in a rural fantasy world that never really existed. In an incredible example of cultural disconnection, the gentle rube, Gomer Pyle, who was introduced on *The Andy Griffith Show*, becomes the proverbial "fish out of water" character when he joins the Marines and lands in his own series, *Gomer Pyle, U.S.M.C.*, which ran from 1964–69. The uneducated but pure-hearted Gomer (Jim Nabors) makes idiotic mistakes but always prevails over the blustery sergeant he torments in a pristine base near Los Angeles called Camp Henderson, a "Never Never Land" where unpleasantries such as guerilla warfare are never mentioned. Gary Kenton addresses the same type of cultural myopia in his chapter on magicoms, a subgenre of sixties sitcoms that he argues are presented as harmless (if inane) escapism but that actually have had the effect of normalizing regressive attitudes and adding momentum to the backlash against the progressive movements of the 1960s that continues to resonate today.

Although the Civil Rights Movement had benefitted greatly from the two-pronged leadership of the consensus builder Rev. Martin Luther King, Jr. and the more militant Malcolm X, television entertainment programming remained in a period of "Whiteout." Over two hundred thousand people marched for civil rights in Washington, D.C. in 1963, a landmark event that culminated in Dr. King's iconic "I Have a Dream Speech" on the Washington Mall. Other marches and acts of civil disobedience followed, giving millions of Black Americans hope for a more just and equitable future and leading to the passage of the Civil Rights Act of 1964 and the Voting Rights Act of 1965. Television producers and networks responded in 1968 with *Julia*, a sitcom that introduced a professional African American woman in a leading role for the first time. The problem was that including such a character in an imaginary, integrated, peaceful world where race doesn't matter did not strike many people as a realistic or sufficient response. On the one hand, the series was groundbreaking in terms of placing Diahann Carroll in a prime-time starring role, and it reflected the liberal sensibilities of its creator Hal Kanter, who wanted to make a statement on race and acceptance. But, on the other hand, it did not reflect the reality of life as experienced by most Blacks and, as Demetria Shabazz argues, the series adopted production techniques that "whitened" Carroll's character and played too much off her beauty and sex appeal.

The Super Bowl made its debut in 1967, and The Children's Television Workshop was formed that same year by a group of women concerned about television's effects on children, resulting in the creation of *Sesame Street* in 1969. Yet, prime-time television programming remained a predominantly reality-free zone. The airwaves were populated by Westerns, variations on detective and lawyer dramas, quiz shows, and variety shows. The magicoms had no monopoly on escapism; they were joined on the air by the first two sitcoms that were exclusively animated: *The Flintstones*, a series following the exploits of a prehistoric cartoon family; and *The Jetsons*, a show devoted to their space-age counterparts. These shows ushered animation into prime time and foreshadowed the success of later series, such as *The Simpsons*, *King of the Hill*, and *Family Guy*.

The most popular sitcoms of the 1960s were *The Adventures of Ozzie and Harriett*; *The Andy Griffith Show*; *The Beverly Hillbillies*; *Bewitched*; *The Bill Cosby Show*; *Car 54, Where Are You?*; *The Danny Thomas Show*; *Dennis the Menace*; *The Dick Van Dyke Show*; *The Donna Reed Show*; *The Doris Day Show*; *Family Affair*; *The Flintstones*; *Get Smart*; *Gilligan's Island*; *Gomer Pyle*,

U.S.M.C.; *Green Acres*; *Hazel*; *Here's Lucy*; *Hogan's Heroes*; *I Dream of Jeannie*; *The Joey Bishop Show*; *Julia*; *The Lucy Show*; *The Many Loves of Dobie Gillis*; *Mayberry R.F.D.*; *McHale's Navy*; *My Favorite Martian*; *My Three Sons*; *The Patty Duke Show*; *Petticoat Junction*; and *The Real McCoys*. By decade's end, some audiences sought more substance in humor and were rewarded, at least for a couple of years, with Rowan and Martin's *Laugh-In* and *The Smothers Brothers Comedy Hour*. Each of these shows landed in the top-30 programs at least one season during the decade. But, for the most part, the situations in 1960s situation comedies posed problems that were small and lent themselves to quick, tidy solutions. Conflict and controversy were relegated to the nightly news as prime-time network schedules remained committed to escapist entertainment, but that was soon to change.

5

The Rural Sitcom from
The Real McCoys to Relevance

RICK WORLAND AND JOHN O'LEARY

For a few years after the beginning of national television broadcasting in 1948, the first successful examples of the domestic sitcom were about people living in New York apartments: *The Goldbergs*; *Life With Luigi*; the initial variety-sketch version of *The Honeymooners*; and, most famous of all, *I Love Lucy*. Outside the sitcom format, New York Jewish comedians Milton Berle and Sid Caesar dominated early television's take on the riotous vaudeville show. Historians attribute this programming pattern to basic realities: television was mostly concentrated in the Northeast where the networks were based, and large segments of its heavily urban audience were composed of assimilated populations of Jewish, Irish, and Italian heritage. After the FCC lifted its four-year broadcasting license freeze in 1952 and the numbers of television stations and receivers began to increase dramatically, the new medium spread through cities and towns across the country. As the audience became truly national, it got much bigger, and accordingly more WASPy, and programming changed significantly in turn.[1]

Moreover, the explosion of suburbanization in the 1950s became a major part of the postwar economic boom and related social shifts. Even *The Goldbergs* moved to the suburbs in 1955, as did the cast of *I Love Lucy* in its later seasons. Now came the durable sitcoms about White, suburban, nuclear families of the 1950s and 1960s, such as *The Adventures of Ozzie and Harriet*, *Father Knows Best*, and *Leave It to Beaver* that are often held up for praise or ridicule as the supposed family ideal of the postwar years. This might have seemed an unlikely point for a rural-based sitcom to appear, but, in fact, a popular cycle began in 1957 with ABC's *The Real McCoys* and thrived until 1971, mainly on CBS. The appearance and decline of such shows after more than a decade is attributable to the expanded national audience and also to the ways in which the series negotiated the increasing social tumult of the 1960s.

Unless one is a fan of these shows, the rural comedy cycle, including *The Andy Griffith Show, The Beverly Hillbillies,* and *Green Acres,* is most often noted for the circumstances surrounding its demise. In 1970–71, the leading network, CBS, abruptly cancelled a string of still top-rated programs because they were appealing to the "wrong"—that is, least desirable—audience segments for major advertisers. The change came from shifts in advertising from reliance on sheer numbers of households watching a given program to identifying and targeting specific demographic profiles of viewers. Rural sitcoms (and variety shows as diverse as *Hee-Haw, The Red Skelton Show,* and even the New York–based *Ed Sullivan Show*) were drawing most of their numbers from rural and small-market areas; moreover, their loyal viewers were older with less disposable income. Instead, networks and advertisers preferred viewers who were young, urban, and better educated with higher disposable incomes. In the 1970s, in what came to be called the shift to "relevance," CBS scrapped all the rural-appeal programs to aim for the new urban audience with shows such as *All in the Family* and *The Mary Tyler Moore Show* that dealt directly with contemporary social issues.[2]

The rural sitcoms had been deemed "irrelevant" in every sense—corny, pandering, and willfully out of touch with the increasing cultural and political turmoil of the decade that saw their greatest Nielsen successes, a monument to network TV's appeal to the lowest common denominator. Still, any number of weakly-conceived shows failed quickly and understandably throughout the 1960s while *The Beverly Hillbillies* remained in the top of the ratings for nine seasons; similarly, *Mayberry, R.F.D.,* the successor to *The Andy Griffith Show* after its star retired from the program in 1968, was still a top-twenty show at its cancellation in 1971. Unquestionably, the shift to evaluating demographics was a major factor in the removal of these programs from prime time, but discussion of their typical themes and extended success merits further consideration.

Though *The Andy Griffith Show* and the trio of hits created by producer Paul Henning (*The Beverly Hillbillies, Petticoat Junction,* and *Green Acres*) are the most famous and often discussed examples of the rural sitcom, we want to survey the formats and themes of programs at its beginning and ending points that have received less attention: *The Real McCoys,* which started the cycle, and CBS's *The Doris Day Show,* which began with Day's character living on a farm with her father and young sons and then transitioned into a show about a single woman working for a magazine in San Francisco. Besides rural characters confronting contemporary urban America, what these shows (and the long-running *Beverly Hillbillies*) have in common are premises involving physical as well as social mobility, notably movement to California, a symbol of the "New West" of the postwar years.

When Disneyland opened in Anaheim, California, in July 1955, the park's permanent attractions included Tomorrowland, which celebrated the possibilities of the American future, but it also enshrined a particular vision of the past: a detailed replica of a small-town Main Street, inspired by Marceline, Missouri, at the turn of the century, where Walt Disney had spent some of his youth. The park evoked nostalgia in balance with an actively "progressive" vision of the future. As part of the opening-day parade, Disney rode down Main Street on horseback wearing his familiar dark blue suit plus a white Stetson hat; beside him rode actor Fess Parker in fringed buckskins and coonskin cap as Davy Crockett, the character behind the popular show that Disney produced just before the park opened.[3] Postwar America was going to the future on the rocket ships of Tomorrowland but not so fast that it couldn't keep Davy Crockett and a hundred other TV horsemen from Frontierland in sight. Buddy Ebsen, who would star as Jed Clampett on *The Beverly Hillbillies*, appeared in the Crockett adventures as Davy's sidekick; he and Fess Parker did shtick in character on ABC's broadcast of the park's opening. In retrospect, the Davy Crockett fan craze marked the leading edge of themes apparent in the coming flood of network Westerns and their modern-day cousins, the rural sitcoms.

These popular shows about down-home characters adapting to or opposing shifts in modern life fit into this schema because they not only offered a reassuring, nostalgic vision appealing to older, small-town viewers but also provided a way for a broader spectrum of Americans to negotiate the rapid social changes affecting every aspect of life in the postwar years. One needn't hail from a small town to feel that "progress" was coming at the cost of traditional values and ways of life. Through the conventions of the domestic sitcom, stories in which traditional, extended families confront a variety of contemporary social shifts enacted a more gradual transition. The rural sitcoms thrived on such thematic tensions with broad slapstick and sometimes near-surreal humor: *Mister Ed*, after all, is about an L.A. suburbanite who owns a (talking) horse. Indeed, as Hollywood studios began to produce most prime-time shows in the late 1950s, sitcoms about "westward" migration for rural characters in *The Real McCoys*, *The Beverly Hillbillies*, and *The Doris Day Show* mark another instance of the near-mythic attraction of postwar California. Yet, before Jed Clampett's family moved from Appalachia or the Ozarks (a state is never specified in the series) to "the hills of Beverly" after improbably striking it rich, the McCoys traveled from West Virginia to Southern California's San Fernando Valley, still semi-rural and partly agricultural in 1957, and began the rural sitcom cycle with a different approach.

THE REAL MCCOYS AND ITS COHORTS

The Real McCoys was developed at ABC while James Aubrey was head of programming. The show marked a successful effort by the perennial third-place network to attract audiences underserved by CBS and NBC. When Aubrey moved to CBS and became president of the network in late 1959, he put *The Andy Griffith Show* on the fall 1960 schedule, and it became an immediate hit. (The show was made under the auspices of Danny Thomas Productions, which had earlier produced *The Real McCoys*.) As television continued to expand to all areas of the country, these shows had strong appeal in the South and Midwest. Subsequently, Aubrey supported a new rural sitcom idea by Paul Henning, who had written for *The Real McCoys* (as did Jim Fritzell and Everett Greenbaum, who later wrote many of the best episodes of *The Andy Griffith Show*). Debuting in 1962, *The Beverly Hillbillies* was an even bigger hit with audiences, if not critics; in fact, it became the most successful CBS show of the decade (Edgerton 191–92, 244–48).

In her fine study *Rube Tube: CBS, Rural Sitcoms, and the Image of the South, 1957–1971*, Sara K. Eskridge provides a more detailed explanation for why CBS became the home of these shows. (Indeed, even after ABC cancelled *The Real McCoys* in 1962, CBS bought the show and continued it for another season.) Eskridge argues that since the Red Scare began in 1947, from Edward R. Murrow's opposition to Senator Joseph McCarthy on *See It Now* in 1954 to the news division's continuing coverage of the Civil Rights movement, White, Southern conservatives had dubbed the network the "Communist Broadcast System."[4] A commitment to rural, Southern characters and settings, however, collectively presented a benign or implicitly positive view of Southern life. What this meant in practice was that virtually all the rural sitcoms of the 1960s presented a world without any Black characters at all, let alone acknowledgment of Jim Crow and the civil rights struggle. Griffith's genial Sheriff Andy Taylor of fictional Mayberry, North Carolina, offers a far more appealing image than the notorious Eugene "Bull" Connor of Birmingham, Alabama, who turned clubs, fire hoses, and police dogs on nonviolent civil rights demonstrators, including children, all in front of network news cameras. Yet, CBS won back White, Southern viewers with its rural sitcom lineup.

Moreover, this more benign view of American tradition minus slavery and segregation clearly had broader appeal. Eskridge notes that Southern viewers alone cannot account for the popularity of these shows. In 1966, roughly the height of the rural cycle, Southerners owned only 14.4 percent of the nation's televisions, according to A.C. Nielsen. Income and education levels were far better predictors of viewership with households at lower levels of both across the nation tending to be the cycle's most faithful viewers (Eskridge 11–15). In any case, themes and conventions of what would become the rural sitcom cycle began with *The Real McCoys*.

Figure 5.1. (top row) Richard Crenna as Luke McCoy, Kathleen Nolan as Kate McCoy, (middle row) Lydia Reed as Hassie, Walter Brennan as Grandpa Amos McCoy, Michael Winkelman as Little Luke, and (bottom) Tony Martinez as Pepino in *The Real McCoys*. 1957–1963. Photo courtesy of Photofest.

When Irving Pincus and his brother Norman proposed the idea for a rural comedy, NBC turned it down—they didn't think it would play in cities. Still, the New York City–raised brothers got financing from Danny Thomas Productions and were able to sell the show to ABC, where it became the network's first sitcom to crack the top twenty in the Nielsen ratings, reaching the fifth position in the 1960–61 season. The show features the McCoy clan, which has travelled from West Virginia to the San Fernando Valley after inheriting a farm. Grandpa Amos McCoy is the patriarch (played by veteran actor Walter Brennan, also a partner in the company that produced the series). Grandson Luke and Luke's wife, Kate, are also part of the family, along with Luke's little sister and brother. They employ an immigrant farmhand, Pepino.[5]

The Real McCoys can be seen as a link between the portrayal of rural America in other media (books, films, radio, comics) and in the rural television sitcoms of the 1960s. Indeed, there is a great deal of intertextuality as well as a continuity of producers, writers, and actors across the history of rural comedy in popular culture from early network radio to the dawn of relevancy television in the Vietnam era. *The Real McCoys* owes something to the popular radio show *Lum and Abner*. (A series of films was also based on these characters.) The plotlines of *Lum and Abner* often revolved around the main characters' attempts at get-rich-quick schemes, an obsession that also afflicts Amos McCoy. The appearance of lethargic farmers Ma and Pa Kettle as secondary characters in *The Egg and I* (1947) can also be seen as influencing the humor of *The Real McCoys* and other rural sitcoms.[6] Both the Kettles and the McCoys get into ridiculous situations due to their lack of understanding of the modern world. Universal-International began a series of Kettle movies with *Ma and Pa Kettle* (1949) with the first installment involving Pa writing a slogan for a tobacco company contest and winning a "house of the future" as the grand prize. The Kettles' new digs notably includes a television set and other modern consumer gadgetry, which they farcically engage like the Clampetts in *The Beverly Hillbillies*.

Yet, *The Real McCoys* also owes a debt to some decidedly noncomic texts. Hy Averback, who directed 101 episodes of the series, felt that the show became a hit due to its "premise of being able to fight poverty" (Harkins 179). As such, this theme links the series to *The Grapes of Wrath* and *Tobacco Road*, two best-selling novels of the Depression, the former a tale of stoic survival, the latter similarly powerful but with lurid elements that were sometimes parodied.[7] Indeed, the McCoys are similar to the Joads in a number of ways—poorly educated farmers who flee to the promised land of California to enjoy a better life. Once there, they have a difficult time assimilating to the new society.

The fight against poverty and local bureaucracy are the central conflicts of *The Grapes of Wrath* and *Tobacco Road*. Similarly, the McCoys lack the consumer products that the majority of the television audience at the time would have been able to enjoy and that national advertisers preferred, displaying the same shabby lack of upward mobility that made the lower-middle-class family of *The Goldbergs* and the working-class cast of *The Honeymooners* less desirable surrogates for ideal TV consumers by the late 1950s. Instead, the McCoys are often portrayed as outsiders who strive to buy commercial goods to try to fit in with their California neighbors. Farmhand Pepino is further marginalized. Although he seems to be a part of the family, he doesn't usually eat meals with them and sleeps in the barn, maintaining a strict race-class hierarchy even among decidedly downscale Whites.

Although *The Real McCoys* is a comedy, an examination of events in one of the episodes illustrates how close the series was to its dramatic ancestors. In a first-season episode, "It's a Woman's World," a woman running for local office asks Amos if he will be voting on Election Day. He says he would if it were not for the poll tax. When she informs him that there is no poll tax and that all he has to do in order to vote is be able to read the Preamble to the Constitution, he worries. Kate promises to teach him to read by Election Day, but he is embarrassed and refuses. He tries to get Pepino, who can read English, to help him memorize the passage, but Pepino fears being sent back to Mexico and refuses his request. Amos blackmails him by promising to let the violent father of one of Pepino's girlfriends know who had his daughter out very late the previous Saturday night. Pepino reluctantly agrees, and Amos memorizes the Preamble. Amos' conscience gets the better of him, and, although more embarrassed, he leaves the county building without his voter registration card. This plot could certainly have been played as straight drama about a socially displaced, elderly man ashamed of his illiteracy.

But, there were crucial differences among the rural sitcoms of the 1960s, too. The narrative thrust of *The Real McCoys* is for characters to integrate with the new culture. In *The Beverly Hillbillies*, on the other hand, the Clampetts don't need to fit in; indeed, they bring so much of their country lifestyle with them that only Jethro constantly strives (and always gloriously fails) to assimilate and assume a modern identity. Furthermore, because they have all of the money in the world, everyone else in Beverly Hills must adapt to the Clampetts, often realizing that the hillbillies' way really is better. A crucial difference is that the Clampetts are blissfully unaware of how they differ from their neighbors, while the McCoys have an acute, often painful, awareness. The conceit of *The Beverly Hillbillies* turns the central conflict of *The Real McCoys* on its head.

Both shows exploit the tension between rural and urban America, between nineteenth-century and twentieth-century American values, and between wealth and poverty. In *The Real McCoys*, the family struggles to negotiate these oppositions; while in *The Beverly Hillbillies*, the oppositions are used for farcical humor but are never reconciled. Throughout the series, the Clampetts continue to use the billiard table as a "fancy eatin' table" and its cue sticks as "pot passers" while Elly May swims in the "cement pond." On the other hand, the McCoys learn, adjust, and move on. For example, in the episode "You're Never Too Old," Grandpa Amos at first hates the idea of adult education, or, as he calls it, "That durn fancy school," but grows to love it when he gets noticed for his whittling expertise. The "modern" (adult education) is reconciled with the "traditional" (whittling). The McCoys learn and prepare for a new lesson the next week. The Clampetts are static characters: Elly May will never outgrow her tomboy pursuits and fascination with collecting "critters"; Jethro will never become a big executive or a "Double-Naught" spy, Army general, or Hollywood agent; and, Granny will never lose her desire to return to Bugtussle. The show's comedy depends on the Clampetts never changing. Meanwhile, Jed is the wise head of the family because he is largely content with himself and is flexible enough to meet the modern world at least halfway in most situations.

Henning was able to do something truly bold with his third rural sitcom, *Green Acres*, which, as David Marc points out, is ". . . essentially a mirror reversal of *The Beverly Hillbillies*" (*Demographic* 59).[8] Oliver and Lisa Douglas are sophisticated New Yorkers who move to the rural hamlet of Hooterville to run a hopelessly rundown farm. Henning gave the majority of producing responsibilities to veteran writer Jay Sommers, who had worked on Henning's other shows. Sommers based the new show on the premise of a short-lived 1950 CBS radio program he created called *Granby's Green Acres* (Hollis 189).[9] As in *The Beverly Hillbillies*, the humor of *Green Acres* lies in the ways the rural folks get the best of the pompous urbanite, represented by Oliver Douglas. Yet, this show pushes the humor further by bringing in surrealistic elements. In many *Green Acres* episodes, for example, the credit sequences are openly self-reflexive, and the characters comment on them. The credits may appear on the eggs being laid by hens or superimposed on Lisa's dreaded "hots-cakes" as she turns them on the griddle. In one episode, the last credit refers to two recurring characters that sometimes work on the farm. It reads, "Carpentry by Alf and Ralph Monroe," to which Oliver comments sourly, "They weren't supposed to get credit." Whenever Oliver is moved to deliver a grandiose speech on the sacred role of farmers in American tradition, a fife and drum rendition of "Yankee Doodle" rises in accompaniment, an apparently nondiegetic sound that is nonetheless heard by the other characters, who remark on the music. The Hooterville of *Green Acres* is not only out of step with the modern world, it is a self-reflexive, fictional world.

The *Andy Griffith Show*, too, has some elements of self-consciousness as exemplified by a series of 1965 episodes in which Andy and his family travel to Hollywood to observe the filming of a movie called "Sheriff Without a Gun," inspired by a magazine article about the sheriff of Mayberry. The movie turns into a farcical crime adventure that makes the "real" Mayberry and its characters all the more powerful and appealing. In any case, the difficulty of maintaining the tensions among nostalgia, fantasy, and assimilation that figured across the rural sitcom cycle reached its endpoint in the contortions of premise and setting in the still surprisingly successful *The Doris Day Show*.

"QUE SERA, SERA"—ANNUALLY

Doris Day's place at a key moment for network TV was fitting. Her great success as a movie star stretched from 1948 to the mid-1960s in what we now recognize as a transitional period for the Hollywood industry and American society alike. A one-time big band vocalist, the versatile Day functioned equally well in comedy and drama. In the tense climax of Alfred Hitchcock's *The Man Who Knew Too Much* (1956), she sings "Que Sera, Sera," an otherwise sunny song that became a hit for her and serves as the opening theme for *The Doris Day Show*. Day remains best known for a string of romantic comedies including *Pillow Talk* (1959) and *Lover Come Back* (1961) opposite Rock Hudson or with stars of old Hollywood like Clark Gable in *Teacher's Pet* (1958) and Cary Grant in *That Touch of Mink* (1962). Fairly or not, however, "Doris Day" has since become dismissive shorthand for an obsolete and out-of-touch image of feminine gender roles, ones that were changing rapidly by the 1960s. In this, she is recalled as a frantic "professional virgin" in plots that revolve around resisting suitors who seemingly want only to get her into bed while she holds out for marriage and true love. Yet, through the years of her TV show, Day rolled through contradictory genre and social changes with a more flexible persona.

Day came to television in 1968 not long before the rural sitcom cycle came to its abrupt end. She was also part of a briefer trend, as other studio era stars took a shot at weekly television about this time: Glenn Ford (*Cade's County*), Henry Fonda (*The Smith Family*), James Stewart (*The Jimmy Stewart Show* and *Hawkins*), and Anthony Quinn (*The Man and the City*) all had limited success, but more than anything these shows represented attempts to court an older audience that had followed their earlier movie careers. What is perhaps most remarkable about Day's five seasons on CBS, though, was the regular revision of the show's cast and format virtually every year, the most direct indication within a single program of the network visibly struggling with the demographic shift that would doom the rural sitcoms.[10]

Figure 5.2. Doris Day as Doris Martin in *The Doris Day Show*. 1968–1973. Photo courtesy of Photofest.

The Doris Day Show drew decidedly negative reviews at its debut yet ran for five seasons even as the producers continually remodeled the basic premise, a testament finally to the popularity of Day herself.[11] At its start in 1968–69, the show joined the rural sitcom cycle, at least on the surface. Recently widowed Doris Martin has moved to a California farm with her two young sons to live with her father Buck Webb. The second season, she commutes from the farm to a job working at the aptly named *Today's World* magazine in San Francisco with her wisecracking coworker and befuddled boss. Buck, the boys, and klutzy farmhand Leroy Simpson still appear in some episodes either on the farm or in quick visits to the city. In season three, 1970–71, Doris and her sons take an apartment (a rather large and elegant one) above an Italian restaurant where the Palucci family's domestic problems intertwine with her own, nearly returning to the milieu of the earliest New York sitcoms. Buck is ostensibly on the other end of a phone call as Doris moves in but is not seen on camera.

By season four, 1971–72, however, a year after the "rural massacre" and debut of *The Mary Tyler Moore Show*, Doris, like Mary Richards, is a single woman living in the city and working in a media job. Kids and father have seemingly never existed; she has a vainglorious new boss and a daffy new sidekick. This season also brings Doris an interesting boyfriend, Dr. Peter Lawrence. For the show's last season, the actors playing her two sons stay on the payroll while emphasis on Doris' career as a reporter with a (cautiously) swinging love life now involves two eligible bachelors, a doctor and a politician. In sum, the quick jettison of the rural sitcom trappings in favor of a working woman's urban apartment is a most telling symbol of social change.

In its first year, *The Doris Day Show* vacillates between rural sitcom themes established in *The Real McCoys* that emphasize the clash or conflict between tradition and modernity while also being a more typical domestic sitcom that happens to be set on a farm. In the first episode, "Dinner for Mom," for example, the boys take Doris out for her birthday. Because they want to treat Mom, they hide her wallet before leaving home. The "restaurant" they choose is really a noisy, working-class bar. After dinner, no one has enough money to pay. Doris can't reach Buck for help because housekeeper Aggie is on the phone with a friend, happily rehashing the plot of *Gone With the Wind* scene by scene. Fortunately, the gruff bar owner has a big heart, and it all ends well. If this were the sample episode screened for the press, no wonder the initial reviews were so poor. Moreover, while the phony soundstage exteriors of *Green Acres* only added to its near-Brechtian presentation of self-conscious irony, *The Doris Day Show*'s "barnyard" set just seems phony, period, as when Doris visits her mailbox in front of a ridiculous painted backdrop of the "countryside" that looks like it came out of an Edison film from 1905.

The show's attempts to draw on rural sitcom conventions are often just as disappointing. "Let Them Out of the Nest" is another familiar domestic sitcom plot. The boys take over a friend's early-morning job delivering fresh eggs; because Doris won't trust their abilities, she supervises everything and ends up doing it herself with semi-disastrous results. Buck chides her for her well-meant meddling, and she realizes the kids must succeed or fail on their own. Lessons are learned all around, but the egg route could be a paper route or any other small task unrelated to rural life with virtually the same script and a suburban cast of characters from a series like *Father Knows Best* or *The Donna Reed Show*. In "The Songwriter," naïve Leroy falls prey to a mail-order songwriting scam. A letter praises his talent, but he must now pay them $50 to add music to his silly lyrics for "You Put Weeds in the Garden of My Heart." Doris tries to break it to him gently by writing her own awful country song ("Your Love Is Like Butter Gone Rancid") and receiving the same glowing letter from the company. At least *The Beverly Hillbillies* and *The Andy Griffith Show* had enough respect for rural music traditions (and more to the point, its major audience) to feature actual bluegrass artists occasionally like Flatt and Scruggs and The Dillards as guest stars and performers.

Season one sometimes employs the rural comedy trope of a primitive group of rural lumpen proletarians intended as broad caricatures out of Al Capp's popular *Li'l Abner* comic strip. Such premodern figures are held up as wildly out of touch in comparison to wise "salt of the earth" characters like Buck Webb, implicitly making a case for the undeniable benefits of "progress"—especially education and hygiene—while neatly avoiding difficult issues of social class. In "The Relatives," Leroy's hillbilly relations drop in while he is away, and Doris and new housekeeper Juanita are trying to redecorate the house. The trio of Rube Stooges makes a shambles of Doris' efforts to paint and wallpaper the house, and she finally must call in the professionals Buck recommended originally. In "Love a Duck," Tyrone Lovey (Strother Martin), a sly and weirdly threatening neighbor who is poaching wild ducks from Buck's ranch, lives in a rundown shack surrounded by hound dogs, trash, and rusting cars and, in one scene, derisively chomps a roast duck leg while goofy Leroy attempts to "trick" him into confessing. That this guy is creeping around Doris' place at night with a shotgun is less humorous on reflection.

Beyond the inability to situate Day's character convincingly in the rural milieu, it is also difficult to contain her exuberance in a "typical" domestic mom role, though Day's movie career indicated solutions. As a Manhattan mom moving to the suburbs in *Please Don't Eat the Daisies* (1960), she gets opportunities for slapstick, talents displayed in many of her romantic comedies and featured in the series, too. Indeed, if Doris Martin serves as a precursor to Mary Richards, she also continues the slapstick tradition of Lucille Ball. Scenes throughout the show's run feature Day in assorted physical comedy bits, from taking falls to teetering on ladders and regularly getting face and hair splattered with eggs, soap, soup, and paint. With her dancer's grace, bright eyes, and rich voice, Day carries most any situation with aplomb, and her deep talents kept the show going until a more compatible format could be derived. In every variation, she is surrounded by fine supporting players working hard, but clearly no one's heart is in the rural setting. Still, Day's function as a transitional figure for women's roles on the big screen similarly aided the shift from the traditional images of the rural sitcoms to the new relevancy programs of network TV.

Surely the most extraordinary moment of the show's five-year run is the revised opening title sequence for season two: in the first shot, Doris is behind the wheel of a red convertible bidding goodbye to Buck and sons on the farm, pulling away with a quick wave, then driving over the Golden Gate Bridge into the rolling streets of San Francisco. As she drinks in the urban landscape via zooms and fast cuts, we see her feet descending from a cable car and hopscotching with sheer joy across a street toward the office building where she works. "Que Sera, Sera" still plays, but instead of the amber light, soft focus, and lap dissolves of the first season opening as Doris stoically adjusts to widowhood with two kids and a big dog, now she charges into the single life in a fast-paced montage. The "winds of change" are literal as she steadies her stylish hat from a sudden gust while dashing across a street. This play with hats to signify joyfully embracing a new life appears more famously in the final shot of *The Mary Tyler Moore Show* opening with Mary Richards twirling and tossing her knitted cap skyward in the middle of a Minneapolis street. Still, its initial images of beaming but awkward Mary leaving her farewell party surrounded by family and friends and driving warily into her new life contrasts with Doris virtually throwing gravel on the family as she flees for the city in her convertible.

The connection between Doris Martin and Mary Richards is actually quite direct, as revealed in a late 1968 episode called "The Job," which was written by James L. Brooks, soon to be co-creator of *The Mary Tyler Moore Show*. The script explains that before moving to the farm, Doris was a reporter for a New York magazine called *Ladies World*, and that she and her family had lived in Manhattan. Doris' old boss, Maggie, entices her to return to New York for a brief assignment to research a story about corruption in charitable organizations, after which the editor schemes to get her to come back permanently. Paying a visit to lobby for her return, Maggie tells Buck, "I respect your kind of life, Mr. Webb; and I can understand why you think so much of it, but. . . ." Doris, like Mary Richards, was meant for another kind of life—and demographic. Doris excels at the opportunity and clearly enjoys the work but decides she should stay with Buck and raise the boys on the farm. Still, Brooks's script laid the groundwork for the format shift of the second season that was evidently pushed by Day herself.

The final word on the death of the rural sitcom might have come in "The Hoax," a 1973 episode from *Doris Day's* last season in which Andy Griffith appears as Mitch Folger, a probable con man who runs a shady talent business. Doris' editor makes her enroll in his school to investigate. After taking more and more money for acting lessons and headshots, and so on, he actually gets her the promised job doing a shampoo commercial but only after discovering that she is a reporter. "Show business is very puzzling," Folger says in condescending tones after making sure she knows he is on to her, offering neither admission nor apology. "Are you for real or . . . a phony?" Doris persists. "Why do people always want to pigeon-hole other people?" comes his bored response. Griffith brings the dark side of his star persona to this one, the split within his early movie hits between innocent yokel Will Stockdale in *No Time for Sergeants* (1958) and gimlet-eyed Lonesome Rhodes in *A Face in the Crowd* (1957). For Sheriff Andy Taylor, he would smoothly blend and transform these poles—good humored and unassuming but also shrewd and smart when he needs to be. With *The Andy Griffith Show* in rerun heaven, though, he was free to indulge cynical Lonesome Rhodes once more.

CONCLUSION

The rural sitcom held an important role in American popular culture from the late 1950s to the early 1970s, serving as a bridge between the rise of the television Western (there were 31 Westerns in prime time in 1957) and the era of viewer demographics when networks searched for the "right" audiences by serving up character-driven, urban sitcoms. In a larger sense, the rural sitcom also links to a very American style of humor: It finds comedy in the social differences among the citizenry and often without directly confronting issues of class in a supposedly egalitarian society. Jibes at the expense of the backward "hillbilly" (or, conversely, demonstrations of the innate wisdom and virtue of such figures) turn sharp, painful class difference into simple, regional variations. For example, the screwball comedy film genre gained popularity during the Depression by bringing together couples from divergent socioeconomic backgrounds. Many scholars argue this was comforting to a nation reeling from economic catastrophe. If a rich woman and a working-class man (or vice versa) could fall in love, perhaps the differences were not so great after all. Prime examples of this genre, including *It Happened One Night* (1934), *The Awful Truth* (1937), *Bringing Up Baby* (1938), and *Sullivan's Travels* (1941), are celebrations of the urban and the urbane. Yet, all include excursions into the wilds of rural America and/or eccentric rural characters as out of step with the moment as the Clampetts or the McCoys were in 1960.

The rural sitcom reached its zenith of popularity at a time when rural America was going through great political changes, many due to the advances of the Civil Rights Movement. Most rural areas were moving from Democratic Party strongholds to loyal Republican regions, and there seemed to be a growing cultural as well as ideological split between cities and small towns. Viewers might have felt a certain comfort in the ways the rural sitcom upheld many of the nineteenth-century values of rural America while acknowledging the arrival of modernity. Perhaps the death of the rural sitcom signaled the complex discordance of these two American "states of mind" and was an early indicator of the red state/blue state divide that would mark American political boundaries in the twenty-first century.

NOTES

1. See Arthur Frank Wertheim, "The Rise and Fall of Milton Berle." John E. O'Connor, ed., *American History/American Television: Interpreting the Video Past.* New York: Ungar, 1983. 55–78. In early 1949, there were 1,082,100 TV sets in the country, 41.6 percent of them in New York City (59).

2. Todd Gitlin, *Inside Prime Time* (New York: Pantheon, 1983) is still one of the best accounts of this decision. See chapter 10, "The Turn Toward 'Relevance,'" 203–20. See also Aniko Bodroghkozy, *Groove Tube: Sixties Television and the Youth Rebellion* (Durham, NC: Duke UP, 2001).

3. The Crocket craze prompted one of the first television-driven consumer fads for children. For more, see Sean Griffin, "Kings of the Wild Back Yard: Davy Crockett and Children's Space." Marsha Kinder, ed. *Kids' Media Culture* (Durham NC: Duke UP, 1999), 102–21.

4. Sarah K. Eskridge, *Rube Tube: CBS, Rural Sitcoms, and the Image of the South, 1957–1971.* Doctoral dissertation. Dept. of History, Louisiana State

University, 2012. See Chapter 1, "The Communist Broadcasting System"; and Chapter 5, "Rural Comedy and the South as a Scapegoat for Racism."

5. This California-based show, along with *The Doris Day Show* in its first two seasons, could include Latino characters but no Blacks. Naomi Stevens, a character actress who often played "ethnic" figures, but was not Latina, played the housekeeper Juanita on *Doris Day*. Doris and Juanita are portrayed as mutually respectful friends, however, and the housekeeper calls her employer by her first name.

6. Based on a 1945 comic novel, *The Egg and I,* starring Claudette Colbert and Fred MacMurray, was also a forerunner of *Green Acres*—an urban couple buys a rundown chicken farm and moves to the country.

7. John Ford directed successful film versions of *The Grapes of Wrath* (1940) and *Tobacco Road* (1941) with the plot of the latter considerably altered and comic elements emphasized. Erskine Caldwell's novel *Tobacco Road* includes an important character named Ellie May. In the book she is a desperately impoverished hillbilly girl with a deformed cleft lip; in the film, she is beautiful Gene Tierney who has a famously attractive overbite.

8. Marc devotes an insightful chapter in *Demographic Vistas* to an auteurist study of Paul Henning's rural sitcoms, and Marc and Thompson include a chapter on Henning in their book about television auteurs, *Prime Time, Prime Movers.*

9. *Granby's Green Acres* starred Gail Gordon and Bea Benaderet; the latter played the lead in *Petticoat Junction* until her death in 1968. Jay Sommers had also written for *Lum and Abner.*

10. For analysis of the show concentrating on Day's negotiation of changing gender roles, see Phyllis Scrocco Zrzavy. "Women, Love, and Work: The Doris Day Show as Cultural Dialogue." *The Sitcom Reader: America Viewed and Skewed,* Eds. Mary M. Dalton and Laura R. Linder. New York: SUNY Press, 2005. 205–16.

11. The show was produced by Day's company, Arwin Productions, which she took over following the sudden death of her husband, Martin Melcher, soon after he sold the show to CBS. Day strongly disliked the show's rural setting, which had been created without her involvement, and actively worked to change it. A.E. Hotchner, *Doris Day: Her Own Story* (New York: Morrow, 1976), 229, 249. Her husband's death and the TV show's run marked the beginning of a long, difficult period for Day involving numerous lawsuits against her husband's lawyer and business partner over her career earnings with the upshot that she virtually retired from show business after the mid-1970s.

6

The 1960s Magicoms

Safety in Numb-ers

GARY KENTON

Sitcoms are us. Whatever is being felt or experienced in a culture bubbles up in its creative works, whether the brow is high, middle, or low, whether consciously or unconsciously. Even though they are often dismissed as craven televisual products packaged for a broad, undiscriminating audience, sitcoms have been shown to mirror society perhaps more accurately than any other genre and have served as a remarkably useful barometer for identifying ideas and points of view that would not otherwise be ready for prime time. But, neither the mirror nor the weathervane metaphor seems adequate to explain a particular group of ten sitcoms that drew large audiences in the 1960s.

Collectively, *Mister Ed, My Favorite Martian, My Living Doll, Bewitched, I Dream of Jeannie, My Mother the Car, The Smothers Brothers Show, The Flying Nun, It's About Time,* and *The Second Hundred Years* constitute a subgenre that represents something new and strange under the sun. Escapism, the catch-all term so often used in reference to situation comedy, only begins to describe the ridiculousness and supernatural elements of these shows. David Marc calls them "magicoms" (*Comic* 107), Lynn Spigel calls them "fantastic family sit-coms" (*Dreamhouse* 119), and they are described by Susan Douglas as creating "a bizarre cartoon world hermetically sealed off from politics and history" (27). The term "magicoms" will be employed throughout this chapter.

These shows reveal much about the American self-image and the evolution of television in its first full decade of cultural dominance, and magicoms may not only be seen as an endpoint to TV's so-called Golden Age but also as a repudiation of the nascent era in which cultural uplift was widely accepted as part of the medium's purpose. Appearing at a time when television was the primary catalyst for a social sea change that had the American public shifting from being primary producers of culture to being passive consumers of it, the magicoms went further, not just encouraging passivity, but demanding it. These shows embedded retrogressive strains of thought, what Arthur Kroker refers to as "invisible assumptions"—including anti-intellectualism, anti-feminism, anti-federalism, anti-environmentalism—that became embedded in civic discourse in the 1980s and 1990s. Although the directors were not monolithic in outlook, and audience interpretations certainly varied, the magicoms' powerful combination of illogic, repetition, and conservatism had the effect of normalizing regressive attitudes, adding momentum to the backlash against the progressive movements of the 1960s that continues to resonate today.

Escapism, of course, is integral to much art. One reason we love radio, movies, and TV is that we are transported on a journey outside the familiar. But, there is a kind of escapist fare that, instead of depicting an alternative reality, departs from reality altogether. And, to be clear, we are not talking about absurdism or existentialism here; the magicoms offer a pure unmooring, making no comment on the human condition in the manner of Monty Python or Woody Allen, no less Beckett or Ionesco. The magicoms don't just rely on viewers' suspension of disbelief but demand an out-and-out surrender of critical faculties. Generally, genres allow television program creators to strike a balance between innovation and convention, but the signal "innovation" in the magicom subgenre is the ingenious contrivances producers seize upon to steer clear of relevance. That these ten shows were almost universally panned by critics mattered not; when reviews are bad but ratings are high, networks pride themselves on having served the pabulum at just the right temperature. To be sure we're on the same wacky wavelength, let us don our pith helmets and take a brief tour of the magicom realm. Abandon credulity all ye who enter here.

The first harbinger, *Mister Ed*, features a talking horse and has its roots in the talking horse short stories by Walter R. Brooks, which first appeared in 1937, and in a series of 1950s movies in which the estimable song-and-dance veteran Donald O'Connor was upstaged by a talking mule named Francis. *Mister Ed* began its TV life in syndication, a rare case of a show moving from the syndication sidelines into the network mainstream. Mister Ed is a palomino that is gifted with speech yet won't demonstrate this ability with anyone other than Wilbur Post, the architect who has purchased the farm on which Ed resides in pastoral semi-retirement.[1] The show establishes two themes common in the magicoms. First, the non-human character is the only one that demonstrates the greatest common sense; the humans are often endearing and sincere, but invariably dimwitted and hapless. Second, the show mines a rich comic vein in the conflicts between Wilbur's city background and his role as rural landowner, paving the way for *The Beverly Hillbillies, Petticoat Junction,* and *Green Acres,* part of a subgenre referred to as the ruralcoms. Progenitors such as *The Andy Griffith Show* and *The Real McCoys* often feature city slickers to comic effect but were far less reliant on stereotypes, generally finding country folk to be sufficiently three-dimensional so that not every plot had to revolve around conflicts with urban foils.

Amid the widespread paranoia of the Cold War, a slice of the American psyche became preoccupied with aliens and outer space. Numerous episodes of *The Twilight Zone* and *The Outer Limits* capitalized on this fascination, but *My Favorite Martian* followed more in the footsteps of print parodies (notably in *Mad Magazine*), playing it strictly for laughs. A less threatening extraterrestrial could hardly be imagined than "Uncle" Martin, who settles in the garage apartment of Tim O'Hara after his spaceship crash-lands near Los Angeles. Unlike Samantha in *Bewitched* (see below), Uncle Martin does not hesitate to use his magical powers to make household chores less onerous (he levitates the furniture when vacuuming) and takes a bemused, anthropological interest in human behaviors. Martin provides a template for Spock (*Star Trek*) and other intellectually oriented, emotionally challenged space invaders, but he is avuncular, barely more eccentric than your real-life uncle. Perhaps it was this lack of edge that caused the show to fade quickly after considerable popularity in its first year on the air.

One show that often crossed the line from escapist to creepy was *My Living Doll,* in which a doctor (portrayed by Robert Cummings, a sitcom stalwart since *My Hero* and *The Bob Cummings Show*) feels obliged to mold a robot, embodied by the curvaceous Julie Newmar, into the "perfect" woman, which for this medical man means strict obedience and no backtalk. The proximate reason for the show's short lifespan was the sudden departure of Cummings, but the show was never able to make viewers care about the doctor or his pet project. Talking animals is one thing, but expecting viewers to believe that Julie Newmar is not human might have been asking too much.

Bewitched also debuted in 1964 and was based on a similar premise, but it was an immediate hit. Produced by William Asher (whose previous claim to popular culture immortality was directing beach movies starring Annette Funicello and Frankie Avalon), the show stars his wife, Elizabeth Montgomery, as Samantha, a witch whose husband, Darrin, is not only mortal but an ineffectual advertising manager to boot. In fact, Darrin is so inconsequential that the actors playing the role changed midstream with few viewers expressing concern, despite the fact that the show was among the ten most-watched shows in the country at the time. It should also be mentioned that, in an October 1964 episode, Samantha and Darrin become the first television couple who were not married to each other in real life to be shown sharing a bed. By trying to suppress her formidable powers in order to be a "normal" American housewife, Samantha became a hero to traditionalists. But, at least one woman was appalled, telling Samantha in no uncertain terms that she was wasting herself on this shlub: her mother, Endora. Played with sarcastic relish by Agnes Moorehead, Endora is probably one of the most radical feminist characters to appear in a sitcom. She

Figure 6.1. Elizabeth Montgomery as Samantha Stephens, Dick York as Darrin Stephens, and Agnes Moorehead as Endora in *Bewitched*. 1964–1972. Photo courtesy of Photofest.

not only mocks Darrin at every opportunity but disdains all the cherished trappings of the American Dream to which her daughter aspires—marriage, children, suburban house, security—all of it. For Darrin, Endora is like most TV mothers-in-law: sticking her nose into his affairs and undermining his authority. But, Endora is another kettle of witch, showing up in one episode in psychedelic garb, cradling a hookah and quoting Coleridge's "Kubla Khan" with a reference to his "opium-inspired pleasure dome." To Endora, Samantha's willing submission is inexplicable. Week after week, she denies herself the pleasures of her own talents—with a wiggle of her nose she can not only travel anywhere in the world, but anywhere in time—unless, of course, she is forced to perform a little magic to help her husband out of a fix (which, admittedly, she often created).

As Fiske and Hartley demonstrated, however, audience readings of TV texts are not monolithic, and "the same message can be decoded according to different codes, corresponding to the social experience of the decoder" (105). While many viewers adopted what Stuart Hall described as a dominant reading, finding nobility in Samantha's loyalty, restraint, and self-sacrifice, many women adopted an oppositional reading, taking pleasure in Samantha's mastery and superiority. "The show often suggested," says Douglas, "that women, especially younger women, were smarter, more creative, and more versatile than men" (128). Even as the storylines reinforced traditional roles, the pent-up power possessed by Samantha added to what Douglas refers to as "prefeminist agitation" (125).

I Dream of Jeannie was designed to capitalize on the success of *Bewitched,* but it adopts an even more strident anti-feminist stance. Samantha's counterpart, Jeannie, is stripped of choice, dignity, and most of her clothes. Portrayed by Barbara Eden, Jeannie is a genie who is seen in the scanty harem-type garb in which she emerged from her magic bottle. This get-up, better suited to a private belly dance than a PTA meeting (though network Standards and Practices dictated that her costume must cover her navel), makes it clear that, unlike Samantha, Jeannie is not eligible for mainstream respectability. In addition to her well-displayed physical attributes, Jeannie is impetuous, devious, and extremely jealous. Although her only purpose in life is to "please her master," astronaut Captain/Major Anthony "Tony" Nelson, sex is never spoken of, especially since the couple is not married.[2] But, lest anyone think that Jeannie exercised domestic power, many episodes ended with Tony literally putting Jeannie back in her place: her genie's bottle.

In one 1965 episode, "The Americanization of Jeannie," the political battle lines are drawn with uncharacteristic clarity. After reading (reading!)

something about women's liberation, Jeannie adopts the rudiments of feminist rhetoric and refuses to perform her wifely duties by way of protest. But, it soon becomes clear that Jeannie is motivated less by any coherent ideology than by her feeling that Tony is taking her for granted, and Jeannie recants when Tony regards her displays of independence and rebellion as unattractive and unfeminine. Once she feels herself to be at risk of losing her sex appeal, the quest for equality and emancipation is abandoned.

If talking horses enthralled Americans, then perhaps they'd get a charge out of a talking automobile. That must have been the thinking behind *My Mother the Car,* later proclaimed by *TV Guide* to be the second-worst TV show of all time.[3] Here we get David Crabtree who, while shopping for a second family car, can't resist climbing into a fixer-upper—a long-neglected 1928 Porter—only to have the car talk to him through the radio. It turns

Figure 6.2. Barbara Eden as Jeannie and Larry Hagman as Major Anthony Nelson in *I Dream of Jeannie.* 1965–1970. Photo courtesy of Photofest.

out that the car is the reincarnation of his mother, and she will only speak to him. Being a good boy, he feels obligated to bring it/her home. Giving new meaning to the term buyer's remorse, David is constantly caught between the demands of his mother's upkeep (in one episode she complains of the cold and then gets drunk on antifreeze) and the scheming antique car collector Captain Manzini. The show, like the car, was a lemon.

Most people associate the Smothers Brothers with their popular and innovative show, *The Smothers Brothers Comedy Hour*. But, before CBS provided the variety format that allowed their comic skills to shine, the network placed them in a sitcom straightjacket called *The Smothers Brothers Show*. Tom Smothers portrays an aspiring angel dispatched from heaven to provide spiritual guidance to his brother, Dick, a buttoned-down publishing executive. Tom sets out to impress his heavenly managers with good works, but only creates havoc. It's Dick, the long-suffering straight man, who has to keep up appearances while cleaning up Tom's messes. The show lasted only one season and was subsumed in TV history by *The Smothers Brothers Comedy Hour*. It did, however, have the distinction of being the last situation comedy filmed by CBS in black and white.

Even more than talking animals, nothing epitomizes the magicom more than the image of Sally Field soaring over the hills of Puerto Rico in *The Flying Nun*. Although it was sometimes suggested that Fields's character, Sister Bertrille, had received her powers from God, vaguely scientific explanations were also offered, having to do with sudden updrafts caught by the nun's cornette (headgear). This literal flight of fancy wasn't the only aspect of the show that made it a target for ridicule.[4] Unlike her previous role as the prototypical California teen named Gidget, Sister Bertrille was more to be laughed at than laughed with. For all her faults, Gidget was flesh and blood, a typical American girl that viewers could identify with, whereas Sister Bertrille was a cipher, a cardboard cut-out of cute. Field, still a teenager, became despondent over the role, saying later that there was "nothing I could make sense of." She wasn't alone.

One of the last, and perhaps least, of the magicoms is *It's About Time*, in which two astronauts, having inadvertently breached the space-time continuum, find themselves stranded in the Stone Age. This single-season show was made watchable primarily by the indefatigable presence of Imogene Coca, although it is a long way from her inspired contributions to Sid Caesar's *Your Show of Shows* and was enough to kill the on-screen career of Joe E. Ross, who played the role of the caveman Gronk but is more fondly remembered as Patrolman Gunther Toody on *Car 54, Where Are You?* This was an attempt by producer Sherwood Schwartz to repackage

Gilligan's Island, in which a yacht-load of vacationers are shipwrecked on a remote island. But, *It's About Time* lacks both of that show's key ingredients: the nudnik charm of the original TV space cadet, Bob Denver (who played Gilligan, as well as Maynard G. Krebs in *The Many Loves of Dobie Gillis*) and the sex appeal of two of the female characters, Mary Ann and Ginger.

The premise of *The Second Hundred Years* emerged from the pages of *National Geographic,* in which archeological discoveries of extinct animals (think woolly mammoth) preserved in polar ice were colorfully described. In magicomland, the storyline practically writes itself: a prospector, Luke Carpenter, killed in 1900 by an avalanche in Alaska, is uncovered by another avalanche 67 years later, impossibly preserved as the same 33-year-old he was in 1900. When reunited with his family, he is 40 years younger (physiologically) than his son Edwin and the same age as his grandson (played by the same actor, setting up a number of plots revolving around mistaken identities). The show features several plots in which Luke's incompatibility with modern life draws potentially thought-provoking contrasts. In an early episode, he sees cowboys shooting guns on a television set and shoots back, and, in another, he "rescues" a go-go dancer from her "cage"—but evidently few thoughts were provoked, and the show was cancelled after 26 episodes.

Two other shows of the mid-1960s, *The Munsters* and *The Addams Family,* are often lumped in with the magicoms, but they are not a proper fit. In these shows, the strange and supernatural are not springboards from which to depart from reality but everyday amusements in an alternative universe. The Munsters are more Halloween/cartoonish and the Addams family more Marx Brothers/gothic, but both families seek nothing more than to roam the nooks and crannies of their haunted houses and enjoy the simple pleasures of monsterdom: ingesting insects, cultivating dead plants, putting one's head in a vise—the usual. Their domestic bliss is disturbed only by intrusions from "normal" outsiders, who are not just spooked but generally intolerant and vindictive. Allegorical and often quite poignant, the escapism of these family sitcoms is balanced by the consistent foregrounding of xenophobia and bigotry.

So, having completed our forced march of the territory, the question arises: from whence all this folderol? Although the networks invariably fall back on the blanket justification of "giving the people what they want," there is more going on here than supply and demand. In the magicoms, the detachment from reality is radical, suggesting that the evasion is not a creative strategy—it's the point. When a group of contemporaneous sitcoms abandon all concern for verisimilitude, we are transported to a realm so assiduously escapist that the particular exit routes taken, although fascinating, are less meaningful than the flight itself.

What was television (and the country) so scared of? An answer is suggested by the speech delivered by soon-to-be-President Kennedy at the 1960 Democratic National Convention in which every inspirational image is offset by a deep sense of disorientation and foreboding. "[W]e stand today on the edge of a New Frontier," Kennedy stated, "the frontier of the 1960s, the frontier of unknown opportunities and perils, the frontier of unfilled hopes and unfilled threats. . . . Beyond that frontier are uncharted areas of science and space, unsolved problems of peace and war, unconquered problems of ignorance and prejudice, unanswered questions of poverty and surplus." Given this admixture of hope and fear, a prevailing explanation for the ridiculousness of the magicoms is that the news as the 1960s progressed was fraught with troubling images—inner cities under siege, women burning bras, hippies and yippies in the streets—that sitcom advertisers (and therefore producers) wanted no part of. As Gerard Jones says, it was "an expression of a particular moment of nervousness in the national consciousness, when the American imagination was plagued by fears that popular culture didn't yet have the nerve to confront directly" (180). But, this description could apply to most TV fare of that time. The magicoms' headlong dive into the deep end of dumb reflects a deliberate aversion to controversy or relevance. Inanity served as a kind of protective shield (like GL-70!⁵), lending deniability and placing the magicoms outside the arena of rational discourse. Magicom writers could slip in sly comments on social issues with the impunity of a fool or court jester, never to be taken seriously. Spigel gives the magicoms credit for "[taking] up the challenge of the New Frontier," but has to acknowledge that "rather than providing a rational—scientific discourse on the public sphere, they presented a highly irrational, supernatural discourse in private life . . ." (*Dreamhouse* 117).

In addition to being irrational and supernatural, the discourse presented by the magicoms is also rigid and highly traditional. The phrase "family values" would not become a conservative rallying cry until the 1980s, but the magicoms serve as the advance troops, mounting a militant defense against all threats to the domestic status quo, with special invective directed at hippies and women's libbers. These shows have little to say about civil rights or tolerance, *The Munsters* and *The Addams Family* notwithstanding.⁶ Only in the late 1960s with leading roles for Diahann Carroll (*Julia*) and Bill Cosby (*The Bill Cosby Show*) does television begin to emerge from what Cedric Clark calls the "Non-recognition Era," a time when the subject of race was neatly avoided by presenting a universe in which people of color simply did not exist except in the occasional celebrity guest appearance (18–22).

Lynne Joyrich goes so far as to argue that the magicoms should be considered in the category of magical realism, alongside other cultural artifacts, especially Latin American literature. *The Twilight Zone* and *The Outer Limits* might have a legitimate claim to such consideration, and the success of those shows clearly paved the way for *The Munsters* and *The Addams Family,* but magical realism is connected to traditional cultural beliefs and amounts to more than a random mix of fantasy and reality, which the magicoms do not. Nickelodeon reran *Green Acres* in the 1990s with the promo slogan "It's not stupid . . . it's surrealism!" (TV Trivia website). But, even this claim is too grand. Surrealism explores the common ground between fantasy and reality; the magicoms were committed to la-la land.

Perhaps the most trenchant argument for the relevance of the magicoms comes from a feminist perspective. The increased presence of women in the workforce, the sexual liberation afforded by birth control pills (introduced in 1960) and other contraceptives, and a series of manifestos, led by the publication of Betty Friedan's *The Feminine Mystique* in 1963, created a serious challenge to the entrenched patriarchy. "It is no surprise," Douglas writes, "that at the moment girls took to the streets in an outpouring of female resistance against the status quo . . . while their mothers flocked to buy a book demanding equal rights for women, the witch and other women with supernatural powers would reappear on the cultural landscape in America" (138). Douglas suggests that the feminist movement posed such a threat to domestic order that counter-revolutionary narratives needed to be provided. The (mostly) reactionary plots in *Bewitched, I Dream of Jeannie,* and *My Living Doll* perform this function with gusto. Fear of sexuality was not new, of course—the networks had been voluntarily complying with the strictures of the notorious Motion Picture Production Code (the Hays Code) from their inception—but the fear was no longer just about fornication but about the entire balance of gender power. Not every show could take place in a convent.

Television enjoyed a short childhood, and its adolescence was nonexistent. In most industries, there is considerable lag time between market entry and saturation, but television went from availability to ubiquity in a remarkably short time. In the late 1940s, television was essentially a regional medium, and the number of television sets in American homes could still be measured in thousands. By the mid-1950s, the medium had reached critical mass, and sets were purchased at the astonishing rate of 20,000 a day (Miller and Nowak 338). As the reach of television extended across the continent, control was increasingly centralized, and the autonomy of local stations was dramatically curtailed. By the 1960s, as the networks were still engaged in the process of standardizing and professionalizing their business practices, theirs was already the dominant communication medium in the country. At the point of development at which most businesses are still committed to the innovative techniques and policies that paved the road to success, the cultural power of television was so great that networks adopted the programming practice known as "dead centerism" (Gerard Jones 34), which avoided content that might offend any segment of the audience.

The process of nationalization was also pushed forward by a geographical shift that saw a large percentage of shows being developed and produced in Hollywood rather than New York. Even though many of the TV producers were transplanted from New York, they quickly adopted the Californian ethos of self-invention. They were free to create their characters in the image of no person or groups in particular, but as projections of generalized, stereotyped, homogenized American types. This ethnic cleansing was not only a by-product of the new Hollywood orientation, but part of a larger detachment from the civic sphere. As Darrell Hamamoto suggests, deep-seated fears over the Cold War, integration, and other hot-button issues of the 1960s led television producers to see escapism as a safe harbor for themselves as well as the audience. If viewers could not be reassured, at least they could be diverted. Any tendency toward experimentation was undermined by a tremendous (often self-imposed) pressure to act as a paternal agent and a bulwark against the darker side of contemporary life in America. But, what begins as paternalism often morphs into an insistence on conformity. The unintended consequence of what Marc called the "deep escapism" of the magicoms (Marc *Comic* 1997 106) was the creation of an "atmosphere of almost radical caution" (Nussbaum 80).[7] Even as cultural upheaval was forcing citizens to consider broadening traditional views regarding families, gender, race, and politics, the spectrum of permissible behaviors and ideas on television narrowed.

Newton Minnow's 1961 speech to the National Association of Broadcasters (NAB), delivered weeks after he became chairman of the FCC, is an inescapable touchstone in broadcasting history. His brutal assessment of television programming as a "vast wasteland" is frequently described as an epiphany for viewers and programmers alike and is often credited as a catalyst for subsequent reforms. In 1963, the evening news was expanded from 15 minutes to a half-hour, more documentaries were aired, and the Public Broadcasting Act of 1967 was passed, creating the Corporation for Public Broadcasting and leading to the development of the Public Broadcasting

Service (PBS) and National Public Radio (NPR) in 1970. But, the great preponderance of programming that came after Minnow's admonishment offers scant evidence of a great awakening among network executives. To the contrary, the painful truth is that the wasteland became considerably vaster after 1961. Since the FCC stopped short of using its one great regulatory weapon—the withholding of license renewals—any hopes for an elevated level of programming relied on producers to voluntarily create salutary shows unlikely to realize significant profits. As Ouellette points out, Minnow never questioned the basic assumptions of the commercial TV model, arguing more narrowly for "worthier" programming in the "public interest." "From a cultural studies vantage point," she says, "his mistake was to dismiss these popular formats [situation comedies, Westerns, quiz shows, soap operas] as worthless instead of advocating more creativity and diversity within them" (55). Despite the creation of public broadcasting, the pressure of conformity at networks predominated.

While the Golden Age might not have produced as much gold as it is credited with, there is no question that the hopes and dreams of the country were projected onto television and that those aspirations were occasionally fulfilled, but once the magicoms had let the genie of pure escapism out of the bottle, the notion of television as an instrument of cultural uplift was no longer supportable. Classical music, documentaries, and theatre would continue to show up periodically on the small screen, safely ghettoized within the confines of PBS and easily dismissed as elitist. Viewed through the lens of political economy, several factors favored the magicoms. First, comedies are cheaper to make than dramas or variety shows (only quiz shows and "reality" shows cost less to produce). Second, since expanding its radio audience measurement service to television in the 1950s, the Nielsen ratings became the preeminent guidepost in the industry, determining what networks could charge for advertising and often dictating which shows were renewed or cancelled. Good "numbers" equated to profits, leading to a predilection for repackaging successful formulas. As soon as shows like *The Flintstones, The Jetsons, Mister Ed,* and *The Beverly Hillbillies* established themselves alongside the dramas, Westerns, variety shows, and domestic sitcoms that had dominated the Nielsens for the previous decade, the race was on to provide more of the same.

In addition to these essential business concerns, technological advancements served to push the TV industry in a conservative direction. First was the wide availability of professional broadcast–quality videotape machines, which Ampex introduced in 1956. To that point, nearly all sitcoms had been broadcast live.[8] Consumer use of videotape was not common until the

1970s, but the networks began to realize significant savings by using and reusing videotape in the early 1960s. But, more important than curbing costs, the shift to tape gave the networks greater control over their shows. When shows were broadcast live, executives could do little more at air time than what other viewers did—sit back and watch. They had already wrested production control from sponsors by going to the spot-ad system, or magazine format, but producers and actors had to be given latitude when programs were going out live, and the networks chafed. Even on shows with little potential for controversy, the fear of a glitch or slip of the tongue was unnerving, and improvisational iconoclasts like Sid Caesar and Ernie Kovacs gave TV executives heartburn. The advent of videotape spelled the end for live television, effectively removing spontaneity for the performers and anxiety for the networks.

One might have thought that videotape technology would liberate producers, allowing them to test ideas and scripts in the safety of the studio where they were not dependent on live performance or immediate audience reaction, but, paradoxically, it had the opposite effect. The producers could now control every aspect of the show, and control it they did. It was as if it dawned on the networks that videotape had given producers greater creative latitude, and oversight suddenly became much more vigilant. With few exceptions, the production process became increasingly sealed off from reality, a no-fly zone in which caution was the paramount concern. The networks went beyond controlling for potentially controversial content to assuring at the concept and script stage that programs would avoid topicality. Moreover, on those episodes on which plots did refer to some current event or trend, the storyline was angled so that traditional values were upheld and countercultural ideas denigrated. Sex could be "tastefully" alluded to for titillation and humor but never addressed directly or realistically. Even as society was becoming more permissive of sexual expression, television continued to voluntarily comply with the spirit of the Hays Code.[9]

The public, of course, was blissfully ignorant of these machinations. Even in retrospect, few of the millions of viewers who came of age watching the magicoms think of themselves as having engaged in "deep escapism"; for most, the ridiculousness only adds to the nostalgic glow. The adult cohort that bemoans the degradations of reality TV and expresses grave concern for the effects of media violence and social networking on the minds of young people seldom views the programming of their own youth through the same critical prism. It defies logic to think that the magicoms, which occupied a significant portion of the prime-time viewing schedule before syndication and has consistently attracted millions of viewers, left no psychological traces. As Neil Postman points out, television is a "meta-medium," an instrument that not only directs our knowledge of the world but our ways of knowing as well (78–79). This is the fundamental idea behind Marshall McLuhan's most famous aphorism, "the medium is the message." The basic tenet of the field of communication known as media ecology is that every communication technology creates its own environment within which we are obliged to experience the world in a particular way by the forms and biases inherent in the medium. Lynn Spigel says that television delivers "not merely an illusion of reality as in the cinema but a sense of 'being there,' a kind of hyperrealism" (*Dreamhouse* 46) and refers to the tropes of the situation comedy—the laugh tracks, the farfetched plots, the harmonious resolutions—as "structures of denial" (117).

The idea that the social impacts are felt far beyond those intended by the content producers is supported by research. Most famously, George Gerbner's longitudinal studies have shown that regular TV watchers, over time, come to see the world as it is portrayed on television. Whether the topic is violence, Gerbner's primary focus, or other social concerns, attitudes expressed in programming are cultivated in the national psyche. McLuhan, Postman, and others have shown how this immersive experience leaves viewers highly vulnerable to covert suggestion. Inducing an unconscious trust, the magicoms not only serve as a smokescreen to hide reality but also as a seeder and spreader for retrograde ideas and attitudes. The fact that exposure to the magicoms has not just been willing but enthusiastic and that the ideologies are seldom foregrounded only increases the likelihood that they have found their way into people's belief systems without being acknowledged or scrutinized.

Although the magicoms were in a class by themselves, it's hard to argue that the portrait of medicine in *Ben Casey* or *Dr. Kildaire* or that of the West in *Bonanza* or *Gunsmoke* can make a significantly greater claim on realism. But, just as Hostess Twinkies become more compelling than broccoli, the viewing public gradually comes to see the pap as preferable to the serious programming. The anti-intellectualism and civic detachment of the magicoms, expressed both in the form of ridiculous plots and subtextual ideology, infiltrated the public subconscious gradually to become a mainstream value. The goal of the networks might have been to avoid the anxieties and controversies of the real world, but the consequence was, in Marc's words, "depoliticization through escapist fantasy" (Marc *Comic* 1997 106).

One last question. Nostalgia aside, why did we fall for the magicoms? McLuhan suggests an answer in his repurposing of the myth of Narcissus. Conventionally, the story of Narcissus is taken as a cautionary tale regarding self-regard and egotism—Narcissus was so enamored with his own reflection in a pool that he could not attend to anything else—but McLuhan suggests that, in a world without mirrors, Narcissus was less taken with himself than he was transfixed by an image created by the medium of the pool that was simultaneously him and not him. For McLuhan, electronic media work on all of us in a similar fashion. Since media are extensions of our senses (the camera extends the eye, radio extends the ear, etc.), it stands to reason that we don't recognize technologies as outside agents. We embrace electronic media as something familiar, which undermines objectivity and leaves us exposed to messages that should be regarded as external intrusions. McLuhan argues that the sensory disequilibrium caused by electronic communication technologies renders us unwittingly and helplessly in the thrall of electronic media, inducing a numb state he called Narcissus Narcosis.

McLuhan was no Luddite; his quest was to increase awareness of the mediation process. If we can't avoid the ideological and commercial messages embedded in media, we can at least improve our ability to detect patterns and resist the most pernicious content. But, as electronic media delves deeper into the fabric of everyday life, there is little indication that media literacy has improved. Mass media products are created through the manipulation of symbols, and the more we are immersed in those products, we become more, not less, susceptible to the persuasion of what Horkheimer and Adorno identified as the culture industry. One hesitates to draw cause-and-effect relationships between television products of the 1960s and the contemporary social situation, but when we live in an era in which the country is divided less by differences of political opinion than by an inability to agree on questions of science such as evolution or climate change, one wants to understand how we got to this state. Perhaps the magicoms are an overlooked piece of the story. There are, of course, many other factors involved, but it is fair to wonder if 50 years ago we had been less enchanted by talking horses and cars, wily witches and genies, and flying nuns then we might not be living in a trance-like, magicom universe today.

NOTES

1. *Mister Ed* may be said to live on in *BoJack Horseman*, an animated sitcom on Netflix in the mid-2010s featuring a horse that once had a hit TV show but is now drinking hard and trying to peddle his memoirs.

2. It has been suggested that NBC hesitated to marry the couple because Jeannie was not fully human, and the audience was not considered ready for

interspecies wedlock. With ratings slipping in 1969, however, Jeannie and Tony were joined in matrimony, only to have the show cancelled a few months later.

3. The top dishonor went to *The Jerry Springer Show*. Many critics feel *My Mother the Car* was robbed.

4. If the producers of *The Flying Nun* had argued for a force field that could counteract gravity, we might have had a physics phenomenon known as the "sally field."

5. The mysterious additive in Gleem toothpaste, a Proctor & Gamble brand popular in the 1950s and 1960s.

6. One exception is "The Flying Saucer," a 1966 episode of *The Beverly Hillbillies* in which the Clampetts think Martians have landed. Initially extending hospitality, Jethro is convinced that the aliens are a menace, and Granny goes after them with her trusty shotgun.

7. Nussbaum was referring to the risk aversion of prime-time programming in the 2000s, but the term applies even more aptly to the magicoms of 40 years earlier.

8. *I Love Lucy* was filmed, the exception that proves the rule and proof of Lucille Ball's foresight and business acumen.

9. When the Motion Picture Association of America established its ratings system in 1968, filmmakers abandoned the Hays Code, but since Congress had never officially applied the Hays Code to television, the networks never felt obliged to walk away from it, and they continued to follow many of its precepts into the 1970s and 1980s.

7

Negotiated Boundaries

Production Practices and the Making of Representation in *Julia*

DEMETRIA ROUGEAUX SHABAZZ

Julia, a television situation comedy that first aired in 1968, signaled a major shift in the broadcast industry. For many media scholars, *Julia* marks the arrival of industry interest in the Black-cast sitcom (Stroman, Merrit, and Matabane 44–56). Featuring Diahann Carroll, a popular Black stage and film entertainer, the show's creators thought they had the right formula for television's first consistently presented image of a Black family. For many African Americans, however, the series failed to satisfy demands that the industry "integrate" itself and show positive Black images (Peters 140–42). Nonetheless, *Julia*'s three broadcast seasons had an enduring impact and were foundational to later, more successful programs like *All in the Family, Good Times*, and *The Mary Tyler Moore Show*, that claimed to be socially relevant, gender sensitive, and ethnically diverse. *Julia* offers an important opportunity for the study of how television production practices shaped the representation of identity, particularly Black identity, during a period of social unrest and changing political views.

Through a multiphased creative process, television manufactures messages. Industry professionals, such as camera operators, lighting technicians, and directors, have a shared language in which they discuss their craft and how to achieve both the technical and aesthetic goals of production. This language, with all its norms and assumptions, shapes not only how they do what they do, but also the end product of their labor itself. Television's standardized language had its own grammar of race and way of encoding racial bias that developed over time within the racially segregated industry. *Julia* both disrupted the color-coded language at the same time its staging techniques and genre repetition reinforced racist stereotypes.

GENRE CONVENTIONS

As with other genres, the situation comedy reflected hegemonic values and dominant aesthetic conventions. It is a recognizable narrative form consisting of a familiar stock of plot lines that centered most often on the family. Barry Putterman, in *On Television and Comedy*, observes how built-in narrative "hierarchies" for specific genres constrain the modes of expression at different phases of production. He argues that such constraining elements demonstrate "fixed moral and utilitarian positions for audience identity and identification" of characters (117). In creating *Julia*, Hal Kanter, NBC executives, and publicity agents faced distinct positions regarding Black family life that ranged from the uninformed and the ill-informed to the decidedly negative (Shayon "Julia Symposium"). Knowingly or not, they confronted a monumental task of harmonizing their ideological intention with the established hierarchies of the sitcom genre. The instant producers chose to cast African Americans in the lead role of *Julia,* the show encountered problems. Reality and affinity are both important ingredients for sitcom success and are a driving force behind the "mobilization of identification" between audience and sitcom characters (Taylor 39). As the widow of a helicopter pilot shot down over Vietnam, Julia Baker could not represent the idealized notion of the two-parent nuclear family common to the genre. In contemporaneous shows such as *The Lucy Show* and *The Doris Day Show*, commercial sponsors supported female-headed sitcoms. Oddly, single-parent shows were among the highest rated programs during the period. The vice president of nighttime programming at ABC explained that the absence of one parent left the "remaining parent" free to "either embark on romantic endeavors" or to "attend to the children" (Weinberg 174). Corporations such as General Foods and Mattel were hesitant to support *Julia* despite its very conventional content ("Program and Production Report"). The show followed a popular trend but with one key difference: race.

The expectation prevailed that if the series came close to portrayals of actual Black experience, then middle-class consumers were certain to tune out. Many commercial sponsors believed that urban poverty and African American discontent were the only credible representations of Black life in the United States. Likewise, industry executives were chastened by what they perceived as the unfair attribution to their television programs as inflaming Blacks to urban uprisings. Arguably, when it came to sitcoms such as *Julia*, the industry downplayed social realism and relevancy. Despite their conservative attitudes, NBC executives made a full-blown media event for the debut of *Julia*, hailing it as a watershed in the history of television and socially responsible entertainment.

In an interview in *Variety*, Kanter vowed to "show it like it is" (qtd. in Shayon, "*Julia* Symposium"). The network's prebroadcast hype also suggested *Julia* would offer a realistic portrayal of a widowed African American nurse and her son. After viewing the pilot episode, one critic questioned Kanter about the contradiction between his advanced press statements and the "degree of lavishness of Julia's apartment." NBC's vice-president of press and publicity, M.S. Rukeyser, Jr., and the publicity agent for the program, Dan Jenkins, responded to the criticism: "It is not, and never has been, the function of a commercial series to 'show it as it is, baby.' On those rare occasions when the medium has taken a stab at limning the unhappy reality of what goes on in much of the world, the public has quickly tuned out" (qtd. in Shayon, "*Julia* Symposium"). *Julia,* like sitcoms of the 1950s and 1960s, relied upon a formula that focused on superficial familial interaction at home or at the workplace. With regards to commercial viability, *Julia* held the most promise as a sitcom. By its power to gain a sizeable portion of female and young viewers and its overall popularity as a genre, NBC executives saw in the sitcom the best means available to introduce controversial subjects and non-mainstream characters. Such economic considerations might have influenced the elevated class status evident in the set design of the series. Like other single television parents of the period, such as part-time bank secretary and widow Lucy in *The Lucy Show*, Julia Baker lived well beyond her means (Weinberg 175). A critic noted that the "upscale" apartment of the Baker household was too "posh" for a nurse's salary ("Julia"). Carroll's portrayal of a glamorous single mother remained a highly contested aspect of the show despite its similarities to other programs.

The series most often featured Julia and Corey in the kitchen and living room areas of their two-bedroom apartment. During this period of consolidation within the television industry, sitcoms became a primary means of commercial revenue for networks, particularly those in which consumerism was a main feature of the set (Taylor 23). As a narrative device, the design of the set helped identify the class status of the family and reflected the tastes and sensibilities of the central female character. Programs that maintained a large female audience keenly appealed to corporate sponsors holding to the belief that American women made most of the purchasing decisions for the home.

Although the series might have wooed commercial advertisers with its middle-class, "posh" decor, it limited the cues available regarding the character's African American culture and identity. Many black viewers felt little affinity with her middle-class lifestyle, and decided that Carroll herself somehow had turned away from the Black community (See 27–30). The middle-class status of the main character, however, represented a common theme in sitcom narratives in which the families portrayed were typically wealthy, White, and suburban dwellers. Set details, prior to 1968, operated mainly to define the gendered and socioeconomic class identity of the main character and her family, but with the introduction of Julia Baker the matter of African American identity required equal expression.

Designed by art directors, Smith and Roth, and decorated by set decorators, Scott and Wickman, the modern high-rise apartment where Julia and Corey resided differed little from mainstream sitcoms featuring White, middle-class characters. Through their choices in costuming, set design, and lighting composition, they literally framed the Black female character as a wholly conflicted and contradictory subject. The set of *Julia* expressed little difference from that of her televisual neighbors, the Waggerdorns, or her prime-time competition on *The Doris Day Show*. Two African carvings sitting on a bare buffet in the Baker home convey the possibility of an Africa-positive aesthetic sensibility, perhaps a nod to the African-centered values that the Black Arts Movement and cultural nationalists pushed for across America. The statues are sometimes visible in head to shoulder shots and, occasionally, Carroll is framed between them. Against this solitary, quasi-cultural cue, set decorators furnished the apartment with a brownish tan couch with green pillows, pastel green curtains and lamps, floral prints, and two prominently displayed photographs of Julia's dead husband. Interestingly, the picture of the absent father was first placed on a shelf in Corey's bedroom. In later seasons, the picture appears near the carved African figures (Kanter). The attention of show personnel to small details of décor and placement on the set help identify Julia Baker as Black, but not too Black, and as the consummate bourgeois woman.

Class values and set design communicated a bourgeois consumer culture in the series, one that was available to Blacks as well as Whites if the necessary income were present. The mandates of television as an advertising medium that Kanter negotiated and the set decor of Scott and Wickman combined to signify a racially pluralistic vision of democratic capitalism. Far from telling it like it is, the show told a story of how the United States could be if Blacks and Whites simply behaved the way they did on television.

CINEMATIC STYLE AND STAGING CONVENTIONS

Camera angles and lighting operate symbolically and literally within the series to strengthen the constructed identity of the character, Julia Baker. Codified aesthetic and technical practices operate to frame her subjectivity in ways at once similar to and dissimilar from the set design. Camera angles and editing styles work to suggest a specific point of view or subject positioning (Messaris 183). Laura Mulvey, in "Visual Pleasure and Narrative Cinema," argues that narrative structure offers a "masculine subject position" for the cinematic "male gaze." As she suggests, camera operators generally take a point of view that tends to objectify the female body while placing men in the position of the spectator, although many modes of spectator identity are potentially available. Thus, interrelated and infused with the masculine, Eurocentric values inherent to the visual and narrative language of television are the identities of the producers to their own production practices. *Julia* offers a complex example of how devices such as editing and camera work function as traditional narrative mechanisms.

The series incorporated a single-camera mode of production into the usual television sitcom form creating unconventional camera angles and edited sequences that differed stylistically from shows of the period. Single camera and multiple camera are the two main modes of production used for broadcast television. Mode of production means the certain technological and economic conventions that govern the aesthetic style of a program. Although multiple-camera shows are less costly and more efficient to produce, programs using single-camera mode are thought to be qualitatively superior to those made in multiple-camera mode (Jeremy Butler 175). Such devices grew out of a confluence of aesthetic styles from cinema and television. As film-trained technicians worked on studio productions for television, the style of representation began to change (Taylor 44). The style had yet to adjust, however, in any relevant way to the inclusion of people of color and other non-mainstream images in television.

Many of the scenes in *Julia* are highly orchestrated and shot in such a way as to position the viewer in a participative role rather than as a remote or passive observer. The ultimate point of view that lurks in the background is definitively male (Metallinos 225). This presentational style brings the viewer into the scene unlike old modes of televisual cinematography that were restricted by one- or two-camera shots of the entire set. The visual style of *Julia* demonstrated a shift wherein lighter-weight cameras and cinema-vérité techniques borrowed from the big screen joined to bring intimate shooting and segmented editing to the small screen (Caldwell 53). Although critics looking at the artistic value of such innovations on television praised the new techniques, the change resulted in literally segmenting Carroll's body into parts, a visual mode routinely used in media to objectify and festishize the female form. Nowhere is this more evident than in the first episode of the series, entitled "Mama's Man."

Figure 7.1. Diahann Carroll as Julia Baker, Lloyd Nelson as Dr. Morton Chegley, and Marc Copage as Corey Baker in *Julia*. 1968–1971. Photo courtesy of Larry Edmunds BooksFair.

Demonstrating a reconciliation to racial and gender inclusion on the part of the production crew, "Mama's Man" employed shots and an editing technique that emphasized the bouncy and percussive rhythm in *Julia*'s introductory theme song. The opening scene has Corey making juice and toast for his mother, who is asleep on the foldout couch in the living room. The shots begin as a series of close-ups on an orange that Corey is in the process of slicing in two. Instead of a slow pull out to the larger room, several views of the orange, Corey, the knife, and the sleeping mother are edited in montage and cut to the beat of the music. The narrative of the vignette and the punctuated rhythmic edits build suspense and tension that, as an opening to a sitcom, commented ironically on the light and airy themes of middle-class domestic life common to the genre. More appropriate for drama, the tense opening is diffused when Julia opens her eyes to see Corey at her bedside holding a tray with breakfast. John Caldwell suggests in *Televisuality* that the sequence "abruptly cuts in from a wide shot to a closeup without moving to another angle, thereby challenging Hollywood's artificially sacred 30-degree cutting rule" (Caldwell 54). The unorthodox editing of the sequence is stylistically risky for a formulaic genre. Nonetheless, the choppy introduction calls attention to the series' underlying discourse on difference.

Segmentation runs throughout the pilot episode of the series, bisecting Carroll's body. Gazed at in almost every episode, her legs signify Julia Baker's femininity (Carroll and Firestone 137). The objectification of Baker was intentional and specific. Male pleasure through spectatorship did not play a significant role in any 1950s sitcom that featured an African American woman. In *Beulah*, for example, Louise Beavers' femininity and sexual attractiveness were downplayed in favor of her maternal and nurturing qualities. Julia's physical appearance and *haute couture* clothing became an important part of the narrative so as to advance an ideological position of racial advancement. By portraying Baker as more glamorous than her White female counterparts, the producers normalized her television image.

Suzanna Walters, in *Material Girls*, identifies one implication of Mulvey's theory of male spectatorship. She writes that "point of view" is "crucial" to "narrative structure and mise-en-scène" and that it "literally act[s] out the male gaze" (61). Visual narrative devices, specifically camera angles and stylized, edited sequences, point to what became one of the most effective symbols of Julia's sexuality, Carroll's calves. In "Mamma's Man," the camera angle rests just past her hemline as she walks into the Aerospace Industries Health Office to apply for the position of nurse. Carroll is dressed professionally in a dark woolen suit, pantyhose, and heels, but the camera angle and costuming draw attention specifically to her legs. The viewer participates in the scene voyeuristically, and the inclusion of a male spectator smiling at the sight of Julia ascending the stairs to the space center cues the viewer to join in the pleasure. A similar angle is used in the 1969 episode, "The Eve of Adam." As the romantic lead in the episode, artist Adam Spencer provides the added point of view, watching Baker's legs from behind. Walking forward, Baker bends slightly and places a portrait of Corey that Spencer painted against a wall and walks away. In the scene, the image of Carroll's legs is visually constructed in such a way as to suggest an omnipresent sexuality framed like that of the portrait Spencer has stopped by to the deliver.

Prior to *Julia*, Black women cast as servants and maids in familial comedies had little sexual appeal. As a rule, the series shied away from images of Julia that portrayed her as wild, aggressive, or hypersexualized (MacDonald *One* 12). The normalizing goal of *Julia* resulted in the series taking on many of the common modes of female objectification in media. One such device used with regularity in the series was the visual segmentation of the female body that, up until 1968, was used primarily to fetishize White women in television and cinema. As a sign of Julia Baker's attractive qualities, however, the series visually segmented Carroll's body by focusing on her legs. Kanter normalized the content of *Julia* by adhering to dominant modes of representation that had been developed for White women in television. The normalization of Julia Baker resulted in critical comparisons of Carroll to other well-known television widows—placing her in the unfair position of seeming less Black to many viewers (See 27; "Did Diahann Carroll 'Sell Out' to Television?" 56).

Beginning in the 1950s, lighting for sitcoms became an important aspect of staging. Like camera angles, lighting arrangement and design have a signifying function. Terry Byrne, in *Production Design for Television*, states that in the days before color television, the intensity of the lighting was the major visual cue as to the seriousness or frivolity of the piece—a comic piece would be lit flat and bright, a serious one darker and more sculpturally (51). These conventions still persist. Soaps and some prime-time dramas are often lit with strong shadows and strong back lights, while comedies are lit brightly and indiscriminately (Byrne 51). The traditional mode of lighting, however, operated differently for Black actors as compared to White ones. The narrative content for *Julia* coincided with the typical high-key lighting design for sitcoms. The lighting used routinely to frame White female characters in domestic sitcoms did not work the same for Carroll. When used on her, the high-key lighting whitened her already light-brown complexion. Without a lighting adjustment, Carroll's image signified black dilution. Byrne confirms this effect when he observes that a "dark-complected [*sic*] person will be lit more intensely and may have a stronger backlight" to "frame the face and hair and provide more reflective highlights from the cheeks, forehead, and chin" than White or lighter-complexioned actors (Byrne 52).

Lack of attention to racial difference in this case produced a washing-out visually of an important aspect of racial difference, skin tone. Traditional sitcom lighting in this case suggests Caldwell showcased Carroll "with a rather conventional sitcom style, that is with effaced direction and flattering high-key studio lighting that made her seem both very elegant and very white" (54). Important to Caldwell's analysis is how the lighting affected not only the representation of race in the series but the image of idealized womanhood, crucial to domestic sitcoms and Carroll's own star image.

CASTING CONVENTIONS

Prior to her role in *Julia*, Carroll's image in popular media signified the attainment of bourgeois refinement, "sweet" sensuality, glamour, and femininity ("Hands and Song" 57–58; "Nightclubs: Bottom of the Top" 48). Kanter cast her with the hope that the discourse inherited from her stage and film performances prior to 1968 might ensure the show's crossover appeal. As an actress connected to both White and Black communities, Carroll's presence communicated a pluralist discourse on race while reifying White over Black cultural norms. As with many other producers, public perceptions of Carroll guided Kanter's casting choice for the lead role. Initially, he did not envision Carroll's image as matching the role of Julia Baker. He changed his mind, however, when she arrived at the interview "simple and understated" in a "black wool" suit "with a short skirt" (Carroll and Firestone 137). Once in production, his choice of Carroll appeared to undermine the concept of Julia and drew criticism that her sophisticated image hurt her "believability" in the role of mother and nurse. Carroll's detractors likened her inappropriateness for the part of Julia to that of White female icons, such as Jackie Kennedy or Doris Day (Shayon, "*Julia* Symposium;" See 27–30). How she compared to an African American woman such as Merlie Evers (Evers 60) or the fact that she was herself a mother did not matter (See 27). Commenting critically in *Time* on the Julia break-through, Black entertainer Harry Belafonte noted how "for the shuffling, simple minded Amos-and-Andy type of Negro, television has substituted a new, one-dimensional Negro without reality" ("Blacks on the Channels" 74). Kanter seems to confirm Belafonte's critique when he states that a goal of the series was to feature "Black characters as people first" and "Black only incidentally" (Kanter 254). Thanks to Carroll's off-screen persona and performance background, the innovative character of Julia Baker began to construct a new "standard of recognition" for Black women on television.

Julia followed the conventions of the genre that placed White female leads at the center of the narrative, maintaining a tradition of actresses who were "well-dressed" and fashionable, but who lacked depth (Mellencamp *Logic* 66). Carroll is always shown in fashionable attire. The *haute couture* designs of fashion designer William Travilla appeared both in the series and were mentioned in editorials on the show. In the episode "Tanks for the Memories," Julia answers a knock at her door in a peach-colored pantsuit trimmed at the collar with cream-colored feathers. This delighted her male guests, who commented approvingly on her appearance. Her highly publicized wardrobe included designer gowns featured in magazines such as *Ebony* and *Good Housekeeping* and was later duplicated as a line of clothes for Mattel's *Julia* doll ("Diahann Carroll Presents the *Julia* Dolls"). The character's identification with White middle-class housewives, fictional and real, and the heightening of her idealized feminine Eurocentric features displaced her racial "otherness."

As with her costuming in *Julia*, Carroll's body itself engendered elements placing her within the boundaries of the dominant culture and signifying an affinity with the status quo and a tangential relationship to African American phenotypic norms. As a legacy of slavery, African Americans with light skin tones were often able to achieve greater social and economic mobility because of a perceived connection to their owners and ability to assimilate within the dominant culture (Omi and Winant 13–18). Such ideas gave way to aesthetic and class perceptions influencing how Black women are perceived historically, both inside and outside of mainstream American culture.

Throughout Carroll's career, her ability to succeed in the entertainment industry, particularly in leading roles, depended substantially on the lightness of her complexion. As with her predecessors Fredi Washington, Dorothy Dandridge, and Lena Horne, Carroll's light skin tone gave her an advantage over darker women, who, as with Louise Beavers, found no other roles in Hollywood except as servants (Bogle *Primetime* 59). Although lighter-complexioned actresses played more romantic leads than darker ones, such roles were not free of racist stereotyping (Lisa Anderson 18; Bogle *Primetime* 58). In the discourse on *Julia*, Carroll's image is "whitened" through frequent comparisons to White female icons, such as former first lady Jackie [Kennedy] Onassis and the static idealized girl/woman image of Barbie (Simonds

917). Ultimately, such whitening of Carroll proved devastating to her career after Black cultural nationalism successfully critiqued Hollywood biases and color-coded practices as anti-Black. One historian compares Carroll's "pert and proper" image to that of Onassis, and declares that she had "far more in common with Doris Day than Angela Davis" (Van Deburg 251). Similarly, Donald Bogle, in *Toms, Coons, Mulattoes, Mammies, and Bucks,* writes that Carroll's portrayal in *Julia* resembled a "black-face Doris Day" due to her poised mannerisms, glamorous image, and light-complexioned skin (Bogle 211). Other critics charge the producers of *Julia* with creating an "assimilationist" discourse at a time when African Americans accelerated their demand for self-determination and celebrated their distinctive qualities. Herman Gray makes this point in *Watching Race,* arguing that programs such as *Julia* "celebrated racial invisibility and color blindness" (85). He contends that such programs had a "normalizing" effect that configured racism as an individualized experience and reduced the possibility of collective resistance against the savage inequities that persisted in the United States (84–85). The lessening of Julia's Black identity maintained a televisual status quo in that it caused White women to identify with her, while estranging African Americans from one of the few Black female characters on television (Bodroghkozy 415). Writing for *Good Housekeeping* in 1969, Rollie Hochstein offered a slightly critical assessment of Carroll's image in popular culture. She wrote, "after starring roles in movies and television dramas as well as musical specials, after the ending of her own interracial marriage, after a famous and serious romance with superstar Sidney Poitier, *Julia* returned her [Carroll] to the sweetness-and-light department" (47). Contemporary and recent criticism of Carroll's physical appearance and performance in *Julia* stresses how television gatekeepers suppressed more radical identities, especially ones with the markers of Black Nationalism. Carroll's image in the series came to mean Black erasure and an elision of racial tensions through an idealized assimilation of people of color within the mainstream. It is not surprising, therefore, that the show was "originally scripted for a white actress" (Shayon, "Julia: Breakthrough").

Carroll performed as if unaware of her sexuality, although she was well aware of her own media image. She knew how the series utilized her body and her overall public image as a means to attract viewers, a standard device of representing sexuality that she chose to exploit and capitalize on. In her biography, Carroll reveals that the sexuality her character's legs signified was part of the initial crafting of the subjectivity of Julia Baker. She confesses that:

> By the time, I finished the script, I had gone beyond understand-
> ing Julia's character—I saw her actual physical presence. I knew
> exactly how she should look. . . . I hunted through my closet
> and found exactly the right dress: black wool with a short skirt,
> simple and understated (The script had made a point about Julia's
> great legs. If mine aren't spectacular, they ain't half bad, and I
> figured that was bound to help.) (Carroll and Firestone 136–37)

The exploitation of Carroll's sexual image facilitated a whitening process
in which Julia became a representation of Black assimilation. To "whiten"
oneself in the United States refers to the accentuating of Eurocentric values
and aesthetics as part of an overall process of assimilation into mainstream
culture. Carroll's physical and cultural integration resulted in a perception
that the struggle to assimilate into mainstream culture, workplaces, and
neighborhoods was attainable for all African Americans. The representation system in *Julia* led to Bodroghkozy's suggestion that Carroll's character
communicated that " 'Black people were just people' to the extent that they
conformed to an unexamined White norm of representation," or normalization through Black erasure (416).

By design, *Julia* was a carbon copy of the "affable family comedies"
of the mid- to late 1950s (Taylor 29). Because attention was to set decor,
color, and lighting, the genre traditions and practices in the industry from
the 1950s continued to have an impact on shows produced in the 1960s.
The makers of *Julia* worked to produce a show that had a well-established
formula, but they added an ingredient that had never before been included—Black actors performing a version of Black life as the central concern of
the series. The experiment disrupted the language of television. Production
techniques were adjusted, however, because of a decision to make Carroll
and other Blacks appear as mainstream as possible, as white as rice. The role
of the productive forces that created *Julia* and television's capacity to respond
to the political climate of the late 1960s flowed together into matrimony
within the holy family of liberal integrationism, democratic capitalism, and
Virginia Slims femininity. The series helped workers and managers in the
television industry realize that a world in living color could be represented
with a measure of artistry and commercial success. Also, it revealed that the
grammar of television had greater fluidity than was commonly recognized;
certainly it was fluid enough to represent non-mainstream facets of the
American experience in a way that was viable and met recognized standards of production. Finally, it demonstrated, perhaps painfully for some,
that audiences—average viewers to professional critics—could read, decode,

appropriate, be influenced by, and contest shows (particularly their ideological content) in relation to their material, psychological, and cultural locations. *Julia* forever changed the face of television. How fitting it is that the character of a nurse at a military industrial complex would bring a new level of comfort, confidence, health, and healing to a television industry steeped in years of the disease of racism and the nervous ticks of racial hierarchy. The show in no way cured television of its ills, but it did inspire the negotiation of new boundaries.

The 1970s

The 1970s picked up where the 1960s left off—with upheaval and unrest. The decade began with continuing protests against the escalating Vietnam War, and the killing of four students at Kent State University by the Ohio National Guard, which received wide television coverage, seemed to provide final proof that the war had come home. The decade ended with the election of former Hollywood movie star Ronald Reagan as President of the United States. Cultural milestones of the 1970s include the Watergate scandal and subsequent resignation of President Richard Nixon; the ignominious end of the war and reunification of Vietnam; the birth of the first test-tube baby; the legalization of abortion; and, the death of music icon Elvis Presley. While Nixon disappeared from public view, Elvis' death did not stop the flow of purported sightings, as his fans refused to admit he was gone, and sales of Presley music and merchandise skyrocketed.

For the first time, a Black tennis pro, Arthur Ashe, won at Wimbledon, and race was discussed openly, if somewhat clumsily, in relevancy sitcoms such as those pioneered by Norman Lear. Gerard Jones makes compelling arguments about the competing messages that are inevitably embedded in television narratives, the ways the personal experiences and perspectives of viewers shape how the stories are interpreted, and the unintended consequences that can arise when producers like Lear fail to foresee some of the implications of their work. Gay rights became a prominent feature of identity politics but not, unsurprisingly, a regular feature of the prime-time lineup. After all, as Judy Kutulas writes, television executives and producers could acknowledge the Women's Movement by depicting a certain type of feminine, liberated woman as acceptable, but continued to disparage more overtly political feminists with negative incarnations on the small screen. If feminism was deemed too dangerous and unsavory for primetime, then the Gay Rights Movement was certainly verboten because of its challenge to the status quo.

Pocket calculators and video cassette recorders were introduced and mass produced in the 1970s, and most sitcoms started to be produced on videotape. Paul R. Kohl looks beyond technological advances to examine modes of media production and subversive moments across three decades (including the 1970s) when television "creatives," the working class in the schema he presents, strike back at the decision makers who typically call the shots and limit creativity on television shows. Kohl's Marxist analysis of the world of television production is particularly compelling since the medium of television has so seldom been used to explore issues of class in America in substantive ways. For the most part, series tend to uncritically promote narratives of meritocracy while minimizing the effects of social class. As two oil embargos fueled a recession in the United States, serving to increase a widespread sense of disillusionment with government and politics, the frustrated mood in the larger culture seeped into some of the sitcoms of the 1970s, most notably into the relevancy programming that is most closely identified with the era.

Early in the decade, Norman Lear's controversial *All in the Family* began on CBS, and it probably remains the best-known of the relevancy sitcoms. But, that wasn't the only game in town. ABC premiered *Monday Night Football* in 1970, PBS imported the highbrow *Masterpiece Theatre* for its new Sunday night show in 1971, and *Saturday Night Live* premiered on NBC in 1975—and is still going strong as of this writing. Other types of programming addressed issues of gender and race, even as social class continued to spark little explicit discussion. ABC brought the first female news anchor to the airwaves in 1976 when Barbara Walters began co-hosting the *ABC Evening News* with Harry Reasoner. In 1977, the groundbreaking miniseries *Roots* aired for eight consecutive nights on ABC, creating a national dialogue about race. And, as a harbinger of the narrowcasting that would start to emerge and fragment large audiences that had marked the heyday of broadcasting, ESPN became the first cable network to specialize in sports programming in 1979. The top-rated sitcoms of the 1970s were *Alice*; *All in the Family*; *Angie*; *Archie Bunker's Place*; *Barney Miller*; *The Brian Keith Show* (*The Little People* during its first season); *The Bob Newhart Show*; *Bridget Loves Bernie*; *Chico and the Man*; *Diff'rent Strokes*; *The Doris Day Show*; *Flo*; *Funny Face*; *Good Heavens*; *Good Times*; *Happy Days*; *Here's Lucy*; *The Jeffersons*; *Laverne & Shirley*; *The Mary Tyler Moore Show*; *M*A*S*H*; *Maude*; *Mayberry R.F.D.*; *Mork & Mindy*; *My Three Sons*; *The New Dick Van Dyke Show*; *On Our Own*; *One Day at a Time*; *The Partridge Family*; *Phyllis*; *Rhoda*; *The Ropers*; *Sanford and Son*; *Soap*; *Stockard Channing in Just Friends*; *Taxi*; *Three's Company*; *The Tony Randall Show*; *What's Happening!!*; and *Welcome Back, Kotter*.

8

The Norman Lear Sitcoms
and the 1970s

GERARD JONES

Long considered one of the most influential voices in American television and founder of the progressive, nonprofit, advocacy group People for the American Way, Norman Lear has produced some of the most popular and controversial situation comedies in the history of the genre. His legacy, like his landmark series of the 1970s, is a mixed bag of liberal intentions and competing, regressive messages. Prior to the 1970s, American sitcoms showed far less inclination for realism and cynicism than did their British counterparts, which often left their protagonists trapped by poverty and social immobility. *Till Death Do Us Part* and *Steptoe and Son* were two edgy sitcoms made possible by Britain's noncommercial television. In the former, an aging cockney and his left-wing son-in-law argue violently about social politics, while *Steptoe and Son* features two generations of junk dealers, bound by blood, futility, and class limitations, storylines Lear would mine for cultural commentary and comic relief in his American sitcoms.

By the time Lear bought the American rights for *Till Death Do Us Part* and *Steptoe and Son*, he had spent years writing and producing TV variety shows. In the 1960s, he'd teamed up with another TV producer, Bud Yorkin, to make movies under the name Tandem Productions. Their specialty was saucy comedy that took advantage of Hollywood's loosening censorship restrictions, marked by slick, titillating wit and sage doses of social comment, including *Come Blow Your Horn* (1963), *Divorce American Style* (1967), and *The Night They Raided Minsky's* (1968). Lear was interested in reentering television if he could shatter the networks' blandness and fear of controversy, and *All in the Family* was the hammer he wanted to use.

ALL IN THE FAMILY

Lear turned *Till Death Do Us Part's* xenophobic Brit into Archie Bunker, a blue-collar warehouse worker, union man, unreconstructed racist, and social conservative. His leftist son-in-law is Michael "Mike" Stivic, a Polish-American graduate student in sociology and knee-jerk liberal. Mediating the verbal combat is Archie's cute, dopey daughter, Gloria Stivic, who loves her father but adopts her husband's worldview, and Archie's wife, Edith, who is timid, tolerant, and politically naïve—a "dingbat" in Archie's parlance. When ABC ordered a pilot, Lear assembled a superb cast. He turned to Carroll O'Connor, a lesser-known Broadway and film actor, who brought Archie to life in all his anger and vulnerability. Another stage veteran, Jean Stapleton, brought the same combination to the character of Edith. Lear cast Carl Reiner's son, Rob, as the mooching, self-important Mike, and young stage actress Sally Struthers as the naïve, emotionally charged Gloria. The chemistry among them was explosive.

Based on poor test audience reactions in early 1970, ABC rejected the pilot; but it caught the eye of CBS President Bob Wood. His test audiences were no more encouraging (Adler xvii-xviii), but Wood fought to get the show on the air. During the previous year, he had been overhauling his network's image, eliminating shows like *The Beverly Hillbillies* that appealed to older, poorer, and more rustic audiences and replacing them with shows that would appeal to the younger, hipper viewers whom advertisers preferred. Wood was also aware that as the Vietnam War wore on, ethnic movements grew more militant, and feminism hit mainstream America, the national debate was growing broader and louder; sociopolitical arguments were no longer restricted to college students and radicals. The show was slated for a January 1971 premiere, but Wood and his fellow executives were nervous. Fearing a backlash, they did what they could to soften the blow. They pressured Lear into withdrawing a sly sexual reference and the word "goddamn" from the first script. A disclaimer was scrolled across the screen before the first episode, assuring viewers that its intention was to "throw a humorous-spotlight on our frailties, prejudices and concerns."

The first episode opens with generational and religious conflicts on full display: Archie and Edith go to church, but Mike and Gloria stay home (with an implication that they do so in order to have sex). A scatological TV taboo is defied when living-room arguments are disrupted by the loudly flushing upstairs toilet. Race enters the picture, as Archie taunts Mike.

ARCHIE: You're the laziest White boy I ever met.

MIKE: Meaning that the Blacks are even lazier.

ARCHIE: Wait a second, wise guy . . . I never said that at all. Of course, their systems are geared a little slower than ours, that's all.

Later episodes continue to air racial, sexual, and religious laundry. Archie parades his archaic, provincial attitudes, filling the airwaves with words formerly taboo: hebe, mick, spic, fag, Polack, jungle bunny. He defends himself in transparent stupidity: "Look, Archie Bunker ain't no bigot. I'm the first to say that it ain't your fault that you're colored." Inevitably, he gets his comeuppance from the world or from his smug son-in-law.

Figure 8.1. Jean Stapleton as Edith Bunker, Rob Reiner as Michael Stivic, Sally Struthers as Gloria Stivic, Mike Evans as Lionel Jefferson, and Carroll O'Connor as Archie Bunker. 1971–1979. Photo courtesy of Photofest.

The network, producers, and advertisers braced themselves for protests from offended conservatives, but the most serious protests came from liberals. Laura Z. Hobson, author of the anti-anti-Semitic *Gentleman's Agreement*, took the show to task in *The New York Times* for making racism acceptable by placing it within an affectionately humorous context. She thought the scripts were particularly dishonest in playing at racial epithets without going all the way: "*Hebe* and *jungle bunny* are quaint, almost funny, but *kike* and *nigger* never pass Archie's lips (Sec. 2, 1)." A snowstorm of letters agreed with Hobson. It became the biggest debate ever engendered by a piece of TV entertainment: Did *All in the Family* ridicule racist behavior or make it seem permissible? Lear presented himself as a misunderstood liberal, maintaining that Archie was a purely negative example, and the plots generally bore him out. Ultimately, most liberal critics praised the show as anti-racist, and schoolteachers across the country requested *All in the Family* study guides from CBS. The TV professionals who voted for the Emmy awards—generally supportive of liberal-centrist messages—endorsed it enthusiastically.

There was one problem with this liberal scenario: Archie is too damned lovable. He's ignorant but never mean-spirited. All he wants is to sit in his easy chair, take care of his family, and enjoy his cigars and coffee. Second to Archie in emotional appeal is Edith, well-intentioned but befuddled. She loves Archie, and he loves her. He might not respect her mind, he might tell her to "stifle" herself, he might demand to be served, but he works every day to support her, and he passes up a flirtatious divorcée to remain faithful to her. Gloria isn't as likable as Edith, but she's sympathetic enough, and she, too, loves Archie. The show's most touching moments come when she bridges the gap of generations and hugs her daddy. Archie's only constant opponent is Mike, the least likable of the four. He has many good lines and fine ideals, but he takes himself too seriously. He can't drop his political position to establish a personal link with Archie, and he's a parasite. He and Gloria live rent-free with the Bunkers while he's in graduate school, a situation that Archie grudgingly endures out of paternal love but that Mike seems to take as his due. As Archie becomes a better-rounded, more sympathetic character, Mike's immutable hostility makes him an insensitive ingrate. When he complains to Edith that Archie won't stop riding him, Edith flashes uncharacteristic indignation. "Do you wanna know why Archie yells are you? Archie yells at you because Archie is jealous of you. You're going to college. Archie had to quit school to support his family. He ain't never going to be any more than he is right now. Now you think that over." Despite all the conscious plot strategies to create a liberal impression, Archie Bunker is the hero.

Lear once said that he "had a strong conviction for some time that you can discuss national issues and deliver a large audience if it's done just right . . . people will watch. And they will learn" (qtd. in Taylor 57). Lear did indeed parade a lot of "national issues" through the Bunker living room: street crime, anti-Semitism, mixed marriage, Watergate. He even put sexual issues on parade, an easy way of breaking TV taboos, getting press coverage, and drawing a curious audience: Archie is impotent, Mike gets a vasectomy, Edith goes through menopause, Gloria has a miscarriage, someone they know is a lesbian, Edith befriends a drag queen, Archie nearly cheats on Edith, and so on. But, for all this parading, political substance was trumped by personal interactions. In "The Elevator Story," Archie is trapped in an elevator with a bunch of "ethnic types." Most vocal among them is an articulate and confident Black man. The subject of military service comes up, and Archie assumes that the man must have been on "latrine duty" during the war. When the man reveals that he was an intelligence officer, Archie looks chagrined, and the studio audience laughs at Archie's embarrassment. Archie is effectively humbled, and by episode's end the man lets him off the social hook with a noble courtesy. This interchange is ostensibly about racism, but what does it say? Only that Archie is so naïve in his stereotyping that he can't conceive of intelligent, responsible Black people. Institutional racism is not addressed. Archie's folly is harmful only to Archie himself.

Like so many mass audience successes, *All in the Family* could be viewed on different levels. Liberals and intellectuals could see their beliefs vindicated while White conservatives found a new hero and felt the world had acknowledged them. Perhaps more important, Archie spoke to the anxieties of those confused masses in between. When he spoke of "jungle bunnies," he released a little internal pressure for millions of Americans who felt socially unacceptable hostilities within themselves. Archie was a sacrificial lamb for an angry, frightened, would-be progressive America. There is such an electric tension to the first couple of years of *All in the Family* that it's difficult to believe this duality was calculated. It seems to spring from the duality within Norman Lear himself, a common split within sensitive middle-aged progressives. He was an intellectual liberal but an emotional conservative.[1] Whatever he may have *thought* about social revolution, he yearned for continuity and family. In the end, it is the emotional, not intellectual, content that bonds an audience with a TV show. Liberals welcomed the overt messages of *All in the Family*, but it was the Archie Bunkers of America who stayed with the character once the novelty wore off. CBS's new programming chief, Fred Silverman, must have intuited this. The network had originally dropped it into a dead time slot—Tuesday night at 9:30, opposite ABC's top-rated

Movie of the Week—perhaps to minimize the trouble it could cause. It came in 58th in the ratings and was considered for cancellation, but the media attention encouraged Bob Wood to give it a push with the start of its first full season. Silverman moved it to 8:00 on Saturday night. That put Archie squarely in the face of the mass TV audience, and that audience made him a tremendous hit. *All in the Family* topped the Nielsens that season with a 34 rating and remained on top for five straight years.[2]

The success of *All in the Family* guaranteed a flood of shows breaking taboos, playing with topical issues, pitting family member against family member, featuring political misfits and working-class louts. Along with *The Mary Tyler Moore Show*, it taught TV entertainment how to grapple humorously with the anxieties of the time and, in so doing, laid the foundation for nearly every sitcom since. For all the success of *All in the Family*, however, 1970s sitcoms had an increasingly hard time reaching the prime advertising market. The sitcoms that followed it put less emphasis on political dialogue and generational dynamics and steadily more on sex, shock value, sentimentality, and lovable buffoons. After a few years, *All in the Family* itself fell prey to its own sentimentality and repetition. But, in its moment of gutsy, self-contradictory glory, it had changed American mass culture. It dared to state that the culture of assimilation and consensus wasn't working; that communication did not necessarily dissolve our differences—in the Bunker household, communication just leads to a lot of yelling. Yet, as pessimistic as the show was about the modern world, it was optimistic about the basic nature of people and families. Without offering any solutions to social ills, it showed the Bunkers holding together, episode after episode, by foolish love alone. Reaction to *All in the Family* convinced NBC that Lear and Yorkin were hot. When Lear reworked the British *Steptoe and Son* into *Sanford and Son*, about a widowed Black junkyard owner, the network snapped it up and shoved it onto the schedule as a midseason replacement in January 1972. At the end of the previous season, NBC had cancelled *Julia* (1968–71) the groundbreaking, integrated sitcom that had seemed so daring in 1968; *Sanford and Son* was not so much a replacement as a repudiation.

SANFORD AND SON

There are no clean, modern settings for Fred Sanford and no kindly White bosses. Fred lives in a cluttered junkyard in Watts, a rundown, Black neighborhood in Los Angeles. The only regular authority figures are cops, who drop by to make sure Fred isn't fencing stolen goods. Fred's world is not integrated; his peers are loudmouthed, Black ne'er-do-wells with names like

Bubba, Rollo, and Skillet. The only prominent nonblack is Julio, the Puerto Rican neighbor who keeps a goat in his yard. Fred feels no political solidarity with his fellow oppressed; when his son, Lamont, lends Julio their pickup, Fred yells, "Now you gone got Puerto Rican all over our truck!" Fred is a Black Archie Bunker: bigoted, provincial, ignorant, trapped in his economic and cultural stratum. Even more than Archie, though, Fred resists change. Archie seems to understand that Gloria should be allowed to marry a graduate student and move out of the working class, even if he resents Mike's mooching, but Fred uses every trick in the book to force the restless Lamont to stay in the junk business. "If it wasn't for you holding me back," Lamont says, "I could be in an office." "Yeah, the welfare office," snaps Fred. Lamont complains that Fred has forced him to quit high school; Fred calls him a dropout and a dummy. Fred and Lamont wage an endless, screaming, guilt-laden debate between separatism and integrationism. It is a debate with few intellectual underpinnings, however. Fred's separatism is born of a simple, deep suspicion of the White world; a conviction that if Lamont tries to raise his head above the color line, Whites will knock him down. His Black-supported independent business, however modest, is his security against that world. Lamont's integrationism is driven by desire for the comfort and prestige of middle-class affluence and by a naïve belief that success is one clever idea away. Fred constantly hurls the word *dummy* at Lamont, a spin on Archie Bunker's *meathead*. But, *meathead* is a goofy word with little bite. Fred systematically undermines his son's self-esteem. No wonder Lamont is unable to break away from him, unable to sustain a romantic relationship, unable to make his success schemes work.

Sanford and Son was a huge ratings hit, largely for the simple reason that it was funny. Fred is played by Redd Foxx, a comedian who had made 49 raunchy comedy albums and the Black-targeted comedy movie *Cotton Comes to Harlem* (1970). Lear's writer's gags were tight, caustic, and racially edged. A White man thinks Fred has been hurt and asks if he wants to go to the hospital.

FRED: I can't waste three days.

WHITE MAN: It only takes a few minutes.

FRED: It only takes you a few minutes. It takes us three days in the waiting room.

Foxx delivers the lines loud and hard and well. Much of the show's appeal, though, lies also in its sociological bluntness: *Sanford and Son* acknowledges that many people are locked out of the American Dream, forced, like Fred, to live off its scraps. Millions have identified with Lamont, a man denied access to the affluent society, not only by the social mainstream itself but also by their own class and ethnic burdens, their own personal Freds. And, there was another element feeding into the show's success, one that alarmed Black commentators. Fred is a stereotype of the petit bourgeois Black, a throwback to *Amos 'n' Andy*. His prissy, appearance-obsessed sister-in-law, Esther, is a redux of Kingfish's wife, Sapphire. And, Fred's drinking, gambling, and scheming cronies are the Kingfish times three. Fred and Lamont, wrote one Black critic, were "conceived by White minds and based upon a White value system." They were "not [B]lack men capable of achieving—or even understanding—liberation. They are merely two more American child-men" (Collier).

The producers responded by hiring Black writers, but the tone barely changed. Yet, the criticism had little effect. No boycotts were organized, no advertisers targeted. By the early 1970s, American racial debates did not revolve around TV programs. After the assassination of Martin Luther King, Jr., moderate civil rights leadership was undermined, and many saw a new radicalism as the next legitimate step in the Black revolution. As the media became obsessed with soaring crime rates, Whites fled cities faster than ever. The contentious 1972 Democratic Convention broke down in a battle of special-interest groups, many of them ethnic and radical, and Richard Nixon won a landslide re-election by playing to the silent (White) majority. When a Black gang called the Death Angels started to shoot Whites at random and the mainly Black Symbionese Liberation Army kidnapped White heiress Patty Hearst, many Whites imagined their worst nightmares coming true. Controversies over school busing and affirmative action aggravated the conflicts. By the time *Sanford and Son* premiered, all sides of the racial conflict were tired. It seemed easier to accept the impermeability of the racial membrane for a while. Negrophobic Whites could laugh at the harmless Fred. Frustrated minorities could enjoy a sympathetic chuckle over Lamont. No one seemed to want to fight over it. NBC ran with its hit, sponsors fought for spots, and only liberal producers and Black actors felt the need to defend themselves. The relatively unchallenged success of *All in the Family* and *Sanford and Son* shattered the timidity of advertisers and network programmers.

MAUDE

Lear continued to produce brazen programming with *Maude*. She was a wife and mother—that much about her was consistent with sitcom tradition—but she was on her fourth marriage, and her daughter was an adult divorcée with a child of her own, living with her mother and stepfather for financial reasons. The series was intended to be an exploration of current issues but with a woman's twist. Unfortunately, but inevitably, it broke down into a series of "shock" shows. Maude gets pregnant. She has an abortion. She goes through menopause. She has a facelift. She goes to a psychiatrist. The neighbors try to talk her and her husband into wife swapping. Her husband has a nervous breakdown. He is revealed to be an alcoholic. One week, much of the audience tuned in because word had leaked that Maude would say "son of a bitch" on the air. She says it, all right. *Maude* strikes an uneasy balance between coarse humor and heavy drama. The studio audience whoops in shocked delight, then falls utterly silent as an emotional bombshell is dropped. The no-laughter, no-applause cliffhanger fade-out becomes a staple. But, the sources of both drama and humor grow cheaper and cheaper as the writers have to top each old shock with a new one. *Maude* became a victim of Maude's modernity.

GOOD TIMES

Good Times exposes the dangers inherent in the Lear approach to television. *Good Times* was intended to portray a believable and admirable Black family in a ghetto housing project, struggling to get by but always sticking together out of love and pride. The mother, Florida (Esther Rolle), attracted Black and White viewers alike as a proud, no-nonsense maid dealing caustically with Maude's liberal condescension. A working mother with three kids, she is the good-natured, emotional heart of the family. Her husband, James (John Amos), is a hardworking traditionalist, a bit of a disciplinarian who has to be softened by his wife occasionally. The teenage daughter, Thelma (BernNadette Stanis), is an average kid, preoccupied with boys and her appearance. The younger son, Michael (Ralph Carter), is serious, studious, political, and proudly Black. But then, there is the older son, J.J. He is intended to be the screw-up, the one who thinks he can get rich by hustling and jiving but who has to be taught the importance of education, work, and family. The trouble was that J.J. is played by young stand-up comedian Jimmie Walker, part of a new wave of depoliticized ethnic comedians. In the exhaustion of the early 1970s, White and non-White TV audiences alike found themselves responding to young comics who made fun of their own ethnic traits. Walker is a skinny kid with a toothy grin, rubbery lips, and big, rolling eyes. He plays off his Blackness with self-loathing glee, tossing out jokes about watermelon eating and "the ghetto" that are guaranteed to provoke shocked, nervous—and occasionally liberating—laughter. He had an electric effect on kids and teenagers, the segment of the public that often made TV-viewing decisions for the family. Every time he yelled his catchphrase, hollered with a huge grin—"Dyn-O-Mite!"—the studio audience exploded into whoops and cheers.

Blending commerce and art is always dangerous—more to the latter than the former—but never more so than on television, where the pressure to deliver a huge audience by any means is intense. Ironically, the use of a live audience—of which Tandem and MTM Productions were so proud—only compounded the problem, as writers and actors played for crowd response. J.J. was the show's laugh-getter, and Lear and his writers

Figure 8.2. (clockwise from left) Ralph Carter as Michael Evans, Jimmie Walker as James "J.J." Evans, BerNadette Stanis as Thelma Evans, John Amos as James Evans, and Esther Rolle as Florida Evans in *Good Times*. 1974–1979. Photo courtesy of Photofest.

responded by centering more and more episodes on him. The plots continued to try to teach him lessons, but the denouements got smaller, and the J.J. bits got bigger. He never learned his lesson anyway. He became the emotional focus of the show. The older members of the cast were unhappy. Esther Rolle said: "I resent the imagery that says to [B]lack kids that you can make it by standing on the corner saying 'Dyn-O-Mite!' He's eighteen, and he doesn't work. He can't read or write. He doesn't think. . . . [N]egative images have been quietly slipped in on us through the character" (qtd. in Louis Robinson 35). John Amos complained along with Rolle (Louis Robinson). Reportedly, Lear was incensed. Although Florida was too central to be cut, James was not. Amos was released from his contract and killed off-camera in a car accident. Now the stable Black family had become a fatherless Black family, a stereotype of Black cultural dysfunction that incensed Black male critics (and Amos himself). J.J. was now the head of the family, and his parts got even bigger. Before the next season, Esther Rolle quit the show. She expected that Florida, too, would be killed by the writers; instead they had her move South for health reasons and stay there with her new husband, leaving her children to fend for themselves. Now J.J. became almost the entire show, and the writing devolved to primitive insult humor and, increasingly, stereotypes of Blacks as oversexed. It was hard to believe this was a Norman Lear program. Norman Lear, the liberal, fearless opponent of conservative broadcast standards who put sitcom arguments about Watergate in American living rooms, was projecting an image of Blacks as horny, eye-rolling, unemployed hustlers. And, this was a quarter-century after the NAACP (National Association for the Advancement of Colored People) had fought to keep the Kingfish off the air. But, people watched, especially Blacks, non-Black minorities, kids, and lower-income Whites.

THE JEFFERSONS

In 1975, Lear and Yorkin followed with a third, less offensive Black sitcom, a spin-off of *All in the Family* called *The Jeffersons*. George Jefferson is a neighbor of Archie Bunker who hits it big with his dry cleaning chain and buys a co-op on Manhattan's Upper East Side. He is a retrograde bigot, a domestic tyrant, and a social idiot, a more frenetic version of Archie. His wife, Louise, is an expansive, tolerant woman, trying to be elegant and remain friends with the White neighbors and the Black domestic helper, whom George consistently alienates. This is a liberal-consensus show in the old mold with an archaic individualist being dragged into the future. It has blustery conflicts but sentimental endings. It has an intelligent, modern protagonist in Louise. George learns valuable lessons: on the first show, to tolerate a Black–White mixed couple living in the building; and, later, to continue loving his son after he marries the same couple's biracial daughter. Yet, in its tone, it is nothing like the old ethnicoms. Nearly every episode is 25 minutes of "zingers," vaudevillian insults. George tells Louise to be careful with a mirror because, "You don't need any more bad luck." She responds, "I know. I already got you." Loud deliveries and long reaction takes increasingly take the place of wit. Embarrassing slapstick fills in when insults run dry. Lear had torn away the phony gentility of 1960s TV, increased the speed and force of humor, and allowed people who loved each other to fight as people really do. But, the emotional honesty and tension that marked the early *All in the Family* episodes could not sustain itself. Each new laugh had to be louder, each topic more sensational, each sexual reference more daring, each insult more extreme. Lear had gone from giving new meaning to prime-time entertainment to overseeing some of the most brutishly offensive shows on the air. He never acknowledged the change. Whatever he learned about television, Lear had certainly learned how to make people watch. Neither *Good Times* nor *The Jeffersons* was a huge hit, but both held audiences well enough to last for six and eleven years, respectively.

CONCLUSION

In the wake of Lear's extraordinary success, other producers developed sitcoms with explosive, caustic characters and varied family configurations. Actor-producer James Komack was one producer who grasped what the Lear comedies indicated about viewing preferences. His *Courtship of Eddie's Father* was as cute and well-mannered as any other series of the late 1960s. But, he made a radical shift with *Chico and the Man*, a vehicle designed to do for Latin Americans what *Sanford and Son* did for Blacks. Chico is an ethnic comic with a routine built around quaint ghetto stereotypes and funny-accent catchphrases. Freddie Prinze was "Hungarican," half Puerto Rican and half Hungarian, though the Chico character is Mexican-American. Chico's co-star, "the Man," is Ed Brown, played by Jack Albertson as a lonely and hostile, old, White man who owns a garage in an L.A. neighborhood that has gradually become non-White. Chico begins to work for Brown and starts to turn the old coot into a loving, tolerant man. The plot is a ritual emotional play in which Chico loves Ed, Ed spurns him, Chico is hurt, then Ed reveals that he loves Chico—and audiences responded. In its first year, *Chico and the Man* was third in the Nielsens, trailing only *All in the Family* and *Sanford and Son*. *Chico and the Man* takes the Bunkers' conflicts a step further from reality; families like the Bunkers fight, but how often does an old racist take in a young Chicano?

Komack played more extensively with generational and ethnic dynamics in his next sitcom, *Welcome Back, Kotter*, a vehicle for another rising New York comedian, Gabe Kaplan, whose stand-up act featured a routine about his old high school classmates. Like Prinze and Walker, Kaplan played off young Americans' pent-up desire to laugh about race after years of liberal-minded silence, but he used his stereotypes with greater complexity. To develop the routine into a sitcom, Kaplan is cast as a permissive teacher, Gabe Kotter, trying to ride herd on a class of challenging students. The "sweathogs," as they are known, are troublemaking, ignorant, but ultimately good-hearted kids of diverse ethnicities, and the series comes up with a new use for ethnic stereotypes. Instead of these characters being *about* Italianness or Jewishness or Blackness, their ethnic identity is merely used to create character eccentricities. Kotter is an alumnus of the school, coming back to teach the kids whatever he can about the big world outside, especially about overcoming conflicts and functioning together. A new synthesis of sitcom elements is being forged here: *Welcome Back, Kotter* blends farcical situations with juvenile life lessons, just like *Father Knows Best* but in a "post-family" context and with racy 1970s elements of ethnic stereotypes and sexual humor. It holds together because the show makes no bones about being synthetic. The writing is a little too wise-ass to be real. The actors overplay their characters with self-conscious cuteness. And then, there is John Travolta as Vinnie Barbarino, a marketable heartthrob to teenage girls on his way to becoming the sex god of the disco era. The way he plays to the pubescent squeals from the studio audience leaves viewers with no doubt that they are watching a show, not participating vicariously in the lives of others.

The 1970s were launched with fire and relevancy, but as the decade wore on, Archie Bunker softened, subsequent Lear sitcoms eschewed progressive impulses and wallowed in broad, negative stereotypes, and relevancy programs lost ground to maintaining a comfortable space for mainstream viewers. Consider the patched-together family dynamics of *Diff'rent Strokes* in which a White millionaire adopts two Black, inner-city kids.[3] Minority males are infantilized, which simultaneously removes the threat and enables the "adult" (read: White) world to extend a paternal hand. On *Diff'rent Strokes*, revealingly, it is the undersize, precocious younger boy, played by an actor locked in chubby, prepubescent cuteness by health problems, who steals the show. His big brother, who might pose a greater threat to viewers by being a streetwise, adult-sized Black teen, is shoved into the background. For timid Whites, the message seems to be: "We don't hate these people; it's just the way they're raised that we hate." The conflicts that characterized Norman Lear's ethnic sitcoms had been submerged into a new, synthetic domesticity by the end of the 1970s. In the ragged aftermath of national division, viewers were eager to buy it. American culture was returning to themes of harmony and family, by whatever contrivances it could muster.

NOTES

1. David Marc suggests that the tension between the plots and the characters reflects Lear's own psychological battles (*Comic Visions* 147). Lear based Archie largely on his own father, transforming a Depression-era Jew into a recession-era WASP. Mike's arguments with Archie echoed the arguments of a young, assimilating Norman Lear with his father, but the anger was eclipsed by the adult Norman's forgiveness of his father's shortcomings, understanding of the forces that shaped him, and distaste for the insensitivity of youth. *All in the Family* contained a deep sentimentality that set it apart from its British inspiration. In part, this reflected the compulsion of American popular culture to soften and sweeten, but the sentimentality also supported Archie's strongest message: that the world is insane and destructive but that somehow, with the support of our families, we endure.

2. The degree to which the Bunkers touched their audience was reflected by the products that sprang up: a tongue-in-cheek book called *The Wit and Wisdom of Archie Bunker*, a collection of Edith's homilies compiled by a Christian publisher; a record of O'Connor and Stapleton singing the show's theme, which asserted that in the good old days we "Didn't need no welfare state, everybody pulled his weight . . . Mister, we could use a man like Herbert Hoover again"; and T-shirts, mugs, and stickers advocating "Archie Bunker for President."

3. A similar show, *Webster* (1983–87), appeared a few years later. A rich White couple adopts a Black boy, and resulting storylines feature paternalistic overtones that diminish Black power and ameliorate White guilt.

9

Liberated Women and New Sensitive Men

Reconstructing Gender in 1970s Workplace Comedies

JUDY KUTULAS

In the early days of television, paid work was an afterthought on sitcoms but one almost exclusively reserved for men. Home and family were the essence of Americanism in the 1950s (May 11), and home and family were at the center of the sitcom. Representations of women on TV demonstrated what Betty Friedan describes as a feminine mystique, the valuing of women's relationships to others (husband, children, parents) over their own independent identities. TV housewives helped soothe postwar social anxieties about gender roles by "naturaliz[ing] woman's place in the home" (Haralovich 112) instead of the factory or office. A clear sense of gender differentiation prevailed in the 1950s on TV and in real life. But, following the sweeping social changes of the late 1960s, women were no longer content to stay invisibly at home doing for others. Although domestic sitcoms addressed the changes, the better venue for exploring gender issues was in the new genre of the workplace comedy. In 1970s workplace comedies, the audience encountered a mainstreamed version of new gender ideals, one that emphasized liberation while containing feminism.

Television does not create gender norms, but it is a vital part of any cultural conversation about them by providing both a frame of reference and a forum in which social contradictions can be explored. Its representations of 1950s women as invisible housewives existed because it was market driven, and therefore reactive to social trends, and because advertisers valued women as *family* consumers. Women have always been disproportionate watchers of sitcoms (Press 18), and their self-images must be reflected in successful programming. Once women chafed at their traditional roles, networks needed to find safe ways to accommodate their rebellions. They had to readapt the traditional sitcom formula to changing norms.

Family sitcoms reinforced the strict gender roles of the 1950s, providing visual compensation for the housewife's role with their lush renderings of suburban life. Women provide "moral backup" (Leibman 118) to fathers who know best, but women also disrupt the family hierarchy, venturing into the workplace or forcing their husbands to do housework. Sitcoms, like other forms of popular culture, provide safe opportunities for rebellion but ultimately reinforce the status quo. Thus, women's challenges on TV inevitably end in amusing failure, although, as Janine Basinger has argued about women's films, female viewers probably enjoyed the rebellion more than the lessons at the end of the show (21). Only rarely have women on television ventured beyond the domestic realm and into the workplace.

When they do, the experience is distinctly gendered. Theirs is an either-or proposition—jobs or families—unlike men, who have both options. Women's jobs on TV in the 1950s, moreover, aren't glamorous; they are teachers and secretaries, echoing the reality of a gender-segregated workplace that limited real women's employment possibilities. In addition, they are denied access to the consumer pleasures TV housewives have. They live in small apartments and wear tweedy skirts, sensible shoes, and sometimes, black framed glasses; they don't have handsome husbands or cute kids. And, it is clear on shows such as *Our Miss Brooks* and *Private Secretary* that they are frustrated. Eve Arden's Connie Brooks, for example, is snippy and snide, irritated yet capable. What TV's frustrated working girls lack most are husbands because, as in real life, a TV husband is "the base of the pyramid on which she would pile washer-dryers and refrigerators-freezers and sterling and fine china" (Bailey 75). The very qualities that make working girls fun to watch, sarcasm and wit, make them poor marriage material. They are a little too mouthy and too masculine, like Sally Rogers on *The Dick Van Dyke Show*. Often characterized as one of the guys, Sally has a successful comedy-writing career, lots of Jackie Kennedy suits, and a cool Manhattan apartment, but she can't even get her mama's-boy boyfriend to propose. Her story offered female viewers the chance to vicariously experience independence and career achievement while reassuring everyone that staying home was the more rewarding choice for a woman to make.

The networks didn't voluntarily alter such programming but were pushed into change for a variety of reasons. By 1968 or 1969, there was no cultural consensus in the United States. The generation gap, political fights, lifestyle changes, and various empowerment movements forced the networks to rethink their strategies. A TV gap existed, too; baby boomers—those most affected by the 1960s—didn't watch much TV, something network executives discovered when they began to segment and study the audience. And, boomers didn't particularly like domestic sitcoms (Bodroghkozy 64). Partly because they rejected their parents' paths—getting more education, marrying later, and having fewer children—they were attractive targets for advertisers; yet, their rejection of traditional domesticity also meant they didn't find family sitcoms compelling.

Television producers responded with what has been called relevancy programs that advance beyond the bland unreality of the traditional family sitcom. Relevancy TV includes shows like *All in the Family* (Gitlin *Inside* 203–20) and champions a new liberal perspective on politics, lifestyle, and gender. Feminism was trickier because the young, target audience didn't automatically embrace it. Consequently, when a feminist appears on relevancy TV, she is safely flawed. *Maude*, an *All in the Family* spin-off, has a feminist as its title character, but a feminist with an angry foghorn voice, a middle-aged body, and a milquetoast husband she can boss (who supports her). Although some audience members might read her as strong and independent, Maude symbolizes the stereotype of the angry, emasculating feminist who was represented even less favorably on the news and on traditional sitcoms, such as *The Beverly Hillbillies* and *Green Acres*, (Douglas 196–202). But, if feminism was too contested a value to be fully endorsed by sitcoms, the women's movement altered women's roles as consumers in ways that influenced the sitcom and forced changes. Where once a woman's value was a function of her familial role, doing (and shopping) for others, by the early 1970s, "a more independently minded female generation was coming of age" (Rabinowitz 145), and they had money to spend. Female viewers could no longer be counted on to watch programs (and commercials) that centered them in the home as wives and mothers. The workplace sitcom became one place where their new desires and possibilities could be represented.

The beauty of the workplace sitcom is its versatility. It doesn't disturb the traditional gender roles that persisted in the next generation of family sitcoms because most of its workers are single. It isn't as confrontational as relevancy TV. It features ensemble casts appealing to a lot of different audiences simultaneously. Such shows are attractive to baby boomers because they focus on people like themselves, making their way in a world they can't control and don't fully support (Taylor 111–12). The first 1970s workplace comedy was *The Mary Tyler Moore Show*. It was successful because it spoke specifically to young women without alienating the rest of its audience, as

Maude might. Its protagonist, Mary Richards, has left her hometown and fiancé for a career in television news in Minneapolis (Dow *Prime-Time* 25), liberating herself from the wife-and-mother trajectory. Mary is liberated but not a feminist. The difference is crucial, for liberation is gender neutral, consumer friendly, and helps build community, while TV feminism is inimical to all those things. Thus, liberation was mainstream enough for TV while feminism was not.

To accommodate Mary and other women, representations of the workplace had to change. Previously, popular culture portrayed it as hostile, hierarchical, and exploitative. In 1970s workplace comedies, coworkers became family, a metaphor that suited the baby boomers' desire for community on

Figure 9.1. (clockwise from lower left) Betty White as Sue Ann Nivens, Gavin MacLeod as Murray Slaughter, Edward Asner as Lou Grant, Mary Tyler Moore as Mary Richards, Ted Knight as Ted Baxter, Georgia Engel as Georgette Franklin Baxter in *The Mary Tyler Moore Show*. 1970–1977. Photo courtesy of Photofest.

their own terms. In the final episode of *The Mary Tyler Moore Show,* Mary asserts that family is "people who make you feel less alone and really loved." Her claim that the family is a construct rather than a biological entity mainstreamed an idea from the hippie counterculture by situating it within the capitalist system and rendering it compatible with biological family. The workplace family facilitated TV women's entrance into the workplace by implying its dynamic was cozy, familiar, and gendered.

Indeed, men are in charge of the workplace in 1970s sitcoms, and women hold mainly service or clerical jobs, which was true of the real world as well. Few, however, perform those jobs without complaint. Their protests against the menial nature of their work and, especially, the expectation that they serve men culturally references the women's movement and models a new workplace etiquette. Receptionist Jennifer Marlowe (*WKRP in Cincinnati*) won't get coffee or take dictation. Carol Kester (*The Bob Newhart Show*) balks at having to collect her boss' dry cleaning. Despite the seemingly conservative family dynamic, viewers saw women who took their jobs seriously and refused to be as servile as their sitcom ancestors.

Workplace women expect to be treated as people rather than women, a concept that, unlike most feminist ideas, quickly found broad popular acceptance because it was a variant of traditional American beliefs about fairness and mobility. Audiences watched as Mary Richards applies for a secretary's job at WJM-TV, is hired as associate producer of the six o'clock news (which pays less), and is promoted to producer several years later. A number of episodes showcase her struggles to be taken seriously and her developing sense of professional expertise. Bailey Quarters of *WKRP in Cincinnati* joins the radio family with a degree in journalism and moves from creating promotions to writing news copy to broadcasting the news. Except for conservatives, who could quibble with this view of the work world? It confirmed that hard work and talent would be rewarded while it also reinforced 1960s values like diversity and equality. For female viewers, there was the added reassurance of seeing both a friendly, supportive workplace and female characters struggling to be assertive. Mary's voice cracks, and Bailey is shy, but they manage anyway, largely because their coworkers respect them.

For younger female viewers, who had few meaningful models of the workplace, images of strong, competent, working women were particularly revelatory. Unlike earlier TV working women, these workplace women are not marking time until marriage and aren't sadly desperate for men. Mary Richards is neither a bitter spinster nor one of the guys. She made a big difference for a generation of women coming of age in the 1970s, a generation *sui generis.* "Mary was my role model, pure and simple," one recalled. "She showed me how to pursue a career, how to keep romance in perspective, how to suffer fools, how to face my own foolishness" (Ode E–3). As Andrea Press has concluded after studying middle-class women's TV watching habits, characters like Mary Richards "captured middle-class women's imaginations at the time these shows were on, particularly for young women imagining and making plans for their future lives" (77). They educated other viewers about the single, working woman's life, too, helping parents understand how their single daughters lived or teaching men how to treat their new female colleagues. Just as June Cleaver (*Leave It to Beaver*) became a cultural symbol of the perfect homemaker and mom, Mary Richards became a shorthand representation of what liberation meant for women.

Perhaps the most radical aspect of *The Mary Tyler Moore Show* was its implicit creation of a feminist ideal—sisterhood. Mary and her best friend Rhoda talk about things TV wives and mothers didn't, things of relevance to the audience, whether it is the mundane details of their jobs or the far more interesting glimpses of their sex lives. They run interference for one another, rescue one another from boring men, and know each other's back-stories. For female viewers trying to imagine how to live single and work, seeing and hearing how other women did it mattered, especially at a time when there weren't many other social models of career women. This ground-breaking facet of the program reflected another MTM innovation, female writers who "relied on their lives for inspiration" (Armstrong 156) and were likewise inspired by Mary's model. Those female writers found their way onto other 1970s series as well, including *Rhoda* and *M*A*S*H*. The female voice behind the cameras helped turn the sitcom single woman from an object into a subject, creating women-defined-womanhood of compelling authenticity.

TV's version of sisterhood was, like its versions of liberation, different from feminism. Many female writers identified themselves as feminists; that identity was too radical for mainstream television, however. Workplace TV helped to stigmatize feminism as extremist and mean. Real women, who worked for a living, had bad hair days and bad dates, were liberated, not feminists. They wanted to be treated fairly, equally, and respectfully, and they treated others with respect. Feminists, often stereotyped in magazines, newspapers, and on TV news, shouted, carried picket signs, and wore trousers exclusively. The media helped shape a picture of the feminist move-ment as disrespectful and divisive, pitting women against men and women against each other. Privileging women while demeaning men—especially while demeaning men—often seemed the point of feminism, as rendered in the media (Douglas chapter 10). On *The Bob Newhart Show*, for example, psychologist Bob Hartley organizes a consciousness-raising group; but, once empowered, the women in the group turn his wife against him and exclude him because of his gender.

So, when sexism rears its ugly head in the TV workplace, feminists don't solve the crisis; instead, the workplace family protects its own, which sometimes verges into the territory of an older scenario, women-who-need-rescuing. After a sleazy photographer takes nude pictures of Jennifer, her WKRP colleagues invent a scam to get them back. When Elaine Nardo (*Taxi*) suspects that taxi dispatcher Louie DePalma is spying on her through a hole in the bathroom wall, her co-workers help her catch him at it. In workplace sitcoms' portraits of feminism and female ambition, we can find the roots of the "I am not a feminist, but . . ." mentality. These shows support women's desire to compete with men in the workplace without alienating them, changing the rules, or otherwise disturbing the structure of the workplace. TV's liberated women manage what few real-world women could; their gains did not come at the expense of men, except perhaps greedy, sexist, undeserving men.

In fact, it was precisely their ability to get along with men that helped broaden the workplace sitcom's audience. While young women might tune in to watch their TV counterparts achieve in the office, they, like the men who watched, also enjoyed the vicarious pleasures of another kind of liberation, sexual liberation. Sexual freedom was a value enthusiastically embraced by a whole generation (Weiss 171). It freed women from the cult of virginity that had consigned them to early marriage or prolonged sexual longing (Breines chapter 3) while making more willing partners available to men. The 1960s definition of sex as a joyous, spontaneous physical act not limited to the marriage bed informed the 1970s workplace comedy. It was the liberated woman who indulged and not the feminist, who was as asexual as the 1950s TV working woman. TV's liberated 1970s working women explore their sexuality, albeit with the same charming nervousness as they approach the workplace. And, with good reason, since the double standard has never quite disappeared.

On *M*A*S*H*, for instance, male characters, married or not, pursue all sorts of sexual relationships without worrying about their reputations. But, *M*A*S*H*'s head nurse Margaret "Hot Lips" Houlihan's sexuality is constantly judged. What the audience saw was not how Margaret feels about her choices but how the men around her perceive her, whether they think her too promiscuous, too emasculating, or too clingy. The male gaze and attendant male judgments about female sexuality prevail, but the woman's perspective is also present, minus either sugarcoating or moralizing. When Mary's friend Rhoda repeats the old saw about men respecting virtuous women, Mary asks if she thinks it is true. "No," Rhoda replies, "but my mother does." Her rueful comment captures a generational identity and a gendered one in its recognition of both possibilities and limits. The 1970s workplace sitcom offers the vicarious pleasure of female sexuality without punishment and its complex containment within a sexual dynamic still controlled by men (Lehman 157).

On workplace sitcoms, as elsewhere in the popular culture, sexual liberation becomes the less threatening substitute for other kinds of power because it reinforces women's traditional role as consumers. Liberation became a commodity because, as one advertising executive notes, "career women . . . are extremely valuable customers . . . who are acutely sensitive to sexist tonality" (Lehman 123). Known as "Life Stylers," "they needed fabulous clothes, beauty products, and furniture to feel like the independent women they wanted to be" (Armstrong 132). While 1950s TV wives dress in housedresses and look comfortably middle-aged, 1970s working women wear clingy dresses and Farrah Fawcett hair and have slender figures that serve as markers of their independent, modern status. The evolution began earlier, but by the end of the 1970s, the TV women who garnered the biggest audience were on *Charlie's Angels*, a show that spawned the term "jiggle TV" because its stars "often went braless" (McNeil 156). Going braless became the symbol of TV's liberated woman, which is different from feminists' bra burning with its evocations of anger. But, once the bras came off, the audience's understanding of female competence changed. Receptionist Jennifer Marlowe (*WKRP in Cincinnati*) lacks ambition but has power thanks to her long platinum hair and skin-tight dresses. While Loni Anderson, who plays Jennifer, didn't want her seen as a dumb blonde, it isn't Jennifer's brain that gets her places (Kassel 24). By the end of the decade, the media's objectification of women and its concomitant emphasis on youth, slenderness, and sexuality was already having an impact on workplace sitcoms.

Female characters were supposed to be all things to all people—sexy (but not too sexual), competent, sweet, kind, and nurturing. They bring culture and class to the workplace, like the flowers on Mary Richards' desk or the paintings Elaine Nardo helps her fellow cabbies buy. Their apartments are impeccable; they go to concerts; they know how to cook. They exemplify the super woman of the Enjoli perfume commercial, who could "bring home the bacon, fry it up in the pan, and never let him forget he's a man." Liberated status required its own set of goods, a theme that advertisers cultivated. Meanwhile, the shows themselves offered visual reassurance that liberated women had more attractive lives than their married housewife sisters. Liberated consumerism, unlike the purchases of the saintly mother, June Cleaver, was about personal care, convenience, and gratification. It proved, to cite another popular commercial for L'Oréal, that liberated women were "worth it," that they had enough self-respect (and money) to buy what they wanted. Workplace comedies, like the ads embedded within them, show their female audiences what clothes they might wear, how they might wear their hair, and what their apartments might look like. By commodifying the image of the liberated woman, television mainstreamed it and further distinguished the liberated woman from the feminist, who didn't wear nice clothes or shave her legs—who didn't, in short, use the kinds of products TV sold.

Another accouterment to the liberated lifestyle was less purchasable: the new sensitive man (Kimmel 293), who complements the working woman in the office and dates her outside it. He was a media creation, a man himself liberated from gender stereotypes and open to his feelings, genuinely interested in women as people, nurturing, and warm, a man not afraid to cry. Alan Alda and talk show host Phil Donahue were prototypical new sensitive men (Sterns 6–8, 125). Andy Travis (*WKRP in Cincinnati*) and Alex

Figurew 9.2. Loni Anderson as Jennifer Elizabeth Marlowe, Gary Sandy as Andy Travis, and Jan Smithers as Bailey Quarters in *WKRP in Cincinnati*. 1978–1982. Photo courtesy of Photofest.

Reiger (*Taxi*) are sitcom representatives of the type, and Hawkeye Pierce, the character Alda plays on *M*A*S*H*, comes close, except that he is too much of a womanizer. In the workplace, the new sensitive man facilitates the liberated woman's achievements because she doesn't threaten him. Off the job, other new sensitive men treat liberated women respectfully, cook them dinner, and cuddle. The new sensitive man stands between the liberated woman and what television suggests are two unattractive extremes: spinsterhood and feminism. He is as much a part of the consumerist dream as the studio apartment, the platform shoes, and the feathery hairdo—the handsome man who supports both the liberated woman's ambitions on the job and her sexuality off the job.

The new sensitive man adds the final critical touch to the portrait of the liberated woman. He provides the legitimacy that separates her from the feminist. He models sensitivity for male viewers, reassuring them that there is still a place for them in liberated women's lives and teaching them how to treat female coworkers as friends and equals. His position in the modern workplace family as a confidant and job coach lessens the need for a Mary-and-Rhoda-style sisterhood, rendering the working woman a little more male-defined. Perhaps more important, the new sensitive man finds his sensitivity rewarded off the job in sexual ways not available from earlier TV working women. More than the cute apartment, new job, and stylish clothes, he promises that being liberated has its own set of payoffs, payoffs that can cycle a working woman into traditional domesticity or, like Mary Richards, keep her proudly careerist.

Together, the liberated woman and the new sensitive man carefully separate the most palatable aspects of feminism and package them into a neat consumer-friendly ideal. From the start, TV's notion of liberation was fraught with contradictions, but a lot of its appeal is its complexity, which signifies its realism. That complexity expressed the frustrations and pleasures of real women's lived experiences in the 1970s, their uncertainty, their sense of being trapped between ideologies, their objectification, and their new consumer identities. That same complexity also provided ample space to accommodate other viewer perspectives and values, whether they looked at Mary, Bailey, and Elaine as friends, sisters, and daughters, or merely sexy office babes.

By the early 1980s, workplace TV began to lose steam (Waldron 466–67) as family sitcoms revived. The next big workplace comedy, *Cheers*, premiered in 1982. Gender is more fixed in *Cheers*. Sam, the proprietor of the title bar, is not a sensitive male but a self-identified "babe hound," which alters the essential gender dynamic in significant ways. Without the anchor of a new sensitive man to support the aspirations of the female characters, they flounder. Workplace equality gives way to a kind of Mars and Venus scenario where men and women are essentially different. Frasier, the new sensitive man in the piece, is rejected by Diane and dumped by his wife Lilith. The women in *Cheers* pour less energy into their careers than their romances, and the men who attract them are what Lilith characterizes as "bad boys" like Sam rather than supportive co-equals like Frasier. Their choices often seem foolish, and their career competence declines.

Further undermining women's workplace status in 1980s workplace comedies is the emphasis on lifestyle over career, a reflection of Reagan-era yuppie-obsession. What Robert Goldman labels commodity feminism, "an apparent détente between femininity and feminism" (131) predicated on consumer choices is very much in evidence. *Cheers'* Diane is a waitress by trade, but her clothes are preppy, she earns a graduate degree from Harvard, and her tastes are elevated. Stephanie Vanderkellan (*Newhart*) is a maid with designer duds, a dashing boyfriend, and a wealthy father. Even a character like Murphy Brown, whose self-identity is work related (and who, tellingly, also identifies herself as a feminist), still has the perks that come with her network newsmagazine anchor status, a fancy car, designer clothes, and a stylish Georgetown townhouse. It has been a long way up from Mary Richards' pitiful Minneapolis TV station and studio apartment to Murphy Brown's lifestyle—a journey measured in commodities. More and more, the pleasures of being independent, but especially of being female, are presented in material terms rather than as doing meaningful work.

As liberation grew more commodified and sensitivity less privileged, the workplace has become a place where barbs, insults, and sexual objectification take place. One 1995 study found a lack of respect between characters and, particularly, sexual harassment of female characters is "routine" on modern sitcoms (Lorando E–1). Gone is the workplace support men offered liberated women; it is replaced by a much more sexual combination of lust and loathing. Sam and Diane started the trend, but it has popped up routinely on workplace sitcoms ever since. Such love-hate relationships take place against the backdrop of critical workplace commentary, most of it devoted to judging the women's looks and behavior and the man's machismo. In these workplaces, it's not hard work that pays off but aggressiveness and cunning for men and sexuality for women.

The gendered dynamic remains complicated on more recent television, clearly built from the base of 1970s workplace sitcoms while reflecting other elements of the culture. On *30 Rock*, show creator Tina Fey's alter ego, Liz Lemon, has a powerful job in the entertainment industry. *The Mindy Project's*

Mindy Lahiri (played by series creator Mindy Kaling) is a doctor, modeled by Kaling after her mother. Lesley Knopf of *Parks and Recreation* is a city councilwoman in a small Ohio town. These female-centered shows have been shaped, at least partly, by highly credentialed women and inspired by series that came before them. They offer a different kind of commentary on the gendered nature of the workplace than 1970s shows do because their stars are in positions of authority and status. These shows reveal the costs of achievement, not just the messy personal lives their high-achieving characters' experience, and feature the remaining inequalities of the workplace, most particularly the harassment and challenges inflicted by workplace men. Second-wave feminism has paved the way for their professional successes; yet, they also live with the contradictions of feminism and, most especially, American society's failure to fully accommodate the modern woman, whether merely liberated or a dedicated feminist. Most modern TV men reinforce this message by only rarely manifesting the qualities of the new sensitive man of the 1970s. Even the nerdy scientists on *The Big Bang Theory* are more interested in women as sex objects or mother substitutes than as co-equals or true partners. While the workplace family still exists to some degree, its members are considerably snarkier with one another than in the 1970s, and sex between coworkers isn't at all taboo. As network television fights to retain some market share among ever-increasing entertainment options, it cannot afford to offend any segment of the market; but, in the modern marketplace, men's perspectives continue to count for more than women's. Just as in other aspects of society, feminism (and true liberation) remains an unfinished revolution.

10

"Who's in Charge Here?"

Views of Media Ownership in Situation Comedies

PAUL R. KOHL

In November 2002, I attended a faculty seminar organized by the Academy of Television Arts and Sciences. The seminar provided an invaluable opportunity to witness the "behind the scenes" workings of the television industry from production meetings to program tapings and to meet those whose job it is to bring America's most popular entertainment into our homes on a weekly basis. The few days I spent in that Hollywood environment impressed upon me what I had been aware of for years but could only imagine until I witnessed it directly. Television is an incredibly collaborative medium. Television writers work in committees to develop storylines and scripts that are then submitted and commented on not only by the creative personnel involved in a particular program, such as directors and actors, but by production executives, network programmers, and representatives of the advertisers who sponsor the programs.

But, perhaps the term "collaborative" is misleading here. Collaboration is generally regarded as working together toward a common goal. In television terms, that common goal is generally defined as attracting the largest audience. There is, however, division between the creators of television programs and the corporate executives who oversee their creations in terms of how best to attract viewers. While creators operate through artistry and instinct, corporate executives depend on ratings and demographics to make content decisions. This eternal tension is perhaps best described by Ben Stein in his 1979 book, *The View from Sunset Boulevard*, "The Hollywood television writer . . . is actually in a business, selling his labor to brutally callous businessmen. One actually has to go through the experience of writing for money in Hollywood or anywhere else to realize how unpleasant it is. Most of the pain comes from dealing with business people . . ." (27). Stein's portrait of the relationship between writers and executives is hardly "collaborative." "Antagonistic" is a word that more quickly springs to mind. This antagonistic relationship is propounded in more theoretical terms in the work of Karl Marx.

The common reference to Marxist thought in critiques of the media is Marx's contention, according to Dominic Strinati, that: ". . . the predominant ideas common to a capitalist society, including its popular culture, are those of the ruling class. These ideas have to be produced and disseminated by the ruling class or its intellectual representatives, and they dominate the consciousness and actions of those classes outside the ruling class" (131). Marx's distinction between the ruling class, who own and control the means of production, and the working class, who provide the labor for production, raises the question of where "intellectual representatives" fit in.

Television writers are, as Stein states, selling labor. They are employees working for the owners of the production apparatus. As such, their interests are aligned more closely with the majority of viewers than with ownership, despite the fact that writers' wealth and position might far outweigh those of the common populace. As Gitlin writes, "However magnificently rewarded, writers and producers have ample reason to resent the power of the corporations they know best: television networks and major suppliers" (*Inside* 270). Television writers are part of the professional and managerial class; as such, they are part of the same class as blue-collar and manual workers.[1] As Fiske and Hartley state, "Managers and professionals may be relatively privileged in the premium they are able to set on their labour power. . . . But it remains the case that many of them are ultimately just as dependent on selling their labour power as blue-collar workers" (103).

The suggestion that the media speak with the voice of the ruling class presupposes that members of the working class must be trained to speak with that voice: thus business people collaborate in suggesting to creators what is appropriate content. There is a long tradition of resistance, however, within the communities of the working class and oppressed, and despite their monetary and social success, television writers can still be defined as oppressed in Marxist terms. As Fiske and Hartley note, "Their lack of control over property, and hence the conditions of their own employment and production, results in an actual or potential insecurity which provides a basis for 'identity of interest'" (103). Thus, even successful television creators may be aligned with the oppressed members of society in the fact that they do not control or own their work.

Some of the dominant voices of resistance in history have been comic ones. In cataloguing cultural texts with the most resistant potential, Scott, in *Domination and the Arts of Resistance*, includes "Rumor, gossip, folktales, jokes, songs, rituals, codes, and euphemisms . . ." (19). The modern television situation comedy, as the product of such a tension, should certainly show evidence of its resistant potential.

What follows are analyses of three classic situation comedy texts that can be read as resistant, works in which the creators have planted seeds of commentary and dissension against those who control the means of production. The first text, an episode of *The Dick Van Dyke Show*, further expands Marx's concept of the alienated worker and comments on the situation of the television creator whose work is controlled by the owners of production. The second text, the final episode of *The Mary Tyler Moore Show*, uses the resistant potential of carnival to ridicule the corporate end of the media. Finally, a series of episodes from *Seinfeld*, in which the show's origins are self-reflexively parodied, uses the carnivalesque technique of the grotesque to comment on the owner-worker relationship.

It is important to note that the textual analyses provided here go beyond the boundaries of the programs themselves. An important part of any cultural text is its intertextuality, which may be defined as the relationships that exist between it and other texts or the real-life practices of its textual production. Fiske notes two types of intertextuality, horizontal and vertical, both of which come into play here. Horizontal intertextuality refers to relations "between primary texts that are more or less explicitly linked" while vertical intertextuality occurs between the primary text and the historical and cultural background of its production (108).[2] In this way, forces from the real socioeconomic system in which the episodes were created can come to bear on their meanings.

ALIENATION OF THE WORKER: *THE DICK VAN DYKE SHOW*

As previously mentioned, the creation of television texts involves inherent conflict between creative personnel and business interests. These conflicts are enhanced by the mysterious decision-making process at the network level. In his study of 1980s programming practices, *Inside Prime Time*, Gitlin reports that those involved in the industry confess to ignorance when asked how television programming works. This, he suggests, is "a gesture of concealment, a way of protecting power from prying eyes" (22). The hidden nature of programming decisions is one manifestation of how the television industry further reflects Marx's theories of conflict between owners and workers, a conflict leading to the objectification of labor and the alienation of the worker. As Marx writes in *Capital*, "The laborer exists for the process of production, and not the process of production for the laborer" (536).

Erich Fromm's analysis of Marx highlights two points: "In the process of work . . . Especially . . . under the conditions of capitalism, man is estranged from his own creative powers, and . . . the *objects* of his own work become alien beings . . ." (48, italics in the original). The gist of Marx's argument is that under capitalism, workers no longer control their own work nor are they rewarded accordingly for it. Although issues of monetary recompense would not appear to be an issue in the highly paid world of television, Fromm says that is beside the point. Marx, he notes, "is not concerned primarily with the equalization of income. He is concerned with the liberation of man from a kind of work which destroys his individuality, which transforms him into a thing, and which makes him into the slave of things" (48–49). The "Coast-to-Coast Big Mouth" episode of *The Dick Van Dyke Show* echoes Fromm's analysis in its own manner, revealing the alienation of the worker at the heart of capitalism.

This episode was written by Bill Persky and Sam Denoff and was first broadcast on CBS September 15, 1965; it subsequently won the best comedy script Emmy for that year. On the show, Van Dyke plays Rob Petrie, a writer on the fictional television program, *The Alan Brady Show.* In this episode, Rob's wife, Laura, is tricked by a television game show host into revealing that her husband's boss, Alan Brady, is really bald, a fact Brady has kept carefully hidden throughout his career. Laura attempts to apologize to a humiliated and furious Brady in order to save Rob's job. She finds Alan in his office, his various toupees lined up before him. As Laura enters, he introduces them: "Fellas! There's the little lady who put you out of business!" Alan ultimately reveals that he is relieved that his secret is out because it was hard to keep, and more people prefer him bald.

Alan Brady's baldness and his complex attempts to cover it up (he has seasonal toupees and toupees of different lengths) are symbolic of the character's alienation from his craft. Despite seeming to play himself on his variety show, Brady is actually playing a character, a situation revisited in the *Seinfeld* episodes to be discussed below. Brady's alienation is suggested in a number of other ways throughout the episode. In his meeting with Laura, he is laid up with a sprained ankle. He has to remove his producer/brother-in-law, Mel Cooley, from his chair, part of a recurring situation in which Alan berates Mel at every opportunity. Mel's own baldness suggests one possible reason for Alan's continued hostility toward the character. We learn during the episode that not only has Alan been keeping his baldness secret, he has also had a nose job. Alan Brady's incompleteness as a character

Figure 10.1. Richard Deacon as Melvin Cooley, Rose Marie as Sally Rogers, Morey Amsterdam as Maurice "Buddy" Sorrell, Mary Tyler Moore as Laura Petrie, and Dick Van Dyke as Rob Petrie in *The Dick Van Dyke Show*. 1961–1966. Photo courtesy of Movie Star NewsFair.

is echoed in Rob Petrie's character when the host of *Pay as You Go*, the game show Laura appears on, believes initially she is the wife of television writer David Petrie, a misidentification of Rob. Since Rob is a writer on Alan's show, he is in a sense subject to the same alienation as Alan, an alienation that removes the individual's true self from his work. The misidentification of Rob signifies this alienation. It is also appropriate that Alan's secret is revealed in the service of winning commodities such as a grill and a vacuum cleaner on a game show since his alienation is a consequence of working within a capitalist system.

"Coast-to-Coast Big Mouth" contains crucial elements of vertical intertextuality to emphasize its conflicts. The actor who appears as Alan Brady, Carl Reiner, is also the creator of *The Dick Van Dyke Show*. Reiner based the show on his own life as a writer/performer on Sid Caesar's *Your Show of Shows* and played Petrie in the original pilot of the series, entitled *Head of the Family*. Reiner's commitment to his show was so great he even went so far as to write thirteen episodes of the show before it was even picked up as a series, commenting that "This would be a nucleus, a bible, for anybody who would help write after that. It would guard against supposition; everything would be spelled out" (Marc *Comic* 1989 93).[3] Ironically, producer Sheldon Leonard had to tell Reiner "you're not right for what you wrote for yourself" (Weissman and Sanders 5). And so, Reiner's Jewish Rob Petrie became Van Dyke's WASP Petrie, complete with a new background that reflected the new actor's own life. Marc even suggests that it was the original character's ethnicity that prompted Leonard to suggest the change, as performers like Sid Caesar and Milton Berle "had proved 'too Jewish' for the vastly expanded television audience of 1960" (98).[4]

Reiner's real-life predicament and that of Alan Brady is emblematic of Marx's alienated worker, despite the differing circumstances of their labor as opposed to Marx's industrial worker. As Fromm notes, "Marx did not foresee the extent to which alienation was to become the fate of the vast majority of people, especially of the ever-increasing segment of the population which manipulates symbols and men, rather than machines." These workers are even more alienated since they are forced to sell their personality, smile, and opinions (Fromm 57).[5] Alan Brady, like Reiner himself, is at the fulcrum of the conflict between the creative and business interests of television. He is the creator of his show yet does not own its property, a fact symbolized by outside pressures to cover his baldness and hire his brother-in-law. Reiner is not in control of the programming decisions of his network, but he does have the power to characterize his superiors, as do the writers of the next two programs to be discussed.

THE CARNIVAL WORLD: *THE MARY TYLER MOORE SHOW*

The Mary Tyler Moore Show aired its last episode on CBS in 1977. Written by the show's highly successful staff of James L. Brooks, Allan Burns, Ed Weinberger, Stan Daniels, David Lloyd, and Bob Ellison, the episode went on to win the Emmy for comedy scriptwriting. In the episode, television station WJM is sold to a new owner, and its employees are marked for termination. In the show's ultimate irony, it is Ted Baxter, the incompetent anchorman, who is kept on while hard-working professionals Mary Richards, Lou Grant, and Murray Slaughter are let go.

The decision of the new ownership is obviously questionable to an audience familiar with the characters and made even more dubious by Ted's own realization that he deserves to be fired. When Lou informs Ted that the new owner wants to evaluate him, he adds "I told him to watch the news and decide for himself," to which Ted tearfully responds, "Oh my God!" As the final decision is made, the new owner announces that he must "get rid of anything that's pulling you down," concluding with a phrase that echoes Gitlin's responses from network executives: "It's not a science, but I have to go with my instincts" (*Inside* 26–27).

The final episode of *The Mary Tyler Moore Show* is, in essence, a world turned upside down. As Mary double-checks to make sure that she was truly fired along with "the guys," she is informed "especially me." This is a carnivalesque world in which the high are made low, and the low are exalted, and the man in charge is made to look like a fool because all present, including the audience, know that his instincts are uneducated and wrong.[6]

Russian literary critic Bakhtin applied the concept of carnival to those medieval festivals and texts in which traditional hierarchies were toppled. As Stallybrass and White note, "Carnival, for Bakhtin, is both a populist utopian vision of the world seen from below and a festive critique, through the inversion of hierarchy, of the 'high' culture" (7). In this case the high culture is that of the corporate decision makers who would valorize a Ted Baxter while firing a Mary Richards.

There is some irony in *The Mary Tyler Moore Show* making such a critique, it being one of the most critically acclaimed series ever, and one of the few allowed to end on its own terms.[7] Its production company, MTM, became synonymous with quality television, prompting Thomas H. Zynda to comment in his essay "The Mary Tyler Moore Show and the Transformation of Situation Comedy," "the MTM story is one of enlightened capitalism finally delivering the cultural promise of television" (133). But, even *The Mary Tyler Moore Show* faced issues with network decision makers in its early stages of development. The original intention of creators Brooks and Burns was to make Mary Richards a divorcée, but network executives objected "because it would seem like she'd divorced Dick Van Dyke, her television husband in *The Dick Van Dyke Show*" (Zynda 132). Marc reports that the head of CBS programming, Mike Dann, stated that "his own research had conclusively proven that there were three types of people Americans didn't want to see in situation comedy: people from New York, people with mustaches, and people who were divorced" (*Comic* 1985 167). The wisdom of those findings would be challenged in the 1990s by *Seinfeld*.

THE GROTESQUE: *SEINFELD*

The "wisdom" of network program executives is similarly portrayed in a series of 1992 episodes of *Seinfeld* in which Jerry is approached by NBC and offered the chance to make a pilot. This plot echoes the real situation in which stand-up comic Seinfeld was given the chance to create a show with writer/producer Larry David. As Seinfeld plays himself on the series, David's alter ego is George Costanza. Together they come up with the idea for Jerry's sitcom to be based on incidents and characters from their own lives. George suggests that it be a "show about nothing," an appellation for which *Seinfeld* became famous. Jerry and George pitch their idea to NBC executives, who are dubious about the merits of a "show about nothing."

The self-reflexive nature of *Seinfeld* gives it an appropriately satirical bent while toying with reality in a carnivalesque manner. Part of the carnivalesque attitude is a celebration of the grotesque. According to Bakhtin, "The essential principle of grotesque realism is degradation, that is, the lowering of all that is high . . . [by] . . . transfer to the material level, to the sphere of earth and body . . ." (19).[8] *Seinfeld* was notable for its use of the grotesque; and in "The Pitch" episode, and its follow-ups, it is used considerably to comment on high/low relationships.

The first appearance of this relation occurs early on, as Kramer suggests that Jerry play the manager of a circus in his proposed show. As Stallybrass and White remind us, "The carnival, the circus, the gypsy . . . play a symbolic role in bourgeois culture out of all proportion to their actual social importance" (20). Or, as Kramer states, "The show isn't about the circus, it's about watching freaks." George articulates the high/low juxtaposition as he expresses anxiety in meeting with NBC executives, men who are quite unlike him with their "jobs, suits and ties, wives, secretaries." Ironically, it is at this meeting that George meets his future fiancée, Susan, a network executive, who will later die in the series from licking the cheap wedding announcement envelopes George buys. Susan is the high brought low as she becomes the victim of Kramer's vomiting attack while announcing to Jerry and George that their show idea has been accepted. The characters of Jerry, George, and Kramer are presented as representatives of the low, who are given authority to bring down the high.

The main target of these carnivalesque practices is the character of NBC president Russell Dalrymple. George manages to convince Russell to back their pilot show about nothing, offering as his credentials a fake off-Broadway play titled *La Cosina*. His agreement to do the pilot is punctuated with another comment reminiscent of Gitlin's interviews: "I've got a feeling about you two." The joke here, that NBC executives are clueless enough to give the go-ahead to a show about nothing written by a stand-up comic and his terminally unemployed, no-talent best friend, is doubled by the fact that the real *Seinfeld* was eventually picked up and became the biggest hit of the decade despite the concerns of executives that the show was "too New York, too Jewish" (Jacobs *Seinfeld* 11), echoing the opinion articulated earlier by Mike Dann. Russell is eventually brought down from his position of power through his infatuation with Elaine, who rejects his advances and refuses to take him seriously. This rejection makes Russell desperate, and he attempts to fire a stagehand for no reason. In an outburst, he screams, "Do you know who I am? Do you know how much money I make? . . . I can have any woman in this city I want." Believing that his job is keeping Elaine from him, Russell throws it all away, joins Greenpeace, and is lost at sea. Meanwhile, his replacement cancels the *Jerry* pilot two minutes after it is broadcast.

Several subplots in this narrative arc celebrate the body and the grotesque, including George's obsession with a growth on his lip and his conviction that his death is imminent, Elaine's attempt to file a discrimination lawsuit against a restaurant owner whose waitresses all have large breasts, and Kramer's incontinence. This last plotline allows for one of the more telling juxtapositions in the story. As the pilot for *Jerry* is about to be filmed in front of a studio audience and Jerry announces "Are you ready to meet our cast," the scene cuts to Kramer preparing to receive an enema to cure him of his ills. This joke is typical of the sophomoric humor that was prevalent on *Seinfeld*, causing Steven D. Stark to reflect on its "evocation of early male adolescence." He notes that, "many psychologists consider that preteen stage of life, when one is acutely aware of being powerless, as the time when individuals are most subversive of society-at-large" (285). *Seinfeld* is ironic in its subversiveness, as evidenced by its self-reflexive portrayal in this series of episodes. For instance, Jerry states his insecurities about the show: "I can't act. I stink. I don't know what I'm doing." He confesses his belief that the show will ruin his career. While it was widely noted during the series' run that Seinfeld himself was not a great actor, the show obviously did not ruin his career.

Just as in the final episode of *The Mary Tyler Moore Show*, this series of *Seinfeld* episodes gave writer Larry David a forum for subversiveness, played out in his portrayal of broadcasting decision makers. While Russell Dalrymple okays the fictional *Jerry* despite George's incompetence, the pilot is ultimately rejected by his successor. The audience, however, knows that the real *Seinfeld*, using the same premise, became the most successful program of the 1990s.

CONCLUSION

As workers selling their labor to the owners of the production apparatus, television sitcom writers have to deal with the realities of the business world. Unless they have achieved uncommon power, they are subject to the decisions of corporate executives and others. Their words and characters may be changed and eventually taken away from them. With the product of their labor removed from their control, writers are subject to alienation. But writers, especially those who work in the comedic vein, are capable of instilling messages of resistance in their texts. They reclaim some power by creating a world where their oppressors are brought low, and in doing so, they speak for more than just themselves. As Fiske writes in *Understanding Popular Culture*, "What people in capitalist societies have in common is the dominant ideology and the experience of subordination or disempowerment" (28). The episodes discussed here reflect that subordination while providing renewed empowerment for both the viewers and the program's creators.

Television creators like Carl Reiner, James Brooks, Jerry Seinfeld, and Larry David may not appear to have much in common with average viewers settled into their living rooms ready to laugh at the latest installment of their favorite situation comedy. But, in Marx's formulation of the classes, they have in common that neither writer nor viewer own the production apparatus. Though obviously more highly rewarded than most workers, television creators still work in an environment in which the product of their labor is not entirely within their control. When a show is as successful as *The Dick Van Dyke Show*, *The Mary Tyler Moore Show*, or *Seinfeld*, however, it is certainly given more power to control its own destiny, and the creators of the episodes discussed here have used that power to comment upon tensions and conflicts prevalent in the television industry beneath a veil of humor. Like all great comedy, there is a good deal of truth behind the laughter.

NOTES

1. Marx notes a distinction between class *in itself*, or the objective reality of social conditions of existence and class *for itself*, in which classes respond to their

situation through solidarity with other classes by creating a common identity (see Fiske and Hartley 101–02).

2. Secondary texts are publicity materials, journalistic, historical, or critical items produced by the professional media. Tertiary texts are produced by the fan audience through fan literature, water cooler discussions, etc. (see Fiske *Television* 108).

3. Reiner also used his experiences as a young actor as the basis for his novel *Enter Laughing*, which later became a Broadway play and a 1967 film that he directed.

4. In the early days of television, 40 percent of television sets were in the New York City area. As television spread across the rest of America, the popularity of Jewish vaudeville comedians like Berle and Caesar waned in favor of the situation comedy (see Marc *Comic Visions* 98).

5. The final episode of *The Dick Van Dyke Show*, broadcast in 1966, brings the Reiner/Brady connection full circle as Rob Petrie's autobiography is bought by Alan so he can play Rob in a television series.

6. Other series that have shown media executives in a less than flattering light include *WKRP in Cincinnati* and *Newsradio*.

7. It should be noted that the other two series discussed here also left the airwaves on their own terms rather than through cancellation.

8. For a discussion of Bakhtin's notion of carnival and the grotesque in relation to rock and roll, see Kohl's chapter " 'Who's in Charge Here'? Views on Media Ownership in Situation Comedies" in this volume.

The 1980s

The decade began with a certain amount of drama, quite apart from the big hair, frosted eye shadow, shoulder pads for women, and punk styles that would come to characterize the era. In a word, everything was big. Mount St. Helens in Washington State erupted for the first time in over a hundred years. Then the nation stood by helplessly as hostages were taken and held in Tehran, Iran, a bellwether of more trouble in the Middle East. A failed attempt by President Carter to rescue the hostages deepened the sense of powerlessness and contributed to the election of Ronald Reagan as president of the United States in November of 1980. Two months later, John Lennon was assassinated on the streets of Manhattan. When launching his presidential campaign in 1991, candidate Bill Clinton referred to the decade in this way: "The Reagan-Bush years exalted private gain over public obligation, special interests over the common good, wealth and fame over work and family. The 1980s ushered in a Gilded Age of greed and selfishness, of irresponsibility and excess, and of neglect" (Troy 16). This is an apt description for an era in which unemployment reached 9.5 percent, and there was a 15 percent overall poverty rate.

Of course, there were also notable signs of progress. During the 1980s, the first woman, Sandra Day O'Connor, was appointed to the Supreme Court; Sally Ride became the first American woman astronaut; the environmental movement became mainstream; and, the Cold War with the Soviet Union ended with the fall of the Berlin Wall in 1989. In the realm of popular culture, MTV was launched; Oprah Winfrey began her talk show career; Ted Turner started CNN, a 24-hour news channel (amid much skepticism); and Rush Limbaugh catalyzed the conservative talk show movement with his AM radio show. On television, the animated sitcom *The Simpsons* debuted, and *The Cosby Show*, a sitcom about an upper-middle-class Black family, was rated the number-one show in America for five years running. Michael Real and Lauren Bratslavsky write about *The Cosby Show*, generally considered a conventional sitcom, and how it recoded ethnicity and masculinity, which explains certain cultural resonances and deepened our appreciation of the popular series, despite the scandal that has unraveled around Bill Cosby in the mid-2010s.

Overall, the decade was one of unease, demonstrated by a number of incidents, including a student massacre in Tiananmen Square in Beijing, China, and a catastrophic nuclear accident at the Chernobyl reactor in Ukraine. In 1986, the Challenger space shuttle exploded, killing all aboard, including schoolteacher Christa McAuliffe, the first civilian and first teacher in space. The AIDS epidemic was discovered early in the decade and declared a pandemic in 1986. A significant increase in violent crime was predicated by a crack cocaine epidemic in urban areas. Through it all, the divide between the rich and the poor was increasing, causing widespread anxiety as the middle class saw its share of the economic pie decreasing. The time was right for a working-class family, bound by love and tight resources, to return to the small screen. Roseanne Barr's standup persona led to the creation of an eponymous character on the popular series *Roseanne*; Susan McLeland writes about how the performer and the series shatter certain myths about the American Dream, the family, and feminine ideals.

Representing a group with a more secure spot on the class spectrum than the working-class, Midwestern Connor family, the term "yuppie" was coined to describe "young, urban professionals." These well-educated members of the new middle class had the purchasing power to unleash a new cycle of conspicuous consumption. Products like personal computers, mobile phones, and video games, each of which debuted in the 1980s, ushered in a digital information age and fueled a boom in the stocks of Silicon Valley technology companies. The cultural clash between two factions within the baby-boom generation—the yuppies and those who still identified with the anti-materialism of the hippies—is a frequent thread running through the popular sitcom, *Cheers*. In his chapter, Robert S. Brown champions the bar as an egalitarian collective space for talking through differences, which compares the community bar to Jürgen Habermas' ideal public sphere. Another term that came into widespread use, this one in reference to President Reagan's economic program, was Reaganomics. This program stressed low taxes and reduced government spending (except for the military) and is said to have contributed to the large budget deficits that plagued the country at the end of the decade.

The top-rated sitcoms of the 1980s were: *AfterMASH*; *Alf*; *Alice*; *Amen*; *Anything but Love*; *Archie Bunker's Place*; *Cheers*; *Chicken Soup*; *Coach*; *The Cosby Show*; *Day by Day*; *Dear John*; *Designing Women*; *Diff'rent Strokes*; *A*

Different World; *Doogie Howser, M.D.*; *Empty Nest*; *The Facts of Life*; *Family Ties*; *Full House*; *Gloria*; *The Golden Girls*; *Grand*; *Growing Pains*; *Happy Days*; *Head of the Class*; *The Hogan Family* (originally *Valerie*, then *Valerie's Family*); *The Jeffersons*; *Kate & Allie*; *Laverne & Shirley*; *M*A*S*H*; *Murphy Brown*; *My Sister Sam*; *My Two Dads*; *Newhart*; *Night Court*; *9 to 5*; *One Day at a Time*; *Roseanne*; *The Simpsons*; *Three's Company*; *Too Close for Comfort*; *227*; *Webster*; *Who's the Boss?*; *The Wonder Years*; and *You Again?*

11

The Cosby Show

Recoding Ethnicity and Masculinity
within the Television Text

MICHAEL REAL AND LAUREN BRATSLAVSKY

While the goal of this chapter is to discuss how Bill Cosby and those associated with The Cosby Show *worked to recode Black masculinity and normalize the representation of an affluent middle class Black family on television, we would be remiss to exclude mention of events in 2014 that, in effect, recast Bill Cosby and his creative works in an alternative light. In the past 10 years, over 30 (at this writing) women have charged Bill Cosby with sexual assault dating back to the late 1960s. News of these allegations had circulated in the media but did not reach the subsequent groundswell of public outcry until a combination of factors emerged, including a new biography that touched on Cosby's reputation as a womanizer, several civil lawsuits, and a viral video of comedian Hannibal Buress calling Cosby a rapist. These led to major headlines and created fodder for the news and social media as more women stepped forward with allegations. Talks of Cosby's new sitcom deal with NBC ended, Netflix pulled a Cosby special, and TV Land quietly removed* The Cosby Show *from its lineup. These charges have seriously damaged the reputation of Bill Cosby as a person[1] and led to his dismissal from corporate boards and the revocation of honorary degrees. The historic role and achievement of* The Cosby Show *itself remains, however, and we have chosen to examine the show apart from the more recently revealed issues concerning Cosby's personal life.*

The Cosby Show has been in syndication for more than two decades, replayed until recently during afternoon and late-night hours on various local and cable channels, and has been available on the Internet. Without doubt, the show has been a staple of popular culture. Within television history lore, it is known as the show that revived the domestic sitcom genre and boosted NBC's ratings dominance (Staiger 143–44). The Huxtables, Bill Cosby's fictional TV family, depict the idealized family while the character of Cliff Huxtable (Bill Cosby) earned canonization in the television fathers' hall of

Figure 11.1. (clockwise from lower left) Lisa Bonet as Denise Huxtable, Bill Cosby as Dr. Cliff Huxtable, Tempestt Bledsoe as Vanessa Huxtable, Sabrina Le Beauf as Sondra Huxtable, Keshia Knight Pulliam as Rudy Huxtable, Malcolm Jamal-Warner as Theodore Huxtable, and Phylicia Rashad as Clair Huxtable in *The Cosby Show.* 1984–1992. Photo courtesy of Larry Edmunds BooksFair.

fame. The program was a wholesome and moralistic model for "family." Rumors of a Cosby family show revival surfaced every few years. Cosby's trademark sweaters were once postmodern, ironic symbols of goofy television fatherhood. Audiences took pleasure in the self-acknowledging appearances of the Huxtable children, especially Theo, as they played along with the show's tropes and moral lessons. Until recently, Bill Cosby was still active, embarking on stand-up comedy tours and sit-down television specials while also periodically making the rounds of news and public forums to comment on the state of African American families and race relations.[2]

Since the show's legacy, its fictional characters, and its real life personas have permeated popular culture and even political discourse to such a great degree, it is easy to overlook the impact of this show in its day (as well as its spin-off, *A Different World*). To underscore and interrogate its historic recoding of African American ethnicity, we revisit the program at the time of its original airing. This was a time when the three major networks still reigned supreme but faced structural changes (e.g., new corporate ownership, FOX as the fourth network, satellite and cable programming, and niche markets). This was also a time when representations of African Americans, particularly men and father figures in sitcoms, tended toward stereotypes of "authentic" ghetto life (e.g., *Good Times, Sanford and Son, What's Happening!!*) or were defined in relation to Whiteness (e.g., *Diff'rent Strokes, The Jeffersons*) (Gray).[3] Why do representations on television matter? Television has a crucial political and ideological influence on how we think and interpret the world, as Sut Jhally and Justin M. Lewis explain in their foundational study of *The Cosby Show* and perceptions of race.

The Cosby Show was the most popular television program of the 1980s, dominating Thursday nights in America from 1984 to 1992 (Fuller). Ideologically and semiotically, the program was significant in recoding public perception of Blackness and, to some extent, masculinity. Challenging the prominent, negative stereotypes of Black males as irresponsible, unreliable underachievers who pervaded popular culture in the previous decade, *The Cosby Show* gave the American public a comfort level that foreshadows its acceptance of a Black man as president two decades later. But, more negatively, the show was also charged with creating a false impression that American racial problems had been resolved and that America had entered a postracial era in which no racially-based structural disadvantages remained (Jhally and Lewis). *The Cosby Show* was part of a broader moment in the 1980s that promoted "the growing 'race doesn't matter narrative,' . . . turning television into a vessel through which to perpetuate color-blind ideologies and uncritical multiculturalism" (Leonard and Guerrero 3). The show was indeed a corrective, yet maintained a particular political point of view, as Blackness was mapped onto upper-middle-class affluence while nearly eliminating issues of racism and structural inequalities (Gray).

The force behind this show, William H. "Bill" Cosby, Jr., emerged in the last third of the 20th century as one of the great popular artists of the age. As performer and producer, Cosby achieved the stature of an institution and was featured on the September 28, 1987, cover of *Time* magazine as "Cosby, Inc." Considering that Cosby had inherited both a strong entertainment tradition and a negative stereotype as a Black, American male, his achievement is especially emblematic. From minstrel shows to *Birth of a Nation*, from Stepin Fetchit to *Amos 'n' Andy*, the Black male in particular has been the subject of stereotyping. *The Cosby Show*'s success occurred in a challenging context. Black scholarship, especially in film theory, was then drawing from semiotic and mythic analysis in order to critique the distorted Black presence in the image industries, and James Snead, Gerald Davis, and Armond White had called for new forms of mythic media construction of the African American experience. The power of prime-time, network television to code and recode dominant cultural myths was brought front and center.

MYTHOLOGY AND ICONS IN THE TELEVISUAL TEXT

Myths construct narratives around types and stereotypes, and in the words of Douglas Kellner, echoing Roland Barthes, "The myths of a society are the bearers of its ideologies" (*Television, Mythology, and Ritual* 134).[4] In this sense, embedded in American mythology are codes about race as well as class, gender, sexuality, and social structure. Kellner summarizes the ability of television to express such myths:

> Television images and stories produce new mythologies for problems of everyday life. Myths are simply stories that explain, instruct, and justify practices and institutions; they are lived, and they shape thought and action. Myths deal with the most significant phenomena in human life and enable people to come to terms with death, violence, love, sex, labor, and social conflict. Myths link together symbols, formula, plot, and characters in a pattern that is conventional, appealing, and gratifying (*TV, Ideology, and Emancipatory Popular Culture* 22).[5]

Semiotically, myths are expressed through signs and codes, through formulas, genres, and icons. An icon is "an object of uncritical devotion" in the words of Marshall W. Fishwick (1970, 1978), drawing from the ideas of Herbert Read and Erwin Panovsky. Bill Cosby personally, and his mythical television family collectively, became icons of American popular culture in the 1980s.

How did Bill Cosby achieve the status of an icon of American culture? Emerging as a successful stand-up comic in the early 1960s, Cosby developed routines about his boyhood friends, his brother and himself, his family and neighborhood, sex and marriage, all delivered with vocal dramatics and masterful timing; they are nuanced and telling stories of everyday experience. These routines became best-selling recordings as well. With Robert Culp, Cosby co-starred in the dramatic television series *I Spy* and then starred in the sitcom *The Bill Cosby Show* from 1969 to 1971. By the early 1970s, Cosby was also providing voices and direction for the popular *Fat Albert* television cartoons, which in turn spun off several Fat Albert books. As the commercial spokesperson for Jello, Coca-Cola, and Kodak, Cosby developed into one of the most credible pitchmen in the history of television, eventually registering the highest "Q Score" for audience popularity and trust in history. Cosby also authored best-selling books; his first, *Fatherhood*, sold a then-record 2.6 million copies in hardback. At this point, Cosby's annual earnings made his the highest earned income in the United States, averaging some $57 million. His iconic presence had become unavoidable. Cosby's personal life was more complex, ranging from regular attendance at parties at Hugh Hefner's Playboy mansion to developing an impressive fine art collection to completing his doctorate in education at Temple University. Cosby was a generous supporter of Jesse Jackson, the anti-apartheid movement, traditional Black universities, and various political causes. One-dimensional, Cosby was not.

Cosby funneled his iconic status, his humor, and sense of American mythology (the nuclear, aspirational, affluent family) into a familiar format (the domestic sitcom, a modern *Father Knows Best*) as a means to shift and challenge popular perceptions of race. The show's contribution was how it "repositioned and recoded [B]lackness and [B]lack (middle-class) subjectivity within television's own discursive and institutional practices" (Gray 83). The following section introduces and situates the ways in which the show recodes Blackness, particularly in conjunction with the myths and codes of American social class and family. The chapter concludes with a look at critical interrogations about *The Cosby Show's* work to promote mythic portrayals of equality and manhood while avoiding (and allegedly erasing) dimensions of racism and structural inequalities.

GENRE, CONVENTION/INVENTION, AND RECODING BLACKNESS

Television situation comedy, like any genre of cultural practice (Mittell *Genre*), reflects both what is customary in the genre, the "conventions" of it, and what is innovative, the "inventions" within a particular expression of the genre (Cawelti). *The Cosby Show* employs the conventions of domestic comedy: humorous situations and clever lines, characters representing defined personality types, plot complications that nevertheless always end well, formulaic productions often taped before a live audience, and filling no more than twenty-two minutes, allowing plenty of time for commercials within the half-hour block. Conventions maintain a predictable stability in cultural products and contribute to the continuity of the culture while operating within industrial logic (Gitlin 1983). In contrast, inventions are those parts of a cultural product uniquely contributed by a particular creation: the distinctive domestic slapstick of Lucille Ball, the dark battlefield humor of *M*A*S*H*, or *Seinfeld's* insights into the trivia of everyday life. Over time, inventions may modify conventions, as in *I Love Lucy's* filming its comedy before a live audience, the creators of *M*A*S*H* fighting to drop the laugh track, or more recent postmodern, ironic sitcoms without moral lessons and with characters who truly never change. Inventions enable a culture to respond to changing circumstances. *The Cosby Show* skillfully employs the conventions of the domestic sitcom to weave in inventions in terms of how Americans see the Black family and the Black male on television.

Beginning from the understanding that race and ethnicity are socially constructed, media institutions and content are major forces in constructing and normalizing but also shifting codes of race and ethnicity (Downing and Husband). Another way to address these shifting codes is through Gray's conception of Blackness, which explains it as "a cultural signifier that although operating on the basis of specific histories, dynamics, and relations of power, nevertheless remains open to multiple and competing claims" (12). Cosby as an icon and creator of *The Cosby Show* worked within the medium's production and representational histories, the conventions of the sitcom genre, and broader social discourses while he used inventions to challenge the dominant modes of portraying Black individuals and families on television. Invoking the power to produce his own media and representations (albeit in the confines of the media industry [see Fuller]), Cosby recodes some but certainly not all dimensions of race in America. He was able to accomplish what White describes as the influence of the producer: "How [B]lack characters might be presented in a politically correct, emotionally resonant situation depends on the filmmaker's mythic or visionary sense of his subject" (40). Indeed, it is essential to recognize Cosby's deliberate effort to code *The Cosby Show* with positive portrayals of family *and* of African Americans; Cosby employed Dr. Alvin Poussaint, a Harvard psychiatry professor (as well as his friend) to consult on the reflection of "psychological reality" (Johnson; discussed by Fuller and by Jhally and Lewis).

Codes organize signs into systems—for example, in the way that grammar organizes words into sentences. Certain structural features, such as binary oppositions of Black and White or male and female, appear in the signs and codes of verbal expression, social relations, and mental categories (e.g., race). These structures exist as codes that relate the signifying practices of media to the personal identity of members of the public. Myths tell a culture's stories through its signs and codes. *The Cosby Show,* in its years atop American television ratings, managed to cleverly entertain as it carefully wound its way around and occasionally challenged the mythic stereotypical structuring of Blackness that preceded it. As evidenced by this show and many other cultural texts, the codes and mythic dimensions of the narrative and representations can work in opposing directions, alternatively seeming to resolve or suppress cultural contradictions. Levi-Strauss emphasizes the ability of myth to resolve cultural conflict and contradictions. In contrast, Barthes sees myth as a vehicle to suppress contradictions and idealize existing conditions. Different readings of *The Cosby Show* draw opposite conclusions on this issue. First, though, let us take a close look at the textual content and structure of the show or, in other words, the codes of the convention as they intersect with Cosby's representational innovations via the recording process.

In the first season, the show's opening credits reveal a normal American family–two parents and children getting out of a van with sports equipment to spend a day at the park. These codes of the sitcom and of domestic life "constructed [the Huxtables] as little more than an average suburban family, who just happen to be African Americans" (Leonard 115). This sets up the first contradiction: the need to use codes of the suburb (the park, the van) to connect this urban, upper-middle class family with the dominant conventions of domestic and, significantly, White, sitcoms. The next and subsequent seasons open with the characters each dancing to a jazz score with Cliff at the center of it all in a move away from the domestic setting and the conventions of past credit openings and, instead, an introduction of the family with signifiers of Black culture, such as African American fashion, jazz icons, and eventually the Apollo Theater sign in Harlem.

PROFESSIONALS AND THEIR NUCLEAR FAMILY: CLASS AND AFFLUENCE CODES

The Cosby Show, following domestic sitcom conventions, takes place primarily in the living room and kitchen, with occasional bedroom scenes, within the Huxtable residence (*Comic* 1985). Moreover, this setting demonstrates upper-middle-class affluence and, thus, codes of televisual normalcy: a well-equipped kitchen, including a table for informal family meals and interactions; a clean, comfortable living room with expansive seating; a writing desk; tasteful art in the background (works by prominent African American artists); and, bedrooms that reflect the personalities of each character. In other words, any typical television family of substantial means, which has been the TV norm, might live in this home

Consisting of two loving parents (an obstetrician-gynecologist and a partner in a law firm), five clever and achieving children (the college-age Sandra, the teenagers Denise and Theo, the preteen and classic middle child, Vanessa, and the adorable preschool girl, Rudy), and frequently visiting grandparents, the Huxtable family seems to have moved right out of sociology texts about the nuclear family and into our living rooms. Cliff Huxtable is the loving, caring, and incredibly present (he has a home office) father of five. His wife, Clair Huxtable, is a busy lawyer, who is also deeply involved in the children's lives. They have a very stable union and have ostensibly worked out how to share household and parenting duties, albeit with Cliff still as head of the household (the show *is* called *The Cosby Show,* not *The Huxtables*). His character is unequivocally established as a well-employed breadwinner, and yet, he is present at home and involved with his children to an unusual, if not impossible, degree for a working parent of any race or circumstance. When they argue over Theo's punishment, Cliff calls from his doctor's office to Clair's law office, and their professional personas are overlaid on their family roles. The show is structured to present Cliff and Clair as role models, busy professionals who protect plenty of time for parenting their children.

In his parenting, Cosby's character shows unwavering understanding, perceptive advice, and good-humored charm in all his dealings with his children (which serves as an extension of both his standup comedian persona and the conventions of the 1950s television family; see Frazer and Frazer). The children are intelligent and well-adjusted; when they have problems with grades or siblings or boyfriends or girlfriends or other day-to-day facets of adolescence, they respond quickly to parental attention. They have predictable conflicts—wearing each other's clothes, demanding the privileges granted another, etc.—but they wind up assisting each other as well as their parents. Against the negative stereotypes of unstable Black families found in news reports and Reagan-era policies, this family is as stable as the Cleavers in *Leave It to Beaver*.

DISPOSABLE INCOME

The Cosby Show presents the antithesis of the stereotypes and discourses about poor and broken Black families; thus, "blackness is not imagined as incompatible with the family but in fact complementary" (Leonard 116–17). The show celebrates not just the possibility of reaching the middle class but the fact of Black middle-class existence; it offers no apologies for the affluence it portrays. The Huxtables own an impressive home, cars, wardrobes, appliances, and other expensive consumer goods. For example, when Clair buys a new sofa, Cliff objects because he is opposed to changes in his habitat rather than for financial reasons. They enjoy nice dinners and nightclubs, take vacations, and send their children to college with no apparent financial strain. Lest their children become financially reckless, however, they instruct them carefully on the realities of living expenses. When Denise wishes to spend all her savings on an attractive and untested used car, Cliff dissuades her by speaking of costs of gas, insurance, and maintenance. When Theo wants to skip college, get a job, and buy a motorcycle, Cliff gets out Monopoly money to explain to him the hard facts of rent, food, clothing, transportation, entertainment, and other costs matched against income. This Black family's enviable affluence has come from planning, hard work, and fiscal commonsense.

THE VALUE OF EDUCATION

Against stereotypes of school dropouts and poorly-educated, unemployable characters, the Huxtable household seems to ooze with affirmation of education and the value of school.[6] Cliff and Clair refer periodically to their years in college and professional school; the children often deal with issues related to homework assignments and grades; and, everyone plans for college. The Huxtables' eldest daughter, Sandra, is a success at Princeton, but Denise, after intense lobbying by her father, chooses to attend his alma mater, a traditional Black college, Hillman. The *Cosby* spin-off, *A Different World*, which aired directly after *The Cosby Show*, is set on the college campus of Hillman. Consistent with the program's validation, Cosby has personally contributed more than a million dollars to Black college funds. *The Cosby Show* features episodes set at college and showcases a professor as "the master teacher" as well as commencement ceremonies complete with educational rhetoric and ceremonial music. Cosby's own credit at the end of the show reads: "William Cosby, Jr., Ed.D."

MULTIRACIALISM

Although the emphasis is Black, the show is carefully inclusive of a variety of ethnic representations. Rudy has a White playmate, Peter, as well as her Black friend, Bud. When the experienced Black actor Roscoe Lee Browne plays a Hillman professor of literature, the equally experienced White actor Christopher Plummer enters as a professor of drama at Columbia. Cliff borrows a saw from a White neighbor, and Rudy, feared lost at the plaza, is found at a Chinese restaurant playing with her friend, the daughter of the owner. Clair collaborates with her White law partners, and Cliff counsels a pregnant Latino woman. All this helps to counter any charge that Blacks or others live with and care about only "their own."

RACIAL PRIDE

Despite its appeal to a broad cross-section of the American television audience, *The Cosby Show* makes deft and frequent reference to elements of Black history and culture. Student essays for school, Black History Week, pictures on the walls, references in conversations, and other opportunities are seized upon to refer to historical personages and events in Black American history and culture. Black jazz receives especially prominent endorsement through the taste and conversations of Cliff and his father and through an occasional guest appearance by Black musicians, such as Lena Horne. One episode centers on Martin Luther King, Jr., when, for a school essay, Theo asks his parents and grandparents to describe the March on Washington. The episode concludes with King's voice delivering the "I Have a Dream" speech as the family watches a television documentary. Family members never speak in Black dialect—although, for example, Theo does perform a rap version of Mark Antony's speech from Shakespeare's *Julius Caesar* with his buddy, Cockroach. Given the show's popularity in South Africa, NBC was uncomfortable with an anti-apartheid poster on Theo's wall, but Cosby insisted it stay put. Overall, the show manages to affirm Black pride in a nonthreatening way, specifically constructed as "cultural, as something as important within the Huxtables' lives but not a defining or constraining reality" (Leonard 122). Racial discrimination and conflict are rarely, if ever, confronted directly. Freed by its setting on a college campus and its focus on youth, *A Different World* is able to move beyond *The Cosby Show's* caution in portraying controversial issues of the time. Under the direction of producer Debbie Allen, the show confronts issues of male domination, unwanted pregnancy, date rape, AIDS, and urban racial uprisings. From the platform of a historically Black college, the show engages racial and economic-cultural issues far more directly than its progenitor *The Bill Cosby Show* had been able to do.

HUMOR MEDIATED BY HUMANITY

Of course, what makes *The Cosby Show* successful is its humor. More obvious than the show's positive values is the crisp writing, the likeability of its characters, and the comic talent of Bill Cosby. His nonverbal skills can be exceptionally expressive. The doorbell rings, he lifts his eyes, does a dance move across the room, and "charmingly" opens the door. Nothing has been said, but the live audience responds with laughter, and home viewers connect. In one episode, Cosby makes the onerous task of caring for a sick child a delightful experience. He imitates the germs inside his youngest daughter, Rudy, in the form of a tight, prissy little face as he mincingly articulates, "Party, party. We're going to party," and then administers the antidote. The spoon with medicine becomes an airplane. Rudy sits up in bed transfixed; she begins to smile, and then to giggle contagiously. Cosby continues clowning with the airplane spoon. He's got Rudy engaged, and he's got the live audience engaged and, one can only assume, he's got the home audience engaged. It is what comedy writer-director Garry Marshall describes as "taking it on out" (Kaminsky 209). The script identifies a comedic action, often near the climax of the episode, and the actor expands and embellishes with improvisational flare: Marshall's sister Penny did this in *Laverne and Shirley*, as did Lucille Ball, the master of taking it on out, in *I Love Lucy*. In a way that parents have tried for decades, Cosby selling the medicine creates classic Aristotelian humor by surprise. It is the common presented in an uncommon way. In contrast to the Stepin Fetchit tradition, Cosby does not demean himself for a laugh. He does not insult others. One laughs *with* Cosby and his family, not at them.

In all of Cosby's work, there is an element seen earlier in Walt Disney (Real): an immediate sense of what the largest portions of the public will respond to, which creates an ability to operate in the middle register between the heights of elite culture and the depths of brutal culture. For Cosby, the mainstream artist, this means a sense of popular taste perceptively and humorously presented in books, recordings, films, television specials, live appearances, and especially, this sitcom. The sitcom is pragmatically designed to appeal to the widest possible audience. Networks and writers (and of course, advertisers) aim for a sweet spot that is unique to television as a popular cultural form: syndication. A show can live in perpetuity, entering people's homes on a regular schedule, and thus potentially reaching far more people than Cosby's other creative outlets. Operating anywhere outside of the sitcom's middle register, such as confronting racism or structural inequalities, would have interfered with Cosby's commercial success and challenged NBC's tolerance for such content.[7]

ACHIEVEMENTS AND LIMITATIONS IN THE COSBY RECODING OF "BLACK"

The Cosby Show rejects past codes of Blackness (e.g., the minstrel, the servant, the poor, the working class, etc.) and instead recodes the representation of African Americans on television using the powerful American Dream myth (that already dominated the sitcom genre; see Marc *Comic* 1997 183). This myth invokes the nuclear family, aspirational and meritocratic social values, and visions of a classless and raceless (or some would say multiculturalist) society. So, while *The Cosby Show* intervenes in television's representational strategies by providing more complex and richer representations, it reifies certain aspects of television mythology while ignoring other realities of racism and structural inequalities (Leonard). Or, as Gray frames it, "the show seemed unable, or unwilling, to negotiate its universal appeals to family, the middle class, mobility, and individualism on the one hand and the particularities of Black social, cultural, political, and economic realities on the other" (81–82). For instance, high unemployment, especially among the young, finds no echo in *The Cosby Show*. Forms of racial discrimination in housing, education, and other areas are not confronted. Police harassment of minority populations receives no attention. What the show omits is significant; it carefully avoids antagonizing any members of the audience. In this sense, as the saying goes, it "comforts the afflicted" far more than it "afflicts the comfortable." But, is the latter even a possibility for any prime-time network sitcom? The show engages in a different political project, an ideological struggle to break the signifier of Black man and Black families from a dominant meaning system within negative racist stereotypes and to reconnect that signifier with an alternative meaning system.[7]

This tension anchors polarized judgments about the show: Does *The Cosby Show*, as a mythology, serve to suppress (Barthes) or resolve (Levi-Strauss) the social contradictions that surround it—namely those concerning the representations of race, class, and family? Does this recoding merely mask and obscure problems through ideological manipulation (the function of myth for Barthes when it replaces history with ideology), or does *The Cosby Show* provide needed catharsis and resolution, as Levi-Strauss sees myths doing? Perhaps the question is a false dichotomy; *The Cosby Show* manages to do some of both. Yet, how did audiences react?

To better understand this contradictory space, Jhally and Lewis approach the complexities that *The Cosby Show* poses concerning race, family, gender, and social context by studying audience reactions. They first situate the show within its critical reception, notably that advocates view the program as "an enlightened step forward in race relations" and detractors critique the episodes as "counterproductive because they reinforce the myth of the American dream" and erase structural inequalities (2–3). Their research supports the critical praise and concerns found outside of academia. *The Cosby Show* indeed offers positive images of an African American family and, moreover, a fictional realism about family life. In terms of representation, Jhally and Lewis argue (and draw from their audience research in which viewers are divided by race and class) that for White audiences the show "wants to make racial differences irrelevant" while for Black audiences, the show represents "the *dignity* of [B]lack American life" in opposition to lived and fictional stereotypes and prejudices (36). But, the authors caution that this is too celebratory, as *The Cosby Show* operates on an ideological level. Given the class-based code system of the American Dream, a show about a successful Black family "symbolizes the fairness of the American system," thereby masking structural inequalities in American social and economic structures (72). While viewers recognize the fictional limits of the show (e.g., how realistic is it to have a doctor and a lawyer frequently available at home), viewers decode *The Cosby Show* as an affirmation that within the constructs of the American Dream, race is not a barrier of entry to upward mobility. Jhally and Lewis argue that ideologically this indicated a resolution that racism is *historical* and not contemporary and that individual ability trumps social structures. *The Cosby Show* might have challenged past stereotypes of Black identity on television, but it does so within the contours of a class(less) value system that both obscures and resolves lived experiences of racism and structural inequality.

Jhally and Lewis argue that *The Cosby Show* recodes race less than gender and family. Race relations is not the butt of jokes, but gender and masculinity are, and, as Jhally and Lewis write, "The show frequently uses humor to expose the inadequacy of the sexist or machismo attitudes of some . . . of its male [characters]" (5). In this respect, the social contradictions inherent in a television sitcom that centers on an upper-middle-class African American family are suppressed *and* resolved by focusing instead on gender and the quirks of family dynamics.

IN THE END

Television is constrained by the demands of its own *consensus narratives* as much as by dominant ideology. David Thorburn finds a consensus narrative has "the ambition or desire to speak for and to the whole of its culture, or as much of 'the whole' as the governing forces in society will permit" (56). The consensus narrative reconciles contradictions within the text and distills the core ideals within easily recognizable genre conventions and cultural codes. In Thorburn's words, its task is "to articulate the culture's central mythologies in a widely accessible 'language,' an inheritance of shared stories, plots, character types, cultural symbols, narrative conventions" (57). This function is accomplished by storytelling in a popular language located within the common understanding of a majority of the culture. Consensus narratives are essentially conservative, serving as a central carrier of the lore and inherited understanding of the culture in which it operates. It is not necessarily, however, a closed text. A continual testing, rehearsal, and revision of cultural experience and values takes place within consensus narratives. The mythologies of the American Dream and aspirations of upward mobility are central stories of *The Cosby Show* and reconcile past representations and contemporary discourses about race by utilizing the domestic sitcom to recode Blackness. *A Different World* offers greater opportunities to recode Blackness alongside and in reaction to our central mythologies while also confronting the issues dodged by the serene world of the domestic sitcom.[8]

As such, *The Cosby Show* demonstrates the operation of consensus narratives in the recoding of what a television family can look like. It catalyzed a change in recoding Blackness, particularly by inserting a positive icon to challenge negative stereotypes of Black males in family life. But, the change was limited, given the centrist demands of prime time as well as the authorial visions of *The Cosby Show* and its comfort level with an American consensus narrative about family, race, ethnicity, and masculinity. Recoding Blackness in this manner serves liberal progress but does not directly threaten the protected interests of media ownership and the dominant class. It is, in the classic phrase of Daniel Hallin, "reformist conservatism."

Placed in the context of codes, myths, icons, genres, and ideology, the positive and negative portrayals of Black males, from Uncle Tom to Bill Cosby, serve to illustrate the mechanisms on a broad cultural level through which television as a whole creates, sustains, and reflects meanings along with the interpretation and structuring of existence. Pro and con, the conflicting portrayals become differentially refracting prisms through which current cultural struggles are observed, expressed, sometimes challenged, sometimes reinforced, and, on rare occasions, held up for all to see through and learn from anew.

NOTES

1. For an overview of public reaction and critical response, see Bambi Haggins, "Losing Cosby" *Flow 22*(1), http://flowtv.org/2015/10/losing-cosby/.

2. To illustrate Cosby's continued status as a pop culture icon, a 2013 segment on *The Today Show* asked viewers to vote for the best Cosby sweater with Cosby announcing the winner. In the realm of public discourse, Cosby has frequently participated in public forums and commented on the state of black youth, families, and education. For an overview, see Chapter 11 in James Patterson's *Freedom is Not Enough: The Moynihan Report and America's Struggle Over Black Family Life–From LBJ to Obama*. New York, NY: Basic Books, 2010; see also Michael Eric Dyson, *Is Bill Cosby Right? Or Has the Black Middle Class Lost Its Mind?* New York, NY: Basic Civitas Books, 2008.

3. Gray also writes about the overall televisual construction of "black as expression of social menace and male irresponsibility (and its opposite—*The Cosby Show* ideal of responsibility and citizenship)," particularly in conjunction with the broader, conservative Reagan era (15). Television news, evening news magazines, dramas, talk shows, and other programming all served to construct and reinforce rather negative and problematic stereotypes (Downing and Husband; Jhally and Lewis)

4. Well before and beyond television, the dominant mythology in Western popular culture has included stereotypical symbols, formulas, and characters for virtually all non-Whites. Roland Barthes' famous description in *Mythologies* of the picture of a Black, African soldier saluting the French flag on the cover of *Paris Match* illustrates the subtleties of these representations. The picture conveys in a single image a mythology and an ideology of French imperialism, racial integration, and the honor of the military, all of which were debated points at the time that

Paris Match, without comment and in all likelihood without self-conscious intent, selected this mythically rich and biased image.

5. This draws on Stuart Hall's work, specifically his work on language, meaning systems, and the power of these systems to structure class and social relations. For example, Hall writes about the word *Black* and its use by both the oppressors and the oppressed, which points to the "ideological struggle to disarticulate a signifier from one preferred or dominant meaning-system, and rearticulate it within another, different chain of connotations" (80).

6. For an analysis of the education specific episodes, see Leonard 128–33.

7. For more on how the structure of the television industry constrains the content, see Mike Budd and Clay Steinman, "White Racism and *The Cosby Show*," *Jump Cut* 37, July 1992; Justin Lewis, *The Ideological Octopus: An Exploration of Television and Its Audiences*. New York: Routledge, 1991.

8. For an in-depth analysis of *A Different World*, see D.J. Leonard, "A Different Sort of Blackness: *A Different World* in a Post-*Cosby* Landscape." In *African Americans on Television: Race-ing for Ratings*, Eds. David J. Leonard and Lisa Guerrero, Santa Barbara, California: Praeger, 2013, 141–58.

12

Roseanne, *Roseanne,* Reality, and Domestic Comedy

SUSAN McLELAND

When Stephanie Coontz states in the introduction to her 1992 history of American domesticity, *The Way We Never Were: American Families and the Nostalgia Trap,* that her students had often confessed their guilt because their families "didn't act like those on television," (7) it's pretty clear they hadn't been watching *Roseanne.* Not only would most of Coontz's research have been completed before *Roseanne* premiered, we also can deduce this based on the myths Coontz dissects throughout the book. These myths are based in the idyllic, self-reliant, upwardly-mobile, suburban, White households of the 1950s and 1960s where sitcom parents are effortlessly wise, kids are generally people pleasers, and material comforts have ensured that there are few problems so big that they can't be solved in half an hour (even if you might require some magic). In the world of *Roseanne,* none of these myths apply.

Roseanne represents a break from the upscale and upwardly mobile network television families of the Reagan era—*The Cosby Show*'s Huxtables and *Family Ties*' Keatons in the sitcom world, as well as *Dallas*' Ewings and *Dynasty*'s Carringtons on the prime-time soaps. Instead, *Roseanne* focuses on the blue-collar Conner family in fictional, small-town Lanford, Illinois, including mom Roseanne, dad Dan, daughters Becky and Darlene, son D.J., and Roseanne's sister Jackie. The show also is distinguished from most other domestic sitcoms in that the overworked, flawed, but loving mother is the narrative center of the show, rather than the bemused patriarch or *Tiger Beat*–ready teens. That focus on the sitcom mom, but especially this particular sitcom mom, gives *Roseanne* its unique, sometimes abrasive, but still appealing blue-collar feminist perspective that challenges traditional sitcom practices in terms of authorship, politics, and representation of motherhood.

Roseanne aired on ABC from the fall of 1988 to the spring of 1997, holding in the Nielsen top 10 for its first seven seasons (and the top five for the first six) before falling to 16 in season eight and 35 in season nine.[1] The Conners both worked primarily menial jobs with occasional stints as entrepreneurs, resulting in more failure than success. While *Roseanne* was never nominated for an Emmy for outstanding comedy series, Laurie Metcalf won outstanding supporting actress three times, and Roseanne Barr won outstanding lead actress once. The show also received a Peabody Award in 1992, as well as numerous Golden Globes, People's Choice, and American Comedy Awards. During 1989, *Advertising Age* named Barr its Cover Queen after Barr's appearances in (and on) virtually all the major women's magazines—*People, TV Guide,* and the tabloids—despite her unconventional (read overweight) appearance.[2] The show distinguished itself immediately from other television programs by its subject matter and casting: the working class couple portrayed by Barr and John Goodman are both overweight, but the major sources of plots and jokes are their relationships and money problems, not their waistlines. And, the show makes it clear that the Conners have a healthy sex life, despite their girth.

The show's popularity with television audiences capped Roseanne Barr's professional rise from wisecracking waitress (and mom of three) to standup comic to memoirist and sitcom star. She achieved all of this with a flamboyant whine, flaunting her un-ladylike manners and appetites. Her standup act centered on her persona as the "domestic goddess," a housewife with a particularly rough-and-tumble, brash, acerbic sense of humor. She was famous for telling hecklers to "suck my dick." Barr made it onto the national stage with a *Tonight Show* appearance in 1985, on *Late Night with David Letterman* in 1986, and in her own HBO special, *The Roseanne Barr Show,* in 1987. Husband Bill Pentland and their three kids followed her to Los Angeles where Pentland signed on as "executive consultant," writer, and actor on *Roseanne*.

Throughout the media blitz that surrounded the premiere of *Roseanne* and its subsequent rise to the top of the Nielsens, a few truisms about Roseanne Barr, Roseanne Conner, and the show were widely accepted. The first is the almost universal conflation of Roseanne Barr (as she was then known, and as I will refer to her in this chapter), Roseanne Conner, the character Barr played on her weekly sitcom, and the show itself, *Roseanne.* In *Newsweek,* Givens describes *Roseanne* as "an extension of [Barr's] stand-up comedy act, which is itself an extension of her life" (62). In *Time*, Zoglin called it "an unmistakable expression of her comic persona" (88). And, *People* quipped, "It's hard to tell where the real Roseanne stops and the comedian and TV star begins; these various Roseannes, like their outsize shirts, simply hang loose" ("Twenty-Five" 46–47).

This type of promotion was common in network television in the 1980s and 1990s, as can be seen by the number of standup comedians playing sitcom characters based on their own material, including fatherly Bill Cosby, master of the mundane Jerry Seinfeld, ironic masculinist Tim Allen, recovering alcoholic Brett Butler, and Cleveland native Drew Carey. As such, in promotion, Roseanne Barr the comedian and actress and *Roseanne* the show worked in concert to erase the boundaries between the fictional

Figure 12.1. John Goodman as Dan Conner, Sara Gilbert as Darlene Conner, Roseanne Barr as Roseanne Conner, Michael Fishman as D.J. Conner, Alicia Goranson as Becky Conner in *Roseanne*. 1988–1997. Photo courtesy of Photofest.

representation of a working-class woman in fictional Lanford, Illinois, and the real, historical woman, who portrayed her on prime-time television. Rooted in an ideology that holds "reality" equivalent to grittiness, sordidness, and their associations with coarse bodily functions, this rhetorical move both overvalued Roseanne's personal narrative and sanitized it for prime-time television.

The "reality" of the Conners' working-class lifestyle tweaked a few critics' noses. Since both Roseanne Barr's and Roseanne Conner's "little woman against the system" persona demanded that she remain somehow "outside" mainstream power structures, even as the show topped the Nielsen's, Barr-as-Conner assaulted the status quo by skewering class-based norms of good taste. The Conner household clearly lacks a decorator and, as Roseanne Conner is fond of pointing out, such modern conveniences as a dishwasher. The Conners are more interested in crafting elaborate Halloween pranks than advancing at work or maintaining the highest standards of hygiene, and they clearly love their television more than their vacuum cleaner. Roseanne and Dan both flout the common television standards of trim and toned protagonists, openly lounging with their sodas, white bread, and bags of chips in their plus-sized wardrobes. Even the most complimentary reviewers regularly refer to Roseanne and her family as "slobs"; commentators seem incapable of writing about her without discussing her weight; the show's fractured grammar and lackadaisical approach to the Conner children's supposedly fragile self-esteem have earned both *Roseanne* and its star a number of reproaches. Writers in both *Mademoiselle* and *The New York Times* even attacked Roseanne's femininity early in 1990.

The equation Roseanne Barr = Roseanne Conner might have assisted network promotions early in the show's run, but it also signaled Barr's position as "author" of the show. This type of authorship-by-actor is unique to U.S. network television series production and contrasts with the relationship between film or theater actors and the characters they play for discrete projects or periods of time. In a few privileged cases discussed elsewhere in this volume (see chapters on *I Love Lucy*, *Seinfeld*, and *Cybill*, for example), television has made this implied authorship manifest with ramifications ranging from a different balance of legal and merchandising rights for the actor and producers to the necessity for changes in the narrative of the series to reflect the star's changing physical state and greater power.

Barr is one of the strongest examples of this case. Her relationship to Roseanne Conner and the show *Roseanne* neatly illustrates two of Michel Foucault's four "author functions": the legal and institutional aspects of authorship and the shifting subjectivities that it calls into play[3] (456–57).

Both the title *Roseanne* and Roseanne's end credit on the show, "Based Upon a Character Created by Roseanne," suggest her legal authorship as well as that the proprietary rights normally attributed to the executive producers/ writers of the show transfer at least partially to Barr. In fact, writer Matt Williams brought a spec script to executive producers Marcy Carsey and Tom Werner about a working-class working mom before Barr achieved national acclaim. When she was brought on board, the writing team worked with her to tailor the pilot to fit her personality and backstory. Barr fought to have the show renamed *Roseanne* (from Williams' *Life and Stuff*) to emphasize this equivalence, but it wasn't enough. In an *Entertainment Weekly* tribute to the show's twentieth anniversary, Barr remembered her reaction to first seeing the credit, "Created by Matt Williams" at a viewing party for cast and crew on the night of *Roseanne*'s premiere. "We built the show around my actual life and my kids. The 'domestic goddess,' the whole thing," said Barr.[4] Williams, Carsey, and Werner countered that the credit was determined by the Writer's Guild of America rules, but Barr was unsatisfied. She settled for her own "Based Upon a Character Created by" credit and the promise of Williams' impending departure from the show. Carsey noted in the same article, "The script Matt [Williams] turned out was about a working-class heroine, really. A woman who, against all odds, was raising the kids and keeping a marriage healthy while working full-time. So, it was the opposite of things [Roseanne] was talking about in 'The Domestic Goddess.'" What Carsey doesn't acknowledge is that the actors who play perfect housewives on television have always been working women. While Barr's standup shtick was about a housewife, the actual woman performing it was working, albeit in comedy clubs instead of a plastics factory. While Roseanne Conner might have started out as Williams' superwoman-like "working class heroine," she quickly developed into a particular, complex character whose philosophical, political, and emotional core is rooted in Barr's personal history.

Roseanne's feminist and populist sensibilities match Barr's experiences and the way that she interpreted them. Compared to its network television predecessors in the 1980s,[5] the show's depiction of working-class life during a recession is remarkably raw and ties neatly with Roseanne Barr's well-publicized biography. Both Barr and Conner had working-class husbands and close relationships with their sisters (at least, Roseanne Barr was close to her sister at times), high school diplomas, three children, histories of low-paid and unfulfilling jobs, a sarcastic sense of humor, and dreams of artistic expression. Both Barr's history and her off-screen life during the run of the show were more scandal-ridden, however. In her teens, she had been committed to a mental hospital and had placed a child for adoption; during the run of the show, she divorced and remarried twice, underwent numerous plastic surgeries, struggled against the tabloids, postponed a wedding while her fiancé went into rehab for cocaine addiction, battled (and fired) many of the production staff on the show, alienated her parents and siblings with accusations of childhood sexual abuse, and sparked a nationwide outcry with a purposefully off-key rendition of the national anthem before a professional baseball game. None of these episodes fit the networks' model for half-hour comedy material at the time.[6]

While the Conners are downwardly mobile, they're a sanitized version of the stressed American working-class family, as well as Barr's working-class family. Roseanne and Dan Conner might fight like tigers, but their mutual affection and understanding lowers the stakes on the blistering battles we witness throughout the series. Their financial troubles might escalate to the point where they have their electricity cut off ("The Dark Ages"), but within a few episodes, Roseanne and her sister are opening a small restaurant thanks to a loan from their mom. Daughters Becky and Darlene do not follow the path that their parents foresee for them, both marrying hometown boys when they are very young. Becky and husband Mark even live in a mobile home for a time, marking them as genuine "trailer trash." But, neither daughter becomes a prototypical unmarried, uneducated, and unemployed teen mom, and Darlene even goes to art school in Chicago on her way to a bright future as a writer.

For Barr, the feminist slogan "the personal is the political" was the source of much of her comedy from the beginning of her career. Kathleen Rowe's *The Unruly Woman: Gender and the Genres of Laughter* explains how just appearing on network television as herself, a loud-mouthed, working-class, overweight, middle-aged woman, Barr transgresses classical standards of femininity and challenges patriarchal norms. In both her standup act and on *Roseanne*, her actions expose the ways that gender and class power structures exclude people like her from the American Dream. Instead of belittling herself for her failures as a housekeeper, she questions patriarchal norms that saddle women with responsibility for the whole family's accumulated grime. On the show, Roseanne Conner allows the kind of chores June Cleaver regularly performs in high heels and pearls to slide. In at least one episode ("Take My Bike, Please"), she even delegates all her household duties to Becky and Darlene when she adds a second shift at Dan's motorcycle shop to her full-time waitressing job. But, her act and the show also work to make the political personal. In "Aliens," a Republican congressional candidate spouting supply-side rhetoric to the penniless Conners meets his debating match in Roseanne's economic analysis (starting from her overdrawn, working-class checkbook), defeating his vague generalities with concrete causes and effects.

Roseanne's progressive positioning doesn't just focus on the identity categories that Barr obviously embodies. The show also is one of the few network programs of the time to depict gay and lesbian characters, especially in recurring roles, and was the first to feature an onscreen kiss between two women ("Don't Ask, Don't Tell"), although the kiss was between Nancy's girlfriend Sharon and the straight Roseanne Conner, rather than a true "lesbian kiss."[7] Barr's sister is a lesbian, and her brother is gay; she responded to queries about these representations on the show by noting her desire to make the show realistic: if there are gay and lesbian people in the world, why not show them on television? Generally, however, gay and lesbian characters' sexuality is downplayed in the series. For example, Nancy is a lesbian, but she is also Arnie's ex-wife and Roseanne and Jackie's business partner and wacky friend. The fact that she is a lesbian is only one aspect of her character, and in most episodes, Roseanne and others are more likely to interact with her based on one of these other facets than merely because of her sexuality.

Just because *Roseanne* is progressive in its depiction of different sexualities doesn't mean that it has always been politically correct. When the show features a gay wedding between Conner's antagonist/business partner/former boss, Leon, and his much more appealing boyfriend, Scott, in the eighth season's "December Bride," the nuptials are a festival of flamboyance, including drag queens and rainbows. The episode makes it clear, however, that the event's gaudiness is thanks to wedding planner Roseanne Conner rather than to Leon or Scott; ABC still aired the episode at a special later time to avoid troubling its (presumably homophobic) audience. Sometimes the show highlights Dan and Roseanne's hypocrisy, as in "A Stash from the Past," in which the Conners prepare to punish David and Darlene for the baggie of marijuana they find in the house only to realize it's left over from their own youth. Dan, Roseanne, and Jackie opt to smoke it themselves with hilarious results but in clear violation of the standards they set for their kids. And, in "White Men Can't Kiss," D.J.'s refusal to kiss an African American girl in the school play forces Dan and Roseanne to rethink the attitudes about race they might have unconsciously passed on to their kids.

But, the primary representation that *Roseanne* redefines for network television is that of the wife/mother, both problematizing and redeeming the role by acknowledging her flaws and her efforts to improve. As other chapters in this anthology attest, domestic situation comedies—sometimes called "domcoms"—have been an essential part of network television programming since TV's first appearance in homes. The families (and therefore mothers) that these shows represent have been almost uniformly White and middle- or upper-middle-class suburban residents, thereby providing appropriate models and environments for the types of consumption they were designed to promote.[8] Mothers in comedy frequently play supporting roles to wise fathers and/or rebellious but appealing kids. Paralleling a range of popular representations (and in denial of demographic trends), domcom mothers in leading roles until *Roseanne*'s premiere tended to be portrayed with either a husband or a job but not both. Roseanne Conner has both, as well as close relationships with her sister, friends, parents, grandparents, in-laws, co-workers, and business partners.

Roseanne's rich network of relationships enables us to see her as more than just a mom, a wife, or a worker. By building a large, multigenerational ensemble surrounding Roseanne, the show makes the argument that it is through the complex web of relationships and subject positions—mother, daughter, sister, wife, friend, granddaughter, co-worker, frenemy, and more—that our concept of the character is formed and experienced. At the same time, the show is careful not to sugarcoat these relationships. Here again, Roseanne Barr's backstory, including the "gritty reality" of childhood abuse and neglect, regularly extolled in popular talk shows like *Donahue* or *Oprah*, evokes a particularly timely empathy with television viewers in the late 1980s and 1990s. These talk shows often brought troubled families and therapists together to explore the ways that each individual's personal history influenced his or her ability or inability to deal with everyday challenges.[9] Characters on *Roseanne* also faced situations that echoed Barr's revelations of her personal history, which included parental abuse, giving a child up for adoption, multiple divorces, and a stint in a mental hospital.

Some of Barr's real-life troubles are revised and narratively displaced onto Jackie Harris, Roseanne Conner's sister. Jackie's search for a soulmate on the show devolves into a combination of aborted relationships and one-night stands, a physically abusive boyfriend, a child born out of wedlock, a loveless marriage ending in divorce, and years of therapy. While she never finds a long-term romantic partner, Jackie grows from a dependent but wacky sidekick into a capable but wacky single mother as the show progresses. Her most active roles in the show, however, are as a foil, sidekick, and amateur relationship therapist for Roseanne. Jackie regularly questions her sister's initial, angry reactions to Dan's or the children's actions in light of the sisters' shared history in a home with an abusive father and checked-out mother. These reminders often lead Roseanne to rethink her current problems and respond more rationally. Jackie makes Roseanne a better mom and a better wife. But, she also supports and escalates Roseanne's wilder schemes, and their competitive camaraderie gives the show some of its most outrageous moments.

Portraying Roseanne Conner as simultaneously a mother, a daughter, and a sister enables *Roseanne* to tap into a therapeutic rhetoric that focuses on acknowledging the ways in which childhood traumas influence us and consciously work to avoid traditional but abusive family relationships. This theme is particularly strong in "This Old House" when Roseanne punishes Darlene harshly for traveling to a comic book convention in Chicago without permission then reminisces with Jackie about their experiences dealing with their father's brutality when they visit their childhood home, which is scheduled for demolition. Roseanne finally listens to Jackie, relents, and apologizes to Darlene for her temper in keeping with narrative patterns on the show. For *Roseanne*, a perfect parent is not one who never makes mistakes. Roseanne Conner's temper and love of wise-cracking, even when it's inappropriate to the situation, preclude that perfection, but she recognizes those mistakes and apologizes for them. Characters on *Roseanne* regularly miscommunicate, misunderstand, argue, shout, and pout as they navigate their relationships, but at the end of the day, in the episode or the story arc, they confess their shortcomings and ask forgiveness.

Such a "realistic" view of parenting contrasts with the ideal of the supermom who manages to "have it all" effortlessly or cheerfully in the 1980s or who obsessively creates a perfect domestic space á la Martha Stewart in the 1990s. It also differs from stereotypical views of working-class parents as overstressed or uninvolved.[10] *Roseanne* highlights these differences by introducing a variety of characters whose attitudes and home lives contrast with the Conners, such as prim neighbor Kathy Bowman in seasons three and four, the abusive Healy parents in seasons four through eight, and clueless neighbor Ty Tilden in season five. Watching these parents micromanage, mistreat, or neglect kids in contrast to Dan and Roseanne's sometimes flawed but loving attempts to raise their three children reinforces the Conner parents' "normal" reactions, wisdom, and goodwill, despite their sarcastic responses or angry outbursts.

Roseanne is the character who most commonly must apologize for her shortcomings, but she is by no means the only one. Dan shares her explosive temper and even spends a night in jail for beating up Jackie's (ex-) boyfriend Fisher when he learns Fisher has beaten his sister-in-law ("Crime and Punishment"). He also goes through periods when his anger won't allow him to speak to either daughter. Both Dan's father and Roseanne's mother are vilified on the show for not apologizing, or not apologizing sincerely, for their parenting mistakes. Darlene shares her mom's sarcastic tone, regularly wounding her sensitive boyfriend David, her parents, her siblings, and a vindictive bully at school ("Therapy"). And, Becky's decision to marry Mark, her parent's worst nightmare, at the beginning of season five ("Terms of Estrangement, Parts 1 and 2"), affects her family relationships through the rest of the series.

Roseanne's creators' decision to embrace the painful adolescence of the Conner children, especially Becky and Darlene, allows them to grow into their own complex and contradictory characters. While Becky starts off as the responsible, book-smart one and Darlene is the tomboy, over the seasons they develop in unexpected ways. Becky falls in love with the "bad boy," Mark Healy, and drops out of high school to marry him and move to Minnesota and then must deal with the repercussions of this decision. Darlene first falls into a long-term depression and then finds a passion (and a future partner) in the zine culture that recognizes, nurtures, and rewards her critical and creative voice in a way that a small-town Illinois high school cannot.[11] Still, even from the first seasons of the show, *Roseanne* deals with subjects that previous sitcom kids never face—at least onscreen. Darlene gets her first period ("Nightmare on Oak Street"), Becky farts in front of the entire student body ("Inherit the Wind"), and D.J. chooses to cross-dress un-ironically for Halloween ("Trick or Treat"). Later, Roseanne and Dan struggle to deal with both girls developing sexual relationships, ("A Bitter Pill to Swallow," "The Dark Ages," and more) and D.J. becomes a compulsive masturbator ("Homeward Bound").

Tied in with the show's focus on family and memory is the way that it portrays the difficulty—the virtual impossibility—of parenting as well as one would like, especially given the cultural and material conditions of the working class in the Midwest during a recession. *Roseanne* is intimate enough with the experience of motherhood to acknowledge that it's possible to love and hate your kids simultaneously and that sometimes your past and your resources are a better determinant of your success as a parent than your knowledge or your intentions. The series undercuts romanticized representations of the work of mothering that leave children mostly off-screen or that focus only on the trials of parenting malleable babies and toddlers. Instead, *Roseanne* revels in the conflicts inherent in raising children to become independent adults with their own missteps, beliefs, feelings, and opinions and explores the ways that this can highlight or open up fault lines even in a normally unified co-parenting relationship like Dan and Roseanne Conner's. As such, *Roseanne*'s narrative arc prepares viewers for confessional tomes celebrating "bad moms" like *The Girlfriend's Guide to Pregnancy* and anticipates the truths that a generation of mommy bloggers would rediscover a decade or more later—parenthood is hard, and you won't know which of the decisions you are making will be mistakes for years to come.

In its final season, *Roseanne* shifts its tone and focus as Jackie and Roseanne win the lottery and revel in the types of excess they could only have imagined in previous seasons, while Dan takes an extended trip to California to help his mother, who is in a psychiatric hospital. Many of these changes were prompted by off-screen events, especially John Goodman's burgeoning film career and Barr's squabbles with ABC and thwarted desire to produce an American version of the British farce *Absolutely Fabulous*. Ratings for the series, which had already dropped in season eight, fell out of the top twenty-five, and the show faced cancellation. The final episode, "Into That Good Night, Part 2," ends with Roseanne Conner's extended monologue where she reveals that the entire series has been a memoir that she has written in the office that Dan and the kids built for her in the basement. But, it's not a straightforward chronicle of the family: the character of Roseanne Conner confesses that she has rewritten herstory to fit her own tastes. There was no lottery win; Dan died from his heart attack; Darlene "actually" married Mark, and Becky married David, rather than the way that the series portrayed them. And, Jackie was really a lesbian. This was a jarring and controversial ending that many viewers found even more alienating than the preceding season. But, it was one last way for Barr to assert her ownership of *Roseanne*, its narrative, and the way that it portrays a unique woman's view of life in the middle of the United States at the end of the twentieth century.

NOTES

1. The show's tone and storylines changed dramatically in season nine. I'll discuss it separately in the conclusion.

2. See Scott Donaton, "Svelte Oprah Slips Past Barr." *Advertising Age* 11 Sept. 1989: 92.

3. Foucault characterizes the four as legal/institutional functions, establishing authority within a particular culture, fulfilling established criteria and procedures, and clarifying the shifting subject positions conjured in and around individual texts.

4. See Tanner Stransky, "A 'Roseanne' Family Reunion: The behind-the-scenes truth about Roseanne Barr's groundbreaking sitcom." *Entertainment Weekly*, 24 Oct. 2008.

5. Network television broadcast shows about working-class families before *Roseanne*. *The Honeymooners* and *The Goldbergs* fit this demographic in the early 1950s, but as Mary Beth Haralovich and others have reported, as the decade continued, networks replaced them with more upscale families whose homes showcase the kind of consumer goods advertisers were selling. In the 1970s, Norman Lear and others developed a number of working-class sitcoms such as *All in the Family*, *Sanford and Son*, and *Chico and the Man* to tie into the movement toward relevance

that drew the young, urban demographic the networks were seeking, but these shows had been cancelled or moved upscale by the beginning of the Reagan era.

6. Roseanne and others described these events in print autobiographies/biographies, including Roseanne's own *Roseanne: My Life as a Woman* (1989) and *My Lives* (1994) and her sister Geraldine Barr's *My Sister Roseanne: The True Story of Roseanne Barr Arnold* (1994), as well as numerous magazine profiles, standup performances, talk show appearances, and two 1994 made-for-television biopics.

7. We will save for another paper the examination of *Roseanne's* practice of casting particularly attractive actors as Nancy's girlfriends. In addition to Sharon, played by the actress and former model Mariel Hemingway, Nancy also had a long-term relationship with Marla, played by the former soap star Morgan Fairchild.

8. See Lynn Spigel's *Private Screenings*, Nina Leibman's *Living Room Lectures*, and Mary Beth Haralovich's "Sitcoms and Suburbs: Positioning the 1950s Home-maker" for analysis and description of the historical precedents of motherhood in televisual representations; Jane Feuer's *Seeing Through the Eighties: Television and Reaganism* updates their arguments to reflect more contemporary developments.

9. Since the talk shows sought buzz for higher ratings, their definitions of "everyday challenges" could be pretty sensational—taboo subjects like transgender family members helped make *Donahue* a syndication champion in the 1980s, Oprah Winfrey shared her own experience as a victim of childhood sexual abuse in 1986, and Jerry Springer regularly confronted parents with DNA tests proving or disproving the dad's paternity during the 1980s and 1990s.

10. Consider the contrast between Roseanne Conner and television contemporary Peg Bundy of *Married With Children* with whom she was frequently compared. Both women are wise-cracking members of the working class, but while Peg is proud of her indolence and the way that she neglects her children, Roseanne cares deeply about her kids and their development.

11. In later seasons D.J. struggles with puberty and finding his place in school, but he isn't showcased as dramatically as his older sisters. The world of *Roseanne* is a matriarchy with Becky and Darlene as future mothers.

13

Cheers

Searching for the Ideal Public Sphere
in the Ideal Public House

ROBERT S. BROWN

The issue of representing a multivocal society within a unified whole has been the subject of debate in education, politics, and entertainment. Making a place at the table for all members of a diverse society challenges its members to create an environment in which all might participate in the sharing of knowledge and the crafting of culture. Jürgen Habermas is known for his theories on the ideal speech situation and further attempted to locate those situations in an ideal public sphere in *The Structural Transformation of the Public Sphere*. Searching through history, he found his ideal sphere in late-medieval Europe, yet failed to find it in the modern world, mainly due to his high, arguably elitist, standards. In a continuing effort to locate that elusive, ideal public sphere, I shall combine Habermas' ideas with those put forth by his critics and apply them to contemporary society to argue that a model for the modern ideal public sphere appeared on television every Thursday night for eleven years in a place called Cheers.

HABERMAS AND HIS CRITICS

Jürgen Habermas, sociologist, political scientist, and cultural critic, studied the problems of legitimation and communication in the creation of the ideal public sphere. In *The Structural Transformation*, Habermas argues that in this sphere, where a community of independent, educated people existed as equals between the state and the masses, opinions on matters of general interest were openly debated in the salons, reading rooms, and coffee houses of Europe. This realm of ideas, brought about by economic and historical circumstances, monitored the tensions of a changing society in the late seventeenth and early eighteenth centuries. According to Habermas, however, this ideal sphere was short-lived, failing to survive in its critical social role due to the intertwining of society and the state through democratization.

Keith Michael Baker offers multiple criticisms of Habermas' bourgeois public sphere. Baker questions Habermas' definition of the sphere's membership, arguing that from Habermas' description, only male property owners had any say in "the needs and interests of civil society in the political public sphere" (186). Baker continues this line of thinking, arguing that the public opinion formed by Habermas' public would represent a single class. Baker also argues that Habermas' public sphere was actually private, representing a select few opinions while leaving out the vast majority. Baker then applies these criticisms to pre-revolutionary French society, concluding that this public sphere was better than the British bourgeois public sphere because it was open to more people and had a special focus on the increased role of women (186–87).

David Zaret's major criticism is that Habermas is too focused on the role of economics in creating a public sphere. While Zaret admits that economics are important, one cannot understand the historical development of the public without taking into account the influence of religion, science, and printing. According to Zaret, these factors are key in the public sphere's interaction with the larger culture, and when included in Habermas' findings, the characteristics of the ideal public sphere are altered for the better. First, the presence of the three new factors allows for more participants in the public sphere, whom Zaret describes as people of "a more popular social milieu than in the learned culture that is the focus of Habermas' account" (220). Next, Zaret points out that while Habermas does mention the role of the press in his study, he reduced its function to the dissemination of information. Zaret argues that the press had a much greater effect as "a causal factor that shaped new modes of thought" (214). These new ways of thinking still have the critical rational traits that Habermas idealizes, but they are not quite as rational or universal (Zaret 221, 223). Zaret also argues that by expanding the identification of the public sphere using his three criteria as well as economics, the public can be involved in "more critical, rational modes of reflection on matters of collective social interest . . . situated in their social context," rather than separated from civilization, as is the case in Habermas' description (215). This idea of a broader public using different styles of rational criticism to discuss cultural issues is important in thinking about the way a public, with an emphasis on diversity, must communicate.

Habermas' historically based study found the elusive ideal public sphere to be a small community of educated socialites practicing social criticism in late seventeenth-century Europe. In order to find a modern equivalent, taking into account changes in society, it is necessary to expand on Habermas' original criteria. Employing Baker's requirement of a more representative community and Zaret's inclusion of multiple social influences and varying forms of criticism allows us to look for contemporary models of the ideal public sphere.

LOCATING A CONTEMPORARY IDEAL PUBLIC SPHERE

The television show *Cheers*, an ensemble comedy based on the antics of patrons of a Boston bar, finished its eleven-year run on television in 1993. Its end was not due to a lack of viewers; it was still a highly rated program when it left the air. As is the case with many long-running programs, however, some members of the cast, most notably lead actor Ted Danson, decided to make career changes. Steven Stark, columnist for the *Boston Globe*, states that while many shows have good writing and acting, *Cheers* has something more. Stark credits the show's appeal to the idea that "the real message of 'Cheers' was an affirmation of the power of the group and of the community" (11). Rarely has any successful television show relied so heavily on dialogue alone. While other programs with ensemble casts may rely heavily on one or two locations—regulars on *The Andy Griffith Show* in Mayberry's jail or Andy's home, the cast of *M*A*S*H* in a few tents, the characters of *Friends* and *Seinfeld* split between an apartment and a local eatery—the citizens of *Cheers* were rarely seen outside of the bar throughout the eleven-year run of the program. While outside lives were mentioned, the whole show was based on how the elements of those lives were discussed from a series of barstools. In fact, most episodes opened with one of the characters, typically Norm, entering the bar and starting a conversation. Certainly, a key to the show's popularity was its tremendous writing, but by considering concepts of community, the program can be seen as demonstrating a higher, more inviting purpose. The environment of Cheers was very appealing to a huge audience because it appeared to be such a welcoming place to sit around and join in the conversation. This ideal discussion space, while basically reflecting Habermas' description of the salon, goes a step further by including the suggestions of both Baker and Zaret, which position Cheers as a model for the modern ideal public sphere.

Both Baker and Zaret agree that Habermas' bourgeois public sphere was too narrow in its representation of the public, leading to public opinion based on the conversations of a singular, literate strata of upper-class men. At Cheers, a wider spectrum of the public was represented, and all had an equal voice in discussions. The cast of characters includes the highly literate, represented by Diane, Frasier, and Lilith, and a seemingly uneducated working class, represented by Coach, Woody, and Carla. Cliff fits the role of what Habermas and Goethe describe as the public person, a "servant of the state,"

Figure 13.1. (clockwise from left) John Ratzenberger as Cliff Clavin, Nicholas Colasanto as Coach, Rhea Perlman as Carla Tortelli, George Wendt as Norm Peterson, Shelley Long as Diane Chambers, Ted Danson as Sam Malone in *Cheers*. 1982–1993. Photo courtesy of Larry Edmunds BooksFair.

who through dress and bearing purposefully tries to appear as a representative of their position (Habermas 13). Norm, spending most of the series as an uninspired or unemployed accountant, appears to represent the average person, the "norm." Sam Malone, a former major league pitcher for the beloved hometown Red Sox now serving drinks from the center of his four-walled castle, represents royalty, looked up to by most of the other characters.

While these characters represent many different levels of education, wealth, and social position in their individual lives, they all have an equal place at the bar once they enter Cheers. Their allegiances seem to shift with the topics, and even the core group of Sam, Cliff, Norm, and Carla is occasionally split by some issue. Yet, by the end of the day, issues have been fully discussed to arrive at a conclusion with which all are satisfied. All of the characters have their chance to shine, just as all are suitably insulted. Cliff appears to get the most constant abuse, perhaps because he exemplifies the tension existing between the public and the state.

The women of the show hold just as strong a position as the men and are rarely excluded from any debate. As Stark comments in his column, "*Cheers* presented a true cast of many equals" (11). It can be argued that the female characters reinforced very negative stereotypes—the pedantic, perky Diane; volatile, oft-unwed mother Carla; the intellectual, ice queen Lilith; and obtuse, gold-digging Rebecca Howe. Yet, the men were portrayed with equally stereotypical characteristics—Sam, the dumb jock; Cliff, the braggart; Woody, the hick; Norm, the sloth; and, Frasier, the elitist, rounding out this cast of characters. They are at once perpetrators and victims of each other's jokes. They often suffer humiliation at the hands of social "superiors," such as the unscrupulous rival Gary, of Gary's Tavern, and the wealthy aristocrat Robin Colcourt. Yet, the gang at Cheers always comes through. Gary loses his bar, and Colcourt is bankrupted and jailed, while the representatives of the larger culture situated at Cheers survive.

The forms of critical rational debate that occur in the bar represent much of what Zaret desires. Bar debates are not always of the high standard that Habermas demanded from his literate bourgeois but, instead, reflect the less rational mode that Zaret expects to exist when influenced by an expanded community. The debates are unstructured, the information often weak or confused, yet the characters take them very seriously and perform rational criticism that a diverse social group would be capable of attaining. The intellectuals, Diane and Frasier, are not granted superior status in this sphere, nor are Coach and Woody relegated to the margin. In the process of discussion, all of the voices are heard, alternately denigrated and respected, all contributing to the marketplace of ideas.

The subject matter of these debates is also not always at the level that Habermas idealizes. Instead, some critical debates fall under the category Zaret refers to as "collective social interest" (215). Sports, television, and movies make up the majority of the debate issues that occurred around the bar—issues that should be expected of a society heavily influenced not by the theater, symphony, and literature of Habermas' elite culture, but by the popular press, television, and movies of Zaret's public sphere.

Michelle Hilmes, in her article "Where Everybody Knows Your Name: *Cheers* and the Mediation of Culture," argues that much of the show's appeal was based on the merging of high and low cultures. Diane and Frasier represent the more intellectual ideals and act as foils for the rest of the bar characters. Having both qualities represented, Hilmes argues, fulfills multiple audience desires for both high and low culture entertainment without viewers being forced to choose (72). Hilmes recognizes that "meaningful critical interpretation is not limited to the high art" while lower standards "are often subtly reinforced through a demonstrated consensus, even when those attitudes are directly critical of such high culture totems" (70). Hilmes fails to go so far as to examine the diversity of the topics discussed and the resulting consensus, although it is not hard to see her argument floating toward that conclusion.

Besides the popular culture and highbrow versus lowbrow debate topics, the gang at Cheers also debates more serious social issues. Topics such as homosexuality, alcoholism, gender roles, and relationships often take center stage. Quite a few shows examine political issues, including an episode in the final season during which a discussion over the state of Boston politics leads to Frasier campaigning for Woody's election to Boston's city council. These bar debates can be seen as clear examples of Habermas' ideal, with the modifications supplied by his critics, as the characters bring their various backgrounds and experiences to the discussion. The issues are then discussed at length until a satisfactory conclusion is reached and a new, often very insightful, understanding is gained.

The social impact of the process of intellectual debate can actually be seen over the course of many seasons. Take, for example, the issue of homosexuality. In the show's first season, Tom Kenderson, one of Sam's old baseball buddies—his former catcher in fact—requests the use of Cheers as the site for the start of his book tour ("Boys in the Bar"). While the catcher urges Sam to read the book first, the less-than-well-read former pitcher schedules the event without even glancing at the volume. What Sam is unaware of is that his old buddy has come out and discusses his homosexuality in the book, a fact later pointed out to Sam by the erudite

Diane. The bar debate then explodes. Some of the obviously homophobic bar patrons take the side that the reputation of the bar, and Sam, could be hurt by hosting the book signing. This would damage business and Sam's image as a ladies' man. Diane, representing a more open-minded opinion, argues that Sam should not throw away the friendship simply because the other man has come out publically. In the end, after discussing the potential outcomes for the length of the program, Sam joins his ex-teammate in the bar in front of the media to support his friend. Sam's reputation is not hurt; his bar business does not fall off, and perhaps more importantly, his friends at the bar change their attitudes about the issue.

The group learns by talking out the issues openly, and this discussion leads eventually to acceptance. By the seventh season, Norm is willing to pretend that he is gay in order to get an interior decorator job ("Norm, is that you?"). By the tenth season, the bar has come to a clear acceptance of people who are openly gay ("Rebecca's Lover . . . Not"). It is Rebecca, a relative newcomer to the bar, who is unaware that her ideal man, an old high school friend in town for a visit, is gay. The community of the bar must work together to find a tactful way of telling Rebecca the news without crushing or embarrassing her. No longer is there any fear of homosexuality or how it will change their lives. The issue has been discussed openly and dealt with in a positive manner, sometimes intelligently and sometimes with base humor, without significant disruption of the community.

The cultural representation at Cheers is not without flaw. Although class and gender differences are clearly present, there is nary a minority. Few African-American, Asian, Hispanic, or other minority group members appear as lead characters or even background customers in the show. What is worse is that when these characters do appear, they are very stereotypical. Sam hires an Asian man to fix his jukebox and supply a Karaoke machine. During the show's second season, Cliff's constant chatter has drawn the ire of a bully ("Cliff's Rocky Moment"), and he brings a Black co-worker named Lewis, a large, athletic male, to the bar as a bodyguard to protect him. While it could be argued that the writers have attempted to duplicate the racist reputation of Boston's Beacon Hill district, this should not be an excuse for the lack of minority representation. Because of this, the bar is not truly representational of all multicultural facets.

Cheers retained its popularity on television in the prime-time schedule for eleven years and continues to do so in syndication. I have argued that this popularity is due in large part to the appeal of its public accessibility. Cheers, as a physical location, invites the public to enter and take its place in the discussion. The banter runs from the most trivial of conversations to heavier dialogues in which contemporary social issues are debated to a peaceful conclusion. The show represents a model of the modern ideal public sphere, as suggested by Habermas and his critics, which fans have obviously found appealing. As a model, it serves as an example of what can be achieved through public discourse. As a popular television show, it invites viewers into the discussions as virtual patrons of the bar, viewer-participants in the discussion of the day. Hilmes points out that through series like *Cheers*, "television, rather than existing in a state of tension between high and low culture demands, becomes the very place where differences are not only mediated but celebrated" (71–72). The sphere, while not measuring up to the demands of Habermas' ideal, instead includes the suggestions of Baker and Zaret, creating a better public sphere in which representatives of the state, royalty, literary, and working class, as well as male and female, and poor and well off, can participate in equal and open social criticism. It is public address at its best: a space where the conversations of the masses overlap with media reports, speeches, and other symbolic exchanges to provide a locus for serious discussion resulting in democratic outcomes. *Cheers* truly provides a place where "everyone knows your name."

The 1990s

The 1990s was bookended by the Persian Gulf War under President George Herbert Walker Bush near its beginning and the impeachment of President William Jefferson Clinton by the House of Representatives (and acquittal by the Senate) at its close. Widely considered a time of economic prosperity with budget surpluses, the passage of the North American Free Trade Agreement (NAFTA) established globalization in international law, and signaled the dominance of the free-market philosophy in commerce and politics. This coincided with the exponential growth of the Internet and much wider availability of personal computers, which also served to make the world seem a smaller place, fulfilling Marshall McLuhan's prediction that information technology would turn the world into a "Global Village." The other news story that dominated the decade was the growing awareness and increasingly successful treatments for AIDS.

Unavoidably, television was also influenced by advances in technology. Stereo television, developed in the 1980s, became increasingly common with MTV an obvious beneficiary but also influencing other youth-oriented shows such as *Miami Vice*. But, the most significant technological story was the gradual but steady laying of cable lines across the country, ushering cable television from the margins into the mainstream of the home entertainment equation. From 1990 to 2000, access to cable television rose from 56 percent of household penetration to 68 percent, outstripping growth in the general population.

In 1990, the documentary *Civil War* ran for five nights and became the highest-rated series in PBS history. Two years later, Johnny Carson's retirement led to a battle between David Letterman and Jay Leno for late-night viewers. The following year, 1993, closed captioning was required on all television sets. In 1995, coverage of the O.J. Simpson trial had millions of Americans glued to their television sets, with particularly large audiences attracted to nonstop coverage on cable. Over 33 million U.S. homes tuned in to live coverage of Princess Diana's funeral in 1997. That same year, Tiger Woods' win at the Masters set a record rating for the golf tournament. According to Nielsen, computer usage topped 58 million in the United States and Canada that year. In 1998, 76 million viewers watched the series finale of *Seinfeld* on NBC, compared to 25 million viewers who watched Mark McGwire hit his then-record-breaking 62nd home run of the season.

It was a great decade for sitcoms. Highly rated shows included popular family sitcoms launched in the 1980s, such as *The Cosby Show* and *Roseanne*, as well as work-family sitcoms, a few of which included biological family members. Shows such as *Cheers, Designing Women, Murphy Brown, Frazier,* and *Friends* regularly landed in the top ten. One unconventional sitcom, often referred to as the "show about nothing," *Seinfeld,* emerged as a television phenomenon. Al Auster writes about the enduring appeal of *Seinfeld* and explains how a show ostensibly "about nothing" can, in fact, be about everything. *The Golden Girls* brought senior citizens into prime time, and *Coach* showed a man curtailing his career to help his wife build hers. Laura R. Linder and Mary M. Dalton write about *Cybill,* a series that goes a step further than *Coach* by actively critiquing sexism in the entertainment industry that produces television and movies.

Of course, sitcoms were not all the networks programmed. *Monday Night Football* and *60 Minutes* remained ratings stalwarts, and the news-magazine genre expanded from CBS to other networks throughout the 1990s with the introduction of *20/20* and *Dateline NBC,* both of which were among the top-rated shows. Successful dramas were also introduced, including *ER* and *N.Y.P.D. Blue,* and the decade ended with the introduction of a hugely successful quiz show: *Who Wants to Be a Millionaire?* The Tuesday, Thursday, and Sunday installments of that quasi-reality program finished first, second, and third in the ratings for the 1999–2000 season.

Focusing on shows that populated the top ten during the 1990s tells only part of the story, however. Conventional genre shows, for the most part, led in the ratings, but cable television made serious inroads into the prime-time arena that had long been dominated by the major networks, which by then had expanded beyond the big three (CBS, NBC, ABC) to include the relative newcomer FOX. Ratings for even the top shows eroded over the period, and by the end of the 1990s, cable had begun to compete on terrain thought to be the exclusive province of the networks: original programming. HBO (Home Box Office) led the way, introducing such landmark programs as *Sex and the City* and *The Sopranos.* But, perhaps the most revealing barometer of the shrinking TV audience could be observed at the lower end of the top thirty list where ratings went from 14.2 for

The Wonder Years during the 1990–1991 season to 8.8 for the shows tied for number thirty in the 1999–2000 season, *Law & Order: Special Victims Unit* and the *CBS Wednesday Night Movie*.

Cable shows such as *Sex and the City* and *The Sopranos* combined high production values, strong writing and performances, and mature subject matter to lure viewers away from conventional network fare to HBO at the end of the decade. Sharon Marie Ross offers a provocative essay on *Sex and the City* that examines women's desire, friendship, and consumerism though the lens of the groundbreaking series, a show that would never have been permitted under network standards and practices. Cable also allowed new networks such as the WB to carve out niche audiences, which catered to viewers interested in seeing programs featuring Black characters. Television network executives tried to compete with cable by offering more sophisticated programs and mature themes but, as in the case of *My So-Called Life* and *Freaks and Geeks*, failed to stick with such programs long enough for them to develop a wider audience.

The top-rated sitcoms of the 1990s were *Baby Talk*; *Becker*; *Blossom*; *Can't Hurry Love*; *Caroline in the City*; *Cheers*; *Coach*; *Cosby*; *The Cosby Show*; *Cybill*; *Dave's World*; *Davis Rules*; *Designing Women*; *Dharma & Greg*; *A Different World*; *Doogie Howser, M.D.*; *The Drew Carey Show*; *Ellen*; *Empty Nest*; *Evening Shade*; *Everybody Loves Raymond*; *Family Matters*; *Fired Up*; *Frasier*; *Fresh Prince of Bel-Air*; *Friends*; *Full House*; *The Golden Girls*; *Grace Under Fire*; *Grand*; *Growing Pains*; *Hangin' with Mr. Cooper*; *Head of the Class*; *Hearts Afire*; *Hiller and Diller*; *Home Improvement*; *Hope & Gloria*; *The Jackie Thomas Show*; *Jesse*; *Just Shoot Me*; *King of the Hill*; *Love & War*; *Mad About You*; *Madman of the People*; *Major Dad*; *Malcolm in the Middle*; *The Martin Short Show*; *Me and the Boys*; *Murphy Brown*; *The Naked Truth*; *The Nanny*; *Phenom*; *Room for Two*; *Roseanne*; *Seinfeld*; *The Single Guy*; *Spin City*; *Stark Raving Mad*; *Suddenly Susan*; *3rd Rock from the Sun*; *Thunder Alley*; *Union Square*; *Veronica's Closet*; *Who's the Boss?*; *Wings*; and *The Wonder Years*.

14

Seinfeld

The Transcendence of the Quotidian

ALBERT AUSTER

Seinfeld, a situation comedy that debuted in 1989 and ran until 1998, has been referred to by some as television's greatest sitcom (Lavery and Dunne). This is certainly high praise for a situation comedy that is famously about "nothing." But, as we've learned from some of the greatest dramatists of the twentieth century, being about "nothing" can, indeed, be at the heart of everything. The plays of Samuel Beckett and Harold Pinter,[1] for example, while ostensibly about nothing, conjure up existential angst and other stark themes germane to modern life. So, despite its claim to the contrary, *Seinfeld* is about a great deal. After all, if it truly had been about nothing, it would not have enthralled a nation for nine seasons.

To a certain extent, Larry David and Jerry Seinfeld, the series co-producers and writers, were trying to distinguish their series from the mega hit series of the seventies, eighties, and early nineties, such as the Norman Lear sitcoms (*All in the Family, Maude, The Jeffersons*), *The Mary Tyler Moore Show*, *M*A*S*H*, and *Cheers* that often confronted hot-button contemporary social, political, and cultural issues. Their series would be a contemporary comedy of manners, dwelling to hilarious effect on the quotidian, the mundane, and petty things, honing in with deadly accuracy on many of the neuroses of contemporary urban life.

Their approach paid enormous rewards, giving us modern, urban, surrealistic narratives that often feature the eccentric playing hide and seek with reality. In "The Doorman," for example, Kramer invents the "bro," or as George Costanza's father, Frank Costanza wants to call it, "the manssiere," after seeing Frank's "man breasts."

Similarly, Frank tires of the commercialization of Christmas and Hanukkah and invents his own holiday, "Festivus" ("The Strike"). An emphasis merely on nothing could never create a gallery of eccentric characters—not only the main four, but also Newman, the Soup Nazi, and the Bubble Boy, to name a few—and bizarre situations—a woman who likes to wear her bra outside her sweater in public ("The Caddy"), George sleeping under his desk at work ("The Nap"), and the death of George's fiancée, Susan Ross, after she licks toxic glue on the cheap envelopes that George insisted they get for their wedding invitations ("The Invitation")—that leave such an indelible cultural mark.

Notwithstanding its bouts with absurdity, one of the series' outstanding features is its revelations about how single, urban Americans might live their lives. By pretending to pose questions—which we are meant to actually ponder—we see our contemporary mores disturbingly offered back to us. For example, after you've had sex with a woman, what is the proper way to end the relationship—on the phone? in person? We glimpse the attenuated lives of professional urbanites who have the freedom never to commit. We see the question reframed over and again. Is it possible for male and female friends to have sex without romantic involvement (what is now referred to as "friends with benefits")? We have watched throughout the life of the series as Jerry and Elaine try rather awkwardly and unsuccessfully multiple permutations of friend/lover/life partner, always giving up on something deeper ("The Deal").

None of Seinfeld's prescriptions are truly a guide for everyone or, for that matter, anyone, but they do point to the series' awareness of these contemporary social, emotional, and romantic dilemmas. Interestingly enough, even when Seinfeld is deepest in the throes of being about nothing, it often lets contemporary events and concerns peek through. For example, in the episode entitled "The Dinner Party," the gang of four—Jerry, Elaine, George, and Kramer—are invited to a dinner party. After totally dismissing George's idea about what to bring their hosts (he wants to get them a bottle of Pepsi and Ring Dings), Jerry and Elaine try to buy a fancy cake for their hosts. While in the bakery, Jerry decides to get one of his favorite treats, a black and white cookie. Jerry bombastically announces to Elaine that Americans could learn a lot from black and white cookies, since they taste so good together. Jerry even coins a slogan that he feels will benefit race relations: "look to the cookie." The irony is that the cookie upsets Jerry's stomach so much it ends his record of not vomiting for the past 14 years. Certainly, the episode is a commentary on Jerry's narcissism and his almost Howard Hughes–like fastidiousness, but it is also a not-so-subtle reminder of what seems like the intractability of race relations in America.

What has also been overlooked in this series that purports to be about nothing is that it frequently serves up brilliant satires on life and work in corporate America. Since neither Jerry nor Kramer have regular jobs, they really don't factor into this dramatically. But, George and Elaine both struggle with employment. George is the epitome of how to succeed

Figure 14.1. Jason Alexander as George Costanza, Jerry Seinfeld as himself, Michael Richards as Cosmo Kramer, and Julia Louis-Dreyfus as Elaine Benes in *Seinfeld*. 1990–1998. Photo courtesy of Larry Edmunds BooksFair.

in business without really trying. Initially, he is fired from job after job for, among other things, having sex with a cleaning woman after work ("The Red Dot"). After deciding to do things differently in his life (by doing the exact opposite of what his impulses tell him in "The Opposite"), he gets a job with the New York Yankees and begins to rise up the corporate ladder by gaining the affection of George Steinbrenner, whom the series portrays as a kind of dithering Mr. Magoo (in a bit of wily satire of the famously autocratic New York Yankees' owner, known only half affectionately as "The Boss"). After George is fired by the Yankees, he gains the affection and trust of the head of Kruger Industries, but unfortunately for George, his new boss happens to be equally averse to work. He thinks nothing of dumping all his work on George ("The Burning").

Similarly, Elaine, who is smarter ("The IQ Test") and far more sensitive in her dealings with people than George but equally capable of falling on her face professionally, has her share of job woes and eccentric bosses, including the very rich Mr. Pitt, who eats his candy bars with a knife and fork. Through all her various employment ups and downs, Elaine finally lands a job at J. Peterman Catalogue where she rises to be interim head of the company during his frequent absences. She also has to deal with his madcap adventures and ironic storylines, such as ghost writing his autobiography ("The Van Buren Boys"), his attempt to purchase at an auction the golf clubs once owned by President John F. Kennedy ("The Bottle Deposit"), and his unwitting consumption of his $29,000 dollar piece of wedding cake from the wedding of the Duke and Duchess of Windsor ("The Frogger").

There are more elemental themes in the series that provide evidence that it is about something. One of the most starkly revealing is the show's sometimes obsessive concerns about male sexuality, masculine maturity, and decidedly tongue-in-cheek concerns about masculine identity. For example, in the third season of the series, George is upset when "it" moves during a massage by a male masseuse ("The Note"). In the same season, Jerry finds himself behaving "like a woman" (waiting for a call, etc.) when he becomes friends with the all-star first baseman of the New York Mets, Keith Hernandez, and he becomes jealous when Hernandez starts dating Elaine ("The Boyfriend, Pts. 1 & 2"). In season four, Jerry and George are mistaken for a gay couple ("Not that there's anything wrong with that" in "The Outing"). For George, this anxiety about his sexuality survives his engagement to Susan, and after her death, he becomes terribly upset when it is pointed out to him that the woman he is currently dating looks exactly like Jerry ("The Cartoon"). Just as disturbing to Jerry and George is their fear that they aren't really men. Thus, in the seventh season, the pair makes a pact to change their lives, which prompts George to run out and become engaged to Susan Ross. Jerry just as promptly breaks their pact, but later he meets a woman, Jeannie, who is the female version of himself. After they become engaged he realizes he can't marry her, thereby revealing his presumed hatred for himself.

Raising the issue of homosexuality and the anxiety that some straight men might feel about it certainly fit in a decade in which the issue was being raised repeatedly on television and when more and more actors were coming out. In 1997, there was the groundbreaking moment when Ellen DeGeneres came out first on the Oprah Winfrey show and then on her sitcom. Interestingly enough, *Will & Grace*, which on occasion was referred to as "the gay *Seinfeld*," debuted in *Seinfeld's* final season. And, by *Seinfeld's* frequent reference to the issue, one might argue that the show paved the way for *Will & Grace*, a series that Vice President Joe Biden referred to in a May 2012 appearance on *Meet the Press* as a show that "did more to educate the American public than almost anything anybody has ever done so far."

The issue of male maturity and masculinity was also more than just nothing. It was an issue that was much on the minds of sociologists and historians during this era. With the decline of the self-made man and the gradual disappearance of the "other directed" male personality models of the 1950s, and especially with the Vietnam War and the rise of feminism in the 1960s and 1970s, the traditional guideposts to male maturity and masculinity seemed to have disappeared or were in disrepute. As a result, men were cast adrift and no longer had any certainty as to what constituted true masculinity and male maturity (Kimmel). For example, Jerry gets concerned about the appearance of masculinity when a woman he is dating orders a porterhouse steak at a restaurant, and he orders a salad ("The Wink"). Similarly, when Jerry has Elaine accompany him to buy a crested blazer and the salesman asks Elaine out, Jerry feels emasculated because the salesman presumes that he and Elaine are not dating ("The Wig Master").

Even marriage as a sign of male maturity is called into question on the series. Just as quickly as George and Jerry make a pact to become real men, George runs out and gets engaged to Susan. He immediately gets cold feet. When Jerry informs Kramer of the pact, Kramer inveighs against it as an infringement on a man's freedom—that marriage is a prison for a man. This impingement on his freedom ultimately takes its toll on George, making him reluctant to share his ATM pin number with Susan because he sees it as the last vestige of his individuality ("The Secret Code").

As significant as the issues of male sexuality and maturity are, there is one great enigma that hovers over the series (which also provides evidence that the show is hardly about nothing): its Jewishness. This probably arose when the late Brandon Tartikoff, then head of programming at NBC, initially proclaimed the series "too New York, too Jewish" (Mirzoeff 74). While there was no getting around its New York qualities, its Jewishness was hardly on display during the first years of the series. Of course, the series could not get away from the fact that Jerry Seinfeld's name was clearly a Jewish one; but, something of a mystery remained about George Costanza, whose father reveled in his Italian roots but whose mother was clearly Jewish, signified by her revulsion at German cars ("The Money") and by how upset she becomes when George tells her of his intention to convert to Latvian Orthodoxy after he falls in love with a woman of that faith ("The Conversion"). While there is no mystery about Elaine, she is clearly not Jewish, which is highlighted when the series explores her "shiksappeal"[2] in an episode in which she has to fend off the advances of a Bar Mitzvah boy, his father, and a rabbi ("The Serenity Now"). But, Kramer has remained a mystery. When the series was first proposed, his name was Kessler (Mirzoeff 76), but that was dropped for Kramer. Even Kramer's first name "Cosmo" (hardly a Jewish name) is a secret until well into the sixth season ("The Switch").

Initially, the issue of Jewishness is approached rather indirectly on *Seinfeld*. Thus, in the episode "The Pony Remark," in the first full season of the series, Jerry is forced by his parents to attend a dinner with a cousin named Manya, who is celebrating her 50th wedding anniversary. At the dinner party, Jerry does a routine about hating people who have ponies. Manya indignantly replies that she had a pony when she was young and is extremely upset by Jerry's remarks. She falls into a rapid decline and dies, and Jerry is haunted by guilt. He feels cursed by Manya's spirit when he makes a number of errors during his softball championship game. Certainly, there is no evidence in this of a great deal of Jewish content, but there are enough indirect hints to make us suspect that Manya is Jewish and a Holocaust survivor. There are several hints about her identity: her name, which was often associated with Polish Jews; that she grew up near Krakow, one of the largest towns in Poland near Auschwitz-Birkenau; and, that she and her husband were married in 1941 during World War II. Of course, none of this is conclusive evidence, but it nevertheless gives some sense of the possibility of her being Jewish.

Not content to leave this issue vague, the series proceeds to fill in the blanks. One issue that stands out in the show as a means of doing this is its evocation of the Holocaust. Needless to say, for American Jewry, reverence for and remembrance of the Holocaust is one of the central pillars of contemporary Jewish identity (Bergmann and Jucovy). In *Seinfeld*, the

Holocaust is dealt with irreverently. For instance, when Jerry dates a Jewish woman named Rachel Goldstein (the only identifiably Jewish woman among his long roster of girlfriends), they have no place to go to make out because Jerry's parents are staying with him in his apartment, and Rachel lives at home with her father, who is a rabbi. Then, when Jerry's parents insist that he go and see *Schindler's List* (1993), he and Rachel are caught making out during the movie by Jerry's arch enemy, Newman, who tells the appalled Seinfelds. Jerry's anger at his dentist, Tim Whatley, for converting to Judaism, not on principle but because he wants to be able to tell Jewish jokes, is also significant. Jerry's anger prompts Kramer to dub Jerry an "anti-dentite" ("The Yada, Yada"). But, the *piece de resistance,* clarifying *Seinfeld's* Jewish identity, is the episode called "The Bris."

In this episode, Jerry and Elaine are invited to be the godparents at a friend's son's *bris* (the Jewish rite of circumcision). Among other misadventures at the ceremony, the *Mohel* (the person who performs ritual Jewish circumcisions) turns out to be a nervous wreck and cuts Jerry's finger, George faints at the sight of the blood, and Kramer tries to steal the baby because he considers circumcision to be a "barbaric" custom. In the final moments of the episode, the couple, whose child has somehow survived all of this unscathed, comes to Jerry's apartment and revokes his status as godfather and gratefully confers it on Kramer.

It is episodes like this one that help establish *Seinfeld's* Jewish identification. They also lend substance to our understanding of Jerry as a secular and cultural Jew with tangential knowledge of Jewish traditions and rituals. One thing, however, that the series rarely mentions is another central pillar of American Jewish identity: Israel. Indeed, any references to Israel are fleeting. Thus, in "The Cigar Store Indian," George is embarrassed to ask an Asian letter carrier for directions to the nearest Chinese restaurant, and Jerry scoffs that he never gets embarrassed when anyone asks him directions to Israel. But, perhaps the key element in *Seinfeld's* Jewish identification is neither intertextual references, an irreverent attitude toward the Holocaust, or even some awareness of Jewish ritual and custom. It is the series' disregard for common civility and its purposeful, anti-puritanical exposé of issues such as masturbation ("The Contest"), nose-picking ("The Pick"), and anxieties about homosexuality ("The Outing"), which confers an outsider status on the major characters that has always been a hallmark of Jewishness.

In a series that was supposed to be about nothing, there are more than a few flirtations with political subjects. For instance, in its second full season, Jerry and George are on their way home from the airport in a limo that they have commandeered by passing themselves off as the person the limo driver is supposed to pick up. They are shocked, and almost lynched by a mob outside Madison Square Garden, after they find out that the limo they had appropriated was supposed to be carrying a neo-Nazi leader ("The Limo"). The major political issue that *Seinfeld* gleefully deals with most often, however, is political correctness. For example, Elaine goes to great lengths to find out if the man she is dating, who has some African American features, is actually African American and is greatly upset to find out he is not ("The Wizard"). When Kramer agrees to take part in a walkathon in support of AIDS victims but refuses to wear an AIDS ribbon, he is beaten up by a pair of gay thugs ("The Sponge"). And, in an episode that prompted a network apology, Kramer stomps on a Puerto Rican flag that catches on fire during the Puerto-Rican day parade ("The Puerto-Rican Day Parade").

The irony of *Seinfeld* purportedly being about nothing is that the series had the latitude to be about anything it wanted to address. So, for instance, the series delves into the manners and mores of the modern urban singles scene. It looks with a satirical eye at the world of contemporary corporate life. More significantly, it ventures into issues of male sexuality and maturity that are prominent in the lives of American men. It also, though somewhat hesitantly, looks at the influence of ethnicity and religion on the lives of its major characters. It even raises political issues. In fact, being about nothing is an advantage for the series, since it raises no political and social expectations, and the series could go wherever the imagination of its creators decided to take it.

But, who among us can argue against being about nothing? Who among us hasn't been annoyed when there is no cream for our coffee in the morning or when there is a surly service person waiting on us in a store where we shop? Who among us can't say that we haven't been frustrated when we can't find a parking space or the couple in front of us talks continuously during a movie? The quotidian is just that and probably unleashes more personal emotion on a daily basis than the biggest political issues of the time. In that way, we are all *Seinfeld* characters, and while one might dispute whether or not it is the greatest of all sitcoms, the source of *Seinfeld's* greatest strength is that we recognize so much of our daily lives, our problems, and ourselves in it.

NOTES

1. The producers and writers of the series did homage to Pinter in their final season with an episode called *The Betrayal* that used Pinter's format of his play

with the same name. It started with the final scene and goes back in subsequent scenes to the beginning.

2. "Shiksa" is the Yiddish word for a young gentile woman. See Leo Rosten, *The Joys of Yiddish*, 346.

15

Cybill

Privileging Liberal Feminism in Daily Sitcom Life

LAURA R. LINDER AND MARY M. DALTON

On January 2, 1995, CBS launched *Cybill,* an overtly feminist situation comedy, named for its star, Cybill Shepherd. Although cancelled in 1998, *Cybill* provides an important case study of a socially relevant sitcom in terms of Shepherd's creative control on both sides of the camera and the program's integration of autobiography, entertainment, and politics.[1] Shepherd and the writers of *Cybill* use the familiar sitcom format to articulate a discourse of liberal feminism in virtually every episode and routinely integrate women's liberation into plotlines based on everyday life. The familiar, even comforting, sitcom format provides a stable foundation for overtly political storylines.

Here we analyze the ways in which the television situation comedy *Cybill* privileges liberal feminism. This process is informed by Shepherd's lived experience and privileges liberal feminism by foregrounding this ideology in the series and integrating it into the everyday life of the eponymous character. Multiple viewings of all of the series' episodes reveal five general but overlapping categories in which discourses of liberal feminism occur consistently: work, culture/politics, dating/romance, friendship, and motherhood. We find meaning from the discursive categories of liberal feminism within the sitcom and in the relationship between the text and the larger culture.

In the series, Shepherd plays a middle-aged actress, Cybill Sheridan, who never made the "A list," despite working steadily in roles ranging from hookers to perfect mothers and from cops to killers. The constant is not the types of roles but the fact that Sheridan continually questions them and the system that perpetuates the stereotypes. Sheridan has two whiny daughters, two lingering ex-husbands, and an outrageous, wealthy best friend. These personal relationships offer opportunities to explore and critique the societal roles assigned to women in a gendered society. *Cybill* chronicles different stages of motherhood and is one of the few television series up to that time that explores the dynamics of post-divorce relationships.[2] Moreover, the sitcom portrays middle-aged women as sexual beings who are not necessarily looking for husbands. In these private contexts of personal relationships as well as the very public context of the main character's work in the entertainment industry, *Cybill* challenges tacit assumptions about the cultural mores of middle-class American life in the late twentieth century.

Cybill is a prime example of a program that satisfies the conventional criteria of the sitcom format as it manages to reflect, comment on, and influence shifting social values by means of a sophisticated, explicit, and self-reflexive discourse of liberal feminism. From her position as a Hollywood star, political activist, and single working mother over 40, Cybill Shepherd consciously used her life to inform the construction of her television alter-ego Cybill Sheridan and to advance storylines that directly engage gender issues and promote the liberation and equality of women in public and private life.[3]

Liberal feminism, radical feminism, Marxist feminism, eco-feminism, womanism, and Third Wave feminism are some of the categories employed to describe strands of discourse and modes of political action dedicated to advancing the rights of women. Some of the terms are fluid with significant overlap among categories. Rather than explore the history and various applications of these terms, we define liberal feminism as a theoretical perspective that advocates for women working within the existing social, political, and economic system to advance their status by establishing rights and opportunities for women equal to those of men. Cybill Sheridan would rather become part of the existing infrastructure than demolish the dominant system. Her protests are related to gender bias instead of race discrimination, heterosexism, unequal distribution of wealth, or other types of injustice. This is not to suggest that Sheridan is *against* righting any of these other wrongs but rather that her political project is more narrowly defined. She makes her critique ubiquitous, applying it to all of the relevant contexts of everyday life found in the sitcom.

Figure 15.1. (clockwise from left) Christine Baranski as Maryann Thorpe, Dedee Pfeiffer as Rachel Blanders, Alan Rosenberg as Ira Woodbine, Alicia Witt as Zoey Woodbine, and Cybill Shepherd as Cybill Sheridan in *Cybill*. 1995–1998. Photo courtesy of Photofest.

LIBERAL FEMINISM AND *CYBILL*

There are obvious similarities between *Cybill* and other sitcoms built around strong women, but one significant difference sets it apart: the ubiquity and overtness of its political content. The most surprising way in which *Cybill* makes points about gender inequality is through Sheridan's critiques of the very system in which she performs—the entertainment industry. During the run of the sitcom, Sheridan encounters directors who sexually harass her, executives who are mercurial or make stupid decisions, and casting and costuming disasters. Furthermore, the critique advanced in the show is based on Shepherd's own experience and is not benign.[4]

Cybill Shepherd and the other producers of *Cybill* manage to portray both how far women have come and how great the distance remains for women to achieve parity with men. Narrative strategies for critiquing the status of women include addressing feminist topics in major storylines and sprinkling pointed one-liners throughout individual episodes. The examples are many, and they often cut across the social contexts identified as major sites for privileging liberal feminism in everyday life. For the character Cybill Sheridan, this involves independence and accountability in her personal relationships and parity with men in her work relationships.

WOMEN AND WORK

Cybill Sheridan is a working mother. Every episode of the show begins with a vignette featuring Cybill at work playing one role or another in commercials, low-budget movies, or tacky television series. These scenes precede the title sequence of the program, and most of them depict Cybill in a role that is demeaning to her, specifically, or generally demeaning to women. In one illustrative example from "Sex, Drugs, Catholicism," the actress is dressed as a centaur and complains, "It's not the costume, it's the dialogue. Listen to this. 'Mount me Hercules and ride me all night.' I can't say that. It's degrading to women." This was risqué dialogue in the mid-1990s, but it is tempered by the stagehand's reply: "Honey, have you seen the show? It's degrading to everyone." This punchline gets the laugh, blunting the force of the feminist line to make the message more palatable, but the subtext— that women are regularly cast in roles that degrade them—remains intact.

Workplace equity is an insistent concern on *Cybill*. In a story arc crossing the episodes "Going to Hell in a Limo 1 & 2," Cybill lands the lead in a fictional television series, *Lifeforms*. When her male co-star begins sleeping with the producer, Cybill finds her role diminished to the point where only her legs and breasts are seen. In one episode, her character is locked in a trunk from beginning to end. She struggles to get her role restored to its original importance, only to see the show cancelled. There are other examples in *Cybill* that parallel Shepherd's own career trajectory and her dissatisfaction with the roles offered to her. Referring to the period between *Moonlighting* and *Cybill*, she writes, "I spent several years doing projects of no particular consequence, playing a collection of wives, nurses, bitches, and sociopaths" (233). Similarly, Sheridan reacts to the paucity of challenging roles. Cast as the superficial sitcom mom in *Earthquake*, she quits because she finds the role too shallow. For Shepherd, it is a scenario of art imitating life.

Although themes related to feminism and the workplace are readily apparent in the majority of *Cybill* episodes, two shows stand out for their explicit articulation of liberal feminist points of view. In "As the World Turns to Crap," Cybill learns that the survival of her role in a soap opera depends on an imminent decision by the producer. Cybill invites the producer, Barry, to her house for dinner to make the case for her character.

CYBILL: Come with me.

BARRY: It's about time. We going upstairs?

CYBILL: We were never going upstairs.

BARRY: You're throwing me out? Interesting career move.

CYBILL: Barry, if you want to keep the best actress, give me a call. If you don't, don't. Either way, I will not compromise my integrity. Plus, if your new soap opera goes—I'd make a terrific lesbian.

This punchline gets her out of a jam because the way the actress delivers the line leaves the producer thinking she's gay—getting a laugh while making (and mitigating) a point. Women are expected to sleep with the boss to get or keep a job, but Cybill takes a stand and refuses. She ends up losing the job but retaining her dignity, offering a powerful role model to viewers. This situation demonstrates a difficult choice women often have to make and valorizes Cybill's choice as the right one.[5]

In a later episode, "Cybill Sheridan's Day Off," Cybill is once again confronted with this dilemma: sleep with the boss or lose the job. George, the director of the movie she's starring in, stops by her house to "discuss script changes." After she introduces him to her best friend, Maryann, as "the nicest man in Hollywood," George flatters Cybill by saying she is a star. The director tries to get Cybill to sleep with him because he cast her in his movie.

CYBILL: Well, then . . . I don't guess I have much choice.

(She walks over to him, runs her fingers through his hair, grabs a handful of hair, and flings his head into the door.)

GEORGE: What are you doing?!

CYBILL: Foreplay!

(Cybill throws the director out the door and wipes her hands to audience applause.)

Rather than fire Cybill, the director punishes her by taking away her dressing room, her wardrobe, and her lines after recasting her as a skydiver with a defective parachute. Cybill eventually gets her revenge, but the use of humor here and elsewhere effectively diminishes any radical threat to the dominant culture while still highlighting injustice and suggesting progressive changes, an approach that is consistent with the aims of liberal feminism.

CULTURAL AND POLITICAL LESSONS

Cybill challenges the female status quo culturally and politically. Not only does the sitcom educate us about how women should be treated in an equitable society, it illustrates the advantages of a progressive feminist stance. Although there are many examples in the series, several stand out as exemplars. In "From Boca, With Love," Cybill ignores the women's guidebook, *The Rules*,[6] and calls a man for a date. In "Sex, Drugs, and Catholicism," she "goes ballistic" when her ex-husband Ira's new girlfriend tells Cybill and Ira's daughter, Zoey, to play dumb to get a guy. In "Bakersfield," she advises her niece, Claire, to ignore the media's unrealistic physical portrayal of women as too thin and too perfect. Through role reversals designed to foreground sexist behavior, Cybill and Maryann spend an afternoon ogling a contractor in "Show Me the Minnie"; Maryann buys her boyfriend a suit in "Bringing Home the Bacon; in "Don Gianni," Cybill tells her age and weight on a talk show, horrifying the female host. In the first three episodes above, Cybill and her best friend challenge viewers' tacit assumptions about gender roles by fighting conventional constructions of femininity and, in the second three examples, by co-opting stereotypical male patterns of behavior.

Another way conventional codes are challenged is through demystifying elements of womanhood that have traditionally denoted gender difference. Cybill and Maryann use humor to openly discuss a formerly taboo topic in "When You're Hot, You're Hot," one of two episodes dealing specifically with menopause.

CYBILL: I've been reading about this pre-menopause and there's a bunch of herbs that are supposed to help. (Dumping lots of bottles on the table.) I've got teas, tinctures, infusions. Yellow doc. I think that's for hot flashes. Skullcap is for sleeplessness.

MARYANN: (Picking up a bottle.) St. John's Wort. You know you can have these burned right off. Cybill, why are you being so medieval? Just take hormones. Think of them as one of the perks of living in the twentieth century, like insulin, tanning beds, personal shoppers.

CYBILL: But, I want to try the natural approach. Oat straw tea, dandelion root, black cohosh for sensitive breasts. Wait a minute, I don't even have that yet. Oh, this is too confusing. I need someone to tell me how to mix this. I don't want to get it wrong and start growing grass on my back.

MARYANN: When you say you're pre-menopausal, does that mean your "friend" has stopped visiting every month?

CYBILL: My "friend?" What are you—twelve?

MARYANN: You know what I mean. Aunt Flo? (Winks.)

CYBILL: (Laughing.) Just say it out: period, period, period.

WAITER: (Overhearing.) Fresh ground Valium? Say when.

CYBILL: Sometimes my period is regular; sometimes I skip a month. But lately, I've been spotting a lot.

WAITER: When!

CYBILL: I know there are a lot of people who are really uncomfortable talking about this, but I tell you one thing, Maryann. No way am I becoming invisible when the wolf whistles stop. I am going to become one loud, brassy, in-your-face menopausal mama!

This was explicit dialogue for network television in the mid-1990s, a period when the topic of menopause was seldom discussed in popular entertainment.[7]

As this scene illustrates, *Cybill* isn't afraid to take on cultural and political taboos, but the entertainment industry executives overseeing the program were not similarly disposed. As Shepherd notes in her autobiography, she tried to demystify female anatomy and bodily functions like menopause and menstruation on her show but received considerable resistance from the network (261–62). By naming that which is seldom acknowledged with openness and humor, *Cybill* marks an auspicious beginning of a demystification process of women and their biological functions—a necessary process in the pursuit of gender equity. Critics might suggest that an episode about menopause still identifies women primarily with their bodies (in this case a body out of control) with the result of sustaining the status quo. We take the opposing view that openly claiming this experience normalizes a natural biological function and eliminates another way of marginalizing women by liberating them from "suffering in silence."

In "All of Me," an episode that epitomizes the series' ability to cut across the contexts of work, culture/politics, and friendship, Cybill is hired to model fashion high-top sneakers for a billboard marketed to 40-something women. When Cybill and Maryann see the billboard, they notice that Cybill's head has been superimposed onto a skinny woman's body. She goes to confront the shoe company representative, Ms. Murphy.

> CYBILL: I saw the billboard. Why did you hire me if you weren't going to use my body? You told me I was what you were looking for.
>
> Ms. MURPHY: Oh, but you are. When we saw your picture in "Fashion Nightmares" in the Hollywood Globe all decked out in your black evening gown and day-glo orange high tops, we thought, "Now there's a woman who says, I don't care what anyone thinks." It's no big deal. We just shaved off a few pounds.[8]
>
> CYBILL: Why? You think only skinny people buy shoes?
>
> Ms. MURPHY: No, but people will buy these shoes because they want to look like the woman on the billboard.
>
> CYBILL: She doesn't exist! She's my head on a stick!
>
> Ms. MURPHY: You just can't get off that, can you?

CYBILL: Oh, I don't know. I just happen to think that my head goes really good with this body. For 46 years it hasn't fallen off once!

Cybill and Maryann redraw Cybill's body on the billboard to add curves in an attempt to combat size-ism. Cybill is let go from the campaign for her objection to having her image altered and for defacing the billboard. The fact that the executive calling the shots is a woman reinforces the idea that women are often complicit in their own oppression, and this episode represents a direct assault on the cultural and political paradigm that says women need to be thin to be beautiful and, by extension, that women are just objects to be manipulated for the pleasure and commercial purposes of others.[9]

These examples challenge the sexism and ageism rampant in society. The scripted situations promote liberal feminism by investing women with the opportunity to voice their needs while modeling ways for them to become part of the dominant system on their own terms. In many cases, the punchline seems to return things to the status quo, but it is not uncontested territory. In all cases, the challenge is articulated and leaves Cybill steadfast in her support of liberal feminism.

DATING AND ROMANCE

In the area of dating and romance, *Cybill* portrays women who are smart, in control, and not dependent on men. Although Cybill and Maryann would like to have boyfriends, they are not driven to acquire them at any cost. Cybill's older daughter, Rachel, has the most traditionally constructed gender role on the show. She is married, has two children during the course of the series, and is defined almost entirely in the context of those relationships. Cybill's younger daughter, Zoey, is as independent and strong as her mother. Maryann evolves over the course of the show from a woman whose identity is tied to her ex-husband to become an autonomous person. The main theme of the series in this area is that women are complete without men (even though men are fun), and women should be able to have the same rights as men when it comes to relationships. In "Going Out With a Bang," Cybill has sex with a hunky cable guy purely for the physical pleasure, which calls attention to the traditional double standard that encourages men to act on their sexuality and women to demur. Conventional boundaries of courtship and marriage are continually challenged by the men Cybill dates (or doesn't), by her ongoing friendships with her ex-husbands, and by her attitudes and actions toward all of the men she encounters.

In the first scene of the first episode, "Virgin, Mother, Crone," Cybill is stuck in a traffic jam on the freeway in her 1964 red convertible, and an attractive man, Teddy, pulls up next to her.

TEDDY: Hey, that's an old beauty.

CYBILL: Thanks. (Pause.) You mean the car, right?

TEDDY: (Laughs.) What is that? A '64?

CYBILL: Yep. Original interior, push-button tranny, and a slant-six engine that'll never die.

TEDDY: I think I'm in love.

CYBILL: It's not for sale.

TEDDY: I wasn't talking about the car.

CYBILL: Still no sale.

TEDDY: My name's Teddy.

CYBILL: Cybill.

TEDDY: Would you like to have dinner tonight, Cybill?

CYBILL: Sorry. I only date guys from the car pool lane.

TEDDY: Did I mention I love animals?

CYBILL: Oh, in that case, give me your phone number.

TEDDY: You want *my* phone number?

CYBILL: What? Now you're playing hard to get?

TEDDY: Here. Call me.

CYBILL: Maybe.

In this scene, Cybill levels the playing field with men. She is knowledgeable about cars. She asks an attractive man for his phone number. Conversely, Teddy tries to show his "feminine side" by saying he loves animals. Establishing a level playing field is a central goal of liberal feminism, and *Cybill* works toward this goal in almost every episode.

In "The Cheese Stands Alone," Cybill begins dating her second ex-husband, Ira. They are both achieving some success in their respective careers: she has a guest role in a sitcom, and his novel is being made into a movie. Ira wants Cybill to go with him to London, but she is offered several more episodes on the sitcom and thinks the role could be expanded into a regular character. Ira wants her to give up the role to come with him, but Cybill says she has to work.

> CYBILL: I'm an actor. I need to work. And, how come your career is more important than mine? Because you're a man?
>
> IRA: You know what the problem is Cybill? You're jealous of my success.
>
> CYBILL: Of course I'm jealous! You're making a feature film with Anthony Hopkins, and I'm in a stupid sitcom with a mouse! But that's not the reason I'm not going to London. I'm not going to London because I have a career of my own—as banal though it may be—and even if I didn't have it, I wouldn't go anywhere with an arrogant windbag who has so little respect for me or what I do.
>
> (She walks out, slamming the door.)

Cybill recounts an earlier time when she gave up a job for her partner, but this time she refuses to make that mistake again. She and Ira break up but remain friends. Once again, *Cybill* integrates the categories of work and romance the way they're integrated in life, and the sitcom successfully privileges the ideals of liberal feminism. In this relationship, the partners are equals despite the relative success of one over the other in the world of work.

A FOUNDATION OF FRIENDSHIP

Cybill explores the role of friendship in many episodes, and Cybill's primary friend in the series is Maryann. They are unlikely friends, perhaps, because Maryann's *haute couture* designs and apparent self-absorption contrast starkly with Cybill's pragmatic approach to clothing and concern for family and larger social issues. In practice, however, Maryann is the perfect foil for Cybill. They forge ahead together, directing viewer attention to gender inequality while striking a perfect balance with their unfailing and mutual friendship.

In "Wedding Bell Blues," Cybill helps Maryann sabotage her ex-husband's wedding. Maryann is invited to the wedding and decides to take Cybill as her guest, but the invitation leads them to a hot dog stand instead of the wedding. Maryann vows revenge, and Cybill agrees to help. They have hot dogs, French fries, and sodas—not the stereotypical food for an actress and a socialite, which puts the pair on equal footing with glutinous sitcom male characters—as they plan to disrupt the wedding. After finding the wedding, all their attempts at sabotage backfire: spiking the pâté with habanero peppers, planting a stink bomb, and turning on the sprinkler system. They only succeed in humiliating themselves. After the ceremony, Maryann offers her congratulations to the bride and walks away—dejected and defeated. Cybill joins her friend at the bar.

> CYBILL: May I have this dance?

> MARYANN: Thanks, pal, but I'm not very good company right now.

> CYBILL: Come on, Ginger. Let's show these kids how it's done.

> (Cybill walks Maryann to the dance floor. They dance. Maryann has her head on Cybill's shoulder.)

> MARYANN: It's over. There's a new Mrs. Richard Thorpe.

> CYBILL: Look at the bright side. You still have his money.

> MARYANN: Oh, money can't buy happiness.

> CYBILL: Yeah, but only rich people get to say that.

> MARYANN: You know why I've spent the last three years tormenting Richard? 'Cause when he walked out on me, he took away

the only identity I ever had. Now he's given it to somebody else. (Crying.)

CYBILL: Maryann, you didn't even start to get interesting until you lost that identity. You are a funny, intelligent, highly dangerous woman.

MARYANN: What I am is a lonely, immature prankster. And look at me. What we did here was the ultimate in childishness.

CYBILL: Well, almost.

MARYANN: What's with the helicopters?

CYBILL: For some reason, the press seems to think that Madonna is marrying Peter Jennings here today.

(Wind gusts from the helicopters cause havoc.)

MARYANN: (Shouting.) Cybill, you always know just what to get me.

CYBILL: Aw. You're easy to shop for.

MARYANN: Cybill, that was perfect.

Cybill rarely tries to talk Maryann out of her harebrained schemes, and she almost always supports her. Maryann, whose identity has been defined by her relationship with her husband, eventually comes into her own through her bond with Cybill. Their friendship allows them to support one another as they tackle personal and political issues. Maryann also functions as someone for Cybill to "educate" about feminist issues. Cybill tries to convince her friend that she is a strong woman, and over time, Maryann adopts a mainstream feminist perspective on the series that complements Cybill's ideology.

MOTHERHOOD

Cybill challenges our assumptions about motherhood in many ways. She talks about sex openly and comfortably; she becomes a grandmother without relinquishing her own sexuality; and, she freely discusses the role of mothers in society. Although liberal feminism advocates for rights and opportunities for women equal to those of men, the challenge in the area of parenting is to engage men more fully in parenting, and Cybill encourages Jeff (her first husband and Rachel's father) and Ira to be involved parents. Since Rachel is out on her own and Zoey is very nearly an adult, the series focuses more on Cybill's relationship with her daughters than on joint-parenting issues. As one might expect, the centrality of Sheridan's role as a mother reflects the importance of motherhood in Shepherd's personal life. Shepherd proves that the personal is political. She has adapted her private life into an overtly political television program, and the discourse of liberal feminism that runs through the series situates Shepherd and her character, Sheridan, into contexts that privilege this discourse.[10] The role of motherhood is highlighted in a number of episodes. In "Cybill Does Diary," Zoey's first sexual experience becomes part of the dominant storyline, and Cybill's concern and honest advice are emphasized. Rather than subscribe to traditional gender roles that penalize female sexuality, Cybill wants her daughters to have agency to act on their sexual desires. Cybill might embarrass her daughters with regularity on the sitcom, but she is always present and involved, modeling independence, responsibility, and commitment to feminist practice.

In "Mother's Day," one of the episodes most directly focused on the issue of motherhood and liberal feminism, Cybill and her mother have a discussion about motherhood. Her mother hears Cybill vehemently assert that she is nothing like her mother (even though everyone around her sees the similarities). After avoiding the issue all week, Cybill and her mother, Virginia, stand by an airline ticket counter as her mother prepares to catch a flight home to Tennessee.

CYBILL: You're not getting on an airplane until we talk.

MOTHER: Cybill, you're making me angry.

CYBILL: Good. I want to see what that looks like. Cut the *Steel Magnolias* crap. Let's duke it out.

MOTHER: Fine. You don't want to be like me. Well, I didn't want to be like me either, but my mom didn't give me any choice. "A lady doesn't raise her voice, Virginia, or work outside the home, Virginia, or get a divorce, Virginia." So I stayed in a miserable marriage until I got lucky, and he divorced me.

CYBILL: Lucky? You were devastated when Daddy left you.

MOTHER: My mother was devastated. I was relieved. You have a career, and you have your freedom. You have a life. I envy that. But I'm proud of it, too. Do you remember what I said to you when you said you wanted to pursue a modeling career in New York?

CYBILL: Yes. You said if I felt like I had to do it, then I should do it. And always put newspaper on the subway seats.

MOTHER: I let you have your choices, Cybill. And, if your daughters turn out half as good as you did, well, maybe it's because you're just a little bit like me.

CYBILL: Wow. That was great Mama. Next time, let's not wait so long to fight with each other.

MOTHER: You're right. I'll call you from the plane.

CYBILL: Happy Mother's Day, Mom.

Cybill Sheridan's mother allowed her daughter choices and the power that goes along with them, even though her upbringing and the proscriptions of the larger culture kept the older woman on a traditional path, and Cybill is extending that gift to her daughters by letting them make their own decisions and to learn from the consequences of what they choose. Of course, Cybill is always there to offer advice, help, and love, but the ultimate choices are theirs; this is a lesson Cybill has learned from her own mother, even if the realization and appreciation of her mother's gift comes long after the fact for Cybill.

CONCLUSION

Fans laugh at Cybill and her family and friends as they watch the series, but viewers also learn strategies for identifying problems in their own lives and working toward solutions by watching Shepherd's television alter-ego in situations that may be loosely or directly analogous to situations in their own lives. Cybill negotiates the public and private spaces of her life with confidence, humor, and a fixed commitment to advancing the cause of women's equality amid the sexism (and related "isms") of the dominant culture. She provides a model for viewers who may or may not embrace the term "feminist" but who fit the definition through their support for the principles of basic fairness and the advancement of social justice.

Liberal feminism is about equality with women securing the same power, opportunities, and choices that men have while accepting the responsibility that goes along with that power. These are not radical precepts, but they are progressive, and the foregrounding of them so centrally into the situational humor of this series is unmatched on any other sitcom with a successful run on network television. Some critics may find these precepts less relevant after embracing postfeminist discourses and "sexcoms,"[11] such as *Sex and the City*. Our viewing of that series suggests that this brand of post-feminism is conflated with consumerism, including a presentation of sexual agency for its own sake absent a larger critical context. Liberal feminism, as we have defined it here, does not offer a panacea for all social ills, but we find that liberal feminism's focus on working toward social justice in a larger cultural context is more promising than many postfeminist discourses, including that articulated in *Sex and the City*, which focuses on individual empowerment through choice and consumption—from sex to shoes.

Of course, Cybill Sheridan enjoys sex and shopping as well, but her purview is more expansive and overtly political than almost all the sitcom women who preceded her and most who have followed. Her intelligence, fearlessness, and even her disobedience lead her to confront the industry that constructs women stars on screens large and small and to point out the deep and ubiquitous sexism of the entertainment industry. *Cybill* advances the discourse of liberal feminism with a seamless integration of the public and private through storylines that include five identifiable discursive categories. In doing so, this sitcom has broken new ground in exploring the landscape of politics and gender in everyday life while pursuing a well-considered, progressive, and explicitly political agenda.

NOTES

1. Although not in syndication at the time of this writing, *Cybill's* 87 episodes are available on Hulu Plus, and DVDs are available through various sources.

2. Since then, other shows have broached this subject, most notably *Cougartown*, *Modern Family*, *Mom*, and *The Millers*.

3. In her memoir, Shepherd describes the character as having a "feminist perspective" (256) based on Shepherd's own life experience (244), and she acknowledges that she provided notes on every script before it went into production (246).

4. In her memoir, Shepherd writes, "I know this: in a company town, I have never been a company girl. I am too blunt and forthright. I will make noise and take chances. All my life I've been diving off cliffs with wings that I had no

assurance would keep me aloft, and I've crashed any number of times" (285). It is important to read her memoir critically as a document providing insight into Shepherd's construction of her own identity. When the series was cancelled, Shepherd notes that "*Cybill* was CBS's highest-rated sitcom for women, number two for young adults, and we finished under budget" (279). Shepherd did not go quietly into syndication (in either *Moonlighting* or *Cybill*), as the criticisms of those involved in straitjacketing her both onscreen and behind the scenes found out with the publication of her aptly titled memoir, *Cybill Disobedience: How I Survived Beauty Pageants, Elvis, Sex, Bruce Willis, Lies, Marriage, Motherhood, Hollywood, and the Irrepressible Urge to Say What I Think.*

5. Cybill plays the "gay card" as a bluff, and even though LGBT liberation is never a central political issue for Cybill, the character's comfort with this pretense has the effect of normalizing lesbianism in the context of the show. In her memoir, Cybill Shepherd recounts participating in rallies supporting LGBT rights (214). And, in her most recent recurring prime-time role, Shepherd appears in *The L-Word* as a married woman with two teenagers who comes out as a lesbian. This role originated on the Showtime series for the 2006–07 season, and Shepherd continued in the role in seasons five and six.

6. *The Rules: Time-Tested Secrets for Capturing the Heart of Mr. Right* by Ellen Fein and Sherrie Schneider, first published in 1995, became a bestseller by telling women that to "get" a man, a woman needs to "play hard to get."

7. Other series, such as *All in the Family* and *Maude,* had broadcast episodes with storylines related to menopause, but such instances are rare, and those episodes are not as candid as *Cybill.*

8. This incident recalls the time when Shepherd wore high-top sneakers with her black evening gown to the 1988 Emmy Awards ceremony (see J.C. O'Connor) and at least one event from Shepherd's memoir. The trip cited below was to promote the short-lived series *The Yellow Rose,* which preceded her starring role in *Moonlighting.*

9. "Sam Elliott and I were asked to come to New York to take part in the network's announcement of fall programming. But, when we went to meet the producers for lunch at the "21" Club, I was refused admittance because I was wearing running shoes, a New Balance model that cost $150. I went down the street and paid $11 for black rubber flats, then made a grand show of sitting in the restaurant's reception area to change, daintily doing a striptease with my socks. No sneakers allowed? *Watch me*" (191). This is another instance of the similar experiences linking Shepherd's lived experience and Sheridan's scripted situations.

10. In her autobiography, Shepherd writes: "I had the temerity to become a grandmother on American television, one experience not replicated in real life, but when my character cooed to her TV daughter, 'And you even got married first!' it was a mocking reference to my own pregnancies before marriage" (7).

11. Christine Scodari has used this term to describe *Ally McBeal* and *Sex and the City,* shows that "deal almost exclusively with the feminine, private-sphere issues surrounding sexual and/or romantic relationships" (Sex and the Sitcom).

16

Talking Sex

Comparison Shopping through
Female Conversation in HBO's *Sex and the City*

SHARON MARIE ROSS

"I know where my next orgasm is coming from. Who here can say that?"

—Miranda, "The Rabbit," *Sex and the City*

Mariana Valverde expresses her frustration with mainstream cultural representations of women's sexual desire when she describes them as part of a "slippery slope," whereby giving a woman an inch of sexual agency will result in her taking a mile (150). Noting that women's sexual desires have been linked historically to a desire for consumable goods, and that such compounded desire has also been seen as social illness in the form of decadence, Valverde argues that "it is consumerism [not erotic desire] which constructs our desire as limitless" (152). As a feminist, I wonder why "limitless desire" is problematic—however it might be constructed. The implication seems to be that a desire that has no end is somehow uncontrollable and ultimately self-destructive, and while this is often the direction that sexually active female characters in media "take," I believe that this is a patriarchal construction working to assuage fears of female power in society. A representation of sexual desire as limitless does not have to be framed in this manner; to position female sexual desire as preferably finite and comprehensible is incompatible with many of the goals of feminism as a political movement.

The HBO comedy series *Sex and the City* speaks to this concern, offering a direct examination of female sexual desire and its connection to other desires. The show elucidates women's desires through three motifs: women discussing with other women sexuality and their own sexual actions, women discussing with other women gender roles in modern-day society, and women discussing with other women their consumption of material goods.

Sex and the City was HBO's first attempt to niche market to an adult female audience, according to Chris Albrecht, President of Original Programming and Independent Production (Higgins 54). In this essay, I focus on how *Sex and the City* works to situate female sexual desire and agency along a spectrum of choice—a spectrum that demands "comparison shopping" and "informed decisions." The show also works to present restrictions

Figure 16.1. (clockwise from left) Cynthia Nixon as Miranda Hobbs, Kristin Davis as Charlotte York, Kim Cattrall as Samantha Jones, and Sarah Jessica Parker as Carrie Bradshaw in *Sex and the City*, 1998–2004. Photo courtesy of Larry Edmunds BooksFair.

on decision making about sexuality and interpersonal relations active in a capitalistic and patriarchal society, and suggests that female friendship is a potential site of resistance to such restrictions. I focus primarily, however, on the connections between consumerism and female sexual desire as the show frames these concepts. Through discussion of sexual choices, gender role options, and literal material goods, the women of *Sex and the City* incorporate personal sexual desire into a consumerist framework that allows them to manage their own sexuality.

MY MOMMA' TOLD ME . . . YOU BETTER SHOP AROUND

Sex and the City first appeared in the summer of 1998 as a new addition to HBO's growing comedy lineup. Based on a 1996 book of the same title by New York newspaper columnist Candace Bushnell, the show's scripts play with Bushnell's essays about the sexual and romantic escapades of wealthy Manhattanites. The show's executive producer, Darren Starr, thought that a focus on four female friends would allow the writers greater flexibility with the book's more circumscribed environment of the world of New York's cultural elite (Cornwell). Many early critics of the show argued, however, that the show's emphasis on shopping, dining, and meeting at exclusive New York establishments creates a lack of realism for the viewers being targeted and that the combination of sex and consumerism is created in part to garner high bids from foreign countries and companies seeking product placement in the show (Bone; Gilbert; Higgins; Jacobs "Let's Talk").

In a standard episode of the show, the narrative links a specific sexual issue to larger sociocultural issues of concern for (primarily, but not exclusively) heterosexual women. A recurring motif of consumerism emerges as one of the primary connections between female sexual agency and desire, sometimes positioning the purchase of consumable goods as analogous and substitutable for sexual fulfillment and at other times positioning the same as the site of power relations. Episodes feature the four friends coming together to exchange their points of view as a way of working through this quagmire of female sexuality and consumerism. Several examples can be provided from the first season of *Sex and the City* to demonstrate this consumerist motif and its conjunction with a motif of female desire.

In "The Turtle and the Hare," the narrative asks what single women will settle for in terms of their desire for sexual fulfillment. After the four friends attend the wedding of a former friend whom they thought would never marry due to her past pleasure in sexual variety, they meet for lunch to ponder why this woman would settle for marrying someone who loves her more than she loves him. Charlotte argues that their friend made a wise "investment" (she gets to take out more than she has to put in), but Miranda challenges her, arguing that the investment is only wise if sexual fulfillment is not lost in the deal. Charlotte argues in turn that sex is not important to a relationship if love is present, and Miranda challenges her to think about whether or not she could live the rest of her life without orgasms.

A subplot emerges in which Charlotte becomes addicted to a vibrator called The Rabbit—a $92 investment that Miranda says could make men and marriage obsolete. Eventually, Charlotte becomes so obsessed with her orgasms that Miranda and Carrie perform a "rabbit intervention," triggered by the fact that Charlotte has been ignoring their friendship. A corollary subplot involves Carrie discovering that her boyfriend, "Mr. Big," does not ever wish to marry. She decides to invest in a marriage with her gay friend, Stanford, so that he can receive an inheritance and she can receive the benefits of being married while retaining sexual fulfillment with her boyfriend. Eventually, Carrie decides that she will forego the marriage and settle for living in the present, wryly noting that Charlotte will not "settle for herself" in terms of sexual fulfillment.

These simultaneous stories resonate with the consumerist trajectory of the Sexual Revolution for women in the United States (Ehrenreich, Hess, and Jacobs). By the 1980s, a market strategy arose targeting women as sexually active and desirable consumers; group outings to see male strippers and group home-shopping parties for sexual aids (modeled on the format of Tupperware parties) were common in middle-class America. Ehrenreich, Hess, and Jacobs argue that the commodified activities of the 1980s emphasized female pleasure in the actual group experience of purchasing *together,* which parallels the behavior of the friends in "The Turtle and the Hare." When Charlotte bought The Rabbit, her friends each bought one also. When The Rabbit threatened the primary group experience of the female friendship, though, The Rabbit had to go. Bonding beat out buying.

The parallel story lines in this episode speak to a late 1980s backlash trend against increased expressions of female sexual desire in the 1970s and 1980s (Ehrenreich et al.; Faludi). This backlash took the form of a cultural emphasis on single women's supposed loss of love and commitment—on sexual desire run amok. Carrie's initial willingness to split her sexual life from her married life, where love is also split from commitment, reveals an ideological contestation over such issues, specifically about what realms love, marriage, and sexual pleasure "belong" in and, indeed, whether love and commitment must be equated with each other. Stanford's dilemma also incorporates a current ideological battle over gay marriages, highlighting the economic benefits of marriage in our culture. While Stanford has the high income associated with many White, gay males in our niche-marketing culture, he still stands to miss out economically on the investment of sanctioned marriage because his grandmother will only give money to her legally married grandchildren. The bottom line is that even though the consumerist-driven ideology of capitalism is pleased to acknowledge Stanford as a "sexual citizen" when it comes to purchasing power, he does not have the same full body of rights that heterosexual citizens of the United States have (David Scott Evans).

In "The Baby Shower," the four women visit yet another friend who has left their single world to get married and raise children. Only Charlotte is excited about the baby shower; she is eager to visit the world she thinks of as wedded and maternal bliss. Sam only wants to see what her former rival looks like pregnant, and she even brings a bottle of scotch to drink in front of her. Miranda is disgusted with the entire concept of the shower, and she warns her friends that she has lost two sisters to "The Cult of Motherhood." Carrie attends the party with the fear that she, herself, may be pregnant—a fear exemplified by her ambivalence about even having a family.

The party ends up devastating Charlotte in particular; she discovers that their former friend has "stolen" her future baby's name. Charlotte is so upset that she later rips up the contents of her Hope Box: her dream man (a picture of John F. Kennedy, Jr.), her back-up dream man (an advertisement featuring a male model), her baby name pillow, and photos of her two dream homes in Manhattan and the Hamptons. Carrie, as she waits to find out if she is pregnant, wonders about the mothers and wives she met at the party—what have they sacrificed and what have they gained? A series of direct addresses to the camera by the mothers at the party reveal a litany of what they had to sacrifice for their current lifestyles, including a powerful position at work, time to one's self, a lesbian lover, sexual freedom, and sexual satisfaction.

Samantha decides that she is tired of married women looking at her and her friends as if they have nothing to live for without husbands and children in their lives; she throws an "I'm Not Having a Baby Shower" to celebrate the fact that her and her friends' lives have not been "squandered" on investing in children and husbands. At the party, Miranda begins a sexual relationship with an accountant, noting her conviction that men will become obsolete does not matter when she can get her taxes done for free. Charlotte eventually decides that she does not need her dreams of marriage and a family to meet the consumerist ideals she had previously laid out for herself and that in the meantime she will enjoy her life as it is. By the end of the episode, Carrie gets her period, and she feels both relieved and slightly sad. This episode's strategy of layering different and changing perspectives on motherhood and marriage results in a more complex representation of sexual fulfillment and self-fulfillment in general for women than TV typically offers. The stories told highlight the double bind still at work in U.S. culture and society that often makes motherhood, career, and sexual agency mutually exclusive, even as they also highlight the legitimacy of women wanting marriage and children.

I am not attempting to argue that such ideological plurality serves as a thorough critique of the restrictions women in capitalism face. I agree with Robin Andersen that television shows in general ignore the world of work in the sense that the majority of series, including this one, follow a "logic of consumption" that focuses on consumerist activities rather than activities of production proper (71). The commodity is, indeed, attached seamlessly in *Sex and the City* to the fulfillment of social and emotional needs in a way that often obscures the failures of society, politics, and the capitalist economic system to support women's needs and desires. Certainly, we rarely see the four lead characters dealing with the demands of work or worrying about where their next meal is coming from. We *do* see women coming together in this series, however, whether it is to shop or try out different activities and ideas related to sex and gender. Ultimately, what can be seen in this show is an emphasis on the value of producing and maintaining female friendships as a source of information and support for making choices when "shopping" for sexuality.

SHOP TALK

Pat O'Connor argues that mainstream culture in the United States maintains "gender-role ideologies about romantic heterosexual love which depict friendships between women as very much second best" (91). Beginning in their teens, girls are trained to come to expect that their friendships with other girls will lessen in strength and importance as girls form romantic relationships with boys. The widespread denigration of women's collective activities culturally reinforces this ideological "given," and denigration of women's activities and desires extends to mainstream texts that offer *representations* of such activities and desires. Thus, for example, there exists a common ghettoization of such subgenres as the "chick flick" and "girl power" shows, as well as soap opera and melodramatic "women's films."

One of the motifs common to these denigrated representational venues is the focus on conversation among women—conversation most often coded as gossip. Many reviews of *Sex and the City* have focused on just this element, noting that the characters "jabber" and "reveal secrets" (Jacobs "Let's Talk") and even that the show itself is an "empty diversion" akin to reading gossip columns (Kelleher). I came across only one critic (Hettie Judah of *The London Times*) who discussed gossiping about men and sex as supportive of the creation of a community with a "secret language" that women can rely on to make informed decisions.

The predominance of discussions revolving around shopping in a text that also focuses on female friendship creates an intriguing intersection of female activities to examine. How is it that shopping can support the creation and maintenance of female friendships? Rachel Bowlby, in her research on the success of department stores in Western Europe during the 1800s, suggests that department stores structure a domestic space based on themes positioning the female shopper as aware and educated about how best to choose. One might argue that shopping, over time, has consistently worked to interpolate female consumers as always "functionally," rather than "frivolously," shopping. Additionally, consumerist cultures tend to position shopping as a "feminine" activity that offers a gendered space for women to call their own, serving the consumerist culture's own ends but offering a site for the maintenance of female friendships and gendered bonding.

There is no doubt that *Sex and the City* positions shopping as a functional activity—be it the purchase of a gift to gain entrance to a social event or the purchase of a material object to enhance one's mood. And, of course, there is the kind of shopping that surrounds sex. These friends do not just *purchase* sexual goods. They shop also through discussions and gossiping—a sort of "comparison shopping by talking." In much the same way that department stores work to manage women's shopping through regular sales and competitive advertising, Carrie, Charlotte, Miranda, and Samantha manage their sexuality through regular comparison of sexual events and competitive perspectives on sexual issues.

Sex and the City's strategy of each of the four friends talking about whatever the episode's topic of the evening might be emphasizes the value of women having access to multiple perspectives. The show seldom offers any definitive "answer" to the sexual questions raised, with the four women often taking divergent paths along the same sexual route. The talking that occurs in this show is an example of what Lorraine Code describes as affective knowing and epistemic negotiation—a knowledge building based on empathy and the ability to imagine other possibilities and perspectives.

This motif of presenting equally valued perspectives on sexual issues and corresponding gender role issues is the source of much of the show's humor and emotional pull. The stories, or gossiping, that emerge in conversations allow these women to explore different possibilities in terms of their sexual desires and agency with the talk functioning as a mode of "window shopping," so to speak.

A specific episode near the conclusion of the first season exemplifies the function of gossip and the process of epistemic negotiation in *Sex and the City*. In "The Drought," the topic of the evening is that the women are not having sex as often as they want. Carrie's particular dilemma appears to her to have been brought on by her farting in bed with Mr. Big, an assessment she hesitatingly takes to her friends one by one. "There is a moment in every relationship when romance gives way to reality," Carrie notes in a voiceover followed by a direct address to the camera informing the viewer that she was "mortified." Sam tells Carrie that she is probably right about why her sex life has dropped off with Mr. Big because "men don't like women to be human." She advises Carrie to "just go fuck him and he'll forget." Miranda insists that Carrie's real problem is that she is trying to be someone she is not around her boyfriend.

Miranda also points out to Carrie that she is not the only one of the four women who is unfulfilled sexually. Miranda herself is in the midst of a three-month "dry spell" that has led her to overindulge in watching Blockbuster movies, even though a group of construction workers harasses her every time she goes to the video store. Charlotte is out of the sex loop because Prozac has squelched her new boyfriend's sex drive; she, too, is watching a lot of Blockbuster movies. Samantha is currently depriving herself of sex, as she has become involved with a yoga instructor who deals in Tantric (read: no intercourse) sex. "Where have I been?" Carrie admonishes herself after she hears all of this. "Having sex," Miranda replies.

With all four women becoming increasingly sexually frustrated, the friends get together at Carrie's house to discuss the fact that Sam's advice to Carrie failed; Carrie went to seduce Mr. Big during a boxing match on pay-per-view, and he ignored her advances. The four friends discuss themselves as starving, and in Samantha's case "fasting," for sex. Carrie tells them that the research she has been doing on their topic (revealed to the audience in a series of "wo/man on the street" interviews) has revealed that no one in New York thinks they themselves are having enough sex. The exception might be the couple who live across the alley from Carrie—Carrie has been watching them through her window, and they have been having sex daily. Curious about this sexually sated couple, the women spend the remainder of their time together watching the "afternoon show" through Carrie's window, eating gummy bears, and discussing the marvel of the couple across the way—especially the fact that the man can stay hard for over an hour. Carrie describes their newfound activity as the 1990s version of ladies going to see a matinee.

After the "show," the women decide to take matters into their own hands. Miranda, returning a movie to Blockbuster, confronts one of the construction workers who has been harassing her and announces that she does not think he can "give her what she wants" because she is looking for an awful lot of sex. She gets some satisfaction from seeing him back down and tell her he is married. Samantha, while in yoga class, begins randomly asking the men surrounding her if they want to fuck until someone acquiesces. Charlotte breaks up with her "Prozac lover." And, Carrie tells Mr. Big that she is tired of trying to be perfect around him. The episode ends with Carrie and Mr. Big deciding that they can "do better" than the matinee couple who are having sex yet again. Carrie foregoes her "free show" and creates her own production instead.

This episode indicates the structural themes at work in many others. Unified by their "outsider" status in terms of sexual fulfillment, the women strategize about how to end their "drought" and simultaneously comparison shop by exploring what other men and women are doing. This is defined as a function of their friendship: to figure out how to achieve sexual fulfillment and to determine what the definitional boundaries of sexual fulfillment are. The episode highlights the friendship among the women, both when Miranda admonishes Carrie for slacking off on their friendship and when the women converge to offer advice to each other. Perspectives for coping are offered, all connected to consumerism either directly (Blockbuster movies and gummy bears) or indirectly (watching the "show" across the way). Through their talk and gossip, the women explore and confront larger cultural issues: Carrie and Samantha's belief that men demand perfection to the point of inhumanity from women is alternately given credence and denied, and Miranda's confrontation with the construction worker deconstructs the notion that such harassment is rooted in male sexual desire rather than gendered power relations. Via empathy, honesty, and "dishing the dirt," these four women not only work through individual dilemmas concerning sexual desire and agency, they also cement their friendship as inextricable from their ability to be sexually fulfilled. Their bonding activities help them make better choices.

CONCLUSION

I have only scratched the surface of the ways in which *Sex and the City* links consumerism with female sexual desire and agency. It is evident, however, that simply because the series focuses on economically privileged women, it does not follow that the high level of consumer activity in this text overpowers all other discourses at work. In fact, the focus on consumer activities to some extent *strengthens* other discourses at work in the show concerning gendered power relations in a capitalistic culture and society. In particular, the show offers female friendship as a potential site for contesting gender-role ideologies that are linked to sexuality. These women's friendships with each other serve to create and maintain healthy female sexual agency with the relationships among the women providing a space for conversation and gossip that encourages informed decision making guided by epistemic negotiation.

Since the first season, the show has maintained its focus on sexuality, consumerism, and female friendship. While episodes continue to make light of consumerist analogies (Charlotte buys a puppy when she cannot find a suitable man; Carrie writes an article for *Vogue* about men as hot, new accessories for the Fall fashion season), other choices have had more at stake. Charlotte gets married and eventually separates from her husband after she finds out that she cannot have a baby easily. Carrie ruins a relationship with a good man when she has an affair with a married Mr. Big. Samantha falls in love twice—first with a woman and then with a man who ends up cheating on her. And, Miranda becomes pregnant and decides to have the baby but not get married.

The show has also begun to address issues of class and economy and how these dynamics interact with women's abilities to make choices and form bonds with other women. Miranda has emotional trouble when buying her own apartment because everyone she deals with financially looks at her askance when she tells them the apartment is "just for her" (i.e., there is no man to live with her or buy for her). When Charlotte gets engaged to a wealthy man, she has to negotiate a prenuptial agreement that she feels underestimates her monetary value as a wife and possible mother. (In fact, the agreement states that she will receive more money in a divorce if she has a boy than if she has a girl.) When Carrie breaks off her engagement with her "good guy," he leaves her potentially homeless because he owned her apartment. Carrie finds out that she is "worth nothing" when she applies for a loan, and she and Charlotte fight when Charlotte does not offer to loan her the money she needs. (Eventually, Charlotte gives Carrie her wedding ring, from her failed marriage, so that Carrie can sell it and buy her apartment.)

The availability of shows like *Sex and the City* is important in a society that continues to simplify representations of female sexuality and female friendship. Feminist scholarship needs to take its passion for discussing female sexual agency and desire in the "real" world and work more diligently to explore this area of representation in its contemporary media forms. There needs to be an exploration of the changing landscape of television as an industry and the complications this affords in terms of commercialism and censorship. It would be helpful to examine differences and similarities in representations of heterosexual and lesbian, bisexual, or transgender agency and desire, given the complex links between the discouragement of the expression of such desires and the need for a consumer society to continually expand its market. We also need to examine the dynamics of race and ethnicity at work in texts that ideologically struggle over these issues along with a more complete exploration of class than I was able to provide here. Representations of female sexuality, friendship, and consumerism are intimately connected to feminism's concern with female empowerment. We cannot afford *not* to "invest" in such research.

ADDENDUM: WHAT *DO* WOMEN WANT?

When I first began studying *Sex and the City*, the show was in the early years of its six season run on HBO. Like millions of other viewers, I eagerly anticipated the end of the series. Romantic relationships came and went, but these women privileged their friendship as a source of strength and knowledge. Carrie, Miranda, Charlotte, and Samantha kept on shopping . . . and talking . . . and talking about shopping . . . and shopping for and talking about sex. This framework stayed intact as richer storylines involving cancer, adoption, and even death wound their way into the mix. Toward the end of the series, the writers even revisit "The Baby Shower" episode by having Carrie register for her wedding—to herself—so that she can get a pair of shoes back from a woman to whom she had given countless wedding and baby gifts over the years ("A Woman's Right to Shoes"). It was this commitment to exploring the range of what women want that kept *me* committed to the show.

I was disappointed, however, with the end result of the series; I felt that the narrative framework and theme of the finale moves away from female friendship. When Carrie faces her penultimate decision (Should she move to Paris to live with her new lover, a Russian artist?), the input of her female cohorts begins to fade in importance. She decides to move after little discussion (in contrast to past discussions about much "smaller" decisions). In fact, *all* of the women begin to turn more often to the men in their lives as they make major decisions, shifting the site of epistemic negotiation in the show's plots.

This shift was not absolute, nor am I suggesting that men should not be involved in women's lives and decision making. Rather, I am posing questions: How powerful is the ending of a television series in defining it ideologically? Is this what women wanted from the show? Is this what women want from their lives? With regard to the first question, I must admit that I am stumped. In this chapter, I argue that we cannot let the consumerist and elitist axes of this series overshadow its feminist rhetoric of choice and female friendship. Yet, I feel that Carrie's final choice overshadows the show's earlier thrust. Carrie dumps the negligent Russian lover just as Mr. Big—her "true love"—comes to Paris to reclaim her; she then makes a second choice to renew her romance with Mr. Big. Clearly, these are "choices," but I was struck by the fact that Carrie's female friends, those women who have stood by her through thick and thin, did not come to her rescue. Instead, they ask *Mr. Big* to "go get [their] girl" (as Miranda put it).

Generally, the pattern of the series is for the women to get together, talk and exchange perspectives, and then make informed decisions. The episodes featuring Carrie in Paris show her becoming progressively more depressed and angry as her lover abandons her, and she eventually realizes that what she is really missing are her friends. I waited for what I thought was inevitable: certainly we would see "the girls" gathering over brunch, discussing a plan, slapping down their credit cards, and taking off for Paris in the final hour of the show. But, in the end, it appeared that all Carrie needed was the right man for the job.

Doing what television does best, *Sex and the City* continues to fulfill different viewer needs and desires. For some fans writing in online fan sites when the show entered syndication in 2004, this is a show about romance and dating, a narrative emphasis that suits the finale of the show. For others, it is about female bonding and lasting friendships. It is striking that in WTBS's promotional spots for syndication, the most noticeable visual pattern involves the four women framed together talking. With regard to the final Freudian question I pose, the final episode of *Sex and the City* may suggest that women ultimately want heterosexual coupling over and above female bonding, but the cyclical nature of the series on television continually revisits its dominant themes of female friendship, shopping, and sex through the glories of televisual repetition.

Then, there are *the films*. While I cannot do justice to the wrench these cinematic narratives throw into my overall argument, it bears noting that everything I find problematic with the series finale looms even larger in the movies from Carrie being won over by a shoe closet after Mr. Big leaves her at the altar to Samantha drifting into cyclical narcissism to the nonsensicalness of Aidan (Carrie's other serious love) somehow showing up in Abu Dhabi. The movies shift female friendship further to the edges of life, centering on men and consumer products that, in the series, serve to highlight the female friendships. Frankly, I simply can't get past the Orientalism of the second film, which makes me feel like I've been blown back to the 1930s.

But, do the films "matter?" I could argue that they so deeply reinforce the series finale that they serve as the definitive message, but I could also argue that ultimately it is the viewers who determine the series' message. Such arguments are for another essay. Meanwhile, the battle continues over how to define "women's TV" and how to represent "what women want." Perhaps *Sex and the City's* greatest success, and the key to its continued popularity after its initial run on cable, might be its refusal to answer this question in a clear-cut way and its ability to advance epistemic negotiations about its meanings outside of its own narrative boundaries. Or, perhaps, I'm just a feminist with a dream, blissfully re-watching and making my own choice to "end" the story before Carrie even leaves for Paris.

The 2000s

The 2000s began with extensive coverage of the Y2K phenomenon and speculation about whether or not computer systems would crash worldwide. Fortunately, the cataclysm predicted by some media sources turned out to be a barely a ripple. True disaster doesn't arrive on a schedule, prepackaged by alarmists on the evening news; it comes like a bolt out of a crystal-clear fall sky. At 8:46 a.m. on September 11, 2001, televisions relayed images of the first of the terrorist attacks on the World Trade Center in New York City. Once again, the nation coalesced into a collective TV audience, reliving the horror, trying to comprehend, and following the exploits of the responders at Ground Zero.

This decade marked an ebb period for the situation comedy. Widely seen in syndication and increasingly available through online delivery systems, the genre hit a rough patch in prime time largely because of the rise in popularity of reality programming, which eventually found its saturation point. Critics and commentators dispute whether the lengthy strike by the Writer's Guild of America in 1988 planted seeds that flowered into a burgeoning garden of so-called reality shows, but the fact of the matter is that reality programming is cheaper to produce than scripted sitcoms and dramas because of production costs and residual payments, and as long as series such as *Survivor, Temptation Island, Who Wants to Be a Millionaire?, Fear Factor, American Idol, The Bachelor/Bachelorette, Dancing with the Stars, Deal or No Deal, Extreme Makeover: Home Edition, Are You Smarter than a 5th Grader?, Amazing Race,* and *Undercover Boss* were bringing in the ratings, they were on the schedule.

While we are confident in predicting that sitcoms will stage yet another comeback in the coming years, the 2000s were not entirely fallow. Animated sitcoms gained in popularity, and H. Peter Steeves pens a suitably iconoclastic accompaniment to *The Simpsons*, exploring postmodernism and possibility in Springfield and other points on the cultural map. Michael

Tueth uses another animated sitcom, *South Park*, to explore the limits of transgressive comedy in the context of its historical roots. Commentators have speculated (with admittedly anecdotal evidence) that rapidly rising rates of acceptance on a range of equality issues were driven at least in part by the weekly appearance of gay men in the living rooms of middle America on *Will & Grace*. It is safe to say that the increasing comfort level of television producers with various aspects of LGBTQ life, however stereotypical, contributed to a climate of tolerance. While measuring the social impact of particular shows is always problematic, Denis Provencher deepens our understanding of the sitcom with his examination of heteronormative strategies on *Will & Grace*. And, in a sense, that is the larger project of this entire volume, to complicate our viewing and enrich our understanding of these cultural artifacts.

In 2001, *American Idol* became a sensation and helped mark the reality boom on television that would rock the industry throughout the decade. The juxtaposition of the tragedy at the World Trade Center with this bit of prime-time fluff exemplifies the contrasts of contemporary life in the United States; sometimes it seems that the defining problems of the era are so large and complex that many people would rather vote for their favorite contestant than become politically active and work for change. By 2003, television newscasts relied on reports from journalists embedded with the troops in Iraq and Afghanistan, which provided many memorable human interest stories but undermined the independence that war correspondents had appreciated historically. With assurances from a battalion of generals on the Sunday morning news programs, many Americans believed President George W. Bush, Vice President Dick Cheney, and Secretary of State Donald Rumsfeld when they promised that the "War on Terror" would be all but won in the hours and days following the first wave of troop invasion. The "shock and awe" bombardments made for strangely hypnotic television, a spectacle that many commentators compared to the visuals of a video game. Delivered less than two months after the bombing commenced, President Bush's made-for-television claim of "Mission Accomplished" quickly rang hollow.

Cable television was still focused on pulling viewers away from the networks with complex and sometimes extraordinary programs such as HBO's *The Wire*. In something of a one-two punch, satellites provided a less costly technology for delivering television signals, which further diminished the influence of broadcast television. By 2006, direct broadcast satellite (DBS) delivery was estimated at nearly 25 percent of U.S. households, while cable penetration fell to about 62 percent. Despite the multiplicity of options available on satellite and cable systems, critics and viewers expressed dissatisfaction with the glut of reality programming, 24-hour cable news outlets that lowered the level of political discourse, and the feeling that there were hundreds of channels available and hardly anything worth watching on them.

The top-rated sitcoms of the 2000s were *Baby Bob; Becker; The Big Bang Theory; Everybody Loves Raymond; Frasier; Friends; Good Morning, Miami; Inside Schwartz; Just Shoot Me; King of Queens; Leap of Faith; My Big Fat Greek Life; The New Adventures of Old Christine; Out of Practice; Rules of Engagement; Samantha Who?; Scrubs; Still Standing; Two and a Half Men; Will & Grace;* and *Yes, Dear.*

17

"It's Just a Bunch of Stuff that Happened"

The *Simpsons* and the Possibility
of Postmodern Comedy

H. PETER STEEVES

At the center of the finest episodes of *The Simpsons* there is absolutely nothing. ("Ummm . . . creamy nothing center. Aghghghgh. . . .") This should be disappointing only if we were thinking that something should have been there, that we deserve something there. Part of the postmodern condition, of our condition, is such frustration of expectation—not just particular expectations but the notion of expectation in general with its linear conception of cause and effect—its reliance on there being a stable and coherent self to do the expecting; its overall naïve innocence about how the world operates. *The Simpsons*, hollow as it is, is anything but naïve; thus, it demands a sophisticated conception of humor.

TRADITIONAL THEORIES OF COMEDY
WORKED FOR MORE TRADITIONAL TIMES

Immanuel Kant's (very Kantian and thus very unfunny) descriptions of what is funny—"the placing of heterogeneous notions under common genera"—explain why jokes about rabbis, priests, and ministers who hang out together on golf courses can get laughs. But, who tells these sorts of jokes anymore, at least unironically? Thomas Hobbes' insistence that all humor stems from a sudden sense of superiority—that jokes bring pleasure precisely because someone is in pain *and it is not me*—might explain why it is funny to watch *The Three Stooges,* why it is funny (for some) to tell ethnic jokes, or why it is hilarious to note that Hobbes is dead and you and I are not. But, so much comedy today is about self-deprecation (think of Larry David and Louis C. K.) that Hobbes seems quaintly out of place—like Don Rickles guest-starring on *Key & Peele.* Henri Bergson's claim that humor arises from involuntary actions, that we expect to find adaptability and pliability in human beings but when met with a stumbling block—literally or metaphorically—we often still stumble, speaks to the human condition. But, in a world where stumbling has become the norm and the possibility of a universal human condition is continually under question, tripping is not as funny as it used to be.

Here, then, is the problem: had this book been published decades ago, a nice chapter could have be written on Kant and *Three's Company* ("Come and Knock on Our Door: Mr. Kant, Mr. Roper, and the Placing of Hetero-Homo-Sexual Notions Under a Common Apartment Roof"), on Hobbes and *Saved By the Bell* ("The Importance of Not Being Screech"), or on Bergson and *The Dick Van Dyke Show* ("On Hassocks, Both Real and Metaphorical"). But, who can speak to *The Simpsons*? Though we might laugh at the improbable coupling of Burns and Smithers, or with a sense of superiority when we watch Chief Wiggum, or with surprise at the eternal lack of adaptability in Homer, this sort of laughing does not seem to get at the heart of what is funny about the show. This is not to say, of course, that *The Simpsons* is *new.* With more than a quarter-century under its belt, *The Simpsons* is not only the longest-running animated TV series but also the longest-running sitcom as well as the longest-running scripted, prime-time television series in general. What was new—and arguably still is new—about *The Simpsons* is its relation to modernity. Springfield is located squarely in a newly postmodern world.

Of course, this is "literally" true. Springfield, the hometown of the Simpsons, is not in any particular American state but is, instead, an eclectic geographic mixture of places. Fans noted this early on, and the show has since made a coyly self-aware running joke out of it. This is as good a place as any to begin our investigation of postmodernity because the way in which Springfield is (dis)located is telling.

Place, for the modern, is unimportant. Modernity's politics, metaphysics, and ethics rejected the importance of context and situation, the possible importance of being one place instead of another. Universal rights and universal conceptions of *Being* were the goals, and universal notions of the individual were thus assumed. From Hobbes' placeless state of nature to the placeless marketplace of capitalism to the American assumption that U.S. democracy is the finest form of government for everyone in the world, there is thus a long history of thinking that the specifics of place are unimportant to anything that really matters. The project of modernity can even be described in terms of the systematic destruction of place: the golden arches of McDonald's look the same around the globe and a Big Mac tastes the same as well; cosmopolitanism destroys true difference even as it commodifies it; the Liberal state would have us treated as generic, isolated, individual selves with generic, isolationist, and individual rights; and, mass communication technologies trick us into thinking that we are near our family and friends—and home—even when we are separated by untold miles. One of the myths of modernity, then, is that we can happily live dislocated.

Postmodernity becomes aware of such false assumptions but without resorting to melancholy over similarly false constructions of the "good old days" with their good old places. Springfield is an embodiment of this ideal. As an artistic representation, it is both generic and specific at the same time. It is not a particular place of this world; yet, it is not placeless. Think of the importance of the town to the show; compare this to the seeming unimportance of "real" locations to other comedies. The Los Angeles of *New Girl* is essentially irrelevant to the identities of the characters and the nature of the action, and the fact that *The Big Bang Theory* takes place in Pasadena, California, is virtually unimportant apart from the fact that some characters are said to work at Caltech. Looking back to the 1960s, the Mayberry, North Carolina, of *The Andy Griffith Show* falls squarely (in more ways than one) into the melancholy category. The small town seems to have created the good-natured neighbors that populate the show, but the maudlin tone and utter lack of race- and sex-politics (even while the show was being produced during the time of the Civil Rights Movement) suggest a whitewashing of true Southern geographic embodiment.

Not so in Springfield. The town may flaunt its inability to be located in one state, but this fluid positioning does not turn it into a placeless every-place. Springfield is unique and rooted. Its history informs the characters, though that history is always ready for rewriting—see, for instance, Lisa's discovery that the town's pioneer founder and namesake, Jebediah Spring-field, was in reality a terrible man, and her refusal in the end to announce this discovery when she realizes that "truth" is always up for grabs and the townspeople are legitimately constructing themselves and their history at every moment ("Lisa the Iconoclast"). Springfield, too, is self-sufficient in a way most towns are not but should be. Though there are moments of disruptive globalism, local products (such as Duff beer) are more prevalent than multinational corporate products (such as Mr. Sparkle). Even the local nuclear power plant is run by a local billionaire, whose mistake in one episode of selling the plant to "the Germans" (who are not all smiles and sunshine) is quickly righted ("Burns Verkaufen der Kraftwerk").

Some critics have suggested that Springfield comes close to the classical *polis*, but that it unrealistically portrays modern local community. "[W]hat are authentic movie stars like Rainer Wolfcastle doing living in Springfield?," goes the argument. "And what about the fact that the world-famous Itchy and Scratchy cartoons are produced in Springfield?" (Cantor 744). In placing the stars and industries in Springfield, though, an important point is being made. The distinction between local culture and global culture is eroded, but not in the way in which it is being eroded today in our world. In our "real" world (or at least, let us say, "nonanimated world"), homogenization of culture works in such a way as to destroy what is local. Architecture, food, language, music, humor, and nearly all customs embedded in local communities are giving way to mass-produced artifacts and thinking. Hence the aforementioned ubiquitous golden arches and Big Macs. *The Simpsons'* twist on this is to make the local culture the dominant culture—to erode the distinction but from the other end. That is, Krusty Burger restaurants are not only a mockery of McDonald's, they are an inversion of McDonald's. Krusty is a local celebrity, and his local business is presented as if it were the homogenizing, corporate, distantly owned fast-food franchise, as if the local were homogenizing the rest of the world. Itchy and Scratchy are world-renowned cartoon characters enjoyed by kids everywhere, but they are created and produced locally. What *The Simpsons* realizes is that commercialization is caught up in webs of global production and consumption, and that the world the show presents—and even the show itself—is complicit in this.

Let us be clear about how this is so. There are three sorts of (television) comedy: traditionalist, modern, and postmodern. Though they tend to be chronologically ordered (roughly, traditionalist television comedies range from the 1950s to the 1960s, modernist comedies from the 1970s to the 1980s, and postmodernists from the 1990s on), there is nothing necessarily chronological about this. Indeed, *Monty Python's Flying Circus* in the 1970s was, perhaps, the first truly postmodern television comedy; *The Cosby Show* of the 1980s was surely traditionalist; and, very few twenty-first century programs are truly postmodern. Still, there is something to be said for such quaint linear classification schemes. Regardless, the types can be defined in part by their reaction to their own status in the culture and, thus, their relation to their production.

All production is somehow complicit in the modern market, including the production that makes television comedies possible. If a show does not acknowledge this, and is even seemingly unaware of it, it would be *traditionalist*. Commercialization never was a theme for *The Donna Reed Show* (though it was undoubtedly so for Donna Reed). If a show realizes this and tries to find a way out, it would be *modernist*. There are multiple modernist tricks toward this end. Some modernist television naïvely attempts to create community by showing local products being consumed as if they were the only products on the shelf. Others cynically exhibit only mass-produced products (thereby accepting their status) and lure us into false community with the characters by naming these as products we all have in common. *Seinfeld*, for instance, chose this latter tactic. Realizing that brand names are everywhere, *Seinfeld* referred to them explicitly, thus making the viewer think that he or she has something in common with the characters ("I love Junior Mints, too!"). Acknowledging the nature of the commercial culture thus makes the show modernist rather than traditionalist. It could have taken the postmodern turn, though, if it had admitted its own complicity and immersion in this culture.[1]

And, *The Simpsons* does just this. It acknowledges what it is and how it is situated in the world. It exposes the artifice that holds it up. It admits its complicity in late capitalism. And, it gives us a reason to smile that does not simultaneously demand bad faith, demand that we either ignore the complexities of the world (as the traditionalist would have us do) or imagine that we can rise above those complexities (as the modernist maintains we can). Thus, for example, by making local products and local culture in Springfield into the assumed mass culture of the world, *The Simpsons* concedes the relation between the two but forces us to think about that relation in a new way. It does not stand outside of that relation but twists it from within. It is hard to do such topological maneuvers when one is immersed in the medium being contorted, but it is the only authentic stance to take in a postmodern world.

Consider, for instance, the Butterfinger candy bar. *The Simpsons*-Butterfinger alliance has been going strong since the late 1990s with Bart and other Springfield residents appearing in various commercials both on television and in print. A package of Butterfinger BB's (an incarnation of the candy consisting of little, round candy bar pieces) is decorated, for instance, with a picture of Bart laughing hysterically and Krusty the Klown saying, "I heartily endorse this product and/or promotion." These are the

Figure 17.1. Marge, Maggie, Homer, Lisa, and Bart Simpson in *The Simpsons*. 1989– . Photo courtesy of Larry Edmunds BooksFair.

moments in which *The Simpsons* confesses its complicity. There are multiple levels to this text. Most obviously, the presentation is different from other product tie-ins. The image of the character or celebrity is typically what is meant to sell the product. It was once enough, then, to have a picture of the Church Lady on a T-shirt, or—more to the point of the tie-in—images of Michael Jordan on the Wheaties box or Jar-Jar Binks on the Pepsi (while Britney Spears gyrated in the Pepsi television commercial, of course, showing us her can). With Butterfinger, Krusty speaks, acknowledging that he is pushing a product, not trying to rise above it. Furthermore, he confesses that this is the norm: that he is a thoughtless shill for capitalism so often that he needs a *generic* pitch statement. The fact that he (and thus the Butterfinger folks) feels comfortable keeping the pitch generic—not changing "this product and/or promotion" for "these Butterfinger BB's"—indicates an assumed cynicism over such commercialism, as if there is no need to go out of the way to point out what the product is since we all know it does not really matter to the spokesperson. And, the fact that Bart laughs at us on the wrapper for buying into it seals the deal. Bart not only laughs because he is aware of his (and our) complicity. He laughs because he knows what we know: he knows that Krusty is famous on *The Simpsons* for endorsing terrible products, for having a line of dangerous household appliances and children's toys with his likeness, even for selling boxes of Krusty-O's cereal with a surprise jagged metal O in each box ("'Round Springfield"). Thus, to buy the Butterfinger endorsed by Krusty (who is, after all, not even interested in knowing what it is he is endorsing) is to buy a shoddy and potentially dangerous product. And, we do so happily.

This does not mean that there is little reason to laugh at traditional and modernist comedy. None of this is to say that *Seinfeld* or *The Donna Reed Show* or even *Three's Company* are not funny. They are (though perhaps in decreasing order, and perhaps in exponentially decreasing order). Defining postmodern comedy is not the same as putting down modernist or traditional comedy. I have been doing quite modernist things throughout this chapter in the name of trying to be a little humorous. Mentioning moments from these sitcoms without explanation (such as an off-hand reference to Mr. Sparkle or Mr. Roper) is a way of cheap inclusion: if you get the reference, you laugh; if you laugh, you are part of the "community." You and I most likely do not have much more in common, so I—the struggling philosopher—take what I can get. It would only turn postmodernly funny if I were to admit to you that I am doing this and you were to find this liberating and humorous. Neither, I fear, is likely to happen.

SO WE CANNOT RISE ABOVE THE WORLD.
THIS IS NOT TO BE LAMENTED. NOTHING RISES.

Language was once thought to rise above it all, or at least to ride on top of it. Language, before postmodernity, was about reflecting the world. Words had meaning because they reached out and denoted things. Propositions had meaning because they reached out and denoted states of affairs. Language magically floated above us, with words mirroring our reality back to us rather than creating it. But, nothing really floats.

Words do not anchor themselves like labels stuck to things. Language does not work like the Post-Its in Ned Flanders's beach house, labeling the world around us and instructing us as to meaning ("Summer of 4 Ft. 2"). Words, instead, are linked in intricate webs of self-reference. They mean each other; they mean what we agree to allow them to mean. And, with them, we carve up an ever-malleable world rather than reflect a rigid world. Thus, when I say, "I love you," there is no stable and universal referent for each word. No necessary self, no Other, no Platonic relation of love to be instantiated in-between. "I love you" has meaning because each word means other words, and because when I speak it I am speaking an echo of every time the phrase has ever been uttered before: it means everything it has always meant. All language is metaphor.

There is, then, no way out, no rising above, no escaping language. But, there is still a chance to speak "truthfully." Doing so requires quote marks; when truth is gone, "truth" is all we have left. And, *The Simpsons* is masterful in its use of quotational discourse. Umberto Eco explains:

> I think of the postmodern attitude as that of a man who loves a very cultivated woman who knows he cannot say to her, "I love you madly," because he knows that she knows (and that she knows that he knows) that these words have been written by Barbara Cartland. Still, there is a solution. He can say, "As Barbara Cartland would put it, I love you madly." At this point, having avoided false innocence, having said clearly that it is no longer possible to speak innocently, he will nevertheless have said what he wanted to say to the woman: that he loves her, but he loves her in an age of lost innocence. . . . [B]oth [the man and the woman] will consciously and with pleasure play the game of irony. . . . (67–68)

Eco is on to something here, but perhaps with a few caveats. Irony is not just a game; it is the only game in town. It is the inescapable, foundational late-modern context of all meaning. Once we realize this—and we realize that our words constantly ring with the echoes of all their past uses, that innocence is not only lost but was never really there to begin with—we need not remain in silence for fear of speaking naïvely. Instead, we must acknowledge our state and our complicity. One way of doing this is to usher in quotational discourse. It is not really that the romance novelists have taken "I love you madly" away from us, making it too cheesy for everyday use. It is that *all* words are simultaneously utterances of other words and other past meanings; and thus, to speak at all is to risk sounding trite and clichéd. Even Eco echoes. We cannot rise above this, but our discourse can acknowledge it. Hence, we speak using quotation marks: "As they have said in the romance novels and on soap operas and in Shakespeare and in parked cars and everyplace everywhere throughout time, 'I love you madly.'"

Sometimes we do this explicitly. When I stub a toe or otherwise hurt myself superficially, I will occasionally respond to a query about my condition in a bad British accent, "It's just a flesh wound." Forced to excuse myself from a room at an inopportune time—during a meal or a conversation, for instance—I have once or twice muttered in a bad Austrian-German accent, "I'll be back." And, I pity the fool who dares say to me, "Surely, you must be joking." Because I am seldom joking. And, I do not like to be called Shirley.[2]

I know that some people do such things to an annoying degree. I know some people who do such things to an annoying degree. I consciously attempt not to be one of them. It is just not funny after a very short while, because one appears a maladjusted show-off, aping every cultural moment of the past, never seeming to speak in one's own voice. But, the point to remember is that we are all doing this, whether we admit to it or not, all the time. And, admitting to it is the only authentic thing left to do. Still, a joke told every five minutes quickly loses its luster.

The Simpsons admits to its involvement in quotational discourse on multiple levels by telling different jokes about the same thing every five seconds. In the ultimate postmodern turn, it often quotes itself (which is another way of understanding the self-references to its own commodification). But, it also quotes other art—linguistically, visually, and thematically. As such, it is a commentary not on the American family but on the American family's appearance in television. Indeed, it could not be otherwise; for the meaning of the family today is (in part) the meaning it has through television. On a more basic level, the show, realizing that it is a visual art and that other works of art have come before, will often conjure a scene in terms of scenes that have come before.

In 2002, season thirteen ended with an episode in which Homer is targeted by the mob, and as Fat Tony and his crew drive to the Simpson's house, the opening credits of *The Sopranos* are recreated with Springfield landmarks rather than Jersey ones ("Poppa's Got a Brand New Badge"). Why? How can one authentically make art about a mob hit today without quoting *The Sopranos* (which itself was often [literally] quoting *The Godfather*)? The sixth season cliffhanger ("Who Shot Mr. Burns?") is, in its entirety, a reference to *Dallas* and the ultimate cliffhanger of "Who Shot

J.R.?" Why? How can one stage a non-naïve cliffhanger without admitting that the ultimate cliffhanger has already been done?

In the fourth season's "A Streetcar Named Marge," there are at least half a dozen references to classic movies: Maggie attempts escape from the Ayn Rand Daycare Center (!) in the style of *The Great Escape*; Homer, Bart, and Lisa show up to the center to find the babies have taken over in the style of *The Birds* (complete with pacified babies perched everywhere and a walk-on cameo from an animated Hitchcock); and, Homer expresses his initial boredom at Marge's performance by tearing his program into a fan and playing with it in the same way that Joseph Cotton's character does in *Citizen Kane* when he is forced to watch Kane's wife in her own terrible performance. Why, why, why? How can one speak to the desire to escape unjust authority, the creepiness of seeing the small and supposedly powerless suddenly take over, and the boredom associated with bad live performance without quoting these past moments of our collective experience? To have Homer say, "I'm bored"—which means, visually, drawing Homer looking bored—is to say, "I love you madly." To have Homer quote someone else in order to indicate his boredom—which means, visually, recreating (quoting) a scene from *Citizen Kane*—is to say, "As Barbara Cartland would put it, 'I love you madly.'"

AS THE COMIC BOOK STORE GUY WOULD SAY, THIS MAY BE THE WORST . . . CHAPTER . . . EVER

The Simpsons, it turns out, is not really hollow. And, all that talk upfront about needing a new theory of comedy to deal with the show was just, well, talk. We have talked a lot about talking, really. About words and language and self-reference. And, though we have taken some time to address the way in which *The Simpsons* is postmodern art, we have not really touched on why it is so funny. There have been hints here and there as to what makes it all so successfully comedic, but no fully-drawn theory of postmodern comedy has emerged.

Of course, this should only be disappointing if we were thinking that something should have been here, that we deserve something at the end. In uprooting modernity, *The Simpsons* uproots the trappings of modernity, including linearity, narrative flow, and expectation, in general. Sometimes the monster at the end of the book has been there all along. Sometimes it is the lovable old narrator himself. And, the end is, thus, the means—and always has been.

When Bart gave blood to a dying Mr. Burns only to be met with a thank you card in place of a reward, Homer responded by writing a nasty letter: "Dear Mr. Burns . . . I'm so *glad* you enjoyed my son's blood. And your *card* was *just great*. In case you can't tell, I'm being sarcastic" ("Blood Feud"). After considering having Homer beaten for his insolence, Burns relents and buys the Simpsons an extravagant gift—a gigantic $32,000 sacred Olmec carved-head statue. At the end of the episode, the Simpsons sit at home trying to figure out the meaning of it all:

HOMER: Save a guy's life and what do you get? Nothing. Worse than nothing. Just a big scary rock.

BART: Hey, man, don't bad-mouth the head.

MARGE: Homer, it's the thought that counts. The moral of the story is a good deed is its own reward.

BART: Hey, we got a reward. The head is cool.

MARGE: Then . . . I guess the moral is no good deed goes unrewarded.

HOMER: Wait a minute. If I hadn't written that nasty letter we wouldn't have gotten anything.

MARGE: Well . . . then I guess the moral is the squeaky wheel gets the grease.

LISA: Perhaps there is no moral to this story.

HOMER: Exactly! It's just a bunch of stuff that happened.

MARGE: But it certainly was a memorable few days.

HOMER: Amen to that! (Everyone laughs.)

It is not, I suppose, that any one moral does not really fit. It is that they all fit. And, in fitting, they draw attention to the plasticity of narrative itself and the clichéd manner in which narrative is necessarily understood.

And so, we have the possibility that an episode—or a chapter of a book—can be content to be aware that it is just a bunch of stuff that happens, headed only where one wants it to head, meaning exactly what it has always meant—itself and, simultaneously, everything else—avowing, especially, that even in questioning the possibility of an ending and a moral, the claim that, "It's just a bunch of stuff that happened" becomes the moral and the ending. In our Fallen era, it is thus, that we can maintain and display what is most important to us: our lack of innocence. What, after all, is not to like about the fall? We have reclaimed it to be the time of season premieres rather than finales. And so, we wear with pride our true achievements: the collection of scarlet letters that comprise our language; our giddy impurity; our proudly mongrel nature and culture; the knowledge that we know what *The Simpsons* knows, *The Simpsons* knows what we know, and we all know that we love each other madly *ad infinitum*. This, then, is how we can maintain our lack of innocence and keep our cool. And, it is, in the end, the only way to avoid the cliché, the moral, and the trite conclusion. Amen.

NOTES

1. There were attempts at this, especially in terms of the storyline involving Jerry and George trying to sell a sitcom to NBC based on their lives—on "nothing"— but the show as a whole was decidedly modernist with postmodern moments (see Auster's chapter "*Seinfeld*: The Transcendence of the Quotidian" in this volume for more on the episode).

2. Of course, you don't need to be told, but the quotational discourse references are—in order—to *Monty Python and the Holy Grail*, *The Terminator*, Mr. T as animated on *The Simpsons*, and *Airplane!*

18

Breaking and Entering

Transgressive Comedy on Television

MICHAEL V. TUETH

Over the years, American television has made various attempts at forms of comedy that dare to violate the accepted norms of middle-class values and good taste. In the television world of the 1950s when *Father Knows Best* and *The Adventures of Ozzie and Harriet* provided the models for husbandly behavior, Jackie Gleason's portrayal of Ralph Kramden, a loudmouthed, working-class braggart, on *The Honeymooners* approached forbidden territory in his threats to retaliate against his wife's remarks "one of these days" by punching her and sending her "to the moon, Alice, to the moon!" Milton's Berle's drag routines, Red Skelton's drunk characters, and Ernie Kovac's effeminate Percy Dovetonsils were similar mild violations of the social taboos of Middle America while keeping well within the traditions of slapstick and vaudeville comedy. In retrospect and even at the time of their airing, however, many viewers did not find such comic presentations amusing, and outlandish comedy often proved to be too risky for the networks. *The Ernie Kovacs Show* managed to survive for only two months in the summer of 1951 on NBC. It did not do much better when it moved to CBS, lasting only four months in the 1952–53 season. It moved back to NBC in the summer of 1956, where it lasted for only three months. *The Honeymooners* lasted only one full season (1955–56) in its half-hour situation comedy format. Gerard Jones claims that its portrayal of a working-class couple barely making ends meet and constantly arguing "played on deep anxieties" and were a "harsh reminder of a conflict being ardently denied by popular culture" (113). Once *The Honeymooners* returned as only one sketch among many on *The Jackie Gleason Show*, Ralph Kramden became more acceptable to viewers as just another example of Gleason's gift for creating eccentric characters.

Fifteen years later, Norman Lear's creations dared to speak the unspeakable, provoking frequent complaints from the guardians of good taste. In Lear's breakout success, *All in the Family*, Archie Bunker's bigotry, his daughter Gloria's feminism, and his son-in-law Mike's liberal atheism all served to shock middle-American sensibilities across the ideological spectrum of the 1970s. Lear continued this pattern with the treatment of abortion on *Maude*, homosexuality on *Mary Hartman, Mary Hartman,* and the anger of successful African Americans on *The Jeffersons*. Two of the most popular situation comedies of the 1990s, *Roseanne* and *Married . . . with Children,* thrived on offensive attitudes, outrageous behavior, taboo topics, and the language of insult.

Almost all of these instances of groundbreaking comedy appeared on major networks during prime time. Most of them were cast in the conventional context of family situation comedies. They were all subject to the pressure of network Standards and Practices policies, the threat of viewer boycotts, the sensibilities of their sponsors, and the usual consensus in favor of "least offensive programming" to appeal to the huge viewership commanded by the three major networks. A new pattern emerged, however, with the advent of cable television. Less burdened with FCC regulations, less dependent on *sponsor*-support, and freed from the need to achieve blockbuster ratings, cable television took advantage of the opportunity to appeal to a narrower demographic. In some cases, this resulted in some bold, new comedy that dared to offend, a transgressive comedy reveling in shock and tastelessness.

At the beginning of its run on the FOX network in 1989, *The Simpsons* shocked many viewers with its subversive portrayal of family life and the shadow side of the "seemingly idyllic" town of Springfield (Brooks and Marsh 1241–42). But, its transgressive comedy paled in comparison with Comedy Central's animated shocker, *South Park,* which made its debut in 1997. Despite its TV-MA rating (unsuitable for children under 17) and its later time slot of 10 PM, it became instantly popular, achieving a record-high rating for a cable series of 6.9 by February 1998. The episode that aired on April 16, 1998, proved to be the highest rated nonsports show in basic cable history. During that season, eight of the ten highest-rated shows on basic cable were *South Park* episodes (Huff 102). And, its popularity has continued.

South Park, with its presentation of "alien abductions, anal probes, flaming farts, and poo" has been described as "gleefully offensive and profoundly silly, juxtaposing cute and crude, jaded and juvenile" (Marin 56–57). With the use of childlike cutout figures, the show follows the adventures of four nine-year-old boys in a small mountain town (named after an actual county in Colorado notorious for alien sightings), which the show's creators, Trey Parker and Matt Stone, portray as a "poisoned place in the heart, a taste-free zone where kids say the darndest, most fucked-up things" (Wilde 34). The foul-mouthed boys—Stan, Kyle, Cartman, and Kenny—constantly heap abuse on each other, utter racist and other politically insensitive epithets ("Stan's dog's a homo"), question all authority, and obsess about flatulence, excrement, and other bodily functions. Stan, the leader of the group, vomits every time he encounters his semi-girlfriend, Wendy. Kenny,

Figure 18.1. (top) Kenny McCormick, (bottom row) Eric Cartman, Stan Marsh, and Kyle Broflovski in *SouthPark*. 1997– . Photo courtesy of Photofest.

who is criticized by the others because he is poor, is horribly killed in many episodes only to reappear the following week. Other prominent characters include Stan's Uncle Jimbo, a gun-rights fanatic; the school cook, Chef, the only African American in the town, who shares his fantasies and advice about sexual matters with the awestruck boys; Mr. Garrison, the delusional teacher who speaks through a hand puppet that he always carries with him; and Cartman's Mom, described by the other boys as a "crack whore." The other adults—teachers, parents, and town officials—are generally portrayed as repressed, frantic, or otherwise unworthy of any child's respect. The one exception may be Jesus Christ, who, dressed in his familiar white robe and sandals, serves as the nice-guy host of a local cable-access show, *Jesus and Pals*. It all adds up to a ribald, irreverent comedy with a "joyous lack of self-restraint . . . stridently, relentlessly, gloriously, and hilariously outrageous" (Mink 89). Like the alien visitors who menace their town, these four nasty boys invaded the world of American pop culture and took it by storm. The inevitable feature film, *South Park, the Movie: Bigger, Longer, and Uncut*, was released to high critical praise and ticket sales in the summer of 1999.

Not everyone shared the widespread enthusiasm for *South Park*. Peggy Charren, founder of Action for Children's Television, suspected that despite the TV-MA rating, many children watch the program. She was particularly concerned about the characters' use of racial slurs, indicting such language as "dangerous to the democracy" (Huff 103). Dale Kunkel, professor emeritus of communication at the University of Arizona, questioned the motives of the producers and the network. He noted that "the humor and the whole orientation of the show is adolescent-oriented humor, rejecting authority, flouting convention. . . . They say they don't want the teen audience, yet the nature of the content is significantly targeted to appeal to that audience" (Huff 103). Many parents and educators tried to quell the appeal of the show. Two grammar schools in New Jersey went so far as to send letters home to parents urging parents to stop their children from watching the show (Starr 120). These are not new issues. Concern about the influence of mass communication on the general citizenry has followed every advance in mass circulation from the penny press and lurid dime novels of the nineteenth century to the nickelodeon at the turn of the century and the hysteria-inducing *War of the Worlds* radio broadcast in 1938. But, the debate increased in volume when television "invaded" the living rooms of the nation where it often served as the new babysitter and the culture's primary storyteller.

The success of *South Park* and similar television comedy represents the "mainstreaming" of a new comic attitude previously displayed only in more marginal settings. This attitude is new enough to television to shock yet creative enough to fascinate viewers. Transgressive comedy had been breaking taboos in burlesque houses, Broadway productions, nightclubs, and even some Hollywood films over the years. Gypsy Rose Lee's suggestive remarks combined with her "dignified" strip teases attracted not only large audiences but many imitators. The male comedians in the burlesque theaters pushed the boundaries of good taste even further with their ribald remarks. Many a Broadway musical would feature a "naughty song": Eddie Cantor's "Making Whoopie"; Cole Porter's "Let's Misbehave" and the number "Always True to You (In My Fashion)" in *Kiss Me Kate*; and, Rodgers and Hammerstein's trio of faux-innocent ditties, "Kansas City," "I Cain't Say No," and "All er Nothin'," in their first collaboration, *Oklahoma*.

Even the more family-friendly medium of Hollywood films tested the waters. Mae West's own ribald screenplays, double-entendres, and her moans and poses in her Broadway hits and her blockbuster films, *She Done Him Wrong, I'm No Angel,* and *My Little Chickadee*, delighted her many fans, made huge amounts of money for the studios, but shocked the censors (Louvish 208–214). The release of Howard Hughes' 1943 film, *The Outlaw*, featuring Jane Russell in her first movie role, was held back for three years because of the objections of Hollywood censors (Brown and Broeske 165–66, 207–08). Russell's other Howard Hughes film, *The French Line* (1954), drew the ire of the Catholic Church, whose Legion of Decency condemned the film and ordered the faithful to boycott the movie (Brown and Broeske 244–45). The jokes and stories of the African American "dirty old woman," Moms Mabley, while primarily serving as satires of racism, lynching, segregation, and other abuses, also shocked audiences with tales of her sexual adventures. Her subversive humor made her a major success in theaters, films, nightclubs, and on many recordings from the 1920s to the 1970s (Elsie A. Williams 119–32).[1]

In *Jokes and Their Relation to the Unconscious*, Sigmund Freud analyzes the purpose of jokes. Freud first considers "innocent" jokes such as puns and other plays on words that are enjoyed for their cleverness and playfulness with no further purpose and usually evoke a chuckle of moderate amusement, for example, "knock-knock" jokes. He then deals with "tendentious jokes," which seem to provoke much more laughter and therefore are probably serving some deeper psychological purpose. Freud sees only two types of such humor. "It is either a *hostile* joke (serving the purpose of aggressiveness, satire, or defense) or an *obscene* joke (serving the purpose of exposure)" (97). His explanation of the higher amount of pleasure derived from these two types of humor, especially the obscene, derives directly from his view of "civilization and its discontents":

It is our belief that civilization and higher education have a large influence in the development of repression, and we suppose that, under such conditions, the psychical organization undergoes an alteration (that can also emerge as an inherited disposition) as a result of which what was formerly felt as agreeable now seems unacceptable and is rejected with all possible psychical force. The repressive activity of civilization brings it about that primary possibilities of enjoyment, which have now, however, been repudiated by the censorship in us, are lost to us. But, to the human psyche all renunciation is exceedingly difficult, and so we find that tendentious jokes provide a means of undoing the renunciation and retrieving what was lost. (101)

Since civilization and education remove "the primary possibilities of enjoyment" found in uninhibited aggressive and sexual activity, certain types of humor allow us to "retrieve what was lost," to regress to the more primal state of childhood with its accompanying lack of inhibitions.

It is particularly pertinent to this chapter that, as Freud proceeds to analyze the operation of the smutty joke, he observes that its sexual material can include anything that is "common to both sexes and to which the feeling of shame extends, what is excremental in the most comprehensive sense" (101). He specifically refers to "the sense covered by sexuality in childhood, an age at which there is, as it were, a cloaca within which what is sexual and what is excremental are barely or not at all distinguished" (97–98). The farting, vomiting, and sexual curiosity of the South Park boys vividly exemplify such interconnection. Freud distinguishes the obscene joke, with its purpose of exposure, from the hostile joke, which serves the purpose of aggressiveness or defense. Satirical comedy is one form of such aggression, attacking its target from a sense of outrage and with the hope of some reform. Juvenal catalogued the moral corruption of Rome; Moliere ridiculed the religious hypocrites, the lying doctors, and the miserly parental tyrants of Louis XIV's Paris; Pope and Dryden depicted the vanity and foppery of London society; Heller, Vonnegut, Kubrick, and other twentieth-century artists have employed absurdist techniques to oppose the stupidities of modern warfare and military culture. Such is the grand aggressive tradition of satire: human reason's warfare on human folly.

Transgressive humor—what Freud would call "obscene" jokes—has no such moral purpose. Instead of trying to change or eliminate human foolishness, certain comic writers and performers deliberately revel in the lower forms of social behavior. Unlike the rational wit and verbal sophistication of true satire, transgressive humor regresses to the infantile. Rather than portraying the objects of its humor in hopes that witty ridicule and public shame might provoke change, transgressive humor does not expect or even desire a change because then the fun would end. Transgressive humor does share one element with satire. Both comic methods depend on a basic consensus of standards and boundaries, otherwise the joke would not be funny. For transgressive comedy, the societal taboos and the misbehavior that satire wishes to end must remain, so that one can experience the delight of the entry into forbidden realms, a childish joy in simply breaking all the adult taboos, a joy indulged in for the sake of exposure of our common human condition, the impulses we have all been forced to repress.

Although they are different forms of comedy theoretically, sometimes there is an overlap between transgressive humor and satire, in which the breaking of a taboo may also serve as a critique. Transgressive humor, purposely or not, can sometimes serve general satirical purposes by its faux-innocent, ignorant, or playful critique of ignorance, prejudice, or stereotypes. For example, in a transgressive context, the articulation of an offensive word or performance of an offensive action operates to transform stigmatization into empowerment. Consider a rapper's use of the n-word, a woman's use of the word "bitch," or the gay comedian's use of the word "queer" or "faggot." Such an appropriation of the insult, which previously had been used to intimidate or threaten a certain group, now disempowers the attacker.

Transgressive humor sometimes adds a subtle twist to this formula. While the comic speaker may not be a member of the target group, the speaker's humor attempts to signify his or her solidarity with the group by joining in their appropriation of the hostile or outrageous language or actions. Such seems to have been the intent of a highly publicized attempt at transgressive humor that resulted in considerable confusion and offense, a blackface act performed by the television star Ted Danson at a Friars Club roast of the African American comedian Whoopi Goldberg in 1993. The routine had been written primarily by Goldberg, who was romantically involved with Danson at the time. In the long tradition of the Friars Club roasts, Danson's routine was sexually explicit with many references to black sexual stereotypes, outrageous sexual positions, and Goldberg's anatomy. Danson also joked about racist social stereotypes, reporting that when he brought Whoopi to meet his family, they asked her to do the laundry and wash the dishes and offered to drive her to the nearest bus stop when she had finished. Many prominent African Americans in the audience were deeply offended, however, including former Mayor David Dinkins and television talk-show host Montel Williams, who cancelled his membership in the Friars (Williams 2D).

Another oblique technique is to place the transgressive remarks or actions in the mouth or body of a character for ironic effect. For instance, in *All in the Family*, when Archie Bunker refers to "jungle bunnies," "wops," or "fags," his obvious ignorance heightens the transgressive humor for audience members who also appreciate the irony as a critique of Archie's attitudes. Similarly, the *South Park* children's emotional and mental immaturity and undeveloped impulse control allow them to speak the unspeakable and act out forbidden behavior. The adults to whom the program is ostensibly targeted are presumed to understand and enjoy the irony.

Precedents for the outrageous comedy of *South Park* can readily be found in the practices of various folk cultures. The more widely known influence, however, can be traced to the long tradition in European societies among the common people as well as the highly educated of organized periods of anarchy and official societies that regularly violated and often criticized the standards and practices of their cultures. In Enid Welsford's classic study of the social and literary history of the fool, she describes the phenomenon of "misrule," which was quite popular in European societies from Roman days until the late Renaissance. She refers us to Lucian's *Saturnalia* and its description of the "Liberties of December," a Roman practice at the time of the winter solstice when "for a short while masters and slaves changed places, laws lost their force, and a mock-king ruled over a topsy-turvy world" (201).

In the Christian era, there were even instances of the clergy engaging in public folly in which "mighty persons were humbled, sacred things profaned, laws relaxed and ethical ideals reversed, under the leadership of a Patriarch, Pope, or Bishop of Fools" (201). In the cathedral towns of twelfth-century France, the Feast of Fools was an annual occurrence during which even the Mass was burlesqued. Instead of waving censors of incense, the clergy would swing chains of sausages. Instead of sprinkling the congregation with holy water, some of the sacred ministers would be doused with buckets of water. Sometimes an ass was brought into the church, and "on these occasions solemn Mass was punctuated with brays and howls." The celebrant would conclude the liturgy by braying three times (*ter hinhannabit*), and the people would respond in similar fashion (202). The official Church, of course, persistently condemned such behavior, so the eventually secular associations took up the role of seasonal fools. Groups such as the *Societes Joyeuses* flourished from the end of the fifteenth century to the middle of the seventeenth century. Welsford describes them as

> associations of young men who adapted the traditional fool's dress of motley, eared hoods, bells and baubles and organized themselves into kingdoms under the rule of an annually elected monarch known as *Prince des Sots, Mere-Folle*, etc. . . . which enabled them to keep up a running commentary on the affairs of their neighbours and to indulge a taste for satire and social criticism. (205)

This practice also continued as a popular tradition among the upper classes in England. Examples include the traditional feast of the "boy-bishop" among the choirboys of the English cathedrals and the Christmas Revels of the Lord of Misrule among university students at the Inns of Court and in the English and Scottish royal courts of the fifteenth and sixteenth centuries. But, in France, the holiday tradition became a permanent feature among the upper classes. As Welsford notes, what had been seen as an annual social safety valve developed into a "permanent and legally recognized institution, whose members were pledged to more or less continuous representation of the whole of society as a 'great stage of fools'" (205).

Eventually the social satire that had been only "the occasional by-product of the Feast of Fools became the whole business of the Societe Joyeuse" (205). Welsford describes the development as a change in the understanding of the purpose of a fool. "The Enfants-sans-souci emphasized the idea of folly as a mask for the wise and armour of the critic. Their 'Misrule' was no temporary relaxation of law and order, but a more subtle and permanent reversal of ordinary judgments. It was the wisdom of Mere-Folle to display the folly of the wise (218)."

One is left with the question of whether the transgressive humor of *South Park* and similar television shows is meant to be a mere relaxation of all prevailing norms, like the early Saturnalia and Feasts of Fools, or as a constant satirical commentary on the powerful and famous. Should the foul-mouthed children of *South Park* be considered our boy-bishops (fools for a day) or our *Enfants-sans-souci* (year-round fools)? Since it appears on a weekly basis throughout the year, the series could be understood as a break in the week's routine or the regular weekly meeting of the global-village idiots. Can the viewing of such programming offer an opportunity for a "more subtle and permanent reversal of ordinary judgments"?

Can such programming be truly oppositional and not just a holiday from the prevailing hegemony? John Fiske's approach to the "pleasure and play" of television viewing seems to opt for the oppositional interpretation, describing some readings of the television texts as expressions of resistance to the prevailing norms. He points to Schwichtenburg's account of the stylistic excess and fetishism in *Miami Vice* in which "it is important to render pleasure out of bounds" (Schwichtenberg 47). Fiske comments:

> This sort of pleasure lies in the refusal of the social control inscribed in the "bounds." While there is clearly a pleasure in exerting social power, the popular pleasures of the subordinate are necessarily found in resisting, evading, or offending this power. Popular pleasures are those that empower the subordinate, and they thus offer political resistance, even if only momentarily and even if only in a limited terrain. (*Television* 230)

With their crude language and the offensive actions, the characters on *South Park* seem to develop what Fiske goes on to describe as "an alternative semiotic strategy of resistance or evasion" (*Television* 240). As a model of such cultural resistance, Fiske uses the example of the carnival:

> . . . not in its more overtly political or even revolutionary [sense] of attempting to overthrow the social system. Rather it refers to the refusal to accept the social identity proposed by the dominant ideology and the social control that goes with it. The refusal of ideology, of its meanings and control, may not of itself challenge the dominant social system but it does resist incorporation and it does maintain and strengthen a sense of social difference that is a prerequisite to any more direct social challenge. (*Television* 242)

One might consider drag performances and post-binary representations of gender as examples of such resistance to still-prevalent gender roles. In *South Park*, if only for 22 minutes a week (with, of course, hours more of reruns), the four boys refuse to accept the social identity proposed by the dominant ideology and the social control that goes with it. They refuse to conform to the prevailing definitions of well-behaved little boys.

One final observation of Fiske's is particularly relevant to the comedy of *South Park* and other animated comedies of recent years. The self-referential nature of much of the humor creates what Fiske has called an "empowering inversion of viewer relations" (*Television* 242). Beavis and Butthead spend considerable time watching and commenting on the music videos typical of MTV, the very channel that carries the show. *The Simpsons* and *King of the Hill* have often provided frequent visual jokes about the art of animation and the existence of their characters as products of animators and not actual persons. One of the most sophisticated examples is *The Simpsons* episode "Behind the Laughter" that takes the viewers behind the show, as VH1 does with *Behind the Music,* and interviews each of the main characters as if they are actual actors looking for other work. This conspiracy between the creators and viewers to acknowledge the artifice of television primes the viewer to question the legitimacy of any televised versions of "reality."

It seems that *South Park* and similar oppositional comedies have spawned several successful imitators, inserting more irreverence and shock into the comic landscape of television. The presence, for example, of blatant womanizers on *Two and a Half Men* and *How I Met Your Mother,* recovering alcoholics on *Mom,* sexually adventurous young women on *2 Broke Girls,* misbehaving older family members on *Mike and Molly,* and others—all of them, by the way, originating on CBS with its older demographic—suggests that such portrayals continue to appeal to a general audience.

Since Gitlin ascribes the softening of *All in the Family's* edges to commercial decisions, perhaps the greatest hope for transgressive comedy lies in the viewer-driven nature of cable television as opposed to the broadcast networks' subservience to advertisers. Alan Ball, Academy Award–winning writer of *American Dream, Cybill, Six Feet Under,* and *True Blood* has remarked that he chose to write *Six Feet Under* for HBO because network TV places too many creative restraints to attract a cheerful audience "primed by the fantasy in the shows for the fantasy in the products" (Friend 82). Ball and others believe that commercial-free cable television offers an alternative situation, connecting more esoteric programming with a more select but highly appreciative target audience. This seems to be borne out by the popularity of classic taboo-breaking cable programs like *Oz, Sex and the City, The Sopranos;* more recent comedies such as *Nurse Jackie* (drug addiction), *Girls* (graphic sexual activity and promiscuity), and *It's Always Sunny in Philadelphia* (crude language and behavior bordering on violence); more dramatic series such as *Game of Thrones* (sex and violence); and the frank depiction of gay life and graphic sexual activity on *Looking.*

The arrival of the Internet has offered many more programs, of various time lengths, to amuse the fans of transgressive comedy. Sites such as Funny or Die and YouTube feature many shorter outrageous presentations, that come and go, some of them moving on to cable television. *Louis C.K.*

Live and *Drunk History*, for example, have recently moved to cable channels. If this is the case, then cable television and the Internet will enable those viewers who delight in the violation of cultural taboos their best hope of indulging their anti-social appetites. Every week, they can join the foolish company of Stan, Kenny, Cartman, and Kyle and enjoy the carnival while it lasts. In one way or another, transgressive comedy has continued to thrive for thousands of years from the days of ancient Greek and Roman festivals to the digital age we live in today. While transgressive comedy has amused audiences in so many public places and occasions, it has finally entered the relative privacy of the home environment where it shows no signs of leaving.

NOTE

1. A transcript of Mabley's hilarious performance at the Greek Theater in 1971 is provided on pages 154–72 of Elsie A. Williams' study.

19

Sealed with a Kiss

Heteronormative Narrative Strategies in NBC's *Will & Grace*[1]

DENIS M. PROVENCHER

Heterosexual desire and romance are thought to be the very core of humanity . . . It is the one thing celebrated in every film plot, every sitcom, every advertisement (Warner 47).

AN INTRODUCTION TO *WILL & GRACE*: (HETEROSEXUAL) PAIRINGS AND THE ON-SCREEN KISS

NBC's situation comedy *Will & Grace* is the most recent prime-time television effort since ABC's *Ellen* to deal with lavender issues in a significant way. In fact, Andrew Holleran refers to *Will & Grace* as the first "gay sitcom" and describes its content as "not merely gay, but hard-edged, LA circuit-queen gay. . . . Nothing of the gay content has been held back, nothing homogenized" (65). Indeed, weekly episodes of *Will & Grace* incorporate many elements of gay experience as depicted through various storylines, themes, and the characters' use of gay English (Leap). Thus, this sitcom (linguistically) subverts many norms related to gender and sexuality in pioneering ways.

Will & Grace has been recognized for its creative and innovative efforts. In September 2000, the show won three Emmy awards, including best situation comedy, best supporting actor, and best supporting actress.

In November 2001, Eric McCormick won the Emmy award for best male actor. Moreover, NBC producers moved the sitcom into their Thursday night "Must See television" prime-time lineup during the 2000–2001 season. In addition, in the spring of 2001, GLAAD (Gay and Lesbian Alliance Against Defamation) presented a media award to the show's producers for their commitment to dealing with gay issues on commercial television. In a sense, *Will & Grace* attempts to present "fresh" and "positive" images of homosexuality and gay men in everyday situations analogous to how *The Cosby Show* normalized African Americans on television during the 1980s.

Nonetheless, in its attempt to mainstream homosexuality on commercial U.S. television, *Will & Grace* still falls short in its visual representations of homosexuality and gay experiences. If we examine the narrative structure of this situation comedy, we see how it resembles many other successful network sitcoms with its use of male-female character couplings. In fact, from the very beginning, this show suggests a heteronormative trap with its title that implies: "the codependent relationship between a man and a woman who can do everything but sleep with each other" (Holleran 65). The show's use of character duos certainly reinforces this notion. Several examples underscore this point.

During the sitcom's first four years (with the exception of season two), the eponymous characters, Will Truman (a gay lawyer) and Grace Adler (a straight interior designer) share a Manhattan apartment, which visually reinforces a heteronormative storyline and "codependent relationship." In addition, throughout the show, they share evenings in front of the television, eat meals together at home and in restaurants, exchange heart-to-heart conversations, and share numerous affectionate moments. These include walking down the street together, holding hands, sitting close together on the couch and in the bedroom, calling each other at work to make "dates," sharing financial expenses, escorting each other to weddings, and kissing on a regular basis (often under the pretense of a "wedding" ceremony).

Moreover, the show's supporting cast follows a similar narrative path. Jack McFarland (an "actor-singer-dancer" and generally unemployed gay character) and Karen Walker (Grace's "office assistant," married to a wealthy business man) hang out together, go shopping, recount outrageous stories, support each other through their respective addictions and character flaws, touch each other inappropriately, share hugs, and exchange tongue-filled kisses. In a similar manner, Jack and Rosario (Karen Walker's straight San Salvadorian maid) get married to keep her in the country, watch television

Figure 19.1. Sean Hayes as Jack McFarland, Megan Mullally as Karen Walker, Debra Messing as Grace Adler, and Eric McCormack as Will Truman in *Will & Grace*. 1998–2006. Photo courtesy of Movie Star NewsFair.

together in bed, share living quarters in Karen's uptown penthouse (during the first and second seasons), and lock lips to convince immigration officers of their long-time commitment.

Hence, this sitcom provides a series of affectionate visual moments for its male-female couplings, many of which take place in domestic settings that suggest "family" values. Moreover, each of these three "couples" engages in some act of kissing during the first four years. Television viewers also regularly observe expressions of affection, kissing, and sexual activity between Grace and her various boyfriends who come and go (i.e., Danny, Josh, Ben, Nathan, etc.). In contrast, the show's two gay characters, Will and Jack never appear in affectionate (or sexual) pairings—neither with each other nor with any other gay male character who drifts in and out of the sitcom. In fact, in many episodes, Will and Jack do not even appear together. Jack often conveniently forgets to meet Will for a prearranged rendezvous. Furthermore, Will regularly appears annoyed by Jack and occasionally ditches him to spend time with his best friend, Grace. In addition, Will rarely goes out on dates, and Jack often complains about Will's "anti-gay" behavior with such remarks as: "Do you *ever* touch men?" Although Jack complains about having to juggle several of his own boyfriends, little visual evidence of this occurs on screen. In essence, virtually no visual display of same-sex affection takes place and certainly no suggestive hugging or kissing appears on the small screen for either of the show's two "gay" characters.

Indeed, the history of same-sex affection and kissing on commercial television is quite precarious. Of course, same-sex affection has found a place on public television in such PBS miniseries as *Tales of the City* and on cable series such as *Queer as Folk* and *Six Feet Under*. Moreover, network television episodes of such series as *thirtysomething, L.A. Law, Roseanne,* and most recently, *ER* and *Dawson's Creek* have included suggestions or expressions of same-sex desire (Bruni 327–28). Some major networks, however, have subsequently retracted from syndication many of these particular episodes. As Bruni points out: "Seeing a same-sex couple kiss makes it impossible for an observer to think about homosexuality only as an abstraction or to interpret warm interaction between two men or two women as something else—something less disturbing" (328). Hence, major commercial networks aim to minimize overt representations of same-sex affection and kissing on prime-time U.S. television so as not to offend the "viewing American majority" or commercial television sponsors (Hantzis and Lehr 119–20; Moritz 140–41; Hubert 35).

The characters on *Will & Grace* are squarely situated in this same "kissing" tradition. The fact that *Will & Grace* represents the "first gay sitcom" yet includes virtually no visual evidence of gay affection or kissing is quite remarkable. In the remainder of this chapter, I analyze the use of the on-screen kiss for both opposite-sex and same-sex couples in *Will & Grace*. I compare and contrast a representative episode that presents an opposite-sex kiss (between Will & Grace) with the only episode to include a same-sex kiss between two men (Will and Jack) during the show's first four years. The one-time occurrence of an "unsentimental" gay kiss in contrast with the continual recurrence of the "straight kiss" between male-female couplings on this "gay sitcom" merits some critical attention and explanation.

YOU MAY KISS THE BRIDE:
SAME-SEX CIVIL UNION OR STRAIGHT LOVERS' QUARREL?

I begin my study of the "semantic smooch" on *Will & Grace* with an examination of the episode "Coffee and Commitment" from the third season. Although a whole chain of other quasi-romantic kisses—that imply Will and Grace's semi-married status—occur during many other episodes, this particular embrace represents perhaps the most problematic example of the opposite-sex kiss and its heteronormative undertones as they emerge on the small screen. In fact, this episode most closely resembles an exchange between husband and wife (or groom and bride-groom) of any storyline during the show's first four years.

In "Coffee and Commitment," Will and Grace drive to Vermont with Jack and Karen to attend Joe and Larry's same-sex civil union, the first ceremony of its kind to be depicted on prime-time television since the law's inception in December 1999. As the civil-union ceremony begins, the female justice of the peace introduces the same-sex couple (Joe and Larry), however, she never utters the names of the two men who participate in this union: "What a wonderful day, and what a wonderful couple." The fact that the justice never verbally recognizes the couple in a direct manner leaves the text open for interpretation as to who actually ties the knot. Directly following this opening greeting, the camera cuts away to Will and Grace who sit as attendants and continue an argument that ensued between them earlier in the day. During the argument, Will expresses his discontent associated with always having to pay for and take care of their common expenses (dinner, bills, dry cleaning, wedding gifts, and cards). He also admits his desire to be invited to such events with a male guest and wonders why his invitations are always marked "Will and Grace" instead of "Will and guest."

As both the argument and the ceremony unfold, the justice of the peace calls upon friends and family members (of Joe and Larry) to share their readings. Again, she never specifies the names of the two people who stand at the altar: "And now, I'd like to call upon your friends here who have some words they'd like to share with you." In turn, both Jack McFarland and Joe's sister Joan offer their individual readings. Again, during Joan's reading, the camera cuts away to focus on the ongoing argument between Will and Grace. In the midst of this "lovers' quarrel," the justice of the peace interrupts Will and Grace and calls on them to stand and do their reading.[2] It is important to note here that both Jack and Joan have been asked to do individual readings. The fact that Will and Grace do a joint reading is exceptional because at most U.S. weddings, in contrast to a song that may be sung in duet, a reading is usually done individually. Thus, considering the circumstances, this narrative situation seems extraordinary as it foregrounds Will and Grace, who must stand side by side in a wedding-like pose while they read from a printed card:

WILL: When I'm feeling like there's no love coming to me . . .

GRACE: And I have no love to give . . .

WILL: When I'm feeling separated from the world . . .

GRACE: And cut off from myself . . .

WILL: When I'm feeling annoyed by every little thing . . .

GRACE: Because I'm not getting what I want . . . I'll remember that there is an infinite amount of love available to me.

WILL: And I'll see it in you.

GRACE: I'll remember that I am complete within myself . . .

WILL: So I'll never have to look to you to complete me.

WILL and GRACE: And most of all, I'll remember that everything that I really need I already have, and whatever I don't have will come to me when I'm ready to receive it.

WILL: (To Grace.) Oh, my God. I am so sorry.

GRACE: Me, too.

WILL: I love you. You know that, right?

GRACE: I know.

(Joe and Larry glance nervously at each other.)

WILL: Don't you?

GRACE: I do. And you know I love you, right?

WILL: I do. (Will and Grace kiss and hug.)

(Everyone claps. Will and Grace hold hands and walk down the aisle.)

GRACE: Thanks for coming!

JOE: Guys? Hey, guys! Guys! We're not really done here.

(Embarrassed, Will and Grace quickly sit back down.)

As Will and Grace do the reading, little by little they turn toward each other. By the end of the recitation, they are actually facing each other and pronouncing the words in unison. Once the reading is complete, Will and Grace remain standing and proceed to share their feelings for each other in a public display that is not unlike exchanging marriage vows. Each one confirms their "commitment" to the other with the traditionally scripted wedding phrase, "I do." Moreover, when Will and Grace exchange their mutual remarks about "love," the camera cuts away to the nervous same-sex couple (Joe and Larry), and the television laugh track intervenes suggesting that viewers take notice of this narrative twist. In addition, they consummate this "relationship" by sealing the narrative with a kiss and proceeding to leave the chapel in the traditional chain of matrimonial events. Finally, the wedding attendants acknowledge this consummation by clapping.

It is important to note that the civil union between Joe and Larry is never visually consummated on screen. There is no exchange of vows or any physical display of affection between the two of them during the ceremony. The only exchange that ensues involves a worried look that subtly suggests their frustration with Will and Grace, who take over, or "steal the spotlight," at their civil-union ceremony. The justice of the peace never delivers any sort of performative declaration or final proclamation ("I now pronounce you . . .") that could consecrate this union or authenticate, naturalize, or normalize such an event for television viewers. The congregation never has the opportunity to recognize the couple as "bound" in any kind of union. After the ceremony, the camera cuts to Joe and Larry, who unwrap various wedding gifts and thank their attendants for their kindness. This image is balanced and to some degree neutralized, however, by the image of Will and Grace who sit nestled in a corner sharing a single piece of wedding cake. Finally, the fact that Will and Grace have offered a single wedding gift with a card signed "from Will and Grace" reconfirms Will and Grace's relationship for both the characters and viewers.

The writers of *Will & Grace* recycle many elements of a "marriage" narrative in several episodes throughout the sitcom's first four seasons. Moreover, the kiss is often recycled to situate their relationship into a heteronormative framework. I would like to stress that it is not one individual episode or occurrence, per se, that makes the straight kiss so problematic on a "gay sitcom." On the contrary, it is the ceaseless repetition of such visual acts throughout the four seasons, not only between Will and Grace, but also between Jack and Rosario and Jack and Karen, that allows a narrative of heteronormativity to emerge. Indeed, to some extent *Will & Grace* parodies both gay and straight relationships. This is certainly the case for Grace and her boyfriend, Josh, (with her constant neglect of him and his annoying forehead kisses), as well as the superficial relationship between Karen and her unseen husband Stanley. Moreover, Karen's character regularly challenges family values through her unapologetic use of alcohol and drugs, disinterest in her children, and her allusions to adulterous acts. Some scholars even argue that Karen represents the "queerest" (most non-normative) character on the show (Holleran 66; Kanner 34–35). Nevertheless, it is important to remember the power of the visual message and the repetition of such messages on actors that makes characters appear "believable," "natural," and "realistic" in both their gendered and sexually oriented roles.

Judith Butler reminds us that the body is but "a passive medium that is signified by an inscription from a cultural source figured as 'external' to the body" (129). Indeed, an individual's (gender or sexual) identity becomes inscribed on the surface of the body through carefully crafted artifice (136). Butler adds that "the action of gender requires a performance that is *repeated* . . . gender is an identity tenuously constituted in time, instituted in an exterior space through a *stylized repetition of acts*" (140). Similarly, sexual orientation, as it appears on the small and big screens is created through a stylized repetition of acts, through both visualized production and reproduction. It is through Will and Grace's repeated affection and exchange of kisses (across multiple episodes) that allow Will to emerge as a "straight character" and for Will and Grace to "come out" as the palatable "straight couple" for television viewers. Similarly, I believe it is Jack's visual coupling with Karen and Rosario that allows him to "pass" on prime-time television despite his outrageously flaming comments and behavior. The repeated acts of kissing that take place between Will and Grace (as well as between Jack and his assorted female sidekicks and between Grace and her assorted boyfriends) authenticates and normalizes straight relationships and negates or nullifies the signs of a homosexual narrative. Indeed, verbal or linguistic parody takes place regularly on the show. Nevertheless, it is the visual message that works with and at times against these verbal messages to create meaning for television viewers.

YOU MAY KISS THE . . . NOT YOUR BOYFRIEND, MY ASS!

In comparison to the opposite-sex kisses that regularly take place between characters on *Will & Grace*, the same-sex (male-male) kiss only emerges once during the show's first four years, and television viewers must wait until halfway through the second season to see such a display. In this episode, "Acting Out," Will, Grace, and Jack all become television spectators as they settle in to watch "the first ever prime-time kiss between two men" on their new favorite television sitcom *Along Came You*. The three characters sit on the couch and hold hands (Grace sits between Will and Jack) as they await the lip lock between the two male characters. The kiss never comes.

At the end of this scene, both Jack and Grace express their shared disappointment with the show while Will reinforces the heteronormative narrative and conservative (middle-class) values with his voice of homophobic reason: "Clearly, nobody wants to see two men kissing on television. Not the network, not the viewers, not the advertiser." This spectatorial disappointment provokes Jack to take matters into his own hands by filing an official complaint at NBC headquarters. Will eventually follows Jack down to the NBC studios where they meet NBC's Executive Vice President in charge of public relations, who tells them: "But you will never see two gay men kissing on network television." Jack responds: "Wha—It's a gay network, for God's sake! The symbol is a peacock!" Indeed, there is room for some queer linguistic maneuver in this episode as Jack mocks the network that produces the very sitcom in which he appears. Nonetheless, Jack does not see any resolution to his complaint from the television executives.

After leaving the NBC headquarters, Jack and Will spot weatherman Al Roker in the street hosting NBC's *The Today Show*. After getting Roker's attention and following a bit of idle conversation with the weatherman, Jack proceeds to make his plea "on national television" to see "two hotties get it on."

> JACK: . . . the reason we're here. Um, I don't know if you're aware, but on this week's episode of *Along Came You*, there was supposed to be a kiss and there wasn't.

AL ROKER: You know, Jack, sometimes a kiss is just not a kiss. Do we have any annivers . . .

JACK: Whoa, whoa, back to Jack. We went to complain, and this closet case upstairs—cute, in an offbeat way, got his number—totally gave us the brush off. And I just want to know how long I'm going to have to wait until I can see two gay men kiss on network television.

WILL: Not as long as you'd think.

(Will grabs Jack and kisses him. The crowd cheers.)

At first glance, it appears that the gay kiss (between Will and Jack) has finally emerged on a major network sitcom. The writers have made the attempt to authenticate the characters of Will and Jack by depicting them going into the NBC studios. This is not unlike the effect of the "live camera" on *Late Night with Jay Leno* or *Saturday Night Live* (or any of the other voyeuristic shows such as *MTV Real World*, *Survivor*, *Big Brother*, etc.) that presents seemingly "real" or "live" situations. This episode, however, becomes sanctified or "authenticated" with the use of Al Roker and *The Today Show* label because the weatherman is a "real life" figure who may listen to Jack and broadcast his message on "live" television. Jack also attempts to make this experience as real as possible for the viewers of *Will & Grace* when he says: "We need to get the message out there . . . I know! I'll write an epic poem and post it on my website—www.justjack. com . . ." In fact, this website did exist when this episode first aired.

Finally, the writers of this episode have tried to authenticate this gay kiss by placing Jack and Will on the street with hundreds of other "real" spectators. Indeed, the event is well strategized; it cannot be missed, and all of New York City is there to see it. In Holleran's words: "[the characters] seemed so free, so believable all of a sudden, out in the open air. There was spaciousness about their world, and suddenly the possibility of their interaction with real life, the real city, and real emotions, rose up" (66). Like many of the kisses that appear on *Will & Grace*, the "gay kiss" is recognized and encouraged by the roar of the on-looking spectators.

This particular episode clearly illustrates the lack of affection between two same-sex characters that continues to persist on prime-time commercial television. First, Will kisses Jack in a "read my lips" fashion to make a political statement about gay representations in the media. It is done out of the blue and is not "passionate" per se. Will admits "four seconds before we did it, I didn't know I was going to do it. And then . . . I just did it." Moreover, Jack's reaction does not indicate any passion directed in Will's direction: "I just pray none of my boyfriends saw that tragic display. 'Cause that's like five serious long-term relationships down the tube." Neither character can explain the precise goal of the kiss or be hopeful of a positive outcome from it.

It is important to remember that at the very moment the kiss occurs, Will and Jack have become actors in a television broadcast (*The Today Show*) within another television show (*Will & Grace*). This is a production within a production or, in theatrical terms, a play within a play (Forestier). So many layers of artifice now exist between the spectator of *Will & Grace* and the two characters (Will and Jack) that the kiss remains virtually impossible to read as an authentic form of expression between two gay men. They are no longer the weekly characters in the first-level text (Will and Jack in *Will & Grace*) but are now characters in the second-level text (Will and Jack in *Will & Grace* in *The Today Show*) involved in the theatrics of this new layer. The other characters from *Will & Grace* have become the spectator-characters of the first-level text who watch Will and Jack on the small screen of the second-level text.

By tuning in to *The Today Show* and watching Will and Jack perform their gay identity, everyone else on *Will & Grace* has become a spectator-character, and in turn this first layer of text has become more "real" and closer to the television audience's lived experience than what transpires between Will and Jack on the set of *The Today Show*. In a sense, the *Will & Grace* set has dissolved as spectator-characters emerge; moreover, as television spectators, we are drawn into the "realness" of this first-level of text. For example, Grace and her boyfriend, Josh, watch *The Today Show* from bed. Karen and her husband, Stan, watch it from the tub. Mrs. Freeman (the assistant to Will's boss, Ben Doucette) watches from the law firm. One would think that this would authenticate the kiss between Will and Jack. As television viewers, however, we become as interested, if not more interested, in the point of view of the spectator-characters who appear almost as real as us watching NBC television. It is also worth noting that the laugh track intervenes here to draw our attention to the reaction of the spectator-characters and detract us from the kissing event itself. Karen gasps at the sight of the two men kissing and sinks into the tub. Mrs. Freeman shares her own acrimonious opinion of Will and Jack's act: "Not your boyfriend, my ass." Finally, Grace freaks out since she has been trying to break up with Josh by convincing him that she is in love with Will. In fact, it is her reaction to this lip event that is the most extreme, as she later storms into Will's apartment and exclaims: "Well, thank you very much! Because of your little on-air lip lock, I am going to spend the next week in an *ashram* with no heat with my undumped boyfriend Josh . . . some big queen on *The Today Show* blew my alibi."

The television audience becomes separated from the gay kiss—not only through the multiple layers of action that take place—but also through the displacement of viewing pleasure. As viewers, we are diverted by the reaction of the new spectators (Grace, Josh, Karen, and Mrs. Freeman), and it is at least in portion from their reactions during this narrative game that we draw our viewing pleasure. Grace's words serve as a reminder that Will & Grace should be together in principle, and it is her reaction coupled with her word choice that counteract, or help to negate, the "homosexual act" that has just occurred. Grace's use of the word "queen" emphasizes how this attempted act of same-sex affection on television was an unusual, if not derogatory, homosexual act. In a sense, her voice of reason intervenes at the end of this episode and acts as a deus ex machina to bring the heteronormative narrative back where it belongs.

CONCLUDING REMARKS:
IN SEARCH OF HOMONORMATIVE NARRATIVES

In this chapter I have emphasized the absence of the "gay kiss" and the problematic recurrence of the "straight kiss" on a gay sitcom. We could argue that *Will & Grace* is just a sitcom, and viewers should not expect more from this show than a few laughs. The fact remains, however, that a limited range of (straight) signifiers, storylines, and plots are recycled on this sitcom and throughout a whole range of commercial television shows that include gay and lesbian characters. It is worth noting that in the fall of 2001, CBS began airing the new sitcom, *The Ellen Show*. In a July 2001 interview, Ellen DeGeneres admitted that her former show (*Ellen*) "got to be too issue-oriented" and promised that her new show would be "all about funny this time" [hence, less political] (Keveney). In *The Ellen Show*, DeGeneres plays a gay character who returns to her small hometown after having just left a relationship. This is the same premise on which *Will & Grace* began in 1998. Hence, in parallel to *Will & Grace* (and their relationship), many commercial prime-time television series still continue to avoid the candid treatment of gay characters and their stories by portraying them as "de-sexed" and "uncoupled" second-class citizens who must participate in heteronormative settings to find a sense of "normalcy" or "belonging." It should come as no surprise that *Will & Grace* has received overwhelming support from (straight) "middle America" since the show produces and reproduces gay characters (and their female counterparts) in multiple heteronormative situations.

Indeed, we must be thankful to NBC, the producers, writers, and actors of *Will & Grace* for tackling such a "touchy" subject and bringing it to the small screen. This show has certainly begun to lead U.S. television out of the closet by putting gay male characters on prime-time commercial television. Nonetheless, as *Will & Grace* still foregrounds heterosexuality, heteronormativity, and family values, especially on the visual level, these gay male characters still remain closeted—with reference to same-sex affection and intimacy. These gay representations obscure the "lived reality" of many gays and lesbians by suggesting that only "good" sexual citizens (those who subscribe to heterosexuality or heteronormativity) are allowed access to "healthy" and "positive" relationships in which they can care for each other and live together (Bell and Binnie 26). We must ask commercial television producers and scriptwriters to rethink the old dominant narratives that only depict long-term, monogamous, heteronormative pairings. The production and reproduction of queer images is truly the only means by which to neutralize compulsory heterosexuality and to create narrative spaces in which gay and lesbian characters and their lifestyles can emerge on the small screen as "desirable" alternatives.

Will & Grace completed its eight seasons on NBC. In the 2002–03 season, Grace marries Leo (a Jewish doctor), and they move across town into a Brooklyn apartment. This does not prevent the two eponymous characters, however, from continuing to spend most of their time together as Leo travels regularly for his work with *Doctors Without Borders*. The sitcom also tempts television viewers with a potential same-sex relationship with the introduction of Barry (Karen's cousin) who "comes out" and goes on respective dates with both Jack and Will before deciding it is too early in his "gay career" to go steady with anyone. Hence, a same-sex relationship still remains strikingly absent. Indeed, faithful sitcom viewers watch patiently to see how NBC (and the other major television companies) will negotiate either a same-sex kiss or relationship that is both passionate and homonormative. We can only hope that the "next generation" of commercial television shows that follows *Will & Grace* will attempt to open new doors and "boldly go where no 'gay' sitcom has gone before" by bravely attempting to represent same-sex narratives in more queerly visible ways.

NOTES

1. I would like to thank both Van Cagle and the Center for the Study of Media and Society at GLAAD for providing the financial support during this research project. An earlier version of this paper was presented as part of the plenary session on *Will & Grace* at the eighth Annual Conference on Lavender Languages and Linguistics held in September 2000 at The American University in Washington, D.C. Several colleagues have read various drafts and offered helpful suggestions during both the conceptualization and rewriting of this essay. In particular, I would like to thank Bill Leap, Melinda Kanner, Susan Crutchfield, Betsy Morgan, and Carmen Wilson.

2. This scene is hauntingly similar to the first-year season finale in which Jack and Rosario get married and Will and Grace argue while sitting in attendance.

The 2010s

The first half of the 2010s was filled with anxiety nationally and internationally. The world was still recovering from the Great Recession of the late 2000s. The spread of radical Islam and the continued war on terrorism around the world was a major focus of foreign policy. A wave of uprisings in the Middle East beginning in 2010, commonly known as Arab Spring, led to the overthrow of governments while protests and uprisings occurred throughout the region. The explosion and sinking of the BP Deepwater Horizon oil rig in the Gulf of Mexico in 2010 created the worst environmental disaster in U.S. history. Political polarization in the United States between Democrats and Republicans continued to grow. The Affordable Health Care Act was passed by Congress in 2010, the most significant healthcare law since Medicare and Medicaid were passed in 1965. Barack Obama was re-elected in 2012, winning a majority of the popular and electoral vote, but by mid-decade, racial tensions were heightened after a series of shootings of Blacks by police.

The tumultuous times we're experiencing around the world are mirrored by the upheavals experienced by the stakeholders in the art and business of television—writers, directors, programmers, producers, advertisers, viewers, business executives, innovators, and inventors—who are being affected by rapid developments in the digital world. How and what television content is produced, how it is consumed, and how it is paid for are all in flux. The way we interface with TV has changed and continues to evolve, although interactions are highly influenced by each viewer's generation and socioeconomic status among other factors. In many ways, however, the situation comedy endures, bridging the gap from old delivery system to new. While the networks are still the dominant platform for sitcoms, specifically, and television programming, in general, the sitcom format is sufficiently malleable to allow for easy migration across viewing platforms. More and more, television is being viewed on screens and devices other than traditional broadcast TV with the Internet representing the wave of the future.

As of this writing, at the midpoint of the 2010s, sitcoms have accounted for 16 to 20 percent of the top fifty network shows in prime time (from 2010 to 2015) with a bigger spread of 10 to 20 percent of the top thirty network shows and a generally upward trajectory in popularity. The shows represented consistently in the top thirty are dramas (especially crime procedurals), reality series, sitcoms, sports, and news magazines, in that order of popularity. Network sitcoms that have breached the top thirty so far this decade are *Big Bang Theory*, *How I Met Your Mother*, *Mike & Molly*, *Modern Family*, *The Crazy Ones*, *The Millers*, *Two and a Half Men*, and *2 Broke Girls*.[1] All but one of them (*Modern Family*) are conventional shows in aesthetic terms, shows that also feature families as the anchor of the comedic situations—extended families, friend families, workplace families, and hybrids of each of those categories. Other notable sitcoms on the four networks include the following: *The Simpsons*, the long-running, animated show about a family that parodies, well, everything; *Younger*, in which a 40-year-old passes herself off as 26; the animated family sitcom *Bob's Burgers*; *Brooklyn 99*, a wacky police room sitcom (à la *Barney Miller*); *New Girl*, in which a young, idealistic woman has three men as roommates; and, *Black-ish*, a series about an upper-middle class, African American family trying to maintain its Black identity in the mostly White world members inhabit. In their provocative history of the Black sitcom, Robin Means-Coleman, Charlton McIlwain, and Jessica Moore Matthews provide a useful analysis and context of *Black-ish*, a popular ABC sitcom launched in the enviable programming slot following the powerhouse sitcom *Modern Family*.

Acclaimed non-network sitcoms (cable network sitcoms) of this era include *Louie*, an experimental sitcom loosely based on stand-up comedian Louis C.K.'s life; *Broad City*, a sometimes fantastical vision of two young women in NYC; *The Game*, a racially mixed spinoff of *Girlfriends* about professional football players and their wives; *Hot in Cleveland*, about three older entertainment industry professionals relocated to Cleveland with 90-something Betty White as Elka, their landlady; *It's Always Sunny in Philadelphia*, the uncomfortably selfish and crude exploits of a group of bar owners; *Playing House*, a narrative about two women supporting each other after one's husband leaves and the other woman's baby is born; *You're the Worst*, which focuses on the toxic relationship between a self-involved writer and a self-destructive PR executive; *The Sarah Silverman Program*, an immature, unemployed, single woman and her friends; and *Young and Hungry*, which is about a wealthy man who hires a female food blogger to be his personal chef. James Schultz takes a look at how the FX sitcom *Legit*, co-created by Australian, stand-up comedian Jim Jefferies, who is also one of the stars of the series, breaks new ground. The series features a major character with a visible physical disability and depicts him in a complex and nuanced way that is unlike any recurring character in previous sitcoms.

The growing presence of sitcoms on premium channels, especially on HBO and Showtime, is an important element of the sitcom landscape in the 2010s. Showtime's sitcoms include programs about: a psychiatrist having a midlife crisis after a patient shoots himself in his office (*Huff*); a pot-dealing suburban mom (*Weeds*); an alcoholic, womanizing, troubled novelist (*Californication*); a suburban housewife with multiple personalities (*United States of Tara*); a wife, mother, high school teacher coping with a diagnosis of terminal cancer (*The Big C*); and an emergency room nurse who abuses prescription drugs (*Nurse Jackie*).

HBO programmed even more sitcoms than Showtime including programs about: a star playing a fictionalized version of himself as a socially awkward, cringe-inducing curmudgeon (*Curb Your Enthusiasm*); a movie star, his posse, and his agent (*Entourage*); film extras (*Extras*); a blocked detective novelist who becomes an amateur detective (*Bored to Death*); a high school coach who becomes a male prostitute (*Hung*); a washed-out major league baseball player who becomes a small-town coach (*Eastbound and Down*); a woman who has a nervous breakdown and seeks an alternative path (*Enlightened*); a group of gay friends (*Looking*); an aging sitcom actress trying to make a comeback (*The Comeback*); a group of twenty-something young women in NYC (*Girls*); a self-centered, clueless female vice president of the United States (*Veep*); the staff and patients in a nursing-rehabilitation facility (*Getting On*); six young men who begin a start-up company (*Silicon Valley*); and, a married couple, her sister, and his best friend (*Togetherness*).

The online outlets Netflix, Amazon Studios, and Hulu also began producing original, edgier programming, including sitcoms that resemble but also diverge from network sitcoms in many ways. On Netflix, *Arrested Development*, about a wealthy, dysfunctional family, was revived by Netflix in 2014 after being cancelled by FOX in 2006; *BoJack Horseman* is an animated show about a washed-up sitcom star (who happens to be a horse) trying to restart his career; *Unbreakable Kimmy Schmidt* is about a young, emotionally stunted, woman experiencing the world anew after spending 15 years underground as a hostage; *Grace and Frankie* features two older women discovering themselves after their husbands come out as a couple; *Wet Hot American Summer: First Day of Camp* is a prequel to the cult classic film *Wet Hot American Summer;* and, *Master of None,* Aziz Ansari's series about the daily life of a 30-year-old actor trying to make it in New York. These shows all tend to push the envelope in terms of story elements and language that are too explicit for the networks and cable channels.

Because of its merchandising reach, Amazon Prime made a big splash when it decided to begin providing original programming. Its first forays into situation comedies include *Alpha House,* about four male senators living together in Washington, D.C.; *Mozart in the Jungle,* about a conductor, musicians, and board members of the New York symphony; and, *Transparent,* about an older, trans woman who comes out to her grown children, some of whom exhibit a fluidity of sexual identity largely unexplored on television. Maria San Filippo writes about sexuality, identity, family, and something really taboo on television—money—in her chapter on *Transparent.* In 2015, Amazon Prime introduced *Red Oaks,* a coming-of-age show set in the 1980s.

Hulu entered the online original programming business with shows such as *The Awesomes,* an animated show about super heroes with unreliable super powers; *Battleground,* a mockumentary dramedy about a senate campaign team in the Midwest; *Deadbeat,* about a man who sees, and tries to help, the dead people who won't leave him alone; *Fugget About It,* an animated show about a former mob boss living in Canada; *Quick Draw,* a semi-improvised Western comedy; and, *The Wrong Mans,* about two British politicians who become involved in crime, conspiracy, and corruption.

Other online venues also started showing original sitcoms during this time. MTV aired *Awkward,* a first-person-narrated show about a teenage girl who struggles after an accident that is seen as a suicide attempt. Crackle joined the fun with the introduction of *Held Up,* a wacky comedy about a cynical, burned-out bank teller; and the website Funny or Die added *Not Looking,* a parody of HBO's *Looking.* On CWSeed, *Play It Again, Dick* is a meta comedy about the creator of the 2000s drama *Veronica Mars* trying to launch a spin-off of *Veronica Mars. High Maintenance* follows a marijuana dealer and the lives of his clients. *Submissions Only* is an online sitcom about Broadway actors and casting directors. Yahoo! Screen gave *Community,* a show about a group of adult students attending community college, a new home in 2015 after the show was cancelled by NBC the previous year.

It might seem ironic that this section introduction is the longest one in the anthology since we are only midway through the decade when writing, but there are two reasons that this makes perfect sense. First, it is much easier to look back at previous decades and shift through the programming to assess impact and relevance using the lenses of history and context—lenses that are not yet available to us for evaluating the 2010s. Second, we are in the midst of a technology explosion that adds to the number of platforms used to deliver content, including the ever-popular sitcom. The expanding number of outlets has given situation comedies of the 2010s a new lease on life. The genre is multifaceted and adventurous in ways that sitcoms of the past never could be. Writers, producers, directors, and actors have more freedom to explore topics previously foreign to sitcomland. Situation comedy continues to be not only a viable but an expanding genre. No matter what the outlet—broadcast network, cable channel, premium channel, or online—and no matter what the delivery mechanism—television, computer, tablet, or mobile phone—situation comedies continue to thrive.

NOTE

1. Interestingly, *How I Met Your Mother* and *Two and a Half Men* ended their runs early in the decade, after more than a decade each on the air. *The Millers* was cancelled after two seasons, and *The Crazy Ones* was cancelled after its first season.

20

The Hidden Truths in Contemporary Black Sitcoms

ROBIN R. MEANS COLEMAN, CHARLTON D. McILWAIN,
AND JESSICA MOORE MATTHEWS

Playwright/literary critic George Bernard Shaw once advised, "When a thing is funny, search it carefully for a hidden truth." Perhaps such counsel becomes foreboding as we consider the "hidden truths" that are embedded in U.S. network television Black situation comedies—those series that attend explicitly to Blackness or Black life, culture, histories, and experiences. Shaw's charge, when applied to the Black situation comedy, an often provocative form of cultural expression, prompts us to consider the following questions: What are the "truths" about Blackness that Black situation comedies might offer? What possible truths might be revealed about those who produce Black situation comedies? And, how might change agents (e.g., watchdog organizations, concerned viewers) have an impact on the manner of cultural truths circulated in the programming?

We describe the Black situation comedy (aka, Black sitcoms) as a genre of weekly, self-contained episodes that relies on gags, one-liners, and physical comedy. It is entertainment programming that employs a core cast of Black characters and frequently focuses on those characters' familial, romantic, sociocultural, political, work, and class experiences (e.g., *Amos 'n' Andy*, *Good Times*, *The Fresh Prince of Bel-Air*). More controversially, Black situation comedies have often been indicted for their overreliance on stereotypical characterizations of Blackness and situations (e.g., a shuffling dimwit) to promote humor (Gray; Hough; Means Coleman).

In this chapter, we discuss how the comedic mediation of Black identity informs understandings of Black lives, that is, how individuals derive meaning—or various truths—from such shows. We also consider industrial power and the influence such power has over the Black sitcom production process. To these ends, we provide a brief overview of an approximately 60-year history of the Black situation comedy. We then discuss how groups and individuals have worked to act as change agents by attempting to inform Black situation comedy content.

BLACK AMERICA VIEWED

The 1984–85 television season brought the unexpected NBC smash hit, *The Cosby Show*.[1] In the mid- to late eighties, the "big three" networks (ABC, CBS, and even NBC) plotted to create programming that would duplicate *The Cosby Show*'s popularity in an attempt to cash in on Cosby-like ratings. For the Black sitcom genre, *The Cosby Show* was socially and culturally seminal for its novel depiction of an upper-middle-class American family that just happened to be Black. The show accomplished this absent any of the expressions of deviance and deficiency traditionally attached to depictions of Blackness, particularly Black families, in other series (e.g., *Baby, I'm Back*, *What's Happening!!*, *Diff'rent Strokes*, and *Webster*[2]). The popularity of *The Cosby Show* systematically spawned a number of network Black sitcoms that portrayed noticeably more diverse depictions of the Black family. The introduction of these new shows elevated the creative worth of Black image-makers in the television industry (e.g., Bill Cosby, creator of *The Cosby Show*, and Debbie Allen, director of *A Different World*) and served as a catalyst for the cross-over appeal of Black programming.

Beginning in 1985, in almost assembly-line fashion, the networks created a veritable glut of Black sitcoms that, over the next few years, made their way into millions of American households. The result: the 1989 and 1990 television seasons alone proved to be watershed periods for Black programming with the strongest showing of Black participation in network television to date. During this one-year period, over a dozen Black sitcoms aired, including *227*, *Amen*, *A Different World*, *Jackee*, *Family Matters*, *The Robert Guillaume Show*, *New Attitude*, *Sugar and Spice*, *You Take the Kids*, and *The Fresh Prince of Bel-Air*. Quantity did not necessarily bring quality, however, and the new influx of shows served as a reminder of how confining and problematic mediated, commercial Black imagery can be.

During this period one (barely camouflaged) truth some series seemed to espouse—those that viewers became increasingly aware of—was that

Black participation in prime-time television continued to be relegated to the realm of the comedic. Despite recent contributions starring Blacks, such as *Scandal, How to Get Away with Murder*, and *Empire*, Blacks continue to be infrequently featured in dramas that focus primarily on Black culture.[3] Instead, confined if not ghettoized within the comedic, messages of inferiority and de-centrality often prevail (Staples and Jones). As Inniss and Feagin observe, "always seeing Blacks in situation comedies indicates that Black life and Black issues are not taken seriously" (707). Additionally, many of the new series that premiered in 1989 and 1990 failed to represent Black life and culture in a way that captured their full diversity and complexity. For example, sassy, "Sapphire"-inspired characterizations were the norm in *New Attitude*,[4] which features a group of smart-mouthed, inept hairdressers. The group presents itself in modernized, outrageous Sambo-esque outfits[5] and liberally engages in discomfiting slapstick.

A hard truth that the industry eventually came to terms with was that the rush of series of this period was poorly conceived, badly written, underpromoted, or unfavorably scheduled. As a result, these Black sitcoms were not attended to by viewers—Blacks (thought to be the core audience) and non-Blacks alike. With little in the way of a Black audience fan base and absent a racial cross-over audience, many Black sitcoms of the mid- to late 1980s of the "Cosby Era" quickly dropped off network schedules. *Charlie & Company, What's Happening Now!!, He's the Mayor, Melba, The Redd Foxx Show*, and *Frank's Place*, were the first wave of Cosby-inspired hopefuls that saw their swift demise between *The Cosby Show* debut year of 1984 and the watershed year of 1989. More devastating to the inclusion of Blackness on network television, in the single year between 1989 and 1990, five additional Black situation comedies were cancelled, including *227, The Robert Guillaume Show, Jackee, New Attitude*, and *Sugar and Spice*. Quantitatively, the impact of losing Black series was devastating to a genre that rarely offered more than two or three series per season. These departures introduced a perplexing dilemma: given the often-troubling nature of Black representations in media generally, and in Black situation comedies (with few exceptions) specifically, were these cancellations-cum-absences a blessing in disguise? That is, is invisibility or absence a lesser evil than the symbolic annihilation of the race?

VIEWING THE SKEWING OF BLACKNESS

While the crisis caused by the loss of many Black sitcoms in the late 1980s and early 1990s was significant, the disappearance of Blackness on network television was not an entirely new phenomenon: Blacks had faced virtual invisibility some three decades earlier during the "Non-recognition Era" (see Cedric Clark; Means Coleman). The Non-recognition Era (1954–1967) describes a 15-year period when Black representations of any stripe, not just starring roles, hit an all-time low on network television due to the total absence of Black situation comedies (rare exceptions included Blacks' appearances on non-Black shows such as *Father of the Bride*, *Car 54, Where Are You?*, and *Hogan's Heroes*). The Non-recognition Era emerged during the rise of the Civil Rights Movement when Blacks were pushing for their civil and human rights while fighting against segregation and other legal and extra-legal discriminations. The happy-go-lucky characterizations of Blackness in television programming, as seen in minstrelsy-based comedic television shows such as *Amos 'n' Andy* and *Beulah* of the early 1950s, seemed a startling disjuncture from the protest marches and sit-ins in the quest for equality, as well as brutalities meted out against Blacks in the form of church bombings, police attacks, and lynchings that appeared on the nightly news. Afraid of alienating viewers on either side of the Civil Rights debate, "[e]ntertainment television chose not to choose sides, opting instead to ignore the crisis and [Blacks] altogether" (Means Coleman 82). Entertainment television, particularly situation comedy, seemingly could not handle the truth around Blacks' increasing power and centrality in American culture. It was a handling of Blackness in which, as Angela Harris describes, "[i]t is not ridiculed, it is not caricatured, it is simply not there" (49).

Blacks eventually did return to television's situation comedies in the late 1960s, coinciding with the ebb of the Civil Rights Movement. Black sitcoms had not been attempted since the early 1950s with *Amos 'n' Andy* and *Beulah*, series whose characters and humor were deeply informed by minstrel theatre of the late 19th century. Television did not dare return to a TV minstrelsy era. Instead, the networks offered what scholars have described as the Assimilationist Era (Dates; Gray; MacDonald [*Blacks and White TV*]; and Riggs). In the Assimilationist Era (1968–1971), Blacks returned to television through Black situation comedies such as *Julia* and *The Bill Cosby Show*. A series in this era was met with a healthy dose of skepticism, however. For example, *Julia*, which emerged during the sociopolitical backdrop of Black Power/Black nationalism, was blasted by some viewers and TV critics for presenting a depiction of Blackness that "evacuat[ed] as much ethnic and cultural difference as possible [and that] conformed to an unexamined White norm" (Bodroghkozy 150). Indeed, Julia is mostly missing Black men and racial, social, or political debates. These are notable omissions given America's troubled climate of war protests, urban riots, and assassinations. Moreover, the show's lack of humor and culturally-savvy references is made all the more obvious with the introduction of comedies such as *Maude*, *All in the Family*, and *Sanford and Son*, all of which work to acknowledge sex(ism), race relations, and economic disparity truths. *The Bill Cosby Show* and *Room 222*, like *Julia*, depict a world that was wholly integrated and generally free of conflict. Overall, though the Assimilationist Era was a marked improvement over the minstrelsy-tinged shows of *Amos 'n' Andy* and *Beulah*, it nevertheless offers a racist ideology that Black culture is most prized when it approaches the norms and values of Whiteness. For those invested in Blackness, imbedded in these series is a message of cultural abandonment and racial assimilation.

Figure 20.1. Louise Beavers as Beulah, Jane Frazee as Alice Henderson, David Bruce as Harry Henderson, and Stuffy Singer as Donnie Henderson. 1950–1953. Photo courtesy of Photofest.

The period from 1972–1983, the era of Social Relevancy and Ridiculed Black Subjectivity (aka, The Lear Era), was a dramatic departure from the Assimilationist Era of the late 1960s to early 1970s. During this time, Black sitcoms began to address the social and political experiences of the nation head-on in large part through the efforts of Norman Lear (along with Bud Yorkin). Marc and Thompson write: "By consistently embedding authorial advocacy into plot and characterization on issues ranging from abortion and homosexuality to foreign policy and Watergate, Lear helped dispel the belief that situation comedy was an intrinsically superficial form that could only support its own status quo" (49–50). *Sanford and Son*, *Good Times*, and *The Jeffersons*, Black sitcoms all, attend directly to race, racism, public policy issues, government, police brutality, discrimination, and Black empowerment efforts. Through Black-centered worlds and Black-centered circumstances, non-Black Americans had an opportunity to see Blackness as canonical while Blacks went about surviving, thriving, and contributing to the citizenry without abandoning their culture. Still, the Black world that Lear and others created during this period was a segregated one. Yes, White invisibility made Blackness central. But, it also shielded the ways that White society was mostly complicit in creating and sustaining the largely unequal conditions that most Blacks experienced as portrayed in these shows. As such, non-Black invisibility amounted to tacitly "blaming the victim" for Black deficiencies instead of grappling with causes for differences or exploring the need for structural changes. In the case of George Jefferson (*The Jeffersons*), Blacks who did "move on up" to the (White) middle class were represented as doing so through a rags-to-riches narrative in which they were often situated as crude and out of place. Unfortunately, most, if not all, of the socially relevant Black situation comedies would ultimately fall back on comedic clichés of trickery, buffoonery, and Sambo-ism that would make the series resemble early minstrelsy television (J.J. Evans of *Good Times* is most illustrative of this slippage).

While social relevancy was, generally, the formula for the Black situation comedy in the 1970s, this period saw programming offer clear messages about the inadequacies and stunning deficiencies of Blackness as well. Series such as *Diff'rent Strokes* and *Webster* emerged during this period, featuring "White saviors" such as the Drummond (*Diff'rent Strokes*) and Papadapolis (*Webster*) families, bringing to their homes Black boys who were unable to be raised in their familial Black households or by other members of Black communities. Simply put, if one were to look for truths about Blackness in this era of television programming, the message here is that Blacks operate in odd, segregated worlds, worlds that might benefit from a normalizing dose of Whiteness, and non-Blacks have no need for the Black world except to visit momentarily to rescue Black youth.

The Era of the Black Family and Diversity (the Cosby Years, 1984–89) is one of the most promising five years that Black situation comedy has seen to date. *The Cosby Show* brought with it a return to the Black subjectivity the Lear programming had promised to supply but failed to deliver. The programming of this era was often family-centered (e.g., *Charlie & Company*, *Melba*, and *227*) and positioned Blacks within their own cultural center, though not wholly segregated from the rest of the world. Series such as *The Cosby Show*, its spin-off *A Different World*, and the critically acclaimed *Frank's Place* introduce Blackness as varied, sophisticated, and culturally relevant. Though *The Cosby Show* has been criticized for its failure to attend to America's racial inequalities—including the struggles Cliff and Clair Huxtable would have faced to become as professionally and financially successful as they are—much of this era of Black situation comedy television shows Blackness as broadly diverse in its politics, economics, cultural practices, and contributions. As discussed earlier in this chapter, however, the networks had great trouble keeping up with this trend of offering more whole and full "truths" about Blackness in their programming, gambling instead on foregrounding fast profits while sacrificing quality.

This abandonment resulted in one of the most notorious periods of Black situation comedy programming since the minstrelsy characterizations of the 1950s. The Neo-Minstrelsy Era (1990–1998) describes a return to Black sitcom tropes popularized on the original minstrel theatre stage. Sambos, coons, Black bucks, and Sapphires proliferated as racial separation and inequality returned. The biggest culprits were the newer networks—FOX, UPN, and WB—that created series such as *Martin* (FOX), *Goode Behavior* (UPN), and *The Wayans Brothers* (WB).[6] Alvin Poussaint, professor of clinical psychiatry and consultant to *The Cosby Show*, offered, "I don't think that *Martin* is a show that's projecting us forward. . . . Shucking and jiving is not representative of Black America" (qtd. in Farley, *Black and Blue*, 81). As an upstart network, UPN initially built its network around Black comedic programming. In addition to *Goode Behavior*, UPN premiered *Malcolm and Eddie*, *Sparks*, and *Homeboys in Outer Space* in 1996 alone. According to television critic Robert Bianco:

> Almost without exception, men in this UPN quartet are portrayed as sex-crazed idiots or stuffed shirts: women as shrews or sexpots. Any behavior that borders on the intellectual is mocked; any sign of "uppity" aspiration is crushed. On *Malcolm [and*

> *Eddie*], a man is ridiculed for reading poetry—and he's a fat
> man which is supposed to make it twice as funny. On *Goode*
> [*Behavior*], a college professor finds his tea party turned into a
> barbecue (ribs, of course). And so on." (4)

WB's *The Wayan's Brothers* was thought to be so offensive that it became one of several comedies airing on the newer networks to be targeted by an NAACP chapter's protest. Billie J. Green, then-president of the NAACP Beverly Hills/Hollywood Chapter, lamented:

> I know comedy is comedy, but there's a fine line when people
> are laughing with you and people are laughing at you. Right
> now people are laughing at us. What's on these shows is just
> horrible . . . It's not a fair representation of Black America.
> What we're seeing is like *Amos 'n' Andy* and Stepin Fetchit. In
> fact, *Amos 'n' Andy* was a better show than what we're seeing
> now." (qtd. in Braxton A1)

To this complaint, Marlon Wayans, star of *The Wayans Brothers*, responded, "The funny thing that strikes me is it's, like, Black people can be so hard on Black people, where White people embrace. If you look at Jim Carrey, he's considered a genius. But if a black person does some physical comedy, I'm considered a buffoon. I don't get it. You're stopping me from making that $20 million" ("Black Sitcoms"). And, yet, there was little to defend during this Neo-Minstrelsy Era when Black sitcoms hit an all-time low in 1998, as UPN premiered the "slave-com" (as it came to be called colloquially) *The Secret Diary of Desmond Pfeiffer*. A slave-era, Black situation comedy set in the Lincoln White House, it featured the character Pfeiffer as a Brit who comes to America fleeing gambling debts and ends up as Lincoln's man-servant. The series' pilot offers darky jokes, and in its regular season episodes, as Lisa Jones writes, "[t]he South was remembered as a peaceful fairytale, largely absent racial animus, and a prime setting to revisit good-old fashioned racial humor . . . its bewildering supposition—that a Civil War story could be divorced from the atrocity of slavery, while treating race like a running gag."

The jury is still out on what the future holds for the Black situation comedy. The inroads into presenting Blackness as relevant and necessary to those inside and outside of Blackness is a notable achievement for series of the new millennium such as *Girlfriends*, *The Bernie Mac Show*, *The Hughleys*, *My Wife and Kids*, and Tyler Perry's longstanding series *House of Payne*.[7] Perhaps most notable of these is the most recent series in this group of

Black sitcoms: *Black-ish*, which places Blackness at the core of the cultural discourse and is primarily the sociocultural experience against which all else is marked. *Black-ish* in particular has been applauded by critics and viewers alike for its discourse about what it means to be both Black and upwardly mobile in modern America. The series centers on advertising executive André "Dré" Johnson—patriarch of an affluent Black family in Los Angeles—and his quest to reinvigorate his family's cultural self-identity in the midst of their White-washed circumstances (ritzy neighborhood, private school, etc.). Dré's comedic mid-life crisis of cultural conscience leads to storylines that address topics such as cultural appropriation, tokenism, and even affirmative action. A particular example exists in the series pilot when Dré is finally promoted to Senior Vice President of his firm's "urban" division, to which he questions: "Wait, did they just put me in charge of Black stuff?" His father sarcastically congratulates him on becoming "the White man's lead puppet." Throughout the series, André is self-consciously aware of his family's Blackness, humorously stressing to his children the importance of cultural traditions such as "the nod" of familiarity when seeing another Black person in predominately White spaces or understanding the significance of the first Black president (to which his youngest children reply defensively: "But, Obama's the only president we've ever known!"). As Dré grapples with his son's desire to join the school field hockey team and have a Bar Mitzvah like the rest of his friends, he brings about rare but relevant conversations about race, not seen since the Lear Era, while also reintroducing the [successful] Black family to the national consciousness.

Pessimistically, however, while *Black-ish* might indicate brighter horizons for the future of prime-time depictions of the Black experience, representation of Blackness remains at risk. There is the obvious concern that Black life and culture remain relegated to the comedic on network television. Some have criticized *Black-ish*, in particular, for leaning too heavily on both its designation as a "family show" and its historically familiar tendency to put most of its comedic emphasis on its Black characters to avoid alienating White viewers. Larry Wilmore, veteran television writer who has produced several episodes of *Black-ish*, noted that the show's ideal audience is "people who have families or are looking to have a family and they feel this push and pull on their identity." Wilmore continues: "Some of these topics, you have to be careful about how you present them, because it's a family comedy" (qtd. in Emami). As a result, André's frenzied fears of his family losing its cultural identity or his commentary and performance when dealing with obtuse White co-workers and neighbors could arguably come across as more paranoid than authentically valid.

Figure 20.2. (clockwise from left) Marcus Scribner as André Johnson, Jr., Tracee Ellis Ross as Rainbow Johnson, Anthony Anderson as André "Dré" Johnson, Laurence Fishburne as Pops, Yara Shahidi as Zoey Johnson, Miles Brown as Jack Johnson, and Marsai Martin as Diane Johnson, in *Black-ish*. 2014– . Photo courtesy of Photofest.

Even more disturbing, Black sitcoms continue to battle against other troubling representations in reality television and in prime-time dramas, which showcase Black people in power-wielding roles while often sacrificing the characters' personal morals. ABC dramas *Scandal* and *How to Get Away with Murder* both feature savvy, professional Black women as the main characters, but they also lead dark double lives as adulteresses and accomplices to crimes of murder among other things. FOX's *Empire* also showcases Black characters in powerful professional positions while playing on their more stereotypical personas as criminals (again, murderers) turned rappers and producers. And, while some might argue that the more varied and complex characterizations in these dramas are many steps forward from the past, the underlying messages across all Black television programming must be critiqued. According to Moss:

> All television programs live in the shadow of the ratings guil-lotine, but does the blade fall more quickly on a Black show? Ask any African American in the television business, and you'll get a long list of classic White sitcoms—*The Mary Tyler Moore Show, Seinfeld, The Drew Carey Show*—that had to be nurtured through difficult infancies by supportive networks. With Black shows, complains Mo'Nique, costar of [the Black sitcom] *The Parkers,* the same white-run establishment "puts us on and pulls us off" as it pleases. (19)

Critiquing media texts is an important step, but it is not the only one. It is essential to look at the industry structures that produce programming and the commercial imperatives that drive that production.

CONCLUSION

Our discussion highlights the central problems surrounding Blackness, representation, and definitions of the Black image in television programming—problems that emerge as hidden truths beyond the comedic maskings of the situation comedy genre. These problems are more complex than what is often depicted in low culture forms such as television and must be fully understood before we undertake any discussion of what we can and should do to help rectify such problems. The first problem we encounter stems from the medium of television itself, which brings to the masses its own interpretations of Blackness. The nature of television as a mediated form, as well as the dominant programming style of network television, presents images and narratives in short, often uncontextualized, segments that are structurally unable to deal with the complexity of human experience in general. For us, this means that we first have to accept the fact that, insofar as this is the case, the fundamental problem is that television programming does not present the diversity of the Black experience. That is, while we must have some expectations with regard to what is presented to us in these shows, we cannot anticipate that a single show or two, premiering every few seasons, will provide us with images that span the spectrum of the lived experience of the Black diaspora. What we can strive for, however, are shows that, in their plurality, can explore the variety of experiences—from the person who lives in a perceived world that consists completely of Blackness to the Black person who, in his or her diverse racial world, does not see himself or herself as invested in Blackness at all. We should expect that enough shows could be produced that present Black characters' lived experience in Black-centered worlds, as well as those in which they interact closely and often with non-Black counterparts, while each is allowed to maintain some distinctiveness.

A second problem is a common perception among television audiences, Black and otherwise, that a dualistic, subject-object relationship exists between them and the television screen. Because television gives us the perception of truth by hiding from the screen what lies behind its programming, many have the sense that television acts while we react. That is, we often get the feeling that the enterprise of television viewing necessarily is one that separates actors from audiences, doers from viewers, and watchers from the watched. The experience of television viewing is an interactive enterprise, however, constituted through reciprocal interaction. This is to say, television programming is a constitutive, rather than a dualistic, process. It is a process whereby lived experience finds its way onto the screen while that which is on the screen is subsequently altered as it is given feedback from the life experience of those watching. This is the reason that such programming ends up with stereotypes, those myopic snapshots of life. The reason we have the perception of television viewing as a separated experience (rather than interactive experience) featuring stereotypical images of Blackness (rather than wider views of Black life on network programming) is because there is a vast disconnect between those who control the images produced and those who watch.[8]

Beyond this, Black actors are often forced to play roles they really do not want to play in order to put food on their tables and are shut out of the creative process of writing and directing television programs. Furthermore, few, if any, Blacks have access to the corporate boardrooms where the rubber of television programming meets the road of money, corporate capital and influence, and where the primary and final decisions are made. A culture of powerlessness is compounded by three factors: the inherent failure of television as a medium to represent the diversity and complexity of Black life; our perception that, as viewers, a vast gulf separates us (mass consumer audiences) from them (those controlling television production); and the barriers of wealth and power that restrict access to decision making regarding the presentation of Black images and the meanings expressed through them. As media consumers, we live in a culture where we are faced with encumbrances to becoming agents of our own experiences—our bodies, our values, our beliefs, our commodities. We forget, as audiences and as consumers, that we are the driving force behind television programming and the financial apparatus that funds it. Precisely by finding the hidden truths expressed in Black sitcoms, and other Black television programming, we are able to bring to the forefront the problems that necessitate human action to alter them in some way. Nevertheless, the options for such action, though not easy, are available to those outside of the television entertainment industry as a way of turning the experience of television viewing from a one-directional, transmission model into a more open and democratic model for informing programming content.

As individuals, we always have the prerogative to choose what we view. As an option of expressing our favor or disfavor with Black programming, whether sitcoms, dramas, or the commercials dispersed throughout programs, the remote control is not only our best friend but a powerful method, in the aggregate, to say to network executives that their productions are farcical. While tuning out seems simplistic, there is some complexity here. Audiences must forego the temptation to concede that they will continue to watch, despite the overall message of the show and its social and political implications, just because a certain show makes them laugh and is entertaining. In order to shape the media landscape, we must be vigilant as viewers (i.e., "resistant spectators") as well as educate ourselves and others to be able to look beyond the surface of the image in order to see the messages embedded in their expression. Only then will we be able to convince ourselves and others that certain programming is unacceptable.

The emergence of fan communities on social media surrounding particular programs and individual actors is proving to be a viable way to educate and to collaborate around these mediated messages. Often such communities are initiated by networks themselves, looking to further promote their shows (and their advertisers) by receiving quick, efficient, mass feedback regarding particular shows and episodes. By being involved in such community forums and urging the networks to create, sustain, and actually pay attention to the feedback given, those of us invested in Black televised images can get a creative foot in the door of production by revealing our opinions, suggesting alternative plots, stories, characters, and so on, and convincing decision makers that alternative content might translate into greater viewership and revenue for a particular series. Our individual efforts can be solidified through collective action that goes beyond persuading others as to the demerits of a given show by urging them to collectively exercise their power of choice of viewing. Such options include collective actions such as boycotts not only of the television shows themselves but actions that have an impact on the television industry's profit-seeking ability.

If it is true, as NBC West Coast President Scott Sassa quipped, that "NBC is the place to buy [advertising time] if you're selling to people who actually shop, not shoplift" (qtd. in Flint "How"), then African Americans, for example, can flex their collective muscles as the largest consumer segment in the country by refusing to purchase products advertised on offending networks (McIlwain and Johnson). Withdrawing millions of dollars from advertisers who support network programs has proven to be an effective tool for demanding that other voices be heard in the decision-making process of television programming (as typified by recent NAACP-led boycotts). In 2014, VH1 introduced *Sorority Sisters*, a reality show that focuses on "Black sorority life" through VH1's trademarked, drama-filled, cat-fighting lens. Despite numerous pre-pilot petitions, VH1 aired the show to reportedly strong ratings. Immediately, droves of people led by members of Black Greek-letter organizations began what would become both a loud social media rebuke and boycott of the show and the advertisers that aired commercials during the series. The pressure led brands including McDonalds, Sports Authority, Victoria's Secret, and the NBA to announce their withdrawal of ads and support from the show. In less than a month, VH1 ended the show with no mention of any rebroadcasts or subsequent seasons. Individual and collective activities are powerful and important in helping address some of the problems described in this chapter. Such action ensures that the process of problem solving is an inclusive one and has as its goal to create more diverse images of Blackness rather than, for example, the frequent and undiscerning Sambo/Sapphire-type caricatures. By doing so, the hidden truths expressed in Black situation comedies will not remain hidden but, instead, become apparent for all to see, debate, and change.

NOTES

1. *The Cosby Show* was rejected by both ABC and CBS before being picked up by NBC.

2. Why were these series bad depictions of Black families? Here, the hidden message is that African-Americans operate in odd worlds marked by bigotry where non-Blacks need not take part except to rescue Black youths from dysfunction and family peril. *Baby I'm Back* tells the story of an African American husband who deserts his wife and two children, only to re-enter and wreak havoc on the family. *What's Happening!!*'s mother's ex-husband is no-good, and the family's better off

without him. In the series *Webster* and *Diff'rent Strokes*, the juvenile characters find themselves living with "White savior" parents.

3. We cannot sing the praises enough of *Under One Roof*, the first (and, to date, only) African American, nuclear and extended family drama to ever air on network television. In 1995, the Langston family graced the airwaves offering one of the most whole, complex, and realistic depictions of a family (Black or non-Black) that we have ever seen. The series lasted only one month on CBS, airing from March 14 to April 18, 1995. Since *Under One Roof*, networks have attempted to offer up Black-centered workplace dramas such as *City of Angels* and *Gideon's Crossing*, both medical dramas. All were fast failures. Some view *Homicide, Life on the Street* as a Black drama due to its setting ("Chocolate City," Baltimore), and its increasingly African American core cast over the run of the series. We believe *Homicide* exemplifies what television, when at its best, can do with the depiction of race: privilege its presence and diversity while not reducing it to the single, focal theme (or gag) or cliché.

4. Recurring African American stereotypes are, at times, described based on the characterization in popular culture that first introduced or popularized the stereotype (e.g., the "Uncle Tom" or the "Sambo"). We can credit the *Amos 'n' Andy* character Sapphire for "naming" the frequent depiction of African American women as smart-alecky, emasculating, nagging shrews.

5. The Sambo characterization is a negative Black stereotype that originated with minstrel theatre (performed by White men in Blackface). The Sambo was a male simpleton who sang, danced, sometimes strummed a banjo, and spoke in heavy Blackvoice. Modern-day Sambos can be seen in J.J. from *Good Times* and Steve Urkel from *Family Matters*. During the minstrelsy era, audiences loved the Sambo for his adoration and unabashed loyalty for the slave master, his docility, and outrageous costuming. The Sambo often found himself in tight spots and would draw on ridiculous superstitions and trickery to get himself out of trouble (though his actions only proved to make things worse). Boskin decodes the Sambo as "an extraordinary type of social control, at once extremely subtle, devious, and encompassing. To exercise a high degree of control meant also to be able to manipulate the full range of humor; to create, ultimately, an insidious type of buffoon. To make the black male into an object of laughter . . ." (13–14).

6. None of these three shows aired on the "big three" networks.

7. Exceptions to the dreck of the 1990s included *Sister, Sister* and *The Parent'Hood*. Tim Reid and Robert Townsend, respectively, produced and starred in these quality, family series that most resembled the efforts of *The Cosby Show*. It was not surprising that these series stood out in their depictions of Black family life (though they hardly stood out in the ratings, and quite honestly did not have the same strong presence or scripts that *The Cosby Show* had), as Reid and Townsend (like Cosby) have spent much of their careers talking about and promoting the need for improved Black imagery in media. During this period, the regular networks all but abandoned Black situation comedy. For example, CBS aired no Black situation comedies in 1992 or 1993, and offered only two in 1996. NBC introduced no

new Black situation comedy in 1993. In 1994, FOX began to move from "upstart" network to more of a mainstay and, upon finding it no longer needed to appeal to African American viewers, made overt moves to pull back on the number of Black situation comedies it offered.

8. Stuart Hall describes racial stereotypes as a "racialized regime of representations." When considering the treatment of African Americans and Blackness in Black situation comedies over the past five decades, Means Coleman has long felt that "racialized" was too subtle of a concept to make sense of the depictions seen in this genre of programming. As elaborated on in Means Coleman's book, *African American Viewers and the Black Situation Comedy: Situating Racial Humor*, positive, negative, or neutral, programming can be "racialized," and that racialization does not always mean racist. Black situation comedy is obviously racialized as it focuses on Black life and culture, but it is a "racist" regime of representations because of its unusual, frequent focus on negatively stereotyping African Americans, and in doing so, drawing on some of the most abhorrent characterizations (e.g., Sambo) to do so.

21

Disability and Sitcoms

A *Legit* Analysis

JAMES SCHULTZ

Disability is an essential identity category as much as race, sex, gender, sexuality, or any other phenotype. A multiplicity of identity categories is increasingly present in television sitcoms, except for disability. What strikes me while watching episodes of sitcoms produced from the 1950s through 2014 is the absence of marked disabled bodies. I say "marked" to denote both visibly apparent disabilities and invisible disabilities that have been declared, not disabilities that are solely implied or remain in the subtext. Even college courses and books on sitcoms and culture that are thorough and inclusive overlook disability. Robert McRuer developed a theory of compulsory able-bodiedness that normalizes an idealized body and mind "free from physical disability" as one that appears natural (*Compulsory* 91). There are a few notable exceptions to the conventional approach to compulsory able-bodiedness including *Malcolm in the Middle* (Stevie), *Becker* (Jake), *South Park* (Timmy and Jimmy), and the first sitcom to feature a recurring character with a disability, *The Facts of Life* (Geri). These characters are all recurring on their respective series, but only Jake from *Becker* is a main character. There are far too few exceptions to disprove the rule; sitcoms participate in compulsory ableism largely by excluding any disabled actors, characters, and storylines.

It is useful and important to analyze shows that include disabled characters, storylines, and actors. This analysis is best when it is earnest in its attempt to be charitable while also being critical. Given that the vast majority of sitcoms do not even visualize disability, every show that runs counter to this process of exnomination disrupts the process of creating able-bodied norms. It is a disservice to disability studies to allow such interruptions of compulsory able-bodiedness to go without applicable criticism. This can assist in creating better understandings of how cultural norms are created and mobilized with regard to disability and how disability contributes to processes of normalization for sex, gender, race, and so on. The sitcom *Legit*, which aired on FX, provides ample opportunity for such analysis.

Acknowledging that *Legit* provides a progressive narrative addressing issues of institutional versus independent living, disability, and sexuality, I seek to criticize the pilot episode for its compulsory heterosexuality and reinforcement of the male gaze. Laura Mulvey explains: "The determining male gaze projects its phantasy on to the female form which is styled accordingly" (9). As a result, the construction of disability is locked in a hegemonic notion of male heterosexuality. The show provides a narrative that successfully provides representations of disability that demonstrate agency, independence, and sexuality. *Legit's* representations of sexuality, however, are indebted to conventional notions of heterosexuality and cinematographic methods locked into the male gaze. Compulsory heterosexuality and the male gaze contribute to a normalization that interrupts the emancipatory potential of non-traditional notions of disability.

Figure 21.1. Dan Bakkedahl as Steve Nugent, DJ Qualls as Billy Nugent, and Jim Jefferies as Jim Jefferies in *Legit*. 2013–2014. Photo courtesy of Fanart.TV.

I am attempting to provide a multifaceted examination of the show *Legit* and its representations of disability and gender. Understanding how television participates in constructing compulsory able-bodiedness and the male gaze, both examples of deeply entrenched privilege, is critical to forwarding an understanding of how hegemonic status is formed and proliferated. I will begin my analysis with a description of how disability is best understood as a rhetorical-relational construct. I proceed by describing the show and the pilot episode's characters and plot. I will then examine the relationship between disability and sexuality in the episode. Finally, I will investigate how the pilot episode of *Legit* participates in reinforcing the male gaze and compulsory male heterosexuality.

DISABILITY

Disability is a rhetorical device used to distinguish diverse bodies from the ideal able body. Disability is best determined relationally in particular contexts and creating the idealized norm is the primary mode of establishing disability. Lennard Davis clarifies:

> To understand the disabled body, one must return to the concept of the norm, the normal body. So much of writing about disability has focused on the disabled person as the object of study, just as the study of race has focused on the person of color. But as with recent scholarship on race, which has turned its attention to whiteness, I would like to focus not so much on the construction of disability as on the construction of normalcy. I do this because the "problem" is not the person with disabilities; the problem is the way that normalcy is constructed to create the "problem" of the disabled person. (3)

Normalcy is not standard, rather, the construction of normal/abnormal, and thus able/disabled, operate through the goal of the ideal. The normal body isn't standard; the normal body is ideal, able to meet the conditions of every situation that is socially and materially constructed for the body to encounter.

Scott Lunsford gives careful attention to his theory of dis/ability and the way these categories are co-constituted. He argues that commentators who are silent on dis/ability are participating in the primacy of able-bodiedness; "we must understand the hegemony which makes dis/ability invisible through silence" (1). This exemplifies the process of exnomination in which able-bodied writers are silent on disability, which creates able-bodiedness as the standard or norm by not referring to itself.

Conventional sitcoms don't need to address ability; the assumption is that everyone is able-bodied. These shows formulate a meaning of normal as compulsory. Norms frequently are circulated through exnomination, and able-bodiedness is not described on those terms because they are the assumed universal embodied experience. Disability is created and given meaning through the assumption that able-bodied is normal. It may be useful to think of disability as a rhetorical construction much like a black hole. Disability/blackholes cannot easily be observed or defined themselves, but the things surrounding them that are not the disability/black hole give shape and context to the surrounding ability/objects.

Disability and able-bodiedness change in given circumstances and across time. Disability is not something that is inherent in an individual. Disability is a mutable category that carries no calcified meaning or objective criteria. Furthermore, disability is rhetorically constructed. Disability can be determined based on physical conditions that are temporary, semi-permanent, or permanent. But, these determinations are made relationally to particular contexts. Thus, able-bodiedness can only be temporary, "No one is ever more than temporarily able-bodied" (Breckenridge and Vogler 349). Despite the limited and finite possibilities of able-bodiedness, disabled people continue to find an unwelcoming attitude from many. Lennard Davis describes the intensity of this situation: "For centuries, people with disabilities have been an oppressed and repressed group. People with disabilities have been isolated, incarcerated, observed, written about, operated on, instructed, implanted, regulated, treated, institutionalized, and controlled to a degree probably unequal to that experienced by any other minority group" (xv). Disparaging attitudes toward and treatment of people with disabilities continues to be pervasive. There is no universal natural standard for mental or physical ability. Rather, situations contingently construct the idealized standard for temporary able-bodiedness. Accompanying the norms of able-bodiedness with positive and negative associations is part of how attitudes and treatments are informed by media representations.

LEGIT

Legit is based on the stand-up routine of the show's lead actor, Jim Jefferies, who plays a characterization of himself. The show is largely centered on the (mis)adventures of Jim and his two roommates, Steve Nugent and

Billy Nugent, who are brothers. In the pilot episode, Billy does not yet live with Jim and Steve; he doesn't move in until the second episode, which is largely focused on Billy's criticism of medical institutionality versus independent living. Throughout the two seasons that aired on FX and FXX in 2013–14, the show deals with Billy's disability as a central theme in storylines that include having a girlfriend, fighting off home invaders, and parenting. These are issues many shows that include disabled characters do not delve into, and, as such, *Legit* deserves recognition for breaking ground in representing disability.

In the pilot episode, Jim accompanies Steve to visit his brother in an institution that cares for disabled people. At first, Jim is not going to go, "It's too depressing," but Jim talks himself into going "to do something nice." This is a rhetorical move that treats Billy's disability as something that is to be pitied and interactions with him as acts of charity. Joseph Shapiro describes the danger in this rhetorical move:

> Disabled people have become sensitized to depictions of disability in popular culture, religion, and history. There they find constant descriptions of a disabled person's proper role as either an object of pity or a source of inspiration. These images are internalized by disabled and nondisabled people alike and build social stereotypes, create artificial limitations, and contribute to discrimination. (30)

Legit gives Billy and his disability complexity with both positive and negative attributes, but this particular bit in the opening of the pilot is ripe for criticism. In a later episode, Billy argues with intruders who have broken into the home he shares with Jim and Steve, yelling, "Don't you pity me!" The episode concludes with Billy defeating the burglars with the alarm device on his wheel chair. Billy, who has muscular dystrophy, is played by DJ Qualls, who does not have muscular dystrophy. Although Qualls does not have a visible or disclosed disability, the show employs a significant number of disabled actors throughout the series. In the pilot episode, autistic Nick Daley plays Billy's roommate Rodney. Casting an actor with muscular dystrophy to play Billy would be difficult with the current health care measures and profit motives in entertainment media.

Billy and Jim talk one on one, and Billy divulges that he is 32 years old, is still a virgin, and wants to go to Las Vegas to hire a prostitute as a sex surrogate. Billy insists that Jim is "the only guy I know that would take me to a hooker." The episode places Billy, his disability, and his sexuality front and center. The episode does not tread lightly, and Billy is not there solely as a prop or a sight gag, although the episode engages in some jokes about Billy's immobility in more than one scene. The show does not make fun of his disability, but it is a crass sitcom with a disabled character as one of the three leads. Many of the jokes border on the edges of what someone may find acceptable. This analysis focuses on how the text constructs meaning in disability, sexuality, and masculine heterosexuality; the political correctness of certain jokes is not central to this project.

After some deliberation, Jim and Steve agree to accompany Billy on a trip to Las Vegas to explore Billy's sexual desires with a surrogate. While in a van to Las Vegas, there is a montage of Jim interacting with Billy: taking off his breathing apparatus, giving him pornography, drinking beer together, smoking pot together, and Jim moving Billy's arms in dance and simulated masturbation as a disability gag. Once in Las Vegas, the trio arrives at a brothel where Jim attends to a lineup of prostitutes. Jim explains that he has a disabled friend with him and that any of the prostitutes who would prefer not to have sex with him should remove themselves from consideration. Some prostitutes leave the lineup. One prostitute asks, "How disabled is he?" Jim replies, "Pretty bad." More prostitutes leave the lineup. This scene constructs disability as sexually undesirable. The lineup of women in bathing suits and undergarments is an example of the show's use of the conventional male gaze. Jim even lists them off by physical characteristics, "Blonde, redhead, tattoos, Asian."

Billy chooses to go with a surrogate named Wendy while Jim and Steve go to the bar. Jim and Steve quickly realize they need to help Billy disrobe and go to assist. While taking Billy's pants off, Jim comes into contact with Billy's penis, the large size of which is a reoccurring feature of dialogue throughout *Legit*. This could be read as participating in myths of disability by offering individuals compensation, or it could be read as creating a more complex, visibly disabled character by including positive physical characteristics. Either interpretation is saturated in male heterosexuality. The idea of a large penis compensating for hardships of muscular dystrophy or providing a narrative of a disabled person with positive attributes through penis size is myopically indebted to male heterosexuality; it fetishizes and valorizes the penis, and situates penis size as central.

Billy consummates his sexual desires with Wendy, and the trio leave the brothel with Billy smiling widely as triumphant, non-diegetic music reinforces the mood. The episode ends with Jim driving the car while Billy and Steve sleep. A police officer pulls the van over, observes Billy's disability, and chooses to let them go without citation. Jim says, "I'm going to get so much pussy" and drives off. This objectification operates in similar ways for women and disabled people regardless of their sex. The show participates in an odd tension in its capacity to provide heterosexual male disabled bodies with agency that is typically denied while participating in the simultaneous objectification of females and queer people.

DISABILITY AND SEXUALITY

Throughout the series, in order to disengage from conversation, Billy will "leave the room" by turning his head. This is not an uncommon tactic by disabled people who have difficulty with ambulation. The discomfort involved in jokes about Billy "leaving the room" illustrates how immobility impedes ending conversation. Billy cannot walk away; his audience can continue to be demanded. These moments of clarity demonstrate why including disability in sitcoms can be an effective way to engage in broader discussions of disability and raise awareness. There are kernels of truth that sitcoms can display effectively by finding ways to analyze culture through humor. Comedy allows a text to examine culture while providing opacity for the writer; the comedic text does not demand transparency. If these are not observable facts that are analyzed, then sitcoms can effectively participate in making meaning that provides a respect and appreciation for difference.

Disabled people are conventionally scripted as asexual, possessing no sexual desires or desirability. Disabled people may choose to participate in asexuality, and they should be afforded this choice, but it ought not be compulsory. Margrit Shildrick clarifies disability's "exclusion from the very notion of sexual subjectivity is so under-problematized that it is taken almost as a natural fact" (116). The pilot episode of *Legit* explicitly and overtly demonstrates Billy as disabled and sexualized. The episode ends with the surrogate and another woman being affectionate toward Billy. Later on in the series, Billy gets a girlfriend, and she is revealed as disabled in the final scene of the episode.

Sexual desirability is a method of creating and enforcing the idealized embodied norm. *Legit* is more successful at constructing Billy as a desirable sexual being without doubling down on the male gaze when it steers away from focusing on the size of his penis. Centering and elevating the importance of the phallus places the biological male fantasy as the hegemonic ideal. Although *Legit*'s ability to sexualize Billy without fetishizing his large phallus may not participate in the male gaze, it is consistently read in a compulsory heterosexual fashion. The pilot episode runs through a homophobic set of jokes when Jim helps Billy disrobe in the brothel.

By having a disabled character as one of the three leads, *Legit* is contemporarily read as counter-hegemonic in disrupting the process of exnomination that builds norms. Shows that only feature characters with no visible or disclosed invisible disabilities construct a narrative reality where all characters are able-bodied. There is no need to show those who deviate from the idealized normal concept of ability because the idealized able body is naturalized and ossified as the norm. Billy is written with agency, and his sexual desire initiates the conflict of the pilot episode. Billy argues with his brother Steve about choices over sexual acts he is planning. Ultimately, Billy argues with his parents and brother Steve about whether it is more important to consider his safety over his enjoyment. This is a core controversy in exercising agency over choices for disabled people in choosing independent living over medical institutionalization. Freedom for disabled people is a core ideal in disability studies—freedom to choose their own housing, freedom to participate in the communities they select, and freedom to exercise movement without the permission of an institution. The second episode of the series is about exercising that freedom, and a number of subsequent episodes revisit the debate.

Legit is successful in creating a disabled character with complicated interests, embodied attributes, sexuality, and so on. Billy is well-crafted, perhaps more so than Jim and/or Steve, which is the most remarkable feature of *Legit*. Despite the fact that this is the first sitcom to develop a character with visible disabilities and a nuanced existence, the hegemony of compulsory able-bodiedness remains pervasive, particularly in the world of sitcoms. Still, *Legit* remains a mixed bag in terms of its progressive messages; the depiction of characters with disabilities is presented in sharp contrast to the fact that the series does not develop any character that is not overtly heterosexual and that does not objectify women.

THE MALE GAZE AND COMPULSORY HETEROSEXUALITY

In the pilot episode, Billy argues with Steve about whether or not Billy is physically capable of having intercourse. Billy says, "I want to feel a vagina." The argument happens twice and is resolved with the same line both times. Compulsory heterosexuality is Adrienne Rich's concept that McRuer explicitly cites to construct his own concept of compulsory able-bodiedness, and this scene offers a direct demonstration of how compulsory heterosexuality functions. The undeniable implication here is that desirable and appropriate sex acts involve a man and a "vagina." The episode, and the series writ large, participates in exnomination in forming norms of heterosexuality in which women are treated as sex objects. The pilot episode also features a series of prostitutes who are reduced to physical characteristics and working for male sexual satisfaction. Prostitution is a complicated issue and can involve sex-positive identification, agency over sexuality, and a litany of feminist issues that *Legit* excludes from narration, which is yet another example of how far *Legit* falls behind in dealing with issues of gender and sex compared to the pace it sets with narrowly constructed but progressive depictions of disability.

The series glosses over connections to disability and gender, and compelling arguments can be made that the issue of disability affects women disproportionately. As Rosemarie Garland Thompson notes, there are 26 million women in the United States who have a disability, and women live an average of four to five years longer than men in the United States. Around the world, women with disabilities are more likely to receive unequal pay for equal work and experience occupational segregation than either nondisabled women or disabled men," and "women with disabilities are more likely to be institutionalized than men with disabilities" (30). *Legit* at least deals with Billy's disabled girlfriend in another episode, but it does not live up to its potential as a progressive narrative on multiple fronts. The series is littered with women being objectified in dialogue as well as instances when the camera focuses on their sexualized bodies. More broadly, the stigma over disability is related to that of sexism in a way that reinforces both. Jay Dolmage clarifies: "Disability has a rhetorical push-and-pull not just wherever we might recover disabled bodies, but also when we find any supposedly "abnormal" body—foreign, raced, feminized, sexualized, diseased, aging. Disability is often used rhetorically as a flexible form of stigma to be freely applied to any unknown, threatening, or devalued group" (4). The lineup of prostitutes includes sexualized bodies and demonstrates how the series reinforces the male gaze. Women are filmed to showcase their bodies, particularly their cleavage and exposed skin in wardrobe that includes bathing suits and lingerie. Other episodes are about picking up women at the bar, and those scenes, too, are filmed in conventional modes that demonstrate the male gaze. The camera continues to find many shots that fragment the female body by focusing on breasts, hips, and derrieres.

CONCLUSION

The pilot episode of *Legit*, and the series as a whole, participates in the circulation of compulsory male heterosexuality and the male gaze. This has an effect of contributing to inequality over sex in society and culture, but also informs how the process of constructing a heterosexual male able-bodied audience ultimately works against the capacity for *Legit* to transgress ableism. *Legit* makes important contributions regarding disability in sitcoms, but the show could have gone further. Since FX did not renew the show after the second season (which ran on FX's sister station FXX), it will fall to other series to take on the important work of writing new, counter-hegemonic narratives that expand our conceptions of what it means to be fully human in culturally acceptable ways.

22

Transparent Family Values

Unmasking Sitcom Myths of Gender, Sex(uality), and Money

MARIA SAN FILIPPO

Seventy years since its carryover from radio made it one of television's first successful genres, the sitcom remains a programming stalwart and the family sitcom its prototype, even as its evolution in both structure and content echoes that of all contemporary television genres into ever more hybridized form. That the Amazon original series *Transparent,* created by Jill Soloway and debuting in 2014, was awarded Golden Globes (for best series and best actor) in the "Television—Comedy or Musical" category demonstrates how contemporary television series might be outgrowing conventional industrial designations such as "sitcom" and indeed even "television" itself, as the half-hour format shifts to encompass dramatic elements and serialized structure, and as online streaming allows series such as *Transparent* to circumvent the traditional televisual apparatus altogether. Though the sitcom's legacy still informs much televised (or streamed) content, its conventional aesthetic (high-key lighting, multiple cameras, fixed studio setting, laugh track) grows more moribund by the year. This hybridized sitcom is then less redolent of Brett Mills' characterization of the traditional sitcom as a "transparent" genre, one that foregrounds its artificiality rather than veiling its means of construction. In so characterizing it, Mills finds that the sitcom's transparency works to inscribe its ideological content as truthful even as its formulaic conservatism "replaces comedy's anarchic social role with a repressively commercial one" (64–65). Conversely, contemporary sitcoms often adopt an aesthetic of reality, exemplified by the comedy vérité (or "mockumentary") subgenre popularized by series such as *The Larry Sanders Show* and *The Office*, that Mills argues "offers a site for subtle, yet powerful, critiques of television media" (78). As with these pioneering comedy vérité shows, the critical acclaim and cultural analysis that *Transparent* sparked upon its release stems from its revising and challenging of sitcom conventions, though *Transparent* aims to signify "the real" at the representational rather than the aesthetic level, so as to recuperate a genre that, Mills notes, ". . . has been criticized for failing to place its representations—whether progressive or not—within a larger social context, and for representing class, race or gender conflict as nothing more than personal squabbles and ignoring broader aspects of ideology" (64).

The most conspicuous way in which Soloway's series has challenged the sitcom's ingrained conservatism is surely in its very premise: a retired professor, divorced and living alone on Los Angeles' genteel West Side, takes a substantial step in her transitional process by coming out as transgender to her three grown children. Like other series in television's historical progression of incorporating LGBTQIA visibility, *Transparent* has been positioned as an American television "first" for putting a trans character—one who is older in age yet early in the transitional process, at that—at the show's center, though dissenting voices claimed that having trans writers, producers, and consultants on the show's staff didn't make up for the fact that the role of the transitioning 70-year-old Maura Pfefferman went to the cisgender man actor Jeffrey Tambor. As Anna McCarthy has written about the analogous case of Ellen DeGeneres' 1997 coming out as lesbian (both as a character and in real life) on her sitcom *Ellen*, discursively heralding these media events as "firsts" effaces other legible traces of queerness throughout television history in favor of an institutionally decreed mainstreaming moment that reinforces "popular and professional understandings of the history of the sitcom: the idea that the genre is a barometer of social change" (595).

One noteworthy segment in that queer television history that holds particular importance for discussions of *Transparent* is that of "tabloid talk shows" in the 1970s and 1980s, which Joshua Gamson argues provided an empowering sounding board for gender and sexual nonconformists even while putting such individuals at risk of media exploitation ("Must"). This dual-voiced queer representational politics of visibility combined with spectacularization is alive and well in contemporary television, nowhere more vividly than in the modern-day "freak show" that supplanted tabloid talk shows beginning in the 1990s: reality television. Though queer-identified performers are no less underrepresented in the reality format than in televi-

Figure 22.1. Jeffrey Tambor as Maura Pfefferman in *Transparent*. 2014– . Photo courtesy of Photofest.

sion at large, it is the low-cost spectacle proffered by reality TV that Jason Mittell sees as providing the competitive force that has urged contemporary television storytelling toward a blending of serial and episodic forms that he terms "narrative complexity" ("Narrative" 31). _Transparent's_ innovations in storytelling structure and content demonstrate the potential that Mittell finds in this newfangled narrative mode, which balances conventional sitcom pleasures with a heightened verisimilitude that revalidates the sitcom as industrially and ideologically relevant. With a media spotlight trained on trans issues in the wake of prominent cultural Americans (including Chas Bono, Chelsea Manning, Lana and Lilly Wachowski, and Caitlyn Jenner) coming out as trans, _Transparent_ was well-timed and poised to profit from the newfound attention.

"At least we're in front of the camera more now and not just on _Jerry Springer_" (qtd. in Tomashoff). So proclaims Candis Cayne, regarded as the first trans actor to perform a recurring role in prime time, as Billy Baldwin's mistress on _Dirty Sexy Money_. With this broadening visibility comes discussion and frequent dispute over the rules of engagement, with _Orange Is the New Black_ performer Laverne Cox applauded for lecturing Katie Couric on the inappropriateness of asking trans people about anatomical or surgical issues, especially as disproportionate instances of violence against trans people goes largely unaddressed in cultural discourse. Occasionally this insistence on respectful inquiry loses sight of context and consent, as when journalist J. Brian Lowder decried comedy show _Inside Amy Schumer's_ interview with self-identified transsexual Bailey Jay for its alleged prurience and then committed his own dehumanizing gesture in judging Jay's perspective misrepresentative given her profession as a sex worker. Soloway was inspired to write _Transparent_ by her own parent's coming out in late middle age, and though she has, in interviews, insisted on observing preferred pronouns and terms (e.g., referencing Tambor's character only as "Maura"), the series itself has not always been seen as articulating the enlightened perspective or avoiding insensitive depictions; Jack Halberstam, for example, laments "the trans sex scene that never happened" alongside the rendering of trans man Dale (Ian Harvie) as its blunderer in "Symbolic Exemplar."

Like the aforementioned tendency toward proclaiming LGBTQAI representational "firsts," there is risk in employing the queer coming out narrative; to do so sustains a representational politics that reasserts binary formations of gender or sexuality that work to fix identity as static, discursively bound, and thus politically containable. It is a risk that _Transparent_ notes and nimbly overcomes in articulating Maura's self-identity in individual more than gendered terms. Although Maura insists that her family members use her chosen (rather than given) name and reference her with feminine pronouns, on a deeper level she seems to dis-identify with binary labels of gender. In "The Letting Go," upon confronting her feminine-presenting parent for the first time, older daughter Sarah (Amy Landecker) asks, "Are you saying you're going to start dressing up like a lady all the time?" Maura responds with the line that has been the most quoted in the show's publicity: "No, I'm saying my whole life I've been dressing up as a man. This is me." Maura's voicing of her identity as encompassing what she calls "my feminine side," but indefinable by de-individuating relegation to an either/or configuration of gender, redefines trans-ness in terms of uniqueness rather than imitation. This individualist understanding is heard again in "Moppa" when, in preparation for her first gathering of trans folks, Maura marvels "Nobody's ever seen me before but me."

Among the misunderstandings about trans subjectivity that stubbornly persist—the scripted description of being "trapped in the wrong body" that trans people have been made to recite before medical treatment would be granted; the fixation on genitalia that trans people are presumed to have but cisgender people more often manifest—one that *Transparent* patently puts to rest is the conflation of trans identity with sexuality identity. The question of Maura's sexual preference is unrelated to either her gender identity or her transition; indeed, Maura seems to experience far less consternation than her children around questions of sexual attraction. When son Josh (Jay Duplass) asks, "Does this mean he's gay?" and Sarah responds, "No, he still likes women," youngest sibling Ali (Gaby Hoffmann) chimes in with a reminder, "Technically, that makes him a lesbian." Their defaulting to the male pronoun and familiar labels suggests the degree to which language restricts us from re-imagining gender and sexuality as both fluid and independent of one another. We see in flashbacks that Maura's first attempts to come out to then-wife Shelly (Judith Light) about her burgeoning trans awareness took the form of sex play, with Maura instigating lovemaking when she dons Shelly's underwear. As Maura's self-awareness develops, however, this seems more symptomatic of cultural conflations of gender and sexuality, with Maura trying to explain, and deal with, her feelings of being trans by sublimating them in eroticism. We subsequently come to understand this distinction as important in "Best New Girl" when, also in flashback, Maura sneaks away with new friend Marcy (Bradley Whitford), another middle-aged family "man" and closeted trans woman, to Camp Camellia, a hedonistic getaway for self-proclaimed cross-dressers that Maura finds less hospitable on learning that a former camper was exiled for starting hormone therapy. Whereas Marcy and the other campers insist "we're still men—

transvestites and transsexuals, never the twain shall meet," for Maura, trans identity exists as more than a part-time sexual proclivity, or what Shelly attempts to dismiss as "his little private kink—everyone has one."

At the same time, *Transparent* underscores that although gender and sexuality are not co-determining, being forced to hide something as substantially self-defining as one's experienced gender identity has unavoidable repercussions in one's sexual/emotional relationships. Attempting to describe her giddiness upon reuniting with college girlfriend Tammy (Melora Hardin), Sarah says to Maura, "It's a thing you do when you're falling in love, you know?" It is heart wrenching to hear the 70-year-old confess, "Not really," and though it may fuel the show's detractors that season one contains no trans sex scene involving Maura either, given ageism in tandem with transphobia, it is an unsurprising omission. Alongside its focus on those trans individuals barred from the media spotlight on account of being neither young nor beautiful, *Transparent* challenges the "it gets better" optimism of so much LGBTQAI cultural discourse and radically counters the coming out narrative's "happily ever after" teleology. As new trans friend Davina (Alexandra Billings) warns Maura in "The Letting Go" in a haunting prophesy that threatens to abandon any measure of sitcom resolution: "In five years you're going to look up and not one of your family members is going to be there."

Also radical, and more hopeful, is *Transparent*'s move away from much of screen representation's reliance on isolating trans characters within narratives that position them as the queer Other. Not only is Maura, the central character of the series, not on the margins, all three children are arguably queer as well in highly individual ways that are not easily categorized. As such, queerness becomes the norm while straightness is defamiliarized, and its extreme form, heterophallic masculinity, pathologized—as in the scene of Sarah's estranged husband Len (Rob Huebel) becoming irate and threatening violence over his son's alleged emasculation at the hands of lesbian parents and a trans grandparent. Show creator Soloway reminds us of the show's less noticed but equally pervasive element of sexual fluidity, proclaiming, "There is so much bisexuality on this show! Forget the forgotten T. Where's the forgotten B?" (qtd. in Kirby). Not surprisingly, given what I describe in *The B Word: Bisexuality in Contemporary Film and Television* as its cultural *(in)visibility*, the term "bisexuality" goes unuttered in season one, but it is not forgotten. Sarah's adulterous tangle with ex-love Tammy does not preclude her continuing attraction—emotional and sexual—to her husband Len, which culminates in their lustful commingling in the season finale, while Syd's (Carrie Brownstein) pained confession that she has "more than friend feelings" for best pal Ali comes on the heels of her disclosing her sexual relationship with Ali's brother Josh. For Sarah and Syd, attraction is not monosexually limited to object choices exclusively of one gender. Moreover, the complex histories informing their libidinal logic (Sarah's unresolved feelings for Tammy coming up against her unfulfilling marriage; Syd's masochistic attraction to Ali and its quasi-incestuous sublimation with Josh) signal the contingency of sexuality. In recognizing how desire is often steered by circumstance and emotional need, *Transparent* demonstrates a willingness to parse the rules of attraction that makes it less urgent that it voice the B word explicitly. Moreover, in seeing sexual fluidity as the norm and thus defamiliarizing the cultural imperative toward what, in *The B Word*, I term *compulsory monosexuality*, *Transparent* may leave the B word silent without silencing bisexuality or isolating it at the margins. Its non-utterance also functions to cast sexuality as continually in flux and its characters as no less irreducible to fixed identities than real people.

Transparent's clear-eyed assessment of what gets its characters off, though refreshingly cognizant of desire's complex logic, makes for flawed and, for some, unlikeable characters—an assessment that actor Gaby Hoffman, who plays Ali, views witheringly: "[*Mad Men's*] Don Draper is the coldest, most repressed fucking asshole who cheats on his wife and treats his kids like shit, and everyone's fawning over him. So we're a little whiny. We have pussies and are a little whiny. America, can you handle it?" (qtd. in Kirby). Hoffman's outspoken irreverence here and elsewhere, combined with her penchant for playing sexually uninhibited, frequently *au naturel* characters in such projects as the film *Crystal Fairy and the Magical Cactus* (2013) and HBO show *Girls*, imbues Ali with a nonconformist aura that, combined with her characterization, makes her the series' embodiment of sexual fluidity. Her desire is often problematically determined, as with her racially fetishizing trainer Derek (Cleo Anthony), and with the analogous trans fetish that her date Dale refers to as being "a chaser: someone who likes being around trans people." She herself characterizes her sexuality identity in terms that privilege ideological alliance ("Politically I'm basically a lesbian— I see male privilege everywhere") and imagines her sexual preference for "dudes—the dude-lier the better"—as very much including the trans man whom she's intent on seducing.

Transparent further affirms sexual fluidity through its defamiliarizing and problematizing of heteromasculinity. Josh's amusement at realizing that "Four out of five Pfeffermans now prefer pussy" attempts to reduce a complex range of desires to a simplistic anatomical determinant, signaling a cis man's wish to minimize the threat posed by his paternal figure openly identifying as a woman ("Boys are the hardest," Davina commiserates with Maura. "They never stop seeing you as their father"). And, as we've seen, Josh's fraught erotic fixation on mother figures suggests his need to construct a delusion of himself as simply straight. Once revealed, the origin of this fixation goes further to outright pathologize Josh and the heteromasculinity he embodies, though in such a way that evokes our empathy rather than judgment. When Sarah discovers old love letters written to Josh by childhood babysitter Rita (Brett Paesel), hidden within innocent-appearing cereal boxes, she is disgusted but not surprised. Ali displays an identical reaction in the flashback sequence in "Best New Girl" that shows Rita and Josh nonchalantly carrying on, which establishes that it was an open secret enabled by look-the-other-way parenting, and demonstrates (as evidenced by the casting of a small for his age actor as young teen Josh) the extreme inequality of their relationship. Questioning Rita in present day whether his parents knew of their relationship, Rita responds in a way that signals their and her disavowals: "Of course they knew. Your parents are strange people. We were in love." Rita and Josh's relationship retains its perverse mother-son bond in present day, visualized in a sex scene in the pilot episode that plays as ritualistic and regressive, with Rita cradling Josh to her breast. But, it has evolved to become more nakedly transactional, wherein Josh is emotionally uncommitted yet expectant of Rita's sexual availability to him exclusively; "Make yourself at home," she calls when he lets himself into her apartment unannounced, late that evening. Moreover, it is implied that she is a kept woman; as he heads out afterward, she reminds him about the air conditioner he'd promised to arrange to be serviced. That *Transparent* elects to show the still-festering aftermath of their abusive relationship not in prodigiously traumatized terms renders it more realistic but no less dismaying, for condemning Rita to dead-end dependency and Josh to emotional stultification. It is one of several Pfefferman family secrets that in remaining unacknowledged and unresolved is shown to have tragically kept its members in arrested development. In letting us in on these secrets, *Transparent* effectively unmasks the American family as quasi-incestuous and sexually exploitative. Praising its "brutally realistic appraisal of the fucked up family," Jack Halberstam comments that "one of the greatest contributions made by *Transparent*, indeed, lies in its willingness to expose the rotten core of American family life," and, I would add, that of the American family sitcom as well.

Explaining her preference for working with Amazon in terms of cultural affinity, Soloway states, "I'd rather that my stuff have to go past somebody that has been to Burning Man than somebody who has been on the golf course all day. . . . That to me is the main distinction" (qtd. in Koblin and Steele). Still in the nascent stages of its foray into producing original programming, Amazon Instant Video debuted *Transparent*'s inaugural episode free for streaming as part of its February 2014 pilot season, soliciting viewers' feedback without clarifying the extent to which it would determine series development and thus, Cory Barker notes, "tak[ing] advantage of their labor, all under the guise of agency and democratic choice." Barker attributes this marketing structure to Amazon's strategy of brand differentiation, whereby it positions itself as the populist alternative to prestige competitors such as HBO and Netflix. Amazon further seeks to differentiate itself with its ostensible disregard of ratings, refusing to reveal viewership statistics publicly and not even sharing them with show producers; "We just want them to focus on making fantastic shows," claims Amazon Studios head Roy Price (qtd. in Sternbergh 88). In its search for more Amazon Prime subscribers (also demonstrated to be more frequent buyers) and access to their mineable data, chasing risky, innovative content was the strategy that Amazon employed to competitive advantage. Adam Sternbergh notes: "It's the kind of show that no network would touch, premium cable would likely approach with caution, and only an upstart outlet looking to make some noise would move quickly to snatch up" (88). In September 2014, Amazon released the ten-episode first season of *Transparent* to overwhelmingly enthused response, and the second season was released in 2015.

Darrell Hamamoto argues that despite the sitcom's attempts to respond to social changes, "the commercial nature of the institutions which produce the programmes inevitably leads to 'repression'" (1). Amazon's rhetoric of risk taking hardly translates as any radical relinquishing of corporate self-interest, yet Amazon's deal with Soloway was less proprietorial than that of premium cable, with Soloway guaranteed that if Amazon didn't pick up the show after financing a pilot, the footage remained hers to do with what she liked. "It literally felt like a production grant," Soloway recalls (qtd. in Sternbergh 88). Precisely because Amazon controls such diversified interests, it is free to be hands off and exploratory in content creation, and with this liberation from commercial dictates and creative oversight came an opportunity to interrogate the very underpinnings of corporate-controlled media representation and with it, capitalism itself. Therein lies what I find to be *Transparent*'s most significant act, even beyond its revelations on gender and sexual fluidity as the repressed of American family values. As homonormative ideologies develop to allow for the sustainment of such values in accordance with capitalist neoliberalism, what still needs shoring up is an even more repressed component of the nuclear family structure: money as the basis for its members' relations. In revealing this most pervasive and disavowed of family secrets, *Transparent* functions to divorce the family sitcom from mythologies of capitalism.

In his landmark 1983 essay "Capitalism and Gay Identity," John D'Emilio locates the emergence of gay identity within the historical development of capitalism's free labor system, the result of transformations since the nineteenth century of Western societies from agrarian into industrialized nations that allowed for young people to live apart from their families and for the growth of (what came to be known as) LGBTQAI communities in urban areas. Another crucial impact industrialization had was in reconstructing the family as an affective unit rather than the productive unit it had been under agrarianism. Alienated from this newly fashioned nuclear family, queer people forged alternative kinship formations even as they became scapegoated as the threat to the family—the true threat being, of course, the concurrent alienation from one's labor that the capitalist system perpetuates and that "weakens the bonds that once kept families together so that their members experience a growing instability in the place they have come to expect happiness and emotional security" (D'Emilio 473). The family is not a refuge from capitalism's ills so much as it is a catalyst for its continued efficient running, assuring new generations of workers and promising respite from and reward for one's labor, hence the need for its continued mythologizing. It seems entirely fitting that *Transparent*'s pilot episode opens with stay-at-home mom Sarah packing school lunches while bellowing for her Latina maid as her white-collar professional husband slips out to work without saying goodbye; the American nuclear family's fragile harmony is thus immediately revealed as being dependent on underpaid, oppressed, feminized, and racialized domestic labor and alienated, masculinized corporate labor.

Perhaps the most prominent if seamless way in which *Transparent* accomplishes this "return of the repressed" buried within the family sitcom and the American family is through its use of frequent flashbacks to when Maura (then Mort) was still married to Shelly and with their three kids still at home. Despite being a frequently used, thus normalized, feature of film and television, the flashback is stylistically radical in its reflexivity and non-linearity, and its use nearly always signals disturbance—whether of a traumatic memory impinging on the present or of a recollection so pleasurable that is causes a yearning to return to the past. Moreover, as Maureen Turim notes, flashbacks serve to interpellate viewers into identifying with characters through the subjective experience of history revealed through flashback:

If flashbacks give us images of memory, the personal archives of the past, they also give us images of history, the shared and recorded past. . . . This process can be called the "subjective memory," which here has the double sense of the rendering of history as a subjective experience of a character in the fiction, and the formation of a Subject in history as the viewer of the film identifying with fictional character's [*sic*] positioned in a fictive social reality. (2)

Put another way, flashbacks revise cultural scripts by resisting ahistorical, noncontextualized narratives, and at the same time convey stylistically William Faulkner's axiom that "The past is never dead. It's not even past." Struggling to explain to daughter Sarah the trials of being closeted in "The Letting Go," Maura invokes not only her own but the collective experience of self-denial and alienation to which entire generations of queer individuals were (and still are, to a distressing degree) condemned: "People led secret lives, and people led very lonely lives." In a tragic rendering of Maura's consummately queer temporal condition of arriving too late at the table, one that seamlessly blends past and present to signify their entanglement, the episode ends with a shot in flashback of former-day Mort arriving home at workday's end and looking warily up at the family home. In an identically framed shot, Mort transforms into present-day Maura, staring in at the fantasy projection of all five Pfeffermans circa 1994 gathered for dinner. The displacement Maura-as-Mort felt from her masculine-gendered self and domestic life is poignantly visualized by her distanced looking-in on the scene that both entraps and excludes her.

Transparent doesn't stop at this distinction between the queer versus straight experience of family life but rather queers family life itself, and with it the domestic sitcom, by revealing its perversity in the secrets it harbors and lies it tells. The "death of the patriarch"—and the birth of Maura—is fittingly conflated with the passing on of property when Maura (still Mort to her kids) fails to come out during the pilot episode, announcing instead her intention to sell the house. A modernist refuge far from Los Angeles' lower-income, racially diverse East Side (which daughter Sarah comments that snobbish husband Len refers to as the "ghetto"), the Pfefferman family seat looms symbolically at the center of *Transparent*'s first season and its unmasking of the family ties that bind. When Maura offers the house to eldest Sarah, younger siblings Josh and Ali explode. "She already has one sugar daddy! Why does she need another one?" Ali demands. These (nominally) grown children will continue to bicker over their inheritance, as the house is excavated by renovations that dredge up still more memories. Transformed but still recognizable, the house, like Maura, is viewed by the siblings both as obligation and as safe haven, with an eye on potential profit; "How did I raise three such selfish kids?" Maura wonders. After leaving Len, Sarah seeks shelter there and soon moves Tammy and their shared family in, having struck a deal with Maura that the house is hers provided she doesn't tell her siblings. Maura similarly doles money out to Josh, who's planning a music business venture, and Ali, briefly interested in a graduate women's studies course. In all three cases, Maura emphasizes that the transaction is dependent on their promising that they won't tell their siblings, secrecy going hand-in-hand with money and family support.

Kelli Korducki finds that although each individual Pfefferman privileges self-actualization, "it is in the shared support and encouragement of the family unit that this ultimately solitary act becomes collective, and even political" in its "fundamental opposition to the good late-Capitalist drone . . . who sees work as a means to inner salvation and purpose." I agree insofar as *Transparent* discounts capitalist-driven labor as fulfilling (the only character who seems to find her work meaningful is rabbi Raquel Fein [Kathryn Hahn]), yet I find *Transparent* less resolved about our society's overvaluation of money and the familial entrapment, rather than empowerment, that financial dependency perpetuates. By wrenching open what Syd calls "the cabinet of Pfefferman family secrets," *Transparent* acknowledges the affective family unit's complicity in capitalism's system of exploitative labor that keeps its members emotionally and, given the Pfefferman children's disinclination toward wage labor, financially dependent.

By ending her silence around her gender identity, Maura unleashes a stream of equally pent-up sentiments that culminate in the season finale—"Why Do We Cover the Mirrors?"—with Ali's revelation that she was allowed to cancel her bat mitzvah only because Maura was eager to attend Camp Camellia. This connection between two ceremonial instances of "becoming women" echoes that of *Transparent*'s credit sequence, which interweaves home movie footage of midcentury bar/bat mitzvahs with clips from *The Queen* (1968), a documentary about female impersonators competing in the 1967 New York Miss All-America Camp Beauty Pageant. Having missed this Jewish rite of passage further ensnares Ali in the regressively childlike state that all three siblings occupy, provoking her defiance of the family code of silence. Dressed in a suit and tie and with newly short hair that manifests her own gender fluidity, an infuriated Ali confronts Maura, "Keep my voice down? That's our family religion, right? Secrecy! 'Here's some money to go to college—but don't tell anyone. Don't tell Josh and

Sarah.' Why are you always pushing money on me?" Maura's own furious response, "Because, my beautiful girl, you cannot *do* anything . . . I'm paying for your life," cements her infantilized status and shackles it to her non-productive citizenry. First seen accepting a "loan" from Maura, clearly not for the first time, in the pilot episode, Ali is the most financially dependent of the siblings, the "baby" of the family who embodies the repressed energies of emotional blackmail that infect family dynamics under capitalism. Hurling dollar bills at Maura in a tantrum against parental authority, Ali is pushed to confess that her ostensibly familial love is in fact conditional. "Now that you're not on the payroll anymore," Maura asks, "do you like me? If I didn't give you any money, would you even talk to me?" Ali's silence in response speaks volumes; she turns on her heel and leaves the house, though only to return, defeated, at nightfall, acquiescing to the ostensible inescapability of family ties by taking her place at the household table.

It is curious, and rather disheartening, to register that such a courageous exposé of American families under capitalism appeared courtesy of Amazon, the online commerce behemoth that crushes brick-and-mortar booksellers, mom-and-pop retailers, and employee unionization efforts in its quest to attain market dominance. In his essay's conclusion, D'Emilio calls for "structures and programs that will help to dissolve the boundaries that isolate the family" in order to construct "a society grounded in equality and justice rather than exploitation and oppression, a society where autonomy and security do not preclude each other but coexist" (475). By season's end, Maura has started forging such affective communities, bonding with new friends and confidantes Davina and Shea (Trace Lysette), both played by trans performers. We also see Maura and Shelly's reconciliation transforming their formerly toxic marriage into a mutually supportive companionship, as evidenced by Shelly's first use of the feminine pronoun to reference Maura when she tells their children, "She takes care of me." Despite these tentatively hopeful notes, in the final moments of season one, *Transparent* distances itself from both D'Emilio's imagining of alternative kinship formations and from the utopian resolutions offered by conventional sitcoms with an extremely tenuous reconnection of the Pfefferman family circle. The degree to which secrets were guarded and their repercussions still being felt culminates with Josh's discovery that Rita gave away for adoption the son he didn't know they had conceived, and who, when the young man shows up at a family function, is initially misread by the Pffermans as "Rita's new teenage boy-toy." Confessing to son Colton (Alex MacNicoll) his concern that he'll be an unfit parent, Josh is assured, "No matter what happens, I'm always going to like you." Yet, Colton's assurance of unconditional love jars with the following scene's outburst between Ali and Maura, and while Colton is welcomed at the table in this final scene, Josh evades revealing his identity while Rita remains noticeably exiled. That *Transparent* chooses to reconstruct the biological family here construes family along conservative lines that seem further fortified by Colton's engagement of the family in Christian prayer. Rebuffing her amorous advances in a previous scene, Len's last words to Sarah, "I don't want to be a secret. Just because you're from this family doesn't mean you're like this family," yielded hope that she might defy the family code. But, Sarah defaults back to disguising her own secret history by announcing her impending marriage to Tammy, another fortification of (homo)normative ritual that prompts Maura to revert to patriarchal authority in saying, "You didn't ask me, but I approve." Hovering warily at the margins, Ali is incited to surrender with one further babying gesture, when Shelly coaxes "C'mon, come sit by Mommy." The image we are left with replicates that of the aforementioned sequence from "The Letting Go" with the rendering of past and present conjoined, leaving the Pfeffermans masked by the same façade of domesticity. Yet, when Maura exclaims "Oy gevault," a Yiddish expression roughly translating as "woe is me," this parting line promises that their family troubles are far from over, and that season two of *Transparent* will continue its probing of the trouble with family.

Conclusion

The Evolving, Resilient Sitcom

Sitcoms are Not Dead!

Situation comedies at the turn of the century were thought to be dead. Not for the first time, headlines proclaimed their demise, and as the number of sitcoms dwindled on television, it seemed as if the sitcom might go the way of the TV Western. Although multi-camera style was still primarily used by most sitcoms, such as *The New Adventures of Old Christine*, *How I Met Your Mother*, and *Two and a Half Men*, some sitcoms returned to the single-camera style that had been popular in the 1960s but seldom used since until recently. These included the family shows *Arrested Development*, *The Bernie Mac Show*, and *Curb Your Enthusiasm*, as well as the workplace sitcom *Scrubs*. Later in the decade, as the sitcom made its most recent comeback, a few sitcoms began using the mockumentary style. These included *Modern Family*, *The Office*, and *Parks and Recreation*. By the end of the decade, not only was the sitcom not dead, it was thriving with the new forms mentioned above, as well as popular traditional shows, such as *The Big Bang Theory*.

Sitcoms are doing well on broadcast and cable networks, premium channels, and online. There is plenty of familiar fare that resembles the production practices codified by Karl Freund's design of the "three-headed monster" to facilitate the production of what is now one of the classic series of the genre, *I Love Lucy*, but there are departures from that formula, too. The more consistent pattern is that whenever people say the sitcom is dead, the form comes back with a tweak or a twist, or occasionally breaks new ground and is resuscitated once again. Situation comedies are still one of the most popular genres on television and are as alive as they were in the early days of television.

If the 1950s were defined by refining production practices inside the studio, the 1960s broadened the scope. Single-camera techniques used in beloved series such as *The Andy Griffith Show* opened up new spaces and, with them, new narrative possibilities but sitcoms still relied on traditional elements, such as the laugh track, which characterizes many sitcoms and both cues the humorous moments and reminds viewers that they are part of a larger audience. The 1960s also ushered in the first of the prime-time animated sitcoms, *The Flintstones* and *The Jetsons*, though in a milder form than emerges on the FOX network beginning in the late 1980s. In the 1970s, there was a resurgence of the three-camera, studio-produced sitcom, but there were some nods to cultural changes. Politics entered the living room, and single women entered the workplace. The work family joined the nuclear family as a sitcom staple reenacting daily routines in front of a studio audience. Just when work families seemed to be running out of steam and sitcoms were declared dying, if not dead, a conventional family sitcom burst onto the scene to become the most highly rated in history. *The Cosby Show* revitalized the genre by taking a traditional approach with one noticeable change: this family is Black. The change is simple on the one hand (in terms of production practices and design) but profound on the other hand (culturally). An alteration of the traditional format became much more obvious in "dramedy" series such as *Days and Nights of Molly Dodd* and *Frank's Place*. Neither one proved as popular with a mass audience as they deserved to be. The complexity and competing emotional tones took root in later series such as Showtime's *Nurse Jackie* and *Enlightened* on HBO in which the business model of subscription programs allows them to survive with small but devoted fan bases. By the 1990s, the warm and fuzzy Cosby family (literally fuzzy if you recall Cliff Huxtable's sweaters) had become a little predictable, and the sitcom was rescued once again, this time by *Friends*, launching a continuing flow of friend families. And, what about the aughts? In addition to the plethora of conventional sitcoms on network and cable television, there were innovators such as *The Office*, *Arrested Development*, and *Scrubs*, and animated shows such as *Futurama*, *King of the Hill*, and *Family Guy*, which continued to expand our understanding of what constitutes the genre. As part of this process, niche channels are now able to bring more risqué and experimental content to viewers than ever before.

It seems the equation for success has tilted a bit from familiarity to novelty to engage viewers and, especially, critics, which explains the cynicism of *Curb Your Enthusiasm*, the crudeness of *It's Always Sunny in Philadelphia*, the surface superficiality and bawdiness of *Veep*, and the heartbreak and profanity of *Louie*. Sitcoms are constantly reinvented, but there is always room for improvement. At no point in history has there been such a range in the genre as now, but there are still underrepresented areas that should be expanded for inclusiveness, such as shows featuring characters with visible disabilities and characters from more expansive ethnic and religious minority groups. It seems remarkable that *Fresh Off the Boat*, inspired by the life and memoir of Chef Eddie Huang, is the first sitcom built around an Asian-American family since Margaret Cho's *All American Girl*, which ran for one season twenty years before *Fresh Off the Boat* premiered. Perhaps even more surprising is the dearth of Latino characters. Programs produced specifically for the Internet by Amazon Studios and Netflix are promising. *Transparent*, a show from Amazon, expands our exposure to transgender characters by focusing on a man who comes out to his children and grandchildren, a scenario based on the real experiences of creator Jill Soloway. The huge success of *House of Cards* and *Orange is the New Black* on Netflix paved the way for more original Internet programming. Perhaps the roster of sitcoms will expand in the wake of *Derek*, a joint production with Channel 4, which is written and directed by and stars Ricky Gervais as the eponymous character who may (or may not) have a disability, though he is clearly positioned as an outsider.

From time to time the canard about the death of the sitcom is raised again, but even without the constant glut of reruns on television, seemingly unlimited on-demand access from a variety of sources, and DVD boxed sets for purchase, the crop of current sitcoms is rich and varied. Perhaps the half-hour slot is also a part of the sitcom's formula for success. It's easy to find 22 minutes to devote to a story amid other obligations, and it's also satisfying to find a resolution at the end of most episodes. The reason we say "most" instead of "all" is that evolution continues. There seems to be more emphasis on the ongoing story in most of the newer sitcoms and often characters have a developmental arc over time, which is a change from most sitcom characterizations over the years.

What does the future hold? No one knows for sure, of course, but we believe viewers can expect more of the same in terms of familiar formats and conventions, but those shows will be augmented, nudged, and occasionally challenged by innovations that will keep the sitcom relevant and fresh. Many of these challenges will come from cable series, which might not match the number of viewers that network shows enjoy even now when competition has eroded ratings. But, cable and online sources will continue to make up for limited market share with outsized influence because of the creative risks they take. To perpetuate the genre, shows like HBO's *Girls* and *Silicon Valley*, with their millennial ethos and raunchiness, are necessary to bring in new viewers. Viewers have a more direct role than ever before in determining which shows make it into production when they literally vote on pilots such as *Transparent* and *Alpha House* on Amazon. This new selection technique and multiple ways to access media content along with edgier storytelling and evolving production practices revitalize the form, but it is the human connections that are depicted that make the sitcom timeless. Situation comedies never die; they just evolve.

Bibliography

Acker, Joan. "Hierarchies, Jobs, Bodies: A Theory of Gendered Organizations." *Gender and Society* (4 June 1990): 139–58.

Adler, Richard (Ed.). *All in the Family: A Critical Appraisal.* New York: Praeger, 1979.

Adorno, Theodor and Max Horkheimer. "The Culture Industry: Enlightenment as Mass Deception." *Dialectic of Enlightenment* (London: Verso, 1979): 120–67.

Albert, Katherine. "Everybody Loves Lucy!" *L.A. Examiner* 6 April 1952: 6–7, 18.

Allen, Dennis. W. "The Marketing of Queer Theory." *College Literature* 25 (1998): 282–89.

Alley, Robert S., and Irby B. Brown. *Love Is All Around: The Making of the Mary Tyler Moore Show.* New York: Delta, 1989.

Alligood, Doug. "Blacks Are Gravitating to Programs with Black Themes That Relate to Them." *Broadcasting & Cable* 26 Apr. 1993: 74.

Altman, Dennis. "On Global Queering." *Australian Humanities Review.* (July 1996): 1–9.

Amory, C. "The Doris Day Show." *TV Guide*, 16 November 1968: 42.

Andersen, Robin. *Consumer Culture and Television Programming.* Boulder, CO: Westview, 1995.

Anderson, Christopher. *Hollywood TV: The Studio System in the Fifties.* Austin: U of Texas P, 1994.

Anderson, Lisa. *Mammies No More: The Changing Image of Black Women on Stage and Screen.* Lanham, MD: Rowman, 1997.

Andrews, Bart. *The "I Love Lucy" Book.* New York: Doubleday, 1985.

Armstrong, Jennifer Keishin. *Mary and Lou and Rhoda and Ted and All the Brilliant Minds Who Made The Mary Tyler Moore Show a Classic.* New York: Simon and Shuster, 2013.

Arnold, Roseanne. *My Lives.* New York: Ballantine Books, 1994.

Arnold, Roseanne. "Roseanne's Own Journal." *Ladies Home Journal* April 1992: 129–34.

Bailey, Beth. *From Front Porch to Back Seat: Courtship in Twentieth-Century America.* Baltimore: Johns Hopkins UP, 1988.

Baker, Keith Michael. "Defining the Public Sphere in Eighteenth-Century France." *Habermas and the Public Sphere.* Ed. Craig Calhoun. Cambridge, MA: MIT P, 1992: 181–211.

Bakhtin, Mikhail. *Rabelais and His World*. Trans. Helene Iswolsky. Bloomington: Indiana UP, 1984.

Ball, Lucille, with Betty Hannah Hoffman. *Love, Lucy*. New York: Putnam, 1996.

Barker, Cory. "Populist or Prestige? Amazon's Attempts to Brand Pilot Season," *Antenna*, 28 August 2014.

Barr, Geraldine, with Ted Schwarz. *My Sister Roseanne: The True Story of Roseanne Barr Arnold*. New York: Birch Lane Press, 1994.

Barr, Roseanne. *Roseanne: My Life as a Woman*. New York: Harper & Row, 1989.

Barthes, Roland. (1972). *Mythologies*. New York: Hill and Wang.

Basinger, Janine. *A Woman's View: How Hollywood Spoke to Women, 1930–1960*. Hanover, NH: Wesleyan UP, 1993.

Bauder, David. "Night of All-Black Comedies Rankle Some of Their Stars" for *Associated Press* in *Tuscaloosa News*. 6 July 2000: 5–6C

"Beauty into Buffoon." *Life* 18 Feb. 1952: 93–97.

Bell, David, and Jon Binnie. *The Sexual Citizen: Queer Politics and Beyond*. Malden, MA: Blackwell, 2000.

Bellafante, Ginia. "Who Put the 'Me' in Feminism?" *Time* 29 June 1998: cover, 52.

Belton, John. *American Cinema/American Culture*. New York: McGraw, 1991.

Bennett, Tony (Ed.). *Popular Television and Film*. London: British Film Institute with the Open UP, 1981: 12–15.

Bentley, Ricky. "Not Your Average Family." *Fresno Bee* 7 May 2002: E1.

Bergmann, Martin S., and Milton E. Jucovy. *Generations of the Holocaust*. New York: Basic Books, 1982.

Bergson, Henri. *Laughter: An Essay on the Meaning of the Comic*. London: Macmillan, 1928.

Bianco, Robert. "For Shame! New UPN Sitcoms Dredge Up Old Racial Stereotypes." *Pittsburgh Post-Gazette TV Guide* 18 Aug. 1996: 4.

Biden, Joe, Vice President. Interview with David Gregory. *Meet the Press*. NBC. May 6, 2012. Television.

"Black Sitcoms—Brilliance or Buffoonery?" (1997, June 16). *Radioscope's Electronic Urban Report*, EUR-MailmanEur@AfriNET.NET.

"Blacks on the Channels." *Time* 24 May 1968: 74.

Boddy, William. *Fifties Television: The Industry and Its Critics*. Urbana: U of Illinois P, 1990.

Bodroghkozy, Aniko. *Groove Tube: Sixties Television and the Youth Rebellion*. Durham, NC: Duke UP, 2001.

Bogle, Donald. *Blacks in American Films and Television: An Illustrated Encyclopedia*. New York: Garland, 1988.

———*Primetime Blues: African Americans on Network Television*. New York: Farrar, 2001.

———. *Toms, Coons, Mulattoes, Mammies, and Bucks: An Interpretive History of Blacks in American Films*. New York: Continuum, 1994.

Bone, James. "Ladies Who Lunch and Lust." *Times* (London) 25 July 1998.

Boorstin, Daniel J. *The Image: A Guide to Pseudo-Events in America 25th Anniversary edition.* New York: Vintage, 1987.

Booth, Wayne C. "The Company We Keep: Self-making in Imaginative Art, Old and New." Ed. Horace Newcomb. *Television, the Critical View.* New York: Oxford UP, 1987. 382–418.

Boskin, Joseph. *Sambo: The Rise and Demise of an American Jester.* New York: Oxford UP, 1986.

Bowlby, Rachel. "Modes of Modern Shopping: Mallarme at the Bon Marche." Eds. Nancy Armstrong, and Leonard Tennenhouse. *The Ideology of Conduct: Essays on Literature and the History of Sexuality.* New York: Methuen, 1987. 185–205.

Boyd, Todd. *Am I Black Enough For You: Popular Culture from the 'Hood and Beyond.* Bloomington: Indiana UP, 1997.

Brady, Kathleen. *Lucille: The Life of Lucille Ball.* New York: Hyperion, 1994.

Braxton, Greg. "Groups Call for Changes in Portrayal of Blacks on TV." *Los Angeles Times*, (1997, February 8): A1, A18.

Breines, Wini. *Young, White, and Miserable: Growing Up Female in the 1950s.* Chicago: U of Chicago P, 1992.

Breckenridge, Carol Appadurai, and Candace A. Vogler. "The Critical Limits of Embodiment: Disability's Criticism." *Public Culture*, 13:3 (2001): 349–57.

Bronski, Michael. "Book Reviews." *Cineaste* 21 (1995): 90.

Brooks, Tim, and Earle Marsh. *The Complete Directory to Prime Time Network and Cable TV Shows 1946–Present* (9th ed.). New York: Ballantine, 2007.

Brower, Neal. *Mayberry 101: Behind the Scenes of a TV Classic.* Winston-Salem, NC: Blair, 1998.

Brown, Les. *The Business Behind the Box.* New York: Harcourt Brace Jovanovich, 1971.

Brown, Peter Harry, and Pat H. Broeske, *Howard Hughes: The Untold Story.* Harmondsworth, England: Dutton Signet, 1996.

Bruce, Donald. *Topics of Restoration Comedy.* New York: St. Martin's, 1974.

Bruni, Frank. "Culture Stays Screen-Shy of Showing the Gay Kiss." Eds. Larry Gross and James D. Wood. *The Columbia Reader on Lesbian and Gay Men in Media, Society and Politics.* New York: Columbia UP, 1999: 327–29.

Bullough, Vern L. "Weighing the Shift from Sexual Identity to Sexual Relationships." *Journal of Homosexuality* 10 (1984): 3–5.

Bushnell, Candace. *Sex and the City.* New York: Warner, 1996.

Butler, Jeremy. *Television: Critical Methods and Applications.* Belmont, CA: Wadsworth, 1994.

Butler, Judith. *Gender Trouble: Feminism and the Subversion of Identity.* New York: Routledge, 1990.

———. *Fuss.* New York: Routledge, 1991: 13–31.

Butsch, Richard. "Class and Gender in Four Decades of Television Situation Comedy: *Plus Ça Change . . .*" *Critical Studies in Mass Communication* 9 (1992): 387–99.

Butsch, Richard, and Lynda M. Glennon. "Social Class Frequency Trends in Domestic Situation Comedy, 1946–1978. *Journal of Broadcasting* 27 (Winter 1983): 77–81.

Byrne, Terry. *Production Design for Television*. Boston: Focal, 1993.

Caldarola, Victor. "Embracing the Media Simulacrum." *Visual Anthropology Review* 10:1 (1994): 66–69.

Caldwell, John T. *Televisuality: Style, Crisis, and Authority in American Television*. New Brunswick, NJ: Rutgers UP, 1995.

Canfield, Douglas J. *Tricksters and Estates on the Ideology of Restoration Comedy*. Lexington: U of Kentucky P, 1997.

Cantor, Paul A. "The Simpsons: Atomistic Politics and the Nuclear Family." *Political Theory* 27.6 (1999): 734–49.

Carbaugh, Donal A. *Talking American: Cultural Discourses on Donahue*. Norwood, NJ: Ablex, 1988.

Carroll, Diahann, and Ross Firestone. *Diahann!: An Autobiography*. Boston: Little, Brown, 1986.

Carter, Bill, "How It Met Big Ratings 7 Years Into Its Run," *New York Times*, 9 April 2012: C–1.

Cartier, Bill, and Lawrie Mifflin, "Mainstream TV Bets on 'Gross-Out' Humor." *New York Times* 19 July 1999: C 1, 10.

Cartmanfan@aol.com. "Transcripts of *The Tonight Show* and *The Daily Show*." Email to Karen Anijar. 16 July 1998.

Caute, David. *The Year of the Barricades: A Journey Through 1968*. New York: Harper, 1988.

Cawelti, J.G. *Adventure, Mystery, and Romance: Formula Stories as Art and Popular Culture*. Chicago: U of Chicago P, 1976.

Cerone, Daniel Howard. " 'Ellen' Finally Says . . . Yes, I Am." *TV Guide* 29 Mar. 1997: 49–53.

Chafe, William H. *The Paradox of Change: American Women in the Twentieth Century*. New York: Oxford UP, 1991.

Charles, Arthur L. "Now We Have Everything." *Modern Screen* April 1953: 32, 84.

Chocano, Carina. "Herman Munster, Rock God." TV Diary. *Salon.com*. 11 Apr. 2002.

Clark, Cedric. "Television and Social Controls: Some Observations on the Portrayals of Ethnic Minorities." *Television Quarterly* 8:2 (1969): 18–22.

Clark, Steve. "It's As If Roald Dahl Had Dropped an Ecstasy Tab and Set a Story in Dysfunctional America. . . . A Coarse But Sharp-witted Adult Cartoon Series Ridiculing Small-town Living is Taking US Television by Storm. And Now It's Coming Here." *Guardian* [London] 16 March 1998: Media Page.

Code, Lorraine. *Rhetorical Spaces: Essays on Gendered Locations*. New York: Routledge, 1995.

Cohen, Lizabeth. *A Consumers' Republic: The Politics of Mass Consumption in Postwar America*. New York: Alfred A. Knopf, 2003.

Cole, Stephen. *That Book About That Girl*. Los Angeles: Renaissance, 1999.

Collier, Eugenia. "'Sanford and Son' is White to the Core." *New York Times* 17 June 1973, sec. 2: 1.

Color Adjustment. Dir. Marlon Riggs. San Francisco: CA Newsreel. 1991.

Coontz, Stephanie. *The Way We Never Were: American Families and the Nostalgia Trap.* New York: Basic, 1992.

Cooper, Brenda. "Unapologetic Women, 'Comic Men,' and Feminine Spectatorship in David E. Kelley's *Ally McBeal.*" *Critical Studies in Mass Communication* 18 (2001): 416–35.

Core, Philip. *Camp: The Lie That Tells the Truth.* New York: Delilah, 1984.

Cornwell, Tim. "Is It Just Dirty Talk for Girls?" *London Times* 15 Jan. 1999.

Cox, Laverne, and Carmen Carrera. Interview with Katie Couric. "Transgender Trailblazers."
 Katie. ABC-TV. 6 January 2014. Accessed 11 May 2015: http://nymag.com/thecut/2014/01/laverne-cox-taught-katie-couric-how-to-interview.html

Craig, Amanda. "Mad, Bad, and the Teenager's Perfect Dad." *Sunday Times (London).* 21 April 2002: 3.

Crane, Robert. "Roseanne." *Good Housekeeping* July 1989, 60+.

Creeber, Glen. *The Television Genre Book,* London: British Film Institute, 2001.

Cripps, Thomas. "'Amos 'n' Andy' and the Struggle for Racial Integration." *American History, American Television: Interpreting the Video Past.* Ed. John E. O'Connor. New York: Ungar, 1983: 33–54.

Croteau, David, and William Hoynes. *The Business of Media: Corporate Media and the Public Interest.* Thousand Oaks, CA: Pine Forge, 2001.

D'Acci, Julie. *Defining Women: Television and the Case of "Cagney and Lacey."* Chapel Hill: U North Carolina P, 1994.

D'Erasmo, Stacey. "The Way We Live Now." *New York Times* 29 Aug. 1999, late ed., sec. 6: 13.

Dalton, Mary M. *The Hollywood Curriculum: Teachers in the Movies.* New York: Lang, 2003.

Dalton, Mary M., and Laura R. Linder (Eds.). *The Sitcom Reader: American Viewed and Skewed.* Albany, NY: SUNY P, 2005

"Danson 'Proud' of Racial Act at Roast." *Arizona Republic* October 25, 1993: B8.

Dates, Jannette L. "Commercial Television." Eds. Jannette L. Dates and William Barlow. *Split Image: African-Americans in the Mass Media.* Washington, D.C.: Howard UP, 1990. 253–302.

Davidson, Bill. "The Change in Doris Day," *TV Guide* 20 February (1971): 30–34.

Davis, Gerald. "Trusting the Culture: A Commentary on the Translation of African-American Cultural Systems to Media Imaging Technology." Ed. Bernice Johnson Reagon. *Black American Culture and Scholarship: Contemporary Issues.* Washington, D.C.: Smithsonian Institution, 1985: 99–105.

Davis, Lennard. (Ed.). 2006. *The Disability Studies Reader.* New York: Taylor & Francis.

De Blois, Frank. "One of These Days, Alice . . ." *TV Guide* 1 October 1955: 13–15.

DeCaro, Frank. "Finally Out, and Suddenly In." *Newsweek* 12 May (1997): 83.

De Cecco, John, and Michael G. Shively. "From Sexual Identity to Sexual Relationships: A Contextual Shift." *Journal of Homosexuality* 9 (1984): 1–26.

Dellinger-Pate, Charlene, and Roger C. Aden. "'More Power': Negotiating Masculinity and Femininity in *Home Improvement.*" Ed. Marian Meyers. *Mediated Women: Representations in Popular Culture.* Cresskill, NJ: Hampton, 1999. 153–64.

D'Emilio, John. "Capitalism and Gay Identity." Eds. Henry Abelove, Michèle Aina Barale, and David M. Halperin. *The Lesbian and Gay Studies Reader.* New York: Routledge, 1993), 467–76.

de Moraes, Lisa. "Black and White Viewers Are More in Tune on Top 20." *Washington Post* 13 Feb. 2001: C01.

Dempsey, John. "MTV Auds Go Gaga for Ozzy's Oddball Antics." *Variety* 1–7 Apr. 2002: 24.

"Desilu Formula for Top TV: Brains, Beauty, Now a Baby." *Newsweek* 19 January 1953: cover, 56–59.

"Diahann Carroll Presents the *Julia* Dolls." *Ebony* Oct. 1969: 148–53.

"Did Diahann Carroll 'Sell Out' to Television?" *Sepia* Aug. 1969: 56–57.

Doherty, Brian. "Interview with Matt Groening." *Mother Jones* 24 March/April 1999: 35–7.

Dolmage, Jay. *Disability Rhetoric.* Syracuse, NY: Syracuse UP. 2013.

Donaton, Scott, "Svelte Oprah Slips Past Barr." *Advertising Age* 11 September 1989: 92.

Doty, Alexander. "The Cabinet of Lucy Ricardo: Lucille Ball's Star Image." *Cinema Journal* 29 (1990): 3–22.

Douglas, Susan. *Where the Girls Are: Growing Up Female with the Mass Media.* New York: Three Rivers Press, 1994.

Dow, Bonnie J. *Prime-Time Feminism: Television, Media Culture, and the Women's Movement Since 1970.* Philadelphia: U of Pennsylvania P, 1996.

———. "*Ellen,* Television, and the Politics of Gay and Lesbian Visibility." *Critical Studies in Media Communication* 18 (2001): 123–40.

Downing, John, and Charles Husband. *Representing Race: Racisms, Ethnicities and Media.* London: Sage, 2005.

Eco, Umberto. *Postscript to* The Name of the Rose. Trans. William Weaver. New York: Harcourt, 1994.

Edge, Steve, and John Lyttle. "Are Homosexuals Gay?" *Independent* [London] 13 Dec. 1996: 20.

Edgerton, Gary R., *The Columbia History of American Television.* New York: Columbia UP, 2007.

Ehrenreich, Barbara, Elizabeth Hess, and Gloria Jacobs. *Re-making Love: The Feminization of* Sex and the City. New York: Doubleday, 1986.

"Ellen Degeneres." *US News & World Report* 4 May 1998: 16.

Ellul, Jacques. *Propaganda: The Formation of Men's Attitudes.* New York: Vintage, 1965, 1973.

Ely, Melvin Patrick. *The Adventures of "Amos 'n' Andy": A Social History of an America Phenomenon.* New York: Free, 1991.

Emami, Gazelle. "How to Make It as a Black Sitcom: Be Careful How You Talk About Race." *The Huffington Post,* 21 October 2014.

Eskridge, Sarah K. *Rube Tube: CBS, Rural Sitcoms, and the Image of the South, 1957–1971.* Diss. Louisiana State University, 2012.

Evans, David Scott. "South Park: Comedy Central's Low-down-Hoe-down Created by Matt Stone & Trey Parker, Roomies." *Gay Today* 29 Dec. 1997. Web.

Evans, David T. *Sexual Citizenship: The Material Construction of Sexualities.* New York: Routledge, 1993.

Evers, Merlie. "A Tale of Two Julias." *Ladies Home Journal* May 1970: 60–65.

Faludi, Susan. *Backlash: The Undeclared War Against American Women.* New York: Anchor, 1991.

Farley, Christopher John. "Black and Blue." 142 *Time* 22 Nov. 1993: 80–81.

———. "How NBC Defies Network Norms—To Its Advantage." *The Wall Street Journal* 20 May 2002: A1, 10.

———. "TV's Black Flight: The Fall Schedules are Out, and the Shows with Predominately Minority Casts Have Landed in the Low-Rent Neighborhoods." 147 *Time* 3 June 1996: 66–68.

Feran, Tim. "For Your Love a Shallow Cosby." *Columbus Dispatch* 17 Mar. 1998: 7E.

Feuer, Jane. *Seeing through the Eighties: Television and Reaganism.* Durham, NC: Duke UP, 1995.

Field, Sally. Interview with Darby Maloney. Los Angeles, CA, March 22, 2004. Archive of American Television. Video. Emmytvlegends.org/interviews/people/sally-field#

Fishwick, Marshall W. "Entrance." Eds. Ray B. Browne & Marshall Fishwick. *Icons of Popular Culture.* Bowling Green, OH: Bowling Green State UP, 1970.

———. "Icons of America." Eds. Ray B. Browne & Marshall Fishwick. *Icons of America.* Bowling Green, Ohio: Bowling Green State UP, 1978.

Fiske, John. *Television Culture.* New York: Routledge, 1987.

———. *Understanding Popular Culture.* Boston: Unwin Hyman, 1989.

Fiske, John, and John Hartley. *Reading Television.* New York: Methuen, 1978, 2003.

Fleming, Anne Taylor. "Roseanne's Tough Act: Is it Too Harsh?" *New York Times* 17 January 1990, C–10.

Flint, Joe. "Fade to White." *Entertainment Weekly* 23 Apr. 1999: 9.

———. "How NBC Defies Network Norms—to Its Advantage." *Wall Street Journal* 20 May 2002: A1, A10.

Forestier, Georges. *Le Théâtre Dans Le Théâtre Sur La Scène Française Du XVIIe Siècle.* Genève: Droz, 1981.

Foucault, Michel. "What is an Author?" Eds. Chandra Mukerji and Michael Schudson, *Rethinking Popular Culture: Contemporary Perspectives in Cultural Studies.* Berkeley: U of California P, 1991.

Frazer, June M., and Timothy C. Frazer. "*Father Knows Best* and *The Cosby Show*: Nostalgia and the Sitcom Tradition." *Journal of Popular Culture*, 27.3 (1994):163–72.

Freeman, Michael. "Black-Oriented Sitcoms Gaining White Viewers." *Electronic Media* 26 (Nov. 2001): 1A.

Fretts, Bruce. "Keep a Watch on TV Do Not Adjust Your Sets—These Three New Sitcoms Are Broadcast in Black and White." *Entertainment Weekly* 27 Mar. 1998: 54.

Freud, Sigmund. *Jokes and Their Relation to the Unconscious*. New York: Norton, 1960.

Friedan, Betty. *The Feminine Mystique*. New York: Norton, 1963.

Friend, Tad. "The Next Big Bet." *The New Yorker*, 14 May 2001: 83.

Fromm, Erich. *Marx's Concept of Man*. New York: Ungar, 1961.

Frum, David. *How We Got Here: The 70s, the Decade That Brought You Modern Life—For Better or Worse*. New York: Basic, 2000.

Fuller, Linda K. *The Cosby Show: Audiences, Impact, and Implications*. Westport, CT: Greenwood Press, 1992.

Fuss Diana. *Essentially Speaking: Feminism, Nature and Difference*. New York: Routledge, 1989.

———. (Ed.) *Inside/Out: Lesbian Theories, Gay Theories*. New York: Routledge, 1991.

Gamson, Joshua. *Freaks Talk Back: Tabloid Talk Shows and Sexual Nonconformity*. Chicago: U of Chicago P, 1999.

———. "Must Identity Movements Self-Destruct: A Queer Dilemma." *Social Problems* 42 (1995): 390–408.

"Gap Between Black and White TV Viewing Habits Narrows." *Jet* 17 May 1999: 65.

Garland Thomson, Rosemarie. "Roosevelt's Sister: Why We Need Disability Studies in the Humanities." *Disability Studies Quarterly*, 30(3/4), 2010.

Garnets, Linda D., and Anthony R. D'Augelli. "Empowering Lesbian and Gay Communities: A Call for Collaboration with Community Psychology." *American Journal of Community Psychology* 22 (1994): 447–81.

Gelb, Alan. *The Doris Day Scrapbook*. New York: Grosset, 1977.

Gerbner. George. "Biography." George Gerbner Archive. Web. 29 July 2014.

Gerbner, George, Larry Gross, Marilyn Jackson-Beeck, Suzanne Jeffries-Fox, and Nancy Signorielli. "Cultural Indicators: Violence Profile No. 9." *Journal of Communication* 28 September 1978.

Gergen, Kenneth J. *Realities and Relationships: Soundings in Social Construction*. Cambridge: Harvard UP, 1994.

Gilbert, James. *A Cycle of Outrage: America's Reaction to the Juvenile Delinquent in the 1950s*. New York: Oxford, 1986.

———. *Men in the Middle: Searching for Masculinity in the 1950s*. Chicago: U of Chicago P, 2005.

Gilbert, Matthew. "'Sex in the City' is Savvy and Cynical." *Boston Globe* 6 June 1998: C6, City Edition.

——. "*For Your Love* Retro and Stale." *Boston Globe* 17 Mar. 1998: B12.

Gitlin, Todd. *Inside Prime Time*. New York: Pantheon, 1983.

——. *Inside Prime Time*. Berkeley: U of California P, 2000.

——. "Prime-Time Ideology: The Hegemonic Process in Television Entertainment." *Social Problems* 26:3 Feb. 1979: 251–66.

——. "Prime-Time Ideology: The Hegemonic Process in Television Entertainment," Television: *The Critical View* 5th Edition, ed. Horace Newcombe. New York: Oxford UP, 1994: 516–36.

Givens, Ron, with Janet Huck. "A Real Stand-Up Mom." *Newsweek* 31 October 1988, 62–63.

Gliatto, Tom, and Alexis Chiu. "Daze of Their Lives." *People* 9 Dec. 2002: 66–71.

Goldman, Robert. *Reading Ads Socially*. New York: Routledge, 1992.

Goldstein, Rachel. "Sitcom-ing Out." *Village Voice* 6 May 1997: 36–38.

Gould, Jack. "Why Millions Love Lucy." *New York Times Magazine* 1 March 1953: 16.

Grahnke, Lon. "Living, Loving in Suburbia; NBC Sitcom Set in Oak Park Offers Up Slices of Life." *Chicago Sun-Times* 16 Mar. 1998: 39.

Gray, Herman. *Watching Race: Television and the Struggle for "Blackness."* Minneapolis: U of Minnesota P, 1995.

Greene, Alexis. "The New Comedy of Manners." *Theater* 23.3 (Summer 1992): 79–83.

Habermas, Jürgen. *The Structural Transformation of the Public Sphere: An Inquiry into a Category of Bourgeois Society*. Trans. Thomas Berger. Cambridge, MA: MIT P, 1992.

Halberstam, David. *The Fifties*. New York: Columbine, 1993.

Halberstam, Jack. "*Transparent* (2014): The Highs, the Lows, the Inbetweens," *Bully Bloggers*.

Hall, Stuart. "Cultural Identity and Diaspora." *Identity: Community, Culture, Difference*. Ed. Jonathan Rutherford. London: Lawrence, 1990.

——. "Encoding/Decoding." *Media Studies: A Reader*. Eds. Paul Marris and Sue Thornham. Edinburgh: Edinburgh UP, 1996: 41–49.

——. "Encoding and Decoding." *Culture, Media, Language*. Stuart Hall, Dorothy Hobson, Hobson, Andrew Lowe, and Paul Willis. London: Hutchinson, 1980.

——. "The Re-discovery of 'Ideology': Return of the Repressed in Media Studies." Eds. M. Gurevitch et al. *Culture, Society, and the Media*. London: Methuen, 1982: 56–90.

——. (Ed.). *Representation: Cultural Representations and Signifying Practices*. Thousand Oaks, CA: Sage, 1997.

Hallin, Daniel. "We Keep America on Top of the World." Ed. Todd Gitlin. *Watching Television*. New York: Pantheon, 1986: 9–41.

Hamamoto, Darrell. *Nervous Laughter: Television Situation Comedy and Liberal Democratic Ideology*. New York: Praeger, 1991.

"Hands and Song." *Life* Dec. 1959: 57–58.

Handy, Bruce. "Roll Over, Ward Cleaver." *Time* 14 Apr. 1997: 80–85.

Hantzis, Darlene M., and Valerie Lehr. "Whose Desire? Lesbian (Non) Sexuality and Television's Perpetuation of Hetero/Sexism." Ed. R. Jeffrey Ringer. *Queer Words, Queer Images: Communication and the Construction of Homosexuality.* New York: New York UP, 1994.

Haralovich, Mary Beth. "Sitcoms and Suburbs: Positioning the 1950s Homemaker." *Quarterly Review of Film and Video,* vol. 11, 1989, 61–83.

———. "Sit-coms and Suburbia: Positioning the 1950s Homemaker." Eds. Lynn Spigel and Denise Mann. *Private Screenings: Television and the Female Consumer.* Minneapolis: U of Minnesota P, 1992.

Harkins, Anthony. *Hillbilly: A Cultural History of an American Icon.* New York: Oxford UP, 2005.

Harris, Angela. "Race and Essentialism in Feminist Legal Theory." Eds. Katharine T. Bartlett and Rosanne Kennedy, *Feminist Legal Theory: Readings in Law and Gender.* Boulder, CO: Westview, 1990.

Harris, Richard Jackson. *A Cognitive Psychology of Mass Communication.* Hillsdale, NJ: Erlbaum, 1994.

Harrison, Barbara Grizzuti. "*Roseanne*: TV Gets Real . . . Or Just Rude?" *Mademoiselle* March 1990.

Havens, Timothy. *Globalizing Blackness: The International Distribution of African American Television Programming.* Unpublished PhD Diss. Indiana U, 2000.

Hecht, Michael L. "2002—A Research Odyssey: Toward the Development of a Communication Theory of Identity." *Communication Monographs* 60 (1993): 76–82.

Hedge, Radha S. "Swinging the Trapeze: the Negotiation of Identity Among Asian Indian Immigrant Women in the United States." Eds. Delores V. Tanno and Alberto Gonzalez, *Communication and Identity Across Cultures.* Thousand Oaks, CA: Sage, 1998.

Henderson, Katherine, and Joseph A. Mazzeo (Eds.). *Meanings of the Medium.* New York: Praeger, 1990.

Henning, Paul. Interview with David Marc. *Television History Collections of the Center for the Study of Popular Television.* Syracuse University Library. 12 September 1996.

Hensley, Dennis. "Hooked On Sex." *Advocate* 23 Nov. 1999: 88–91.

Higgins, John M. "HBO Tries to Pick Up Women." *Broadcasting & Cable,* 26 Oct. 1998: 54.

Hilmes, Michelle. "Where Everybody Knows Your Name: 'Cheers' and the Mediation of Cultures." *Wide Angle: A Film Quarterly of Theory, Criticism, and Practice.* 12.2 (Apr. 1990): 64–73.

Hirst, David L. *Comedy of Manners.* New York: Methuen, 1979.

Hobbes, Thomas. *Leviathan.* New York: Penguin Classics, 1982.

Hobson, Laura Z. "As I listened to Archie Say 'Hebe'. . . ." *New York Times* 12 Sept. 1971, sec. 2: 1.

Hochstein, Rollie. "Diahann Carroll's Juggling Act." *Good Housekeeping*, May 1969: 38+.

Holleran, Andrew. "The Alpha Queen." *Gay and Lesbian Review* 7:3 (2000): 65–66.

Hollis, Tim. *Ain't That A Knee-Slapper: Rural Comedy in the Twentieth Century.* Jackson, MS: UP of Mississippi, 2008.

Horst, Carole. "*For Your Love.*" *Variety* 21 Sept. 1998: 47.

Hotchner, A.E. *Doris Day: Her Own Story.* New York: William Morrow, 1976.

Hough, Arthur. "Trials and Tribulations—Thirty Years of Sitcom." Ed. Richard Adler. *Understanding Television: Essays on Television as Social and Cultural Force.* New York: Praeger, 1981. 201–23.

Hubert, Susan J. "What's Wrong with This Picture? The Politics of Ellen's Coming Out Party." *Journal of Popular Culture* 33.2 (1999): 31–36.

Huff, Richard. "'South Park' Fuels Truth-in-Labeling Debate." *New York Daily News* 5 March 1998.

Hughes-Freeland, Felicia, and Mary M. Crain (Eds.). *Recasting Ritual: Performance, Media, Identity.* New York: Routledge, 1988.

Hustler Magazine vs. Jerry Falwell, 485 US 46. US Supreme Court 1988.

Inniss, Leslie B., and Feagin, Joe. "'The Cosby Show': The View from the Middle Class." Ed. Robin Means Coleman. *Say It Loud! African American Audiences, Identity and Media.* NY: Routledge, 2002: 187–204.

———. "'The Cosby Show:' The View from the Black Middle Class." *Journal of Black Studies*, 25 (1995): 692–711.

"In or Out." *Newsweek* 14 Sept. 1998: 72.

Iovine, Vicki. *The Girlfriends' Guide to Pregnancy.* New York: Pocket Books, 1996.

Jacobs, A.J. "Let's Talk About Sex and the City." *Entertainment Weekly* 5 June 1998: 32.

———. "*Seinfeld.*" Ed. Alison Gwin. *The 100 Greatest Television Shows of All Time.* 1998: 10–11.

James, Caryn. "That Lovable Sitcom Dad Who Likes to Nibble Bats." *New York Times* 5 Mar. 2002: E8.

Jenkins, Henry. *Fans, Bloggers, and Gamers: Exploring Participatory Culture.* New York: New York UP, 2006.

Jhally, Sut, and Justin Lewis. *Enlightened Racism: The Cosby Show, Audiences, and the Myth of the American Dream.* Boulder, CO: Westview Press, 1992.

Johnson, Robert E. "TV's Top Mom & Dad." *Ebony* Feb. 1986: 29–30, 32–34,

Jones, Gerard. *Honey, I'm Home: Sitcoms: Selling the American Dream.* New York: St. Martin's, 1992.

Joyrich, Lynne. "The Magic of Television: Thinking Through Magical Realism in Recent TV," *Transformative Works and Cultures*, no. 3, 2009.

Judah, Hettie. "Real Living." *Independent* (London) 31 Jan. 1999: 4.

"Julia." *Variety* 25 Sept. 1968.

"June Cleaver without the Pearls." *New York Times* 16 October 1988, II, 1.

Kaler, Anne K. "Golden Girls: Feminine Archetypal Patterns of the Complete Woman," *Journal of Popular Culture* 24.3 (1990): 49–61.

Kaltenbach, Chris. "*For Your Love* Tries for Three Times the Laughs." *Baltimore Sun* 17 Mar. 1998: 4E.

Kaminsky, Stuart M. *American Film Genres.* Chicago: Nelson-Hall, 1985.

Kanner, Melinda. "Can *Will and Grace* Be 'Queered'?" *Gay and Lesbian Review* 10.4 (2003): 34–35.

Kant, Immanuel. *The Critique of Judgment.* Indianapolis: Hackett Publishing, 1987.

Kanter, Hal. *So Far So Funny: My Life in Show Business.* Jefferson, NC: McFarland, 1999.

Karonen, Jenni. "Ally McBeal (and all that followed)." *U.S. Popular Culture Papers.* March 2000.

Kassel, Michael B. *America's Favorite Radio Station: WKRP in Cincinnati.* Bowling Green, OH: Popular, 1993.

Katz, Richard. " 'Ellen' Episode a Big Ratings Winner, Except in the South." *MediaWeek.* 5 May 1997: 4.

Kelleher, Terry. "Tube." *People* 8 June 1998: 31.

Kellner, Douglas. *Media Culture.* New York: Routledge, 1995.

———. "Television, Mythology, and Ritual." *Praxis 6* (1982): 133–55.

———. "TV, Ideology, and Emancipatory Popular Culture." *Socialist Review* (May-June 1979): 13–53.

Kelly, David, and Louis Chunovic. *The Complete Guide to "Ally McBeal."* London: Boxtree, 1999.

Kelly, Richard. *The Andy Griffith Show.* Winston-Salem, NC: Blair, 1981.

Kennedy, John. F. "Democratic National Convention Nomination Acceptance Address 'The New Frontier.' " *American Rhetoric.* Web.

Keveney, Bill. " 'It's All About Funny This Time,' Ellen Says." *USA Today* 26 July 2001: 3D.

Kimmel, Michael. *Manhood in America: A Cultural History.* New York: Free, 1996.

Kirby, Brandon. "6 Things to Know About Amazon's Extremely Promising New Series 'Transparent,' " *bent,* 20 July 2014. Accessed 11 May 2015: http://blogs.indiewire.com/bent/6-things-to-know-about-amazons-promising-new-series-transparent-20140720.

Kitzinger, Celia. *The Social Construction of Lesbianism.* London: Sage, 1987.

Koblin, John, and Emily Steele. "At the Head of the Pack: HBO Shows the Way Forward," *New York Times,* 12 April 2015.

Kohl, Paul R. "Looking Through a Glass Onion: Rock and Roll as a Modern Manifestation of Carnival." *Journal of Popular Culture* 27.1 (1993): 143–61.

Komarovsky, Mirra. *Blue-Collar Marriage.* New Haven, CT: Yale UP, 1964.

Korducki, Kelli. " 'Instead of Doo-Doo Brown': *Transparent,* Assholes, and Jill Soloway's Existential Feminist Collective," *cléo* 3.1, 20 April 2015.

Kroker, Arthur. "Digital Humanism: The Processed World of Marshall McLuhan," *Ctheory.net* 5 June 1995. Web.

Landay, Lori. "Millions Love Lucy: Commodification and the Lucy Phenomenon." *National Women's Studies Association Journal* 11.2 (Summer 1999): 25–47.

———. *Madcaps, Screwballs, and Con Women: The Female Trickster in American Culture*. Philadelphia: U of Pennsylvania P, 1998.

Lavery, David, and Sara Lewis Dunne. *Seinfeld, Master of its Domain: Revisiting Televisions Greatest Sitcom*. New York: Continuum, 2006.

Leap, William. *Word's Out: Gay Men's English*. Minneapolis: U of Minnesota P, 1995.

Lehman, Katherine J. *Those Girls: Single Women in Sixties and Seventies Popular Culture*. Lawrence: University Press of Kansas, 2011.

Leibman, Nina C. *Living Room Lectures: The Fifties Family in Film and Television*. Austin: U of Texas P, 1995.

Leibrock, Rachel. "Who's Your Daddy? If Your Family Values are Closer to the Osbournes than the Nelsons, TV Programmers Want You to Know—You're Not Alone." *Modesto [California] Bee* 19 May 2002: G1.

Leonard, David J. "Post Racial, Post-Civil Rights: *The Cosby Show* and the National Imagination." Eds. David J. Leonard and Lisa Guerrero. *African Americans on Television: Race-ing for Ratings*. Santa Barbara, CA: Praeger, 2013: 114–40.

Leonard, David J., and Lisa Guerrero. "Introduction: Our Regularly Scheduled Program." Eds. David J. Leonard and Lisa Guerrero. *African Americans on Television: Race-ing for Ratings*. Santa Barbara, CA: Praeger, 2013: 1–15.

Levine, Elana. *Wallowing in Sex: The New Sexual Culture of 1970s American Television*. Durham, NC: Duke UP, 2007.

Levi-Strauss, Claude. *Structural Anthropology*. New York: Basic Books, 1963.

Lewis, Nick. "Osbournes Are a Smashing Success: But Their 'Madness' is Tough to Duplicate." *Calgary Herald* [Alberta, Canada] 2 June 2003, final ed.: B14.

Lichter, S. Robert, Linda S. Lichter, and Stanley Rothman. *Prime Time: How TV Portrays American Culture*. Washington, D.C.: Regency, 1994.

Lipsitz, George. *Time Passages: Collective Memory and American Popular Culture*. Minneapolis: U of Minnesota P, 1990.

Lopez, Steve. "Death of the Sitcom." *Entertainment Weekly* 16 Apr. 1999: 30.

Lorando, Mark. "Sexual Harassment Played for Laughs on Television Sitcoms." *Times-Picayune* (New Orleans) 5 January 1995: E-1.

Louvish, Simon. *Mae West: It Ain't No Sin*. New York: St. Martin's, 2007.

Lovell, Terry. "Writing Like a Woman: A Question of Politics." Eds. Francis Barker, Peter Hulme, Margaret Iversen, and Diana Loxley. *The Politics of Theory*. Colchester: U of Essex P, 1983.

Lowder, J. Bryan. "Amy Schumer's Transphobia-Encouraging Misstep," *Slate*, 22 April 2015.

"Lucille Ball—Love Is Her Favorite Career." *Quick* 27 Nov. 1950: cover, 51–53.

Lunsford, Scott. 2005. "Seeking a Rhetoric of the Rhetoric of Dis/abilities." *Rhetoric Review*, 24(3): 330–33.

MacDonald, J. Fred. *Blacks and White TV: African-Americans in Television Since 1948*. Chicago: Nelson, 1992.

———. *Don't Touch That Dial: Radio Programming in American Life From 1920 to 1960*. Chicago: Nelson-Hall, 1979.

———. *One Nation Under Television: The Rise and Decline of Network Television.* Chicago: Nelson, 1994.

Marc, David. *Comic Visions: Television Comedy and American Culture.* Boston: Unwin Hyman, 1989.

———. *Comic Visions: Television Comedy and American Culture.* Malden, MA: Blackwell, 1997.

———. *Demographic Vistas: Television in American Culture.* Philadelphia: U of Pennsylvania P, 1996.

Marc, David, and Robert J. Thompson. *Prime Time, Prime Movers: From I Love Lucy to L.A. Law—America's Greatest TV Shows and the People Who Created Them.* Syracuse, NY: Syracuse UP, 1995.

Marin, Rick, "The Rude Tube." *Newsweek* 23 March, 1998: 55–62.

Marling, Karal Ann. "Disneyland, 1955: Just Take the Santa Ana Freeway to the American Dream." *American Art* 5 (Winter-Spring 1991): 168–207.

Marx, Karl. *Capital I.* Chicago: Kerr, 1906.

Mathews, Gordon. *Global Culture/Individual Identity: Searching for Home in the Cultural Supermarket.* New York: Routledge, 2000.

Matthews, Glenna. *"Just a Housewife": The Rise and Fall of Domesticity in America.* New York: Oxford UP, 1987.

May, Elaine Tyler. *Homeward Bound: American Families in the Cold War Era.* New York: Basic, 1988.

McCarthy, Anna. *"Ellen*: Making Queer Television History," *GLQ* 7.4 (2001): 593–620.

McConnell, Frank. "How *Seinfeld* Was Born: Jane Austen Meets Woody Allen." 123.3 *Commonweal* (9 Feb. 1996): 19–20.

McDowell, Jeanne. "Television's Coming-Out Party: Gay Characters Have Quietly Become Hot. Can Their Love Lives?" *Time* 25 Oct. 1999: 116+.

McFadden, Kay. "New on TV—*Lateline*—For Your Love." *Seattle Times* 17 Mar. 1998: E8.

McIlwain, Charlton D., and Lonnie Johnson Jr. "Headache and Heartbreak: Negotiating 'Model Minority' Status Among African Americans." Ed. Eric Mark Kramer, *The Emerging Monoculture: Assimilation and the Model Minority.* Westport, CT: Praeger, 2003.

McInerney, Jay, Daniel Howard Cerone, and Rick Schindler. "Is *Seinfeld* the Best Comedy Ever?" *TV Guide* Kentucky ed. 44.22 1 June 1996: 14–22.

McLuhan, Marshall. *The Gutenberg Galaxy.* Toronto: U of Toronto P, 1962, 1964.

———. *Understanding Media: The Extensions of Man.* Corte Madera, CA: Gingko Press, 1964, 1994.

McNeil, Alex. *Total Television.* New York: Penguin, 1996.

McRuer, Robert. "Compulsory Able-Bodiness and Queer/Disabled Existence." *The Disability Studies Reader,* 4th ed. New York: Routledge, 2013.

———. *Crip Theory: Cultural Signs of Queerness and Disability.* New York: NYU Press, 2006.

Means Coleman, Robin. *African American Viewers and the Black Situation Comedy: Situating Racial Humor.* New York: Garland, 2000.

———. (Ed.) *Say It Loud! African American Audiences, Identity and Media.* New York: Routledge, 2002.

Mellencamp, Patricia. *Logics of Television: Essays in Cultural Criticism.* Bloomington, IN: Indiana UP, 1992.

———. "Situation Comedy, Feminism, and Freud: Discourses of Gracie and Lucy." Ed. Tania Modleski. *Studies in Entertainment: Critical Approaches to Mass Culture.* Bloomington: Indiana UP, 1986: 80–95.

Messaris, Paul. "Visual Literacy vs. Visual Manipulation." *Critical Studies in Mass Communication* 11 (June 1994): 180–203.

Metallinos, Nikos. *Television Aesthetics: Perceptual, Cognitive, and Compositional Bases.* Mahwah, NJ: Erlbaum, 1996.

Michaels, Marguerite. "Norman Lear, Television's Most Successful Producer, Leaves Sitcoms Behind to Take on a Different Kind of Challenge." *Boston Globe* 3 Sept. 1979: H4.

Mietkiewicz, Henry. "New Sitcom Flashes its Own Death Knell." *Toronto Star* 18 Mar. 1998: D4.

Mifflin, Lawrie. "Of Race and Roles." *New York Times* 20 Jan. 1999: E9.

———. "Shared Favorites." *New York Times* 3 Feb. 1999: E7.

Millar, Steve. " 'Peanuts on Acid' Bring Anal Probes Down to Earth on TV: American Cartoon Erudities Hit Terrestrial TV Screens." *Guardian* [London] 1998: PSA-2139.

Miller, Douglas T., and Marion Nowak. *The Fifties: The Way We Really Were.* Garden City, NY: Doubleday, 1977.

Miller, Nancy. "American Goth." *Entertainment Weekly.* 19 April 2002: 22.

Miller, Toby. *Television Studies,* London: British Film Institute, 2002.

Mills, Brett. "Comedy Verite: Contemporary Sitcom Form," *Screen* 45:1 (Spring 2004): 63–78.

Mills, David. "What's So Funny?" *Washington Post* 26 October, 1993: 5.

Mink, Eric. " 'South Park' Comes Up a Hallo-Winner." *New York Daily News* 29 October, 1997: 89.

Mirzoeff, Nicholas. *Seinfeld.* London: British Film Institute, 2007.

Mittell, Jason. *Genre and Television: From Cop Shows to Cartoons in American Culture.* New York: Routledge, 2004.

———. "Narrative Complexity in Contemporary American Television," *Velvet Light Trap* 58 (Fall 2006): 29–40.

Morehead, Albert. " 'Lucy' Ball." *Cosmopolitan* January 1953: cover, 15–19.

Morgenthau, Henry, III. Interview with David Marc. *Television History Collections of the Center for the Study of Popular Television.* Syracuse University Library 6 May1998.

Moritz, Marguerite J. "Old Strategies for New Texts: How American Television is Creating and Treating Lesbian Characters." Ed. R. Jeffrey Ringer. *Queer*

Words, Queer Images: Communication and the Construction of Homosexuality.
New York: NY UP, 1994: 122–42.

Moss, Robert F. "The Shrinking Life Span of the Black Sitcom." *New York Times* 25 Feb. 2001: 19, 35.

Mulvey, Laura. "Visual Pleasure and Narrative Cinema." *Screen* 16 (1975): 6–18.

Mumford, Laura. *Love and Ideology in the Afternoon: Soap Opera, Women, and Television Genre.* Bloomington: Indiana UP, 1995.

Neale, Steve, and Frank Krutnik. *Popular Film and Television Comedy.* London: Palmer, 1990.

Nelson, Angela M.S. *The Objectification of Julia: Text and Contexts of Black Women in American Television Comedies.* Paper presented at the Feminist Generations Conference, Bowling Green, OH, 1996.

Nelson, Peter. "Roseanne Yea!" *Esquire* August 1989: 98.

Newcomb, Horace. "*Magnum*: The Champagne of Television?" *Channels of Communications* (May/June 1985): 23–26.

Newcomb, Horace, and Paul M. Hirsch. "Television as a Cultural Forum." Ed. Horace Newcomb. *Television: The Critical View.* NY: Oxford UP, 2000: 561–73.

Nicholls, Mark. *Scorsese's Men: Melancholia and the Mob.* North Melbourne, Australia: Pluto, 2004.

Nielsen Ratings. *Broadcasting & Cable* 18 May 1998: 6.

"Nightclubs: Bottom of the Top." *Time* 7 Dec. 1959: 48.

Nochimson, Martha. "*Ally McBeal*: Brightness Falls from the Air." *Film Quarterly* 53.3 (2000): 25–32.

Norris, Chris. "Bernie Mac Smacks a Nerve." *New York Times* Magazine, (12 May 2002).

Nussbaum, Emily. "Faint Praise," *New Yorker* 28 Oct. 2013: 80.

O'Connor, J.C. "TV View; 'Moonlighting' Delivers Wit and Style." *New York Times* (1 Dec. 1985): TV View.

O'Connor, John E., (Ed.). *American History/American Television: Interpreting the Video Past.* New York: Ungar, 1983.

O'Connor, Pat. *Friendships between Women: A Critical Review.* New York: Harvester, 1992.

Ode, Kim. "After All These Years, It's Hats Off to Mary." *Minneapolis Star Tribune.* 5 Feb. 2000: E–1.

Omi, Michael, and Howard Winant. "Racial Formations." Ed. Paula S. Rothenburg. *Race, Class and Gender in the United States: An Integrated Study.* New York: St. Martin's, 1998. 13–22.

Oppenheimer, Jess with Gregg Oppenheimer. *Laughs, Luck . . . and Lucy: How I Came to Create the Most Popular Sitcom of All Time.* Syracuse, NY: Syracuse UP, 1996.

Oppenheimer, Jess. "Lucy's Two Babies." *Look* 21 April 1953: cover, 20–24.

Ouellette, Laurie. "Public vs. Private: PBS: The 'Oasis' in the Wasteland." Ed. Toby Miller. *Television Studies.* London: BFI, 55.

Owen, Rob. *Gen X Television: The Brady Bunch to Melrose Place.* Syracuse, NY: Syracuse UP, 1997.

Perigard, Mark. "Race and Reality; Four New Shows are Adjusting the Color Balance of Prime Time." *Boston Herald* 29 Mar. 1998: 6.

Peters, Art. "What the Negro Wants From Television." *TV Guide* Southeast and Gulf Coast Editions 16 January 1968: 140–42.

Peterson, Kyle. "*Ally McBeal*: George Greenberg." *Advertising Age* 28 June 1999: 16+.

Poniewozik, James. "Color Crosses Over." *Time* 25 Feb. 2002: 64.

Postman, Neil. *Amusing Ourselves to Death*, New York: Penguin Books, 1985.

Press, Andrea Lee. *Women Watching Television: Gender, Class, and Generation in the American Television Experience.* Philadelphia: U of Pennsylvania P, 1991.

"Program and Production Report." *Television Index.* New York: Television Index, Inc. May 27–June 2 1968.

Putterman, Barry. *On Television and Comedy: Essays on Style, Theme, Performer and Writer.* Jefferson, NC: McFarland, 1995.

Rabinovitz, Lauren. "Ms.-Representation: The Politics of Feminist Sitcoms." Eds. Mary Beth Haralovich and Lauren Rabinovitz. *Television, History and American Culture: Feminist Critical Essays.* Durham, NC: Duke UP, 1999.

Rabinowitz, Aniko. "Is This What You Mean by Color Television? Race, Gender, and Contested Meanings in NBC's *Julia.*" Ed. Gail Dines and Jean M. Humez *Gender, Race and Class in Media.* Thousand Oaks, CA: Sage, 1995: 413–23.

"Ratings." *Cable World.* 21 July 2003: 29.

Ray, Robert. *A Certain Tendency of the Hollywood Cinema: 1930–1980.* Princeton, NJ: Princeton UP, 1985.

Real, Michael R. *Mass-Mediated Culture.* Englewood Cliffs, NJ: Prentice-Hall, 1977.

Reed, Rex. "*Women's Wear Daily Television Reviews.*" Reprinted in *Big Screen Little Screen.* New York: Macmillan, 1971.

"Returning Shows: Roseanne." *Entertainment Weekly* 13 September 1996, 58.

Rich, Adrienne. *Blood, Bread, and Poetry, Selected Prose 1979–1985.* New York: Norton, 1986.

Richmond, Ray. "TV Sitcoms: The Great Divide—Few Shows Bridge Black, White Audiences." *Variety* 13 Apr. 1998: 1.

Riggs, Marlon, dir. *Color Adjustment.* San Francisco: CA Newsreel, 1991.

Ringer, R. Jeffrey (Ed.). *Queer Words, Queer Images: Communication and the Construction of Homosexuality.* New York: NY UP, 1994: 107–21.

Robinson, Bonnie. "Why Did America's Funniest Housewife Leave Home?" *Redbook* November 1989, 54.

Robinson, Louie. "Bad Times on the 'Good Times' Set." *Ebony* Sept. 1975: 33–42.

Ross, Chuck. "Funny About HBO . . . It Works." *Advertising Age* 6 Dec. 1999: 20+.

Rosten, Leo. *The Joys of Yiddish.* New York: Pocket Books, 1970.

Rowe, Kathleen. "*Roseanne*: Unruly Woman as Domestic Goddess." *Screen* 31.4 1990: 408–19.

———. *The Unruly Woman: Gender and the Genres of Laughter*. Austin: U of Texas P, 1995.

Sanders, Coyne Steven, and Tom Gilbert. *Desilu: The Story of Lucille Ball and Desi Arnaz*. New York: William Morrow, 1993.

San Filippo, Maria. *The B Word: Bisexuality in Contemporary Film and Television*. Bloomington: Indiana University Press, 2013.

"Sassafrassa, the Queen." *Time* 26 May 1952: cover, 62–68.

Scharrer, Erica. "From Wise to Foolish: The Portrayal of the Sitcom Father, 1950s–1990s." *Journal of Broadcasting and Electronic Media* 45.1, 2001: 23–40.

Schatz, Thomas. "Desilu, *I Love Lucy* and the Rise of Network Television." Eds. Robert J. Thompson and Gary Burns. *Making Television: Authorship and the Production Process*. New York: Praeger, 1990.

———. *Hollywood Genres: Formulas, Filmmaking, and the Studio System*. New York: McGraw, 1981.

Schneider, Michael. "TV Racial Divide Narrows." *Daily Variety* 11 Feb. 2000: 1.

———. "Where Are All the Minorities?" *Electronic Media* 18.16 (19 Apr. 1999): 23–25.

Schulman, Bruce J. *The Seventies: The Great Shift in American Culture, Society, and Politics*. New York: Free, 2001.

Schwichtenberg, Cathy. "Sensual Surfaces and Stylistic Excess: The Pleasure and Politics of *Miami Vice*." *Journal of Communication Inquiry* 10.3 (1987): 45–65.

Scodari, Christine. " 'No Politics Here': Age and Gender in Soap Opera 'Cyberfandom.' " *Women's Studies in Communication* 21 (1998): 168–87.

———. "Sex and the Sitcom: Gender and Genre in Millennial Television." Eds. Mary M. Dalton and Laura R. Linder. *The Sitcom Reader: America Viewed and Skewed*. Albany, NY: SUNY Press, 2005: 241–52.

Scodari, Christine, and Jenna L. Felder. "Creating a Pocket Universe: 'Shippers,' Fan Fiction, and *the X-Files* Online." *Communication Studies* 51 (2000): 238–57

———. "Possession, Attraction, and the Thrill of the Chase: Gendered Mythmaking in Film and Television Comedy of the Sexes." *Critical Studies in Mass Communication* 12 (1995): 23–29.

Scott, James C. *Domination and the Arts of Resistance: Hidden Transcripts*. New Haven, CT: Yale UP, 1990.

Scully, Alan. "A Few Moments with Metal's Big [Expletive] Daddy." *Providence Journal Bulletin* 14 July 2002: I1.

See, Carolyn. "I'm a Black Woman with a White Image': Diahann Carroll Explains Some of the Reasons Behind Her Success." *TV Guide: Southeast and Gulf Coast Editions* 18 (1970): 27–30.

Seldes, Gilbert. "The Errors of Television." *Atlantic Monthly* May 1937: 531–41.

Shales, Tom, and James Andrew Miller. *Live From New York: An Uncensored History of "Saturday Night Live."* New York: Little, Brown, 2002.

Shalit, Ruth. "Cagney and Lacey: Betrayal of Postfeminism in Television Portrayals of Women." *New Republic* 6 Apr. 1998: 24+.

Shalit, Wendy. "Sex, Sadness, and the *Sex and the City*." *City Journal* 28 July 2000.

Shapiro, Joseph. *No Pity: People with Disabilities Forging a New Civil Rights Movement*. New York: Random House, 1993.

Shayon, Robert Lewis. "*Julia* Symposium: An Opportunity Lost." *Saturday Review* 51 May 1968: 36.

———. "*Julia*: Breakthrough or Letdown?" *Saturday Review* 51 April 1968: 49.

Shepherd, Cybill with Ball, A.L. *Cybill Disobedience: How I Survived Beauty Pageants, Elvis, Sex, Bruce Willis, Lies, Marriage, Motherhood, Hollywood, and the Irrepressible Urge to Say What I Think*. New York: HarperCollins, 2000.

Shildrick, Margrit. 2009. "Prosthetic Performativity." Ed. C. Niagianni, *Deleuze and Queer Theory*, 115–34. Edinburgh: Edinburgh Univ. Press.

Shugart, Helene, Catherine Waggoner, and D. Lynn Hallstein. "Mediating Third-Wave Feminism: Appropriation as Postmodern Media Practice." *Critical Studies in Mass Communication* 18 (2001): 194–210.

Silvian, Leonore. "Laughing Lucille." *Look* 3 June 1952: 7–8.

Simon, Ron. "*The Honeymooners*." *Encyclopedia of Television*. Ed. Horace Newcombe. Chicago: Fitzroy Dearborn Publishers, 1997: 789–91.

Simonds, C.H. "Wanted: Black Jackie: Electronic Pipeline." *National Review* 20 (1968): 917.

"Sitcom." *Life* Magazine 24.2 18 Sept. 1964: 24. Cited in *Online Oxford English Dictionary*.

"Situation Comedy." *TV Guide* N.Y. Metro ed. 23 Oct. 1953: 19. Cited in *Online Oxford English Dictionary*.

Skolnick, Arlene. *Embattled Paradise: The American Family in an Age of Uncertainty*. New York: Basic, 1991.

Smith, Anna Deavere. *Fires in the Mirror*. New York: Anchor, 1993.

Snead, James. "Recoding Blackness: The Visual Rhetoric of Black Independent Film." *New American Filmmakers Series 23*. New York: Whitney Museum of American Art. 20 June 1985. 1–2.

"Speaking Out." *People-Weekly* 15 Sept. 1997: 208.

Spigel, Lynn. *Make Room for TV: Television and the Family Ideal in Postwar America*. Chicago: U of Chicago P, 1992.

———. *Welcome to the Dreamhouse*, Durham, NC: Duke UP, 2001.

Spock, Benjamin. *The Common Sense Book of Baby and Child Care*. New York: Duell, 1946.

Staiger, Janet. *Blockbuster TV: Must-See Sitcoms in the Network Era*. New York: NY UP, 2000.

Stallybrass, Peter, and Allon White. *The Politics and Poetics of Transgression*. Ithaca, NY: Cornell UP, 1986.

Staples, Robert, and Terry Jones. "Culture, Ideology, and Black Television Images." *Black Scholar* 16 (1985): 10–20.

Stark, Steven D. *Glued to the Set: The 60 Television Shows and Events That Made Us Who We Are Today*. New York: Free, 1997.

———. "Cheers! It's Been Fun." *Boston Globe* 17 May 1993: 11.

Starr, Michael. " 'South Park' Net Cries 'Foul' " *New York Post* 20 March, 1998: 120.

Stein, Ben. *The View from Sunset Boulevard.* New York: Basic, 1979.

Stern, Jane, and Michael Stern. *Encyclopedia of Pop Culture.* New York: Harper, 1992.

Sternbergh, Adam. "The 'Moneyball' Network," *New York* (4–7 May 2015): 87–89, 129.

Sterngold, James. "A Racial Divide Widens on Network TV." *New York Times* 29 Dec. 1998: A1.

Stransky, Tanner, "A 'Roseanne' Family Reunion: The Behind-the-Scenes Truth about Roseanne Barr's Groundbreaking Sitcom." *Entertainment Weekly* 24 October 2008. Web. 15 Jan. 2014.

Strinati, Dominic. *An Introduction to Theories of Popular Culture.* New York: Routledge, 1995.

Stroman, Carolyn A., Bishetta D. Merrit, and Paula W. Matabane. "Twenty Years After Kerner: The Portrayal of African Americans on Prime-time Television." *Howard Journal of Communications* 2 (Winter 1989–90): 44–56.

"Study Shows How Blacks Differ from Whites in TV Choices." *Jet* 23 May 1994: 58–62.

Sullivan, Andrew. *Virtually Normal: An Argument About Homosexuality.* New York: Knopf, 1995.

Taylor, Ella. *Prime-Time Families: Television Culture in Postwar America.* Berkeley: U of CA P, 1989.

Teachout, Terry. "The New Media Crisis of 1949." *Wall Street Journal* 22 Aug. 2009. Web.

Thomas, Karen. "Friars Take the Heat for Their Tradition of Tasteless Humor." *USA Today* 12 October, 1993: 3D.

Thompson, Robert J. *Television's Second Golden Age: From* Hill Street Blues *to* ER. Syracuse, NY: Syracuse UP, 1996.

Thompson, Robert, and Gary Burns, eds. *Making Television: Authorship and the Production Process.* New York: Praeger, 1990.

Thorburn, David. "Television as an Aesthetic Medium." Ed. James Carey. *Media, Myths, and Narrative: Television and the Press.* Newbury Park, CA: Sage, 1988: 48–56.

Tichi, Cecilia. *Electronic Hearth: Creating an American Television Culture.* New York: Oxford UP, 1991.

Toll, Robert. *Blacking Up: The Minstrel Show in 19th Century America.* New York: Oxford UP, 1974.

Tomashoff, Craig. "Transgender Stories, Characters Are at a Turning Point in TV History," *TV Insider,* 26 March 2015.

Troy, Gil. *Morning in America: How Ronald Reagan Invented the 1980s.* Princeton, NJ: Princeton UP, 2005.

Tueth, Michael V. "Fun City: TV's Urban Situation Comedies of the 1990s." *Journal of Popular Film and Television* 28:3 (2000): 98–107.

Turcotte, Louise. "Foreword." *The Straight Mind and Other Essays.* Marlene Wildeman. Boston: Beacon, 1992. vii–xii.

Turim, Maureen. *Flashbacks in Film: Memory and History.* New York: Routledge, 1989.

Turner, Victor Witter. *The Drums of Affliction.* Oxford: Clarendon, 1968.

———. "Process, System, and Symbol: A New Anthropological Synthesis." *Daedalus* 106.3 (1977): 61–79.

Turow, Joseph. *Breaking Up America: Advertisers and the New Media World.* Chicago: U of Chicago P, 1997.

"TV Trivia." *Trivia Playing.* Web. 20 May 2014.

"The Twenty–Five Most Intriguing People of the Year: Roseanne Barr." *People* 26 December 1988: 46–47.

"Unaverage Situation." *Time* 18 Feb. 1952:

Valletta, Robert G. "Changes in the Structure and Duration of U.S. Unemployment, 1967–1998." *Economic Review—Federal Reserve Bank of San Francisco* 3 (1998): 29–40.

Valverde, Mariana. *Sex and the City, Power, and Pleasure.* Toronto, Ontario: Women's Press, 1985.

Van Deburg, William L. *The Black Power Movement and American Culture, 1965–1975: New Day in Babylon.* Chicago: U of Chicago P, 1992.

Van Gelder, Lawrence. "Arts Briefing." *New York Times* 2 June 2003, late ed.: E2.

Vidmar, Neil, and Milton Rokeach. "Archie Bunker's Bigotry: A Study in Selective Perception and Exposure." Ed. Richard Adler. All in the Family: *A Critical Appraisal.* New York: Praeger, 1979. 123–38.

Waldron, Vince. *Classic Sitcoms: A Celebration of the Best in Prime-Time Comedy.* New York: Collier, 1987.

Walters, Suzanna. *Material Girls: Making Sense of Feminist Cultural Theory.* Berkeley: U of California P, 1995.

Wandersee, Winifred D. *On The Move: American Women in the 1970s.* Boston: Twayne, 1988.

Warner, Michael. *The Trouble with Normal: Sex, Politics, and the Ethics of Queer Life.* Cambridge, MA: Harvard UP, 1999.

Watkins, Mel. *On the Real Side: Laughing, Lying, and Signifying.* New York: Simon & Schuster, 1994.

Weinberg, G. "What is Television's World of the Single Parent Doing to Your Family?" *TV Guide* Southeast and Gulf Coast editions, Aug. 1970.

Weiss, Jessica. *To Have and To Hold: Marriage, the Baby Boom and Social Change.* Chicago: U of Chicago P, 2000.

Weissman, Ginny, and Coyne Steven Sanders. *The Dick Van Dyke Show: Anatomy of a Classic.* New York: St. Martin's, 1983.

Welsford, Enid. *The Fool: His Social and Literary History.* Gloucester, MA: Peter Smith, 1966.

White, Armond. "Telling it on the Mountain." *Film Comment* Oct. 1985: 39–41.

Whitney, D. "All Sugar, No Spice," *TV Guide* 28 Dec. 1968: 2.

"Who's Watching What." *Austin American-Statesman*. 24 Apr. 2000: E10.

Whyte, William H., Jr. *The Organization Man*. New York: Doubleday Anchor Books, 1956.

Wilde, David. "South Park's Evil Geniuses and the Triumph of No-Brow Culture" *Rolling Stone* 19 Feb. 1998: 34.

Wilk, Max. *The Golden Age of Television Comedy*. New York: Delacorte Press, 1976.

Wilke, Michael. "'Ellen' Legacy: Gay Television Roles Are More Acceptable: But Number Drops for Fall Season." *Advertising Age* 22 Jun. 1998: 31.

Williams, Elsie A. *The Humor of Jackie Moms Mabley: An African American Comedic Tradition*. New York: Routledge, 1995.

Williams, Jeannie. "Whoopi's Shock Roast/ Danson in Blackface Leaves Many Fuming." *USA Today* 11 October 1993: 2D.

Williams-Harold, Bevolyn. "Not All Channels Are in Color." *Black Enterprise* Dec. 2000: 38.

Wittig, Monique. *The Straight Mind and Other Essays*. Boston: Beacon, 1992.

Wolcott, James. "Twinkle, Twinkle, Darren Star." *Vanity Fair* Jan. 2001: 64–72.

Wolters, Larry. "They All Love Lucy!" *Chicago Sunday Tribune* 23 Mar. 1952: 6, 25.

Zaret, David. "Religion, Science, and Printing in the Public Spheres in Seventeenth-Century England." Ed. Craig Calhoun. *Habermas and the Public Sphere*. Cambridge, MA; MIT P, 1992. 212–35.

Zoglin, Richard. "Sharp Tongue in the Trenches." *Time* 5 December 1988: 88.

Zook, Kristal Brent. *Color by Fox: The FOX Network and the Revolution in Black Television*. New York: Oxford UP, 1999.

Zynda, Thomas H. "The *Mary Tyler Moore Show* and the Transformation of Situation Comedy." Ed. James W. Carey. *Media, Myths, and Narratives: Television and the Press*. Beverly Hills, CA: Sage, 1988. 126–45.

Contributors

ALBERT AUSTER is a Professor in the Communication and Media Studies Department at Fordham University. He is co-author of *American Film and Society from 1945* (4th ed.) and *thirtysomething: Women, Men and Television.* He has written for the *Journal of Popular Film and Television, Television Quarterly,* and *The Chronicle of Higher Education.*

LAUREN BRATSLAVSKY is an Assistant Professor of Mass Communication at Illinois State University. She is currently working on a book about how television entered archives. Her academic interest in sitcoms began with her master's thesis about *30 Rock* and satire and continues in her teaching and research.

ROBERT S. BROWN is an Associate Professor of Business/Sport Management at Mount Ida College. His research interests include sport communication and the combination of popular culture with politically oriented speech.

MARY M. DALTON is Professor of Communication, Film Studies, and Women's, Gender, and Sexuality Studies at Wake Forest University. She is the author of *The Hollywood Curriculum: Teachers in the Movies,* a documentary filmmaker, and a media critic.

GERARD JONES is the author of *Honey I'm Home: Sitcoms Selling the American Dream; Killing Monsters: Why Children Need Fantasy, Superheroes and Violent Entertainment; Men of Tomorrow: Geeks, Gangsters and the Birth of the Comic Book;* and other books about mass entertainment and its audiences.

GARY KENTON has taught every level from Head Start to college. His chapter, "'Come See About Me': Why the Baby Boomers Liked Stax but

Loved Motown" appears in *Baby Boomers and Popular Culture: An Inquiry Into America's Most Powerful Generation.* He earned his Master's Degree at Fordham University. His current book project is *The Great Divide: Rock 'n' Roll, Television, and the Making of the Generation Gap.*

PAUL R. KOHL is Professor of Media Studies at Loras College in Dubuque, Iowa. In addition to television, Kohl teaches courses in film and popular music and has been published in the *Journal of Popular Culture* and *Popular Music and Society.*

JUDY KUTULAS is Professor of History and American Studies and a founding member of the Media and Film Studies Program at St. Olaf College. Her upcoming book on 1970s popular culture is called *After Aquarius Dawned.*

LORI LANDAY is an Associate Professor in the General Education Department at Berklee College of Music in Boston. She is the author of *Madcaps, Screwballs, and Con Women: The Female Trickster in American Culture* as well as essays on *I Love Lucy,* the flapper, and digital culture; she consulted on and appeared in the PBS American Masters documentary, *Finding Lucy.*

LAURA R. LINDER is a semi-retired media studies professor. She is the co-author of *Teacher TV: Sixty Years of Teachers on Television* (with Mary M. Dalton) and the author of *Public Access Television: America's Electronic Soapbox.* Her interest in situation comedies began at an early age while watching *I Love Lucy* reruns.

DAVID MARC is one of America's leading cultural critics. His books include *Demographic Vistas: Television in American Culture; Comic Visions: Television Comedy and American* Culture; *Bonfire of the Humanities: Television, Subliteracy,* and *Long-Term Memory Loss;* and, most recently, *Leveling the Playing Field: The Story of the Syracuse Eight.*

JESSICA MOORE MATTHEWS is a Social Media Strategist at *The New York Times.* She completed her master's degree in Media, Culture, and Communication at New York University and is pursuing research interests in social media and its convergence with race and social justice.

CHARLTON D. McILWAIN is an Associate Professor of Media, Culture, and Communication at New York University. He is the co-author of the award-winning book, *Race Appeal: How Candidates Invoke Race in U.S. Elections*, and four additional books and numerous articles about race, media, and politics in scholarly journals. His current work focuses on digital media and racial justice activism.

SUSAN McLELAND is an independent scholar living in Austin, Texas.

ROBIN R. MEANS COLEMAN is Professor of Communication Studies and of Afroamerican and African Studies at the University of Michigan. She is the author of *African American Viewers and the Black Situation Comedy: Situating Racial Humor*, as well as numerous other books and articles on media and identity. Her current project focuses on the NAACP's media activism.

JOHN O'LEARY is an Assistant Professor in the Communication Department at Villanova University. He is the co-founder and co-director of Villanova's Social Justice Documentary Program. He is the co-author of a screenplay based on the book *Not Going Home Alone* and is the director of Villanova's Cultural Film and Lecture Series.

DENIS M. PROVENCHER is Professor of French and Department Head in French and Italian at the University of Arizona. He is the author of *Queer French: Globalization, Language, and Sexual Citizenship in France* and *Queer Maghrebi French: Language, Temporalities, Transfiliations* as well as editor-in-chief of the international journal *Contemporary French Civilization*.

MICHAEL REAL is Professor of Communication and Culture at Royal Roads University in Victoria, B.C., Canada. His books include *Exploring Media Culture, Super Media, Mass-Mediated Culture*, and most recently, *Bodies of Discourse*. He has written scores of scholarly studies and hosted television and radio programs. His work focuses on media, culture, and social responsibility.

SHARON MARIE ROSS is an Associate Professor at Columbia College in the Television Department where she teaches TV history, criticism, and programming strategies. Her work focuses on television reception, with a focus on youth markets.

MARIA SAN FILIPPO has taught film and media studies and gender and sexuality studies at Harvard University, Indiana University Bloomington, MIT, UCLA, University of the Arts, and Wellesley College. She is author of *The B Word: Bisexuality in Contemporary Film and Television*. Her new book project examines sexual provocation in contemporary screen media, and she blogs about twenty-first century film and film-going at *The Itinerant Cinephile*.

JAMES SCHULTZ is an independent scholar. The title of his master's thesis, written at Wake Forest University, is "Compulsory Ableism in the Rhetorical Situation: The Imperfection of Exigency in *The Case Against Perfection*." His research interests include disability, gender, and sexuality.

DEMETRIA ROUGEAUX SHABAZZ is a faculty member in the Department of Communication at the University of Massachusetts at Amherst. Her published work focuses on diversity issues in media, especially television and film, as well as mass media and the development of democracy, particularly through media literacy education among youth. Shabazz is the author of a forthcoming book entitled *Television's "Race" of 1968: The Making of Black Representation in the TV Sitcom* Julia.

STEVEN T. SHEEHAN is an Associate Professor of History at the University of Wisconsin-Fox Valley. His published research examines the intersections between gender, social class, and consumer culture in 20th-Century America.

H. PETER STEEVES is Professor of Philosophy at DePaul University where he specializes in ethics, social/political philosophy, and phenomenology. He is author of *Founding Community: A Phenomenological-Ethical Inquiry*, *The Things Themselves: Essays in Applied Phenomenology* and editor of *Animal Others: On Ethics, Ontology, and Animal Life*.

MICHAEL TUETH is Professor Emeritus in the Communication and Media Studies Department of Fordham University. He has moved to St. Louis, where he continues to write film and theater reviews for *America* magazine and is doing research on Tennessee Williams' many years of living in St. Louis.

RICK WORLAND is a Professor in the Division of Film & Media Arts at Southern Methodist University. His research has concentrated on popular film and television in the Cold War Period. He is currently completing a book on Hollywood movies in the Vietnam era for Wiley-Blackwell Publishing.

Index